FEMINIST FIELDS

CONTENTS

FEMINIST FIELDS:

ETHNOGRAPHIC INSIGHTS

EDITED BY

RAE BRIDGMAN
SALLY COLE
& HEATHER HOWARD-BOBIWASH

broadview press

Canadian Cataloguing in Publication Data
Feminist fields : ethnographic insights

Includes bibliographic references.
ISBN 1-55111-195-0

1. Feminist anthropology.   I. Bridgman, Rae.   II. Cole, Sally Cooper.   III. Howard-Bobiwash, Heather.

GN33.8 F45 1999   301'.082   C99-930744-4

Broadview Press Ltd., is an independent, international publishing house, incorporated in 1985.

North America:
P.O. Box 1243, Peterborough, Ontario, Canada K9J 7H5
3576 California Road, Orchard Park, NY 14127
TEL: (705) 743-8990; FAX: (705) 743-8353;
E-MAIL: 75322.44@compuserve.com

United Kingdom:
Turpin Distribution Services Ltd.,
Blackhorse Rd., Letchworth, Hertfordshire SG6 1HN
TEL: (1462) 672555; FAX (1462) 480947; E-MAIL: turpin@rsc.org

Australia:
St. Clair Press, P.O. Box 287, Rozelle, NSW 2039
TEL: (02) 818-1942; FAX: (02) 418-1923

www.broadviewpress.com

Broadview Press gratefully acknowledges the financial support of the Book Publishing Industry Development Program, Ministry of Canadian Heritage, Government of Canada.

Cover image: *Poppy Fields*, by Rae Bridgman. 1999. Crazy quilt of velvet, satin, silk, and cotton, embroidered by hand.

Design and composition by George Kirkpatrick

PRINTED IN CANADA

Canadä

ACKNOWLEDGEMENTS

THE EDITORS of this volume are first and foremost grateful to the contributors for their patience throughout the editing process and for their enthusiastic collaboration, which has made this collection an exciting project. We also acknowledge the careful and attentive support given by Michael Harrison and Barbara Conolly at Broadview Press and by Richard Tallman, the copy editor. Their thoughtful and efficient treatment of our manuscript every step of the way has been greatly appreciated.

ONE

INTRODUCTION

Rae Bridgman, Sally Cole, and Heather Howard-Bobiwash

This book began as a murmur in a crowded room where women anthropologists had gathered to talk about the work they had been doing, to report on the kind of support they were receiving from the institutions with which they were affiliated, and to brainstorm on possibilities for the future of women in anthropology in Canada. It was a meeting of the Women's Network/Réseau des femmes at the annual Canadian Anthropology Society/Société canadienne d'anthropologie at Brock University in St. Catharines, Ontario, in 1996. At that time it was noted that there was a dearth of presentations at the conference on topics related to gender, women's work, women's everyday lives, and feminist ethnography. Yet, scholarship by and about women in anthropology is a growing field internationally, and students in anthropology (undergraduate and graduate) in Canada and the U.S. are primarily women. It was agreed that efforts would be made to ensure that women's work and feminist scholarship would be well represented at the 1997 annual meeting.

This volume arises, then, from a core of papers presented at the June 1997 conference in St. John's, Newfoundland. A general call for papers had been circulated in the fall of 1996 for a session we titled "Feminist Interrogations in Anthropological Fieldwork and Texts." The call for papers read:

> Our theme is broadly defined in relation to three key domains in feminist scholarship: 1) the essential dialogue/dialectic between fieldwork and theory; 2) the continuing salience of empirical studies of women's work; and 3) the questions (ethical, epistemological, political) that surround text, writing, and representation. We are seeking contributions from those both in the academy and within community practice. Contributions may focus on the place of feminism in anthropology; historical perspectives on women in anthropology; ethical issues in research/fieldwork, administrative duties, teaching, writing, and home-life obligations, and how we cope with/resolve them; critical perspectives on feminist theory and practice; or other

related topics. Submissions from all subfields of anthropology are welcome and we encourage the participation of emerging to senior practitioners/contributors. The papers presented in this session will serve as the core for an edited collection which we plan to submit for publication.

We received more than forty responses to the e-mail call. Where attendance in St. John's was possible, a number were invited to present papers there. Other contributions were invited for possible inclusion in the volume when, for various reasons (mostly time and financial constraints), these authors were unable to make the trip to Newfoundland. After the conference, the editorial collective met to discuss both the papers presented at the conference and those received as written submissions. It was clear we had abundant material for a volume that would offer a rich and varied portrait of both the current work and the future possibilities of the dialogue between feminism and anthropology. It was also clear that a number of the contributors were questioning what, in fact, is meant by "feminism" and were exploring the diverse faces of feminism emergent in local contexts around the world (for example, see Dossa, Ertem, Howard-Bobiwash, Judd, Ortiz Barillas, and Roseman in this volume). Following the practice of Cole and Phillips in *Ethnographic Feminisms: Essays in Anthropology* (1995), the only existing volume of feminist essays in anthropology published in Canada, we planned a volume that would meld the voices of both younger practitioners and more established scholars. Also following that earlier volume, we considered it critical that the essays should be revised and rewritten in language that would be friendly to lay and undergraduate readers – our own view being that current feminist scholarship is often exclusive in ways that make the issues and debates of feminism inaccessible, and thus unmeaningful, to novices and to women in the communities where we work.

In editing this volume we have heeded the words of editors Joan Catapano and Marlie Wasserman (1998), who in a recent article in the *Women's Review of Books* argue for the democratization of feminist scholarship and writing. Catapano and Wasserman remind us that "writing for students, as well as non-academics, is a legitimate goal for feminist (and indeed all) scholars. Feminist discussion should be open and non-hierarchical." With this goal in mind, we encouraged authors to enliven their texts with stories and first-person narratives to bring tangled theoretical concepts to life. We also invited authors to explore and highlight the complex ways in which women's lives around the globe exhibit both commonalities and differences.

This volume brings together recent feminist scholarship in anthropology in papers that are both theoretical and ethnographic and that speak to areas of continuing concern to feminists working within the discipline. These topics include: (1) the history of feminist anthropology (Cole, Gordon); (2) the location of feminist theorizing in anthropology and processes of legitimation (Cole, Gordon, Silverstein, Su); (3) change, transformations, and women's work (Dossa, Ertem, Judd, Zhurzhenko); (4) the importance of reflexivity in fieldwork and practice and an ongoing interest in bringing forward submerged perspectives (Bridgman, Clarke, Dossa, Ertem, Frohlick, Howard-Bobiwash, Judd, Roseman, Rothenberg); (5) the questions of text, representation, and the politics of feminism (Clarke, Cole, Dossa, Gordon, Howard-Bobiwash, Roseman, Silverstein, Su); and (6) the plurality of feminisms emergent in diverse historical and political contexts (Clarke, Dossa, Ertem, Howard-Bobiwash, Judd, Ortiz Barillas, Roseman).

Feminist Fields contributes to the growing international body of literature on feminist theory and practice in anthropology and, while Canadian-based, includes numerous international contributors and presents a diversity of ethnographic contexts. It draws together theory, ethnography, field-based research and textual experimentation, and cultural and political economic analytical frameworks. Several of the authors situate their writing in the context of the work of a feminist foremother (see Cole, Su, Silverstein, Howard-Bobiwash, Rothenberg), acknowledging that their work has drawn inspiration and knowledge from women predecessors in their fields. This lends the volume a place in the development of a historical consciousness of the place of women, gender, and feminisms in anthropology.

The first paper clearly makes the argument that the future productivity of feminist scholarship in anthropology will benefit from the development of a historical perspective. In "Pilgrim Souls, Honorary Men, (Un)Dutiful Daughters: Sojourners in Modernist Anthropology," Sally Cole looks at some of the tensions permeating the ongoing "project of building feminist spaces in anthropology." Her essay focuses particularly on women's presence in the anthropology program at Columbia University in the interwar years of the 1920s and 1930s. Through considering the life experiences and work of Ruth Landes, and Landes's mentoring relationships with Ruth Benedict and Margaret Mead, Cole explores the negotiations and complexities of mentoring and patronage in academe and exposes the constraints under which women were able to engage in anthropological research – constraints that in many ways continue to this day. Drawing extensively on the personal correspondence of these anthropologists, Cole historicizes the place of women within the discipline through a close analysis of one feminist career trajectory. She also locates Landes's experiences as an immigrant daughter within the colonialist project that anthropology historically embodies. The paper resonates as a "cautionary tale" for those of us today who may assume that the position of women in the discipline or the status of gender in anthropological theory has been secured.

Writing of both literary foremothers and literal mother-daughter relationships, Karen Su, in "Translating Mother Tongues: Amy Tan and Maxine Hong Kingston on Ethnographic Authority," explores the dynamics of power as these are exposed in acts of translating between languages and cultures. Her paper takes us inside debates about representation, translation, authenticity, and the relationship between ethnography and fiction. She highlights how these debates clearly embody the politics of current discussions of "native anthropology," ethnographic authority, and experimental writing by women in anthropology. Her own position as an Asian-American literary critic infuses her analysis of the predicaments, sometimes humorous, sometimes filled with pathos, faced by mothers and daughters in Amy Tan's *The Joy Luck Club* (1989) and Maxine Hong Kingston's *The Woman Warrior* (1976). Both narratives focus on American-born daughters struggling to understand the cultural sensibilities of their Chinese mothers within a dominant American culture. "Translating mother tongues" simultaneously invokes literal – "ethnographic" – translations (that have been disputed by Chinese scholars) of the Chinese language for Western audiences and the language of mothers in these texts. Su contrasts the tensions between universalizing feminist translations and an emphasis on the differences in women's positions that are not at times easily bridged.

The politics of developing a historical consciousness are highlighted by Deborah Gordon in "U.S. Feminist Ethnography and the Denationalizing of 'America': A Retrospective on *Women Writing Culture*." In response to critics who challenge that U.S. feminist ethnography participates in élitism and the dominance of "the West" through being silent on its national location and through representing itself as born of a "placeless place," Gordon reconsiders the politics of national location in feminist ethnography. In what she describes as an exercise in self-reflexivity, Gordon situates *Women Writing Culture*, the 1995 volume she co-edited with Ruth Behar, in her understanding of the history of feminist ethnography in the United States. Gordon locates the "U.S." character of the volume in its "relative inarticulateness around class." She initiates a "feminist ethnographic accounting" for the way *Women Writing Culture* failed to articulate how "performative" class relations rule the everyday life of the majority of American feminist scholars in the large, urban, increasingly privatized, public universities where they labour. In these workplaces, "class is less a relatively stable identity than a compulsion to perform." Gordon argues that the culture of these "corporatizing" universities is less about research and teaching than it is about marketing, fundraising, and publicity. This workplace produces what she calls a "disoriented" feminist subject position. Gordon locates the emergence of feminist ethnography in the U.S. in the historical moment of the 1980s when this "disoriented" feminist subject engaged with the anti-racist politics of radical women of colour and with the critiques of feminist social science by "Third World" feminists. Gordon describes feminist ethnography at the end of the century as "mutual self-reflexivity among women" and argues that this project will be furthered both by listening to the voices of feminists elsewhere and by becoming articulate about the nature of class relations in contemporary American universities.

In an era dominated by post-modern perspectives on the conceptualization of identities in terms of fragmented selves and others, Cory Silverstein, in "Beyond Selves and Others: Embodying and Enacting Meta-Narratives with a Difference," proposes an alternative analysis of identity formation and representation. She critiques the internalized pervasiveness of binary oppositions within Western culture, in particular within neo-colonial and neo-patriarchal relations. Citing early work of Margaret Mead and Gregory Bateson, Silverstein maintains that a primary source of our understandings of self emerges from the inscription of cultural conceptions of location and orientation on our bodies. Concerned with the feminist goals of achieving a more just and equitable society, Silverstein challenges feminists to consider practical ways in which we can expose and dismantle systemic forms of oppression such as racism and patriarchy as well as the ubiquitous structure of binary oppositions itself. This structure not only dominates social relations but permeates the core of our shifting and multidimensional identities – "borderline" spaces – that are never fully grasped or socially acknowledged, according to Silverstein. Her aim is to break open the idea of "multiple selfhood." She presents narratives that speak to the manifestation of our senses of location and orientation to our surroundings in daily life. She suggests that a reflexive analysis of, and a more holistic approach to, how location is inscribed on the body, particularly in relation to the dominant structures of globalization and displacement, may serve to recast the prevailing social hierarchy and help us to "imagine new ways to enact a new social order."

In "'Home Has Always Been Hard for Me': Single Mothers' Narratives of Identity, Home, and Loss," Susan Frohlick explores multiple layers of meaning attached to home places and the contradictions that permeate the life stories of single mothers she interviewed in Vancouver, British Columbia.

Challenging the idea of home as a naturalized, safe, stable, familiar and fixed container of domestic bliss, Frohlick disentangles how the "sense of oneself" for single mothers is so integrally located in the embodied experiences of home. Their narrations of "struggle" and, for some, "loss" and "incompleteness" are punctuated with tenacious cultural scripts about what constitutes a "proper home." For all mothers, tensions arise between cultural expectations and daily lived practices in homemaking. The appeal of Frohlick's analysis, in which she focuses on the experiences of two women of quite different backgrounds, is heightened by the reflexive interweaving of her own history as a single mother and her questioning how this experience has coloured both her field practice as an anthropologist and her understanding of the life stories the women told her.

In a different exploration of the concept of "home," Rae Bridgman, in "'Oh, So You Have a Home to Go To?': Empowerment and Resistance in Work with Chronically Homeless Women," reflects critically on feminist practice in the field. In her research among homeless women in Toronto, where she is "with home," the very notion of the "field" is in question. In Bridgman's essay, the "awkward" space occupied by feminist anthropologists is accentuated by her ambivalence towards the anthropological expectations of social distancing and othering that are made immediate and constant in the context of working in a familiar urban setting. Through her documentation of the establishment and implementation of an experimental housing initiative for chronically homeless women, Bridgman interrogates the concepts of empowerment and resistance. With "non-intervention" being a fundamental principle guiding the development of the project, Bridgman's questioning emerges "from the street up" and is grounded in the daily practical, intellectual, ethical, and social challenges faced by shelter staff and residents, as well as her own quandaries as a researcher among them. Bridgman explores and uncovers new dimensions of feminist practice in both fieldwork experience and textual representation.

Heather Howard-Bobiwash reports on her experimental research in an urban Aboriginal community in "'Like Her Lips to My Ear': Reading Anishnabekweg Lives and Aboriginal Cultural Continuity in the City." Howard-Bobiwash formed a reading circle with three Native women she has come to know on a daily basis through her work as editor of the monthly bulletin of the Native Canadian Centre in Toronto. Together, the four women read and discussed two published Anishnaabekweg (Ojibway women's) autobiographical accounts. Howard-Bobiwash contrasts non-Native literary critics' readings of such autobiographical accounts with the readings of these texts by the women in the reading circle and describes how these texts were read in a highly interactive fashion by the Native women, for whom they evoked lengthy and personal discussions of cultural traditions and values. Their reading is in sharp contrast to non-Native readers' descriptions of such texts as lacking "intensity of language or emotional pitch." Howard-Bobiwash's analysis of the reading circle reflects on how, for members of the urban Aboriginal world, "Native culture may be simultaneously preserved and transformed." Her essay offers a strong critique of writing on urban Aboriginal life that assumes a traditionalist-assimilationalist opposition. She argues instead for recognition of the histories, memories, and new forms of consciousness in urban Aboriginal communities.

Celia Rothenberg, in her essay "Who Are We for Them? On Doing Research in the Palestinian West Bank," also adopts a reflexive stance to fieldwork. Defining reflexivity as critical reflection on the research process itself and in particular on the relationship between the researcher and the researched so that they are placed "in the same critical plane," Rothenberg argues that reflexivity is a critical characteristic of feminist practice. She frames the process as one in which the question asked is not only "who are they for us?" but also "who are we for them?" Rothenberg describes how the villagers of the Palestinian village, Artas, constructed a direct genealogical relationship between herself and two women scholars, Hilma Granqvist and Louise Baldensperger, who had conducted research in the village in the early decades of the twentieth century and whom the villagers had incorporated as "family" into their narratives of village history. It was only upon taking seriously the villagers' determination to "locate" the young anthropologist within their local history and social networks that Rothenberg was able finally to understand the cultural meanings of family, personhood, and, especially, womanhood in Artas. Interestingly, Rothenberg traces a strand of her intellectual lineage to Granqvist, and one of the contributions of Rothenberg's chapter is in making better known Granqvist's detailed and sympathetic early ethnographic description of Palestinian women's lives.

Parin Dossa documents new forms of women's work in the context of social change and economic development in her essay, "Narrating Embodied Lives: Muslim Women on the Coast of Kenya." Her focus is on the historical and emergent gender roles and identities of the Muslim women of the island of Lamu. The central literary and analytical device of her paper is the paralleling of her own autobiographical narrative as an East African Muslim woman living "in between spaces of Africa and Canada" with the life story of Zeinub, a Swahili Muslim woman. Describing herself as a "border ethnographer," not an "insider," Dossa maintains, following Aihwa Ong (1995: 352), that occupying border positions frees one from the "conflation of identity and location" and offers new vantage points for exploring other possibilities and other ways of being. Dossa argues that women's work constitutes embodied knowledge. She uses examples of her own ignorance of local practices to illustrate the "disembodiment" of knowledge that comes from absence of cultural understanding and that dooms most formal development schemes to failure. Zeinub's narrative also illustrates how the veil is one means through which women occupy multiple spaces.

In "Off the Feminist Platform in Turkey: Cherkess Gender Relations," Gönül Ertem introduces us to internal debates within women's movements in Turkey that intersect with local discourses of ethnic identity, nationhood, and gender identity. Ertem describes the ambivalence ethnic Cherkess women feel towards the national Turkish feminist movement. Points of difference centre on notions of "public" and "private" and, more importantly, on everyday experiences of life in the so-called public and private spheres. Offering ethnographic illustration of diverging local experiences of public and private for Turkish and Cherkess women, Ertem argues for recognition of the importance of experience and history in creating diversity in feminist political practice in local contexts. Contemporary Turkish feminism has carved itself a political space in opposition to "state feminism" and targets both the "desexualized" public sphere and the hierarchical private sphere. Ertem argues, however, that the emphasis on the autonomous female subject by the Turkish feminist movement has distanced women, like the ethnic Cherkess, who historically have been differently positioned to the Turkish nationalist project and who have diverging definitions of modernity.

In "Colonial and Post-Revolutionary Discourses and Nicaraguan Feminist Constructions of Mestiza: Reflections of a Cultural Traveller," Milagros Ortiz Barillas weaves her critiques and explorations of Nicaraguan feminist constructions of Mestiza identity with her own personal narrative. Like Ertem, she examines the schisms between nationalist forms of feminism and indigenous frameworks for gendered and national identities. Ortiz Barillas suggests that deconstructing the combination of hegemonic discourses (colonial, revolutionary feminist, and post-revolutionary), which historically have contributed ingredients to the recipe of Mestiza identity in Nicaragua, demonstrates how gender is highly relevant in understanding the political processes that have taken place in that country. She introduces the notion of the "cultural traveller" to frame her analysis. Her discussion is frankly grounded in her personal experiences, and dialogues, with the raw realities of war and the indoctrination of nationalist discourses in the revolutionary and post-revolutionary contexts, and this personal narrative, which explores her painful desire to sort out her own Aboriginality, illuminates the conceptualization of identity in terms of "cultural travelling."

In "'*Fixo Ben*' (She Did the Right Thing): Women and Social Disruption in Rural Galicia," Sharon Roseman offers a narrative ethnographic account of her fieldwork in Galician villages in northwestern Spain that extends the reflexive objectives of feminist anthropology in two innovative and refreshing ways. First, through her cultivation of a feminist practice approach she presents a critical analysis of how Galician women configure gendered social structures and behaviour within the constraints of their worker-peasant economy. As she relates the circumstances surrounding two separate incidents involving the self-destructive and socio-economically detrimental effects of male alcoholism in the villages, Roseman describes the direct and indirect performance of social "disruptions" by women that result in curtailing both the men's behaviour and their marriageability. Second, Roseman addresses the sense of "paralysis" felt by feminist and other critical anthropologists who occupy an ambivalent position between acting on our convictions and questioning the ethics of our interventions within the context of fieldwork. This feeling of disempowerment, described by Marilyn Strathern (1987) as the "awkward relationship between feminism and anthropology," has received little frank and practical analysis. Roseman, through her reflexive acknowledgement of the power and knowledge frameworks of our shifting positions in the field, offers a perspective on this dilemma that highlights the possible positive results of our interventions and participation in the field, particularly in situations that involve violence or other locally sanctioned behaviour.

In "'To Reclaim Yoruba Tradition Is To Reclaim Our Queens of Mother Africa': Recasting Gender through Mediated Practices of the Everyday," Kamari Clarke, like Roseman, highlights women's agency in determining the shifting contours of the social constraints of small village society. She applies a reflexive bearing on the narrative of her ethnographic experience in the Yoruba community of Oyotunji African Village in South Carolina. In contrast to Roseman, however, Clarke describes women's deployment of structural constraints on gendered behaviour to reinforce the social order of the village. Emerging out of the context of the segregationist South of the United States, Oyotunji is a self-contained village of African Americans founded on the revitalization of Yoruba religious and cultural practices and in response to racism and the need for Black empowerment. In this hierarchically structured society, authority is mediated by "constant reformulations of Yoruba tradition" through which Clarke explores the "navigations" of village women. She documents the women's participation in determining village understandings of collective identity and historical legitimation through "performing Yorubaness." In particular, Clarke examines these "performances" in relation to discourses around purity, polygyny, notions of royalty, and anti-fraternization laws, all of which define the contours of both female and Yoruba identity in this particular transnational context.

Writing of the impact on women of the transition to a market economy in post-socialist Ukraine, Tatiana Zhurzhenko, in "Gender and Identity Formation in Post-Socialist Ukraine: The Case of Women in the Shuttle Business," describes the work and vulnerability of women in the informal economy – in this instance, the unregulated shuttle trade. Based on interviews with women *chelnoks*, or "shuttles," who travel outside Ukraine to purchase cheap consumer goods to transport back to Ukraine for resale at higher prices, Zhurzhenko's essay describes the rigorous physical and emotional stresses on these women traders and argues that they are carrying much of the cost of recent market reforms. While new entrepreneurial opportunities characterized the first stage of economic reform (1987-94), the most recent years have been marked by increasing hardship and poverty. Zhurzhenko identifies three different life strategies that lead women to engage in this arduous and semi-legal activity and correlates these different strategies with new gender identity formations. Ultimately, however, she argues that all of the women identify this work with their historical role as managers of peasant household consumption. The women accept the risks of the shuttle trade to help meet the consumer needs of their families and in response to the decreasing possibilities for legal employment. Zhurzhenko reflects on how the vulnerable conditions of work that affect most women in post-socialist Ukraine – including scientists like herself – intersected her relations with the women she interviewed. A further irony is that women's attempts to meet the consumption needs of their households through their transport and sale of consumer goods from countries like Turkey and China undercut the prices of Ukrainian-produced goods and thus contribute to high local levels of unemployment for women in the domestic manufacturing sector.

Ellen Judd's essay, "Rural Women and Economic Development in Reform Era China: The Strategy of the Official Women's Movement," based on more than two decades of anthropological research in China, offers an invaluable introduction to the goals and strategies of both rural women and the state-sponsored Women's Federations in China. Judd documents how, during the period of economic reform of the 1980s, the official Women's Federations became virtually the only legitimate channel for organizing women in China and other organizations were prohibited unless officially linked with and supervised by a state body. Judd describes how the official Chinese women's movement performs the complex dual role of representing and negotiating both state and women's interests. Refusing the label "feminist," which is understood as a specifically Western construct, the Chinese women's movement favours instead the notion of "woman-work." This essay goes a long way towards assisting Western feminist readers in understanding the ways that women's goals and needs are defined in contemporary China.

Finally, the conclusion to the volume is experimental. Towards the end of the editing process, we initiated an e-mail dialogue among our contributors around the open-ended question: "Where do you place your work as a feminist within contemporary anthropology, and what directions do you see the relationship between anthropology and feminism taking in the future?" The result is a frank exchange of the experiences and ambivalences of situating feminism in anthropology. We hear a diversity of voices. The chat is, in essence, an electronic "talking circle" — clearly an antidote to the conventional conclusion or summary of an edited volume. The result, we believe, is thoughtful, honest, and hopeful.

References

Catapano, Joan, and Marlie P. Wasserman. 1998. "Is Publishing Perishing?" *Women's Review of Books* 15, 5 (February): 22.

Cole, Sally and Lynne Phillips, eds. 1995. *Ethnographic Feminisms: Essays in Anthropology*. Ottawa: Carleton University Press.

Ong, Aihwa. 1995. "Women Out of China: Traveling Tales and Traveling Theorists in Postcolonial Feminism," in Ruth Behar and Deborah Gordon, eds., *Women Writing Culture*. Berkeley: University of California Press, 350-72.

Strathern, Marilyn. 1987. "An Awkward Relationship: The Case of Feminism and Anthropology," *Signs* 12, 2: 276-92.

TWO

PILGRIM SOULS, HONORARY MEN, (UN)DUTIFUL DAUGHTERS: SOJOURNERS IN MODERNIST ANTHROPOLOGY

Sally Cole

How many loved your moments of glad grace,
And loved your beauty with love false or true,
But one ... loved the pilgrim soul in you...
                    — W.B.YEATS
                    ("When You are Old and Full of Sleep")

BETWEEN 1921 and 1940, nineteen women and twenty men received doctoral degrees in anthropology at Columbia University in New York. This phenomenon was not duplicated at any other institution at the time, nor did similar proportions of women begin to enter anthropology again until the 1980s. The history of women in twentieth-century anthropology parallels that of women in other disciplines. In 1930, 15.8 per cent of full professors in the social science departments at American universities were women; by 1960, that number had plummeted to an all-time low of 3 per cent (Parezo, 1993; Rossiter, 1982). Rates of participation of women in higher education have been directly correlated with the strength of the women's suffrage movement in the early twentieth-century and with the second wave of feminism in the 1970s.

The attraction of women to anthropology in the interwar years was bolstered by the legacy of the Victorian lady traveller, the influx of immigrants, especially Eastern European Jews, to New York (and the subsequent opening up of its universities), and the location of the mentoring team of Franz Boas and Ruth Benedict at Columbia. The decrease in women's participation in anthropology after World War II, on the other hand, was correlated with a retrenchment of domestic roles for North American women and with increasing professionalization and positivism in anthropology, a reaction against the inductive particularism and "romantic motives" (Stocking, 1989) of the Boasian anthropology of the interwar years.

This chapter, through a portrait of the anthropological career of Boasian anthropologist Ruth Landes, illustrates the different reasons women may have from men for entering anthropology, the ambiguity in women's relations with one another in academic contexts, and the complexities and contradictory tensions that comprise the project of building feminist spaces in anthropology. Through an exploration of Landes's relationships with fellow Boasians Ruth Benedict and Margaret Mead, this historical case study highlights the complexities of mentoring and patronage in academe and serves as a cautionary tale for feminist practitioners as they begin a new century of anthropology.

The experience of being a woman in anthropology has, of course, not been a uniform one. The guises of women have included: the social reformist: Alice Fletcher in the late nineteenth century (Lurie, 1966; Mark, 1988); the wealthy patroness, feminist, and New Woman: Elsie Clews Parsons (Deacon, 1997); the mentor and poetess: Ruth Benedict (Babcock, 1995; Modell, 1983); the honorary male: Margaret Mead (Parezo, 1993); the "wife" (see Tedlock, 1995); the African-American and Native American Boasian daughters who humanized and "voiced" colonized experience: Zora Neale Hurston and Ella Deloria (Finn, 1995; Hernandez, 1995; hooks, 1990); the dutiful daughter: Gladys Reichard (Lamphere, 1993); and the unruly daughter/disruptive woman: Ruth Landes.

In *Hidden Scholars: Women Anthropologists and the Native American Southwest*, Nancy Parezo refutes the myth of anthropology as the "welcoming science." Parezo instead documents the barriers to women and the accommodation strategies women have adopted and continue to adopt in order to find intellectual and social spaces within the discipline. Following Aisenberg and Harrington (1988: xii), she argues that "for the academic profession there is such a thing as *women's* experience." This experience is of the necessity of strategy-building to overcome marginality. Barriers have included: the required reliance on a male patron; higher IQ requirements for women for acceptance into some universities; employment in untenured positions and at non-élite institutions; employment as field and lab assistants but not as co-researchers; and less frequent citation of women's scholarship, citation being critical to the establishment of scholarly careers and reputations. Furthermore, Parezo (1993: 342) notes: "rarely were professional women able to organize groups of like-minded women. To succeed, women had to align themselves with men, especially those in positions of power .... The lack of support networks ... was a common theme for all women. It required that women strive for self-sufficiency ...." Parezo identifies four strategies that women have followed to fulfil career aspirations in anthropology: acceptance, modified acceptance, confrontation, and compartmentalization.

These strategies manifest in choice of research topics, of fieldsite, of writing style, and of career goals and result, ultimately, in different anthropologies.

"Acceptance" as a style involved adopting the comportment of a dutiful daughter – of a "good girl" – and conducting research on topics that reflected "traditional" female concerns, were not threatening to men, and were "considered of minor theoretical importance," such as culture and personality, child-rearing and socialization, and acculturation (ibid., 337). A "modified-acceptance strategy" also minimized competition with men. This involved adopting a non-theoretical, descriptive style of writing, working on peripheral topics such as art or child-rearing, emphasizing one's role as teacher rather than researcher, and popularizing anthropology. As Parezo (ibid., 338) writes: "[Women] tried to work around [the barriers] – to whittle away at the edges – by working hard, ignoring the discrimination, hoping no one noticed them, demonstrating they were not bad risks." This is what Margaret Rossiter (1982: 129) refers to as "a strategy of deliberate overqualification and personal stoicism." Commonly, successful women have used the accommodation styles of acceptance and modified acceptance. Less successful were those who fought against gender stereotypes and adopted either an uncompromising "bad girl" or confrontational style or what Parezo calls the "modified confrontational style" of "compartmentalization." Compartmentalization, she says, characterized the anthropology of Ruth Benedict and Elsie Clews Parsons, who "compartmentalized their discourse, writing poetry under pseudonyms, disguising or eliminating their feminist writings under pressure to conform to standards of scientific, objective, and apolitical academic anthropology" (Parezo, 1993: 339-40). Barbara Babcock (1995) has further developed this argument, describing how, for women anthropologists, writing about "race and ethnicity may stand in for gender." That is, some women mobilized the anthropological study and writing about cultural "others" as a way to write metaphorically about (their own) gendered experience as "other."

As a "self who is also an other" (Abu-Lughod, 1989), the woman practitioner was/is simultaneously required to live her daily life in institutional structures that place her in the position of subordinate other, as daughter and helpmate but not intellectual heir. The reliance on a male patron or mentor establishes a set of social relationships in which individuals are never equal and one is either patron or client. Friendships and mentoring among women are intersected and undermined by the ultimately confined spaces available to women in the discipline. Thus, the very experiences women may have sought to escape by entering graduate study in anthropology (for example, to escape the domesticity of middle-class marriage, as in Landes's case) are reproduced in the institutional relations – with both men and women – in which women necessarily become entwined within the profession. This study of Ruth Landes's life in anthropology highlights these central contradictions for women in the discipline.

The Making of an Undutiful Daughter:
A Pilgrim Soul Grows in Brooklyn

Born in New York in 1908, Ruth Landes was the daughter of Jewish immigrants. Her mother, Anna Grossman, had middle-class roots and aspirations, completing a high school education in Berlin and coming to America as a young adult to join her older brother and sister-in-law and to practice "medical massage." Ruth's father, Joseph Schlossberg, had emigrated to America from Russia at the age of thirteen and, having had no formal schooling, immediately went to work in the garment trade. Their marriage was not atypical within the endogamous Jewish immigrant community. Anna's brother had introduced her to Joseph (who was six years her senior) as his friend and co-worker in Yiddish press and trade union circles. After their marriage, Anna continued to work for a few years until Joe began to receive a salary for his work as secretary of the Amalgamated Garment Workers' Union of America, at which time she assumed the expected roles of wife and mother.

Class and age differences between Anna and Joe, Anna's relative disinterest in motherhood and domesticity, and Joe's increasingly prominent public life in unionist politics all created an emotional distance between the parents and a coolness in home life. Ruth was the first child born to the couple and a son, David Matthias, was born two years later. Anna seems not to have been particularly affectionate with either child but was especially harsh on Ruth, criticizing her comportment and looks (she was an extraordinarily attractive child) from a young age. In childhood, Ruth was a favourite with her father whom she adored, and the father and daughter were a strongly bonded unit within the household. Ruth often accompanied her father to the union halls, where he was a frequent speaker, while Anna remained at home.[1]

The birth of Ruth's restless spirit and her confirmed individualism (and what she came to describe as "my lone-wolf anthropology") in her childhood home is well represented in the fictional writings of such early twentieth-century Jewish writers as Fannie Hurst and Edna Farber. These novelists describe close, almost claustrophobic, immigrant families, loveless marriages, and restless female protagonists who, finding little to celebrate in their parents' relations, wholeheartedly embrace American individualism. According to literary critic Joyce Antler (1997: 151): "The centrality in [early twentieth-century Jewish women's] writing of family relationships, particularly mother-daughter bonds, reveals how closely the creation of a modern American self was entwined with the process of leaving both filial and ethnic identity behind." Ruth Landes's embracing of anthropology followed closely upon her rejection of prescribed feminine roles in immigrant Jewish households and parallels the choices for individualism made by female protagonists in these novels.

As the Schlossberg household was a secular one, Ruth grew up with little knowledge of Jewish custom and instead identified Jewishness as a particular immigrant experience and identity. Until early adulthood, at least, her life was bounded by the immigrant world. She attended a public high school and the family holidayed at the Jewish summer colony, Tamiment, where she met her first husband, Victor Landes. Although in their premarital relationship the young couple had negotiated a marriage where both would be free to pursue their graduate studies (he in medicine and she in social work), the marriage soon unravelled under the pressures of conformity. In 1931, within two years of their marriage, Ruth had left the marriage and the expectations of "wifely domesticity." She took with her only her husband's name, cognizant, as she noted later in her life, that marital status and a "less Jewish-sounding name" were strategic necessities for her in seeking a professional career.

After completing a Master's thesis in social work in 1929 on Caribbean storefront churches in Harlem – in the heyday and heartland of the New Negro Renaissance – Landes sought to continue study of African-American culture (Landes, 1969). Through her father's friend, anthropologist Alexander Goldenweiser, she was introduced to Franz Boas and, through Boas, to Ruth Benedict. Boas and Benedict became lasting and significant adult models and spiritual touchstones who guided Landes throughout her life. Landes later said that she transferred her daughterly dependence from her parents to Benedict.

Landes conducted her doctoral research among the Ojibwa of Minnesota and northwestern Ontario (1933-35) at Ruth Benedict's suggestion. Benedict arranged post-doctoral research fellowships for Landes to undertake further fieldwork among the Sioux and the Potawatami (1935-36) and proposed Landes as a member of the first group of Columbia University researchers sent to Brazil in 1938-39. The result for Landes was five books and numerous articles (1937a, 1937b, 1937c, 1938a, 1938b, 1940a, 1940b, 1947, 1968a, 1968b, 1970).

In a letter written on November 11, 1939, Landes told Benedict that "I was never happy until I began to study with you and I owe you far more than my Ph.D. The Ph.D. was incidental to the things I was doing through your inspiration"(RFB). And as late as December 9, 1946, despite more than a decade of irregular employment after receiving her doctorate in 1935, Landes wrote to Benedict: "I wish you could know how I love you for setting me on this path – the many times that you did and the steadiness of the doing" (RFB).

It was unfortunate for Landes that Boas, in 1931, was in his last year of teaching when she entered the anthropology program and that, with his retirement, Benedict's status also became insecure. Although Benedict could mentor Landes's anthropological imagination, she was not structurally positioned to serve as an effective patron for her future career. Indeed, once Benedict was passed over to replace Boas as chair of the Department of Anthropology at Columbia (when, as the anthropological daughter, she did not inherit the mantle and Ralph Linton did), Benedict herself began to withdraw from the institutional world of anthropology and to locate her life fulfilment in new relationships with women partners. Although she continued her writing in anthropology (1934, 1940, 1946), she was disenchanted with the politics of placing her students in the profession. On March 19, 1939, she wrote to Margaret Mead from a sabbatical in California:

> With [Edward] Sapir dead and with the Harvard department manned by little people and with Chicago minus Radcliffe-Brown, the real centers of anthropology have become fewer. This hasn't meant, however, that Columbia has been asked to propose candidates for jobs; of course this year there haven't been any but last year there were. It may be that next time jobs come up, we'll have a better chance; time will tell. Of course, I'm a bad contact-man, for I don't like to sell myself or my children and besides I get so swamped in things that have to be done that I cut out the other things – the "things that have to be done" being work on anthropology, and not the business of selling anthropology. (MM, B1)

In adopting Benedict as her mentor and patron, Landes chose to follow a female role model and develop a friendship in anthropology rather than to nurture the requisite relationship with a male patron needed to establish herself in an academic career in anthropology.

Disciplining Women: Landes, Benedict, and Mead

"Mrs. Landes, this is Mrs. Benedict. Mrs. Benedict, this is Mrs. Landes" was Franz Boas's introduction when, one September day in 1931, he took the new student, Ruth Landes, down the hall to meet Ruth Benedict, who was his "right-hand" (Mead, 1959) and was to be Landes's main supervisor. Landes remembered: "I never had the courage to inform him that the marriage was dissolved when I joined his Department. For it was still considered disgraceful when a woman lived unmarried" (Landes, n.d.: 4). Although neither woman in fact lived with a husband, Boas allowed himself to assume that they were somehow economically provided for and did not require secure paid employment; thus, their pursuit of anthropology could be seen as a vocation motivated purely by intellectual curiosity and love. In fact, Landes reported, Boas was frank that day that "There aren't any jobs [in anthropology]. Then Ruth [Benedict] hastened to comfort, 'But I don't know any anthropologist who has no work'" (ibid., 2). Landes appreciated Benedict's layered notion of "work."

Benedict later told Landes that the solution to all private problems is to "work, work, work," (ibid., 16) and, in the years to come, Landes herself turned to "work" (paid and unpaid) in anthropology to help chart the course of her life. With time, however, she became less sanguine about the absence of paid work, writing to Benedict in 1940:

> There are no jobs. I just hate to get out of anthropology. Things look so black for me, I mean, that I can only suppose that I've to learn a technique of playing the game .... I suppose one's got to be quite pedestrian or quite extraordinary, and I'm neither. It seems so silly and wasteful to equip an eager and intelligent person with something that can't be marketed. And, in the case of anthropology, the "world situation" isn't to blame. I've been trying to get somewhere for several years. (RFB, June 11, 1940)

Landes recalled the moment of meeting Benedict:

> Boas had taken me, a bewildered young creature, into her office to explain that he had invited me to study with them. He had in fact invited me a whole year before, when I had ventured to consult him about Negro movements that were bursting out all over the United States, in all social groups. I had taken the year to ponder this very recondite discipline, to consider spending time on the luxury of it

during the profound economic depression when I actually had a social work job ..., to appraise my intention against the threat of my young husband to depart if I adopted graduate study. My final decision promised a very difficult if interesting life .... (Landes, n.d.: 1)

On that day in the fall of 1931, Mrs. Benedict, then in her forties, looked at the attractive young novice and invited her to sit down. Boas withdrew, leaving the two women to begin a friendship that became the most signifi- cant in Landes's life. Landes was captivated by Ruth Benedict:

She was the sole woman employed in graduate anthropology at a major American university .... To see her was looking at a star .... She met her appointment with brilliance, of a special sort; and we, her stu- dents, shone in the reflection .... From such as she, none doubted who worked with her, were goddesses made .... Her physical self was important though not principal. Her face was elegantly lovely – oval and olive-skinned, graced by a dainty aquiline nose, long watching grey eyes that lipread to compensate for her partial deafness, prema- turely white cropped hair that crowned her considerable height. Her dress was often dowdy, even for Academia and the Great Depression; and her strong body moved rigidly erect, awkward on turned-out feet, as if trained in ballet .... What mesmerized students and others were the attentive, unblinking, luminous eyes. There was her hushed voice also, hushed in volume always, as if restraining something .... It put restraints on the listener. Then we who came into her hospitably open office to discuss our studies – we remember that receptiveness all our lives – we would look to her still face with the wide eyes intent upon the speaker and project upon its seeming serenity the approval we longed for. (ibid., 6)

In Benedict's office, Landes poured out the story of her unfulfilled expec- tations of marriage, her intellectual concerns, and her personal longings. Benedict listened, understood, and shared her own experience of marital discontent and her life quest for meaning and belonging. In her response to Landes's description of the recent dissolution of her brief marriage, Benedict summed up her own profound sense of loss and defeat at the elusiveness of intimacy: "One has only one husband, just as one has only one mother" (ibid., 1). Ruth Landes had found, she thought, a kindred spirit.

Landes was led to anthropology in the course of her immigrant's pursuit of individualism and modernity. Like many Jewish intellectuals of the time, the fascination with African-American culture that had taken her to Boas also provided a discourse for talking about the experiences of hegemony, difference, and marginalization that moulded immigrant consciousness. Meeting anthropology in the persons of Boas and Benedict, Landes was seduced by the social and emotional climate that studying anthropology also appeared to offer her: where Boas exemplified the commitment to science and the study of culture, Benedict appeared to offer to Landes a model for a life in anthropology.

Benedict, however, was not comfortably located in anthropology. In 1934, when she had just published *Patterns of Culture* (a landmark in anthropology and a best seller) and had fallen in love with a younger woman, Natalie Raymond, Benedict wrote in her journal:

> I ought to have enough self-knowledge to know what would make life meaningful to me. Not my work in anthropology, much as I owe to it. Like eating and drinking it has a necessary place in my life and adds to it, but the role it plays in Margaret [Mead]'s life or Boas's is impossible. Companionship comes close to the core of the matter, and loving Nat[alie Raymond] and taking such delight in her I have the happiest conditions for living that I've ever known. (quoted in Modell, 1983: 214)

Benedict's search for both meaningful work and the companionship of a kindred spirit resonated strongly for the young Landes and, curiously, Landes's subsequent life bears strong parallels to Benedict's. Although Landes never achieved a public position of stature in the discipline, her pilgrim soul, like Benedict's, guided her life through travels in search of both work and intimacy.

Benedict is widely remembered as an abysmal lecturer. Landes, however, describes being "mesmerized" by Benedict in the classroom and stimulated by her open, non-authoritative, extemporaneous style of presenting concepts and ideas:

> When Ruth lectured to us, standing, unconcerned with her chalk-smeared black dress, her voice small, soft, hesitant, she sounded as if she was thinking, in sound. The sentences came slowly, incompletely; words were begun and abandoned; corrections moved back and forth; there were pauses in the parts of speech to incubate a thought. I found

it wonderful, wonderful, because the style prompted myriad ideas in me. I sat usually in the front row ... looking up her dusty length to the intense, half-stricken face; and I felt I was about entering that head where the furnace of concepts blazed. (Landes, n.d.: 12)

Benedict's teaching was very much based on establishing personal relationships from which, inevitably, some students were excluded. However, recognizing Landes's individualistic spirit, her intellectual curiosity and capacity, and the "woman's dilemma" she faced, Benedict took Landes under her wing.[2] In retrospect this was both a blessing and a liability, but Landes's faith in Benedict's mentoring was unshakeable for years to come.

> Ruth was a great teacher because she was a unique personality to responsive minds. She pursued anthropology to answer her own private questions about the individual's fate. Her lectures focussed on the cultural designs and their sanctions that in each of the various societies mark out the scope of individual lives, bringing torment, dreary suffering, and occasionally special fulfilment. The overwhelming designs or "patterns" must imprison the soul of each "culture carrier," or member of society, and they accomplish this in ways that vary from place to place and from one era to another. (ibid., 13-14)

Like Benedict, Landes, in her Ojibwa and Brazilian field research, employed anthropology as a tool in an attempt to discover the ways in which the individual spirit — the pilgrim soul — can thrive within the constraints of culture (Cole, 1995a).

Beyond her captivation by Benedict and her admiration for Boas, the study of anthropology at Columbia suited Landes well. Studying anthropology in the 1930s was a lifestyle choice. Although Boas and Benedict were in their offices seven days a week, the program was unstructured: few courses were required and little guidance was given either in defining a research question or in methods of fieldwork. At the same time, Boas set high standards for students and assumed a breadth of knowledge that few possessed. A large part of student learning took place when other students returned from the field and presented their experiences to the weekly Wednesday afternoon graduate seminar. Students also gathered daily at "Al's place," a stationery store and luncheonette just off campus, to discuss and debate their reading. Both community and factionalism ruled. Anthropology at Columbia under Boas was "more in the nature of a debating society" than a "school of thought" (McMillan, 1986: 56).

Boas's first generation of students, who were almost all male (Kroeber, Lowie, Sapir, Herskovits), had gone on to establish anthropology programs at other major American institutions, but by the 1930s the student cohort at Columbia comprised equal numbers of women and men, including a significant number of mature students who brought a variety of life experiences into the classroom with them. Like Landes, the students were highly individualistic, propelled by personal and romantic optimisms and motivated by the social urgencies of the time: race relations, poverty, fascism, socialism, and the imminence of war.

Also significant and particular to Columbia is that by the 1930s a large proportion of the students in anthropology were second-generation Jews for whom Boas's anthropology provided a conduit out of their immigrant world into the wider American scene. These students were cosmopolitan, urban, theoretical, and intellectual – unlike the Middle Western or New England Anglo-American population that comprised the student body in other American anthropology departments. Socially and intellectually, the environment perfectly suited Ruth Landes:

> I cannot remember any textbook style data that Ruth taught; I do not remember any discussion with her of my five productive field trips during my apprenticeship in anthropology; and I know that neither she nor Boas wasted time on class examinations. What I do remember is that she expected students to produce serious written works, inducing in all of us a grim sense of that responsibility. She conveyed the *attitude* that made scholars of the survivors, receiving us when we wanted to talk, reading every scrap of our manuscripts for eventual appearance in print, finding stipends to support us during the writing, editing the final drafts, and forgetting to congratulate us when the article or book appeared .... She paid the inspiring compliment of taking our little achievements for granted .... I think she did not gladly release students to full self-determination, but she did not actively interfere. However, the student who took a professional initiative without consultation would find her warm openness shift to coldness in manner and phrase. (Landes, n.d.: 14-15)

In this last statement, Landes begins to express some of the ambivalence that was also part of the experience of Benedict's mentorship.

Under Benedict's direction, Landes conducted her first fieldwork in the summer of 1932 at Manitou Rapids in northwestern Ontario. Here she met Maggie Wilson, her second key mentor in anthropology. Mrs. Wilson, an

Ojibwa grandmother and visionary, through her storytelling directed Landes to the cross-cultural study of women's experience. With Maggie, Ruth was free to explore the questions of work and marriage from the perspectives of women who, despite cultural and historical differences, shared dilemmas over the life course that were not dissimilar from Landes's own (Cole, 1995a, 1997). After publishing her Ph.D. thesis, *Ojibwa Sociology*, a conventionally written description of social and political organization, Landes presented a manuscript that Benedict and Nat Raymond helped to edit for publication as *The Ojibwa Woman* in 1938. This book initiated Landes's public life of controversy in anthropology. Critics charged that the book, based on Mrs. Wilson's narratives of women's autonomous lives, resourcefulness, and skill, represented merely "an idiosyncratic female point of view" (Alexander, 1975). Further, Landes's analysis of individualism and contestation within Ojibwa culture was disputed by anthropologists for whom Ojibwa society represented a hunter-gatherer society where social relations are communal and egalitarian (see Cole, 1995a).

Then, in 1938-39 Landes conducted field research in Bahia, Brazil. Here, she was drawn to describe the singularity of the women ritual leaders of the Afro-Brazilian *candomblé* possession religion and the harsh lives of women for whom the cult houses were havens from marital strife and from daily lives of grinding poverty. In this research, first published in 1940 in an article entitled "A Cult Matriarchate and Male Homosexuality," Landes also described the roles played by men in the cults. Her research was lambasted by critics, notably anthropologists Melville Herskovits and Artur Ramos, who objected to the ethnographic focus on women, to the discussion of male homosexuality, and, not incidentally, to Landes's personal comportment in the field – Landes had had a love affair with a young Black Brazilian folklorist, Edison Carneiro, during the fieldwork (see Cole, 1995b). At the time, Landes was vulnerable to the attacks. As a result of their censuring, she was unable to find an academic publisher for her Bahian study and she rewrote the book in a popular style seeking a wider reading public and finding a trade publisher. *The City of Women* was published in 1947 by Macmillan. At the time this may have represented a "modified acceptance strategy" (in Nancy Parezo's terms), but towards the end of her life Landes reflected on the experience:

I hardly think it was an accident that only I have ever described the Brazilian priestesses. Or for that matter, the Ojibwa women of Ontario's Rainy River. Male and female scholars preceded me and followed me in both places for decades. Neither set of women, Indian and Brazilian Black, gained me straight professional attention .... *The Ojibwa Woman* has been manhandled in our leading anthropological publications to the effect that I had followed some bias, either in selecting the women or in giving a warped picture. That is, my personality was focussed on, not theirs .... I was the presuming woman. (Landes, 1980: 10)

Landes made these remarks in a 1980 address to the Department of Anthropology at the University of Calgary, which she concluded by cautioning her audience: "Keep in mind that our women anthropologists are often depreciated as being emotionally prejudiced. It means they are not scientific; or intellectually as powerful as men; or even reliable. I was told this by no less an authority than Linton. Boas was dead" (ibid., 16).

With the death of Franz Boas, the key male patron of women students and scholars in anthropology was lost – and support from women colleagues in the discipline could not be assumed. After her return from Brazil in June of 1939, Landes was again seeking employment in anthropology. Benedict had withdrawn from the daily operation of the department at Columbia (now headed by Linton) and was on sabbatical in California, where she was beginning life with a new partner, Ruth Valentine. In Benedict's absence, Landes turned to Margaret Mead for collegial advice on the job search and for intellectual mentoring in writing up her Brazilian data. In the winter of 1935-36, just after receiving her Ph.D., Landes had been a member of Mead's Cooperation and Competition Seminar and her chapter, "The Ojibwa in Canada," was published in the resulting book edited by Mead (Landes, 1937c).

Mead, however, was unsympathetic both to Landes's personal style and to her theoretical perspectives. Specifically, Mead failed to appreciate the theoretical importance of the urban context and historical legacy of slavery in Afro-Brazilian culture and disagreed with Landes's writing on male homosexuality in Brazilian *candomblé*. In a letter to Benedict, on October 2, 1939, Mead laments that Landes's portrait of the men is of "prostitutes indifferently turned priests" and not "the more typical primitive picture of integrated socially accepted transvestism." Mead urges Benedict that Landes should be encouraged to "transform ... the urban, complex, disorganized society picture with prostitution into the more typical primitive picture of integrated socially accepted transvestism." In the same letter, she also expresses her personal frustration with Landes: "If there were some way of teaching her to be either (a) a lady or (b) an ordinary academic female who would behave in a routine way in academic situations, it would be a help"

(MM, B1). And, in a letter written a few weeks later, on October 22, 1939, Mead wrote: "she does seem to have a very definite capacity to learn, and I can see how you think she is worth taking trouble over. I still find her personally trying"(MM, B1). Where Benedict appreciated Landes's individualism and her originality in scholarship, Mead found Landes's personality irritating and disagreed with her theoretical frames for cultural analysis. Landes's analysis of Afro-Brazilian *candomblé* described internal contestations over meaning and social roles rather than highlighting the integration and coherence central to Mead's and Benedict's portraits of culture.

After Benedict's death on September 17, 1948, Landes, still without permanent employment since receiving her doctorate in 1935, sought Mead's support. On October 13, 1948, she wrote to Mead:

> May I ask you for advice? Now that my war-borne activities are ended, I am at a loss. You know that when the National Defense was created, I was sent for, first by the Co-ordinator of Inter-American Affairs [in 1940] ... and then by President Roosevelt's Committee on Fair Employment Practises ... where I remained until the end of the war. These took me far from academic work, though to my eyes they look like applied anthropology, and I was offered the jobs because I am an anthropologist .... when the program ended at the close of 1945, I felt I *had* to return to anthropology. My way was to write *The City of Women* .... [In 1946] I was hired by the Los Angeles Metropolitan and Welfare Council specifically by its Youth Project which was concerned with Mexican and Negro ... children. In June 1947, I finished [writing the report for the Council] .... I always felt that Ruth Benedict was my lifeline to anthropological developments – as she had been, in fact. So now I do not know where to turn. I prefer research above all, but having gone without a salary for over a year, my first need is for a job – not a temporary one .... Burdened as you are, I was reluctant to add my troubles – but where else would I turn for anthropological advice, if not to you? I am not asking for an immediate solution. If you could however keep me in mind for anything pertinent that might come your way, I will be once again your debtor." (MM, C18)

In December 1948, through her family's position in Jewish community service work in New York and with Mead's support, Landes returned to the immigrant world she had sought to escape and began a contract as research director with the American Jewish Committee in New York.

Margaret Mead could not be the mentor Ruth Benedict had been. The two Ruths had loved the "pilgrim soul" in one another and neither was as single-minded about anthropology as Mead. Mead was also suspect of Landes's attractiveness, her open sexuality, and her experiments in interracial intimacy. In 1944, when Landes was for a short time engaged to marry Salvador Lopez, a Mexican lawyer working for the rights of migrant farm labourers, Mead told her: "I don't know if that isn't the best thing for you! You've always had a yen to marry into the minority group. You'll toy with the aristocracy but you'll marry minority" (RFB, June 18, 1944, Landes to Benedict). Speaking from a position of security in mainstream White ("aristocratic") America, Mead is referring here to Landes's affairs with African-American men and with Edison Carneiro in Brazil and, at the same time, reminding Landes of her minority status in America (see Cole, 1995a, 1995b).

In an October 2, 1950, letter of reference to the Committee on International Exchange of Persons, to whom Landes had applied for a Fulbright Fellowship,[3] Mead wrote:

> Dr. Ruth Landes ... is thoroughly trained in anthropological field methods and untiring as a field worker .... During the years since she received her degree she has been unencumbered by economic responsibilities beyond her own support and therefore has been free to follow research opportunities rather than to seek any sort of steady professional advancement. This leaves her without a teaching record, but I believe that she would do a competent job of lecturing to advanced students. She has continued to grow intellectually, and has during the last year taken considerable steps ahead in integrating her work with current personality theory. She has serious professional interests and commitments and would take the responsibility of a grant from the Committee on International Exchange of Persons as something not to be handled lightly. *I think I should add that Dr. Landes is considerably better looking and more attractive than many of her sex who seek academic careers and that this circumstance may be looked upon not without acrimony by both male and female colleagues.* (MM, D34; emphasis added)

And, in a May 15, 1957, letter of reference to the School of Social Welfare at the University of Southern California, after describing Landes as "a gifted fieldworker" with "original first class training, and [a] wealth of experience," Mead went on to note: "She was once extraordinarily beautiful, and her role as a woman tends to get confused – more by other people than by herself – with the things that she does" (MM, D34). Significantly, as noted above, Landes and Mead also disagreed about the nature of anthropology's subject.

Landes's interest in documenting the complexity, heterogeneity, urbanity, politics, and history of African-based cultures in the New World was, at a fundamental level, not shared by Mead, who considered culture to be "an integrated whole" and Landes to be "obsessed" on the subject of African-American culture.

On February 2, 1965, shortly after the American Anthropological Association had begun its job placement service and thirty years after Ruth Landes had received her doctorate, Margaret Mead wrote to Ruth Landes and suggested that she register with the placement service: "There are jobs going everywhere, big, little and middle sized .... Everyone who registered with them is getting showered with offers from the US and Canada" (MM, C74). In April 1965, thanks to Mead's drawing her back into the circles of academe, Landes was offered and accepted a tenured position in the new Department of Anthropology at McMaster University in Hamilton, Ontario. It should not go unnoted that this appointment was in Canada – not in Mead's America – and that Ruth Landes acutely experienced her life in Canada (where she died in 1991) as a life in exile.

Sojourners in Modernist Science:
Feminist Moments in the History of Anthropology

A pilgrim from an immigrant world, a sojourner in anthropology, Ruth Landes and her "lone-wolf anthropology" represent one feminist career trajectory in the discipline. Her gender-conscious individualism was nurtured by Ruth Benedict as teacher and fellow pilgrim and moderated by Margaret Mead. Richard Handler (1990: 164) has described the quest for self-realization and self-expression as a "hallmark of modernism" and a tension in the modernist science of Boasian anthropology whose project was to develop a theory of culture that could accommodate both cultural holism and human individuality. The feminist "moment" of the interwar years in Boasian anthropology was both created and ultimately undermined by the modernist aspirations of early twentieth-century American culture. Where modernist America upheld self-development as a value, its realization was structurally less possible for women. Women like Benedict and Landes were contained within institutions – whether marriage or academe – that required reliance on a male patron and that, through hierarchical processes, compromised women's relations with one another. The clustering of women in anthropology in the interwar years was a product of the openness immigration had created in New York society and the political activism and community work of the women's suffrage movement. The numbers of women in anthropology and the emergence of feminist anthropologies in the second half of the twentieth century are similarly contingent on historical moments such as the civil rights movement and second-wave feminism. Young women anthropologists entering the discipline at the end of the century thus cannot assume that the position of women in the discipline or the status of gender in anthropological theory has been secured. Women must still make the choice of strategy: accommodation or confrontation.

As a product of history, feminist anthropology is as dependent on its relationship to the wider society as it is to intellectual currents within the discipline. It is critical that feminist anthropologists remain committed to practice, to communities of women in real social contexts, and to their relationships with one another both within and without the academy. The institutional context of anthropology, however, creates ambiguity among women in the discipline. As the complex relations of Landes, Benedict, and Mead illustrate, differences among women in anthropology – of social class, ethnicity, race, age, familial status, mentoring, professional recognition and security, theoretical orientation, and political commitment – are not new. The challenge for feminist anthropologists, now as in the past, is to reject the hierarchical processes of disciplinary canon-making and to mobilize differences among women as creative forces in the innovation of theory, method, and practice. This challenge constrained the relations of Landes, Benedict, and Mead during the "modernist" moment of interwar anthropology. It was almost insurmountable during the "scientific" moment of the post-World War II period when women were frozen out of the academy and into domestic roles. And it faces women in the "reflexive" moment of cutbacks at the century's end when they are being "welcomed" as cheap labour in underfunded academic institutions.

Notes

Primary sources consulted and cited are: the Ruth Schlossberg Landes Papers (RSL) at the Smithsonian Institution, the Ruth Fulton Benedict Papers (RFB) at Vassar College, and the Margaret Mead Papers (MM) at the Library of Congress in Washington, D.C. I thank Ruth Landes's executor, the Research Institute for the Study of Man in New York, and Mary Catherine Bateson, executrix for Ruth Benedict and Margaret Mead, for permission to quote from these papers. The research is part of a larger work on the life and writing of Ruth Landes, funded by the Social Sciences and Humanities Research Council of Canada and the Faculty Research and Development Program at Concordia University.

1 This portrait of the Landes home relies on my reading of Ruth Landes's letters and journals and on my interviews with family members. See Susan Bordo's "Missing Kitchens" (1997: 214-41) for an uncannily similar portrait of a daughter's experience in an immigrant Jewish household.

2 The "woman's dilemma" refers here to the historical reality that many women have felt they must make a choice between marriage and career and that the search for intimacy conflicts with the search for meaningful work or profession. Toni Morrison (1983: 122) has argued that this is a dilemma particular, however, to White women and that "Black women seem able to combine the nest and the adventure."

3 Landes, in her forties, did receive the Fulbright Fellowship and went to Britain in 1951-52 to study Caribbean migration. She continued the life of a migrant scholar for more than a decade after this, during which time she taught anthropology in the School of Social Welfare at the University of Southern California and in the Faculty of Education at the Claremont Graduate School, and was married briefly to Ignacio Lopez, a Mexican-American journalist.

References

Abu-Lughod, Lila. 1990. "Can There be a Feminist Ethnography?" *Women and Performance* 5, 1: 7-27.

Aisenberg, Nadya, and Mona Harrington. 1988. *Women of Academe: Outsiders in the Sacred Grove*. Amherst: University of Massachusetts Press.

Alexander, Herbert. 1975. "Review of *The Ojibwa Woman*," *American Anthropologist* 77: 110-11.

Antler, Joyce. 1997. *The Journey Home: Jewish Women and the American Century*. New York: Free Press.

Babcock, Barbara. 1995. "'Not in the Absolute Singular': Rereading Ruth Benedict," in Ruth Behar and Deborah Gordon, eds., *Women Writing Culture*. Berkeley: University of California Press, 104-30.

Benedict, Ruth. 1934. *Patterns of Culture*. Boston: Houghton Mifflin.

_____. 1940. *Race: Science and Politics*. New York: Modern Age.

_____. 1946. *The Chrysanthemum and the Sword: Patterns of Japanese Culture*. Boston: Houghton Mifflin.

Bordo, Susan. 1997. *Twilight Zones: The Hidden Life of Cultural Images From Plato to O.J.* Berkeley: University of California Press.

Cole, Sally. 1995a. "Women's Stories and Boasian Texts: The Ojibwa Ethnography of Ruth Landes and Maggie Wilson," *Anthropologica* 37: 3-25.

_____. 1995b. "Ruth Landes and the Early Ethnography of Race and Gender," in Ruth Behar and Deborah Gordon, eds., *Women Writing Culture*. Berkeley: University of California Press, 166-85.

_____. 1997a. "Dear Ruth, This is the Story of Maggie Wilson, Ojibwa Ethnologist," in Elspeth Cameron and Janice Dickin, eds., *Great Dames*. Toronto: University of Toronto Press, 75-96.

_____. 1997b. "Introduction" to Ruth Landes, *The Ojibwa Woman*, 3rd ed. Lincoln: University of Nebraska Press.

Deacon, Desley. 1997. *Elsie Clews Parsons: Inventing Modern Life*. Chicago: University of Chicago Press.

Finn, Janet. 1995. "Ella Cara Deloria and Mourning Dove: Writing for Culture, Writing Against the Grain," in Ruth Behar and Deborah Gordon, eds., *Women Writing Culture*. Berkeley: University of California Press, 131-47.

Handler, Richard. 1990. "Ruth Benedict and the Modernist Sensibility," in Marc Manganaro, ed., *Modernist Anthropology: From Fieldwork to Text*. Princeton, N.J.: Princeton University Press, 163-80.

Hernández, Gabriela. 1995. "Multiple Subjectivities and Strategic Positionality: Zora Neale Hurston's Experimental Ethnographies," in Ruth Behar and Deborah Gordon, eds., *Women Writing Culture*. Berkeley: University of California Press.148-66.

hooks, bell. 1990. "Saving Black Folk Culture: Zora Neale Hurston as Anthropologist and Writer," in bell hooks, ed., *Yearning: Race, Gender and Cultural Politics*. Toronto: Between the Lines, 135-43.

Lamphere, Louise. 1993, "Gladys Reichard among the Navaho," in Nancy Parezo, ed., *Hidden Scholars: Women Anthropologists and the Native American Southwest*. Albuquerque: University of New Mexico Press, 157-88.

Landes, Ruth. 1937a. *Ojibwa Sociology*. New York: Columbia University Press.

_____. 1937b. "The Personality of the Ojibwa," *Culture and Personality* 6: 51-60.

_____. 1937c. "The Ojibwa in Canada," in Margaret Mead, ed., *Cooperation and Competition Among Primitive Peoples*. New York: McGraw-Hill, 87-127.

_____. 1938a. *The Ojibwa Woman*. New York: Columbia University Press.

_____. 1938b. "The Abnormal Among the Ojibwa," *Journal of Abnormal and Social Psychology* 33: 14-33.

_____. 1940a. "A Cult Matriarchate and Male Homosexuality," *Journal of Abnormal and Social Psychology* 35: 306-97.

_____. 1940b. "Fetish Worship in Brazil," *Journal of American Folklore* 53: 261-70.

_____. 1947. *The City of Women*. New York: Macmillan.

_____. 1968a. *Ojibwa Religion and the Midéwiwin*. Madison: University of Wisconsin Press.

_____. 1968b. *The Mystic Lake Sioux*. Madison: University of Wisconsin Press.

_____. 1969. "Negro Jews in Harlem," *Jewish Journal of Sociology* 9, 2: 247-76.

_____. 1970. *The Prairie Potawatomi*. Madison: University of Wisconsin Press.

_____. 1980. "Women in Anthropology," paper presented to the Department of Anthropology, University of Calgary.

_____. n.d. "Ruth Benedict: Teacher," unpublished paper.

Lurie, Nancy. 1966. "Women in Early American Anthropology," in June Helm, ed., *Pioneers of American Anthropology: The Uses of Biography*. Seattle: University of Washington Press, 29-81.

McMillan, Robert. 1986. "The Study of Anthropology, 1931 to 1937, at Columbia University and the University of Chicago," unpublished Ph.D. dissertation, York University, Toronto, Canada.

Mark, Joan. 1988. *A Stranger in Her Native Land: Alice Fletcher and the American Indians*. Lincoln: University of Nebraska Press.

Mead, Margaret. 1959. *An Anthropologist at Work: Writings of Ruth Benedict*. London: Secker and Warburg.

Modell, Judith. 1983. *Ruth Benedict: Patterns of a Life*. Philadelphia: University of Pennsylvania Press.

Morrison, Toni. 1983. "Interview with Claudia Tate," in Claudia Tate, ed., *Black Women Writers at Work*. New York: Continuum, 117-31.

Myrdal, Gunnar. 1944. *An American Dilemma: The Negro Problem and Modern Democracy*, 2 vols. New York: Harper.

Parezo, Nancy, ed. 1993. *Hidden Scholars: Women Anthropologists and the Native American Southwest*. Albuquerque: University of New Mexico Press.

Rossiter, Margaret. 1982. *Women Scientists in America: Struggles and Strategies to 1940*. Baltimore: Johns Hopkins University Press.

Stocking, George, ed. 1989. *Romantic Motives: Essays on Anthropological Sensibility*. History of Anthropology, vol. 6. Madison: University of Wisconsin Press.

Tedlock, Barbara. 1995. "Works and Wives: On the Sexual Division of Textual Labor," in Ruth Behar and Deborah Gordon, eds., *Women Writing Culture*. Berkeley: University of California Press, 267-86.

THREE

TRANSLATING MOTHER TONGUES:
AMY TAN AND MAXINE HONG KINGSTON ON
ETHNOGRAPHIC AUTHORITY

Karen Su

TRANSLATION between languages and cultures involves the negotiation of power – who must translate for whom? As an Asian-American, I feel the act of translation thrust upon me all too often. Many Asian-Americans are held to an "ethnographic imperative" to explain "Asian" culture to a Western audience or to translate what's perceived as our "mother" culture. Exacerbating the situation is the dominant culture's lack of recognition of what an Asian-American cultural identity, as distinct from an Asian one, might be. The central conflicts between mothers and daughters in Amy Tan's *The Joy Luck Club* (1989) and Maxine Hong Kingston's *The Woman Warrior* (1976) involve predicaments that are emblematic of the contexts within which cultural translations must be negotiated by Asian-Americans. Both narratives focus on American-born daughters struggling to understand their Chinese mothers' cultural sensibilities within a dominant American culture. Their struggles are worked out through acts of translation – in Tan's text the mothers act as translators while in Kingston's text, the daughter must translate. Both Tan and Kingston translate "mother tongues" in more than one sense. In their texts, they literally translate Chinese language, but they also figuratively translate the language of mothers. Scenes of translation in both authors' texts engage with issues of cultural representation, ethnographic authority, and "authenticity."

Amy Tan's *The Joy Luck Club* and Maxine Hong Kingston's *The Woman Warrior* present texts relevant to current discussions within anthropology and literature highlighting the intersection of ethnography and fiction. I situate my discussion of translation in Tan's and Kingston's works within the context of current work in feminist ethnography, which both emphasizes experimental writing by women within anthropology and, of particular importance, attempts to recover and recognize the contributions of women of colour (see Behar and Gordon, 1995; Finn, 1995; Harrison, 1995; Hernández, 1995; Visweswaran, 1994). In the introduction to the recent anthology *Women Writ-*

ing Culture, Ruth Behar spotlights the juncture in anthropology of generic interventions (the literary/textual turn) and the interrogation of power relations regarding gender and race. Behar explains that she and co-editor Deborah Gordon intend *Women Writing Culture* to address "the poetics and politics of feminist ethnography as a way of rethinking anthropology's purpose in a multicultural America" (Behar, 1995: 22). My aim, here, is to showcase the relevance of Tan's and Kingston's works to feminist ethnography's rethinking of anthropology's purpose, especially within the multicultural context of ethnic literature. An examination of their translation practices allows us to discuss how their positions as ethnic women writers parallel the positions of "native" women anthropologists. Both Tan and Kingston have had to write under the constraints of the "ethnographic gaze." I begin by highlighting some general issues that concern Asian-American cultural "authenticity" and literary representation in order to focus on the significance of translation to "ethnographic authority."

Translating "Sugar Sisters" and "Heavenly Chickens"

Critical debates about Amy Tan and Maxine Hong Kingston have persistently centred on issues of representational and cultural authenticity. As is the case with works by many writers of colour, theirs have been frequently scrutinized as ethnographic/sociological documents of *the* Chinese-American women's experience. On the one hand, they confront a dominant culture that persistently exoticizes the "Chinese" content of their work. An overwhelming number of mainstream book reviewers as well as a number of mainstream feminist critics associate authenticity with a Chinese female experience rather than a Chinese-American one. On the other hand, Tan and Kingston also face Asian-American reviewers and critics who often hold them accountable for providing correctives to such stereotypical premises. To this Asian-American audience, authenticity tied to Chinese culture is inimical to an alternative authenticity tied to Chinese-American culture.

How these notions of authenticity have played out within Asian-American literary discussions and how they have come to be interlinked with the ethnographic genre must first be outlined. We can trace a critique of so-called ethnographic writing to the early attempts to sever what was deemed authentic Asian-American writing from ethnographic writings catering to mainstream American readers. In other words, the idea of "audience" was deemed crucial. At this early stage, the battle over authenticity involved the attempt to define Asian-American identity as separate from Asian identity. In early assessments of Asian-American writing, ethnography was demonized because it most often presented Asian culture to mainstream reader-ships and set a precedent for what kind of writing by Asian-Americans would be appealing to mainstream audiences. In *Asian American Literature: An Introduction to the Writings and Their Social Context* (1982), Elaine Kim classifies writers of early autobiographical ethnographic writings such as Etsu Sugimoto, author of *A Daughter of the Samurai* (1925), and Lin Yutang, author of *My Country and My People* (1937), as "Ambassadors of Goodwill." Their texts bridged cultural gaps by presenting Asian culture for Western audiences, and they offered views of Western life in America from an Asian point of view (Kim, 1982: 24-29).

This genre set the model for subsequent generations of Asian-American writers in the 1950s and 1960s who also wrote successfully as cultural ambassadors. Their access to native Asian culture, however, was often available to them mainly through Western historical and ethnographic documents to which they turned under the pressure to act as "authentic" authorities on Asian culture. For example, Kim describes *The House That Tai Ming Built* (1963), by second-generation Chinese-American writer Virginia Lee, as a "quasi-autobiographical" book that "is aimed at explaining something to non-Chinese. Lee relies on research about Chinese art for her presentation of Chinese 'culture' .... [A]t times, the narrative degenerates into mini-lectures on Chinese bronzes and philosophy" (Kim, 1982: 291 n. 29). Similarly, in *Aiiieeeee! An Anthology of Asian-American Writers* (1991 [1974]), the editors offer a critique of American-born authors such as Lee, who assumed the role of "native informant" and "cultural expert" in response to the ethnographic imperative to explain Asian culture. At this early stage, the *Aiiieeeee!* editors and Kim call on Asian-American authors to refuse the ethnographic stance of being "native informant/cultural expert" with an authenticity tied to Asia. They encourage an alternative authenticity for Asian-American writers. Under these circumstances, ethnographic writing is targeted as something to be avoided for understandable political reasons.

The rejection of ethnography has continued in more contemporary Asian-American critical assessments. Stringent criteria demarcate boundaries between non-fiction and fiction, between "authentic" and "inauthentic" Asian-American voices. In the attacks launched against Kingston in the late 1970s, for instance, Benjamin Tong and Jeff Chan both vociferously denounce *The Woman Warrior*, accusing the text of being an "obvious fiction" passing for autobiography (see Chan, 1977; Tong, 1977). They take issue with the book being labelled as "autobiography," insinuating that her "fiction" is an assimilationist misrepresentation of Chinese-American culture. In these debates over cultural authenticity and misrepresentation, mistranslation becomes one of the major signifiers of cultural misrepresentation. Kingston is criticized for mistranslating: Ben Tong hones in on how she mistranslates "frog" as "heavenly chicken"; Jeff Chan claims her use of "ghost" for the Chinese word *kuei* is suspect; Frank Chin attacks Kingston's remark that there is a female "I" that means "slave" (see Tong, 1977; Chan, 1977; Chin, 1992; Chan *et al.*, 1992). Their use of the misogynist metaphor "traitor/whore" has been well publicized (see Chung, 1991). I won't rehearse all of the stages of these debates around Kingston. Very cogent and rigorous critiques against these polemical anti-feminist stances have been influential in dismantling a cultural nationalist cultivation of ethnic authenticity within Asian-American literary studies (Kim, 1990; Cheung, 1990; Lowe, 1996; Wong, 1992).

Many feminist counter-critiques of these attacks against Kingston, however, offer a defence that rests precisely on her text's "fictionality" and her mixing of fiction and non-fiction techniques (see Cheung, 1990, 1993; Homsher, 1979; Kim, 1990; Lidoff, 1991; Lim, 1992; Schueller, 1989; Smith, 1987; Wong, 1988, 1992; Yalom, 1991). We can see the intricate ties being made between genres and translation within these debates. Sau-ling Wong, for instance, pinpoints the strong correlation between translation and a realist notion of mimetic verisimilitude that Kingston's detractors make in their polemical stance:

> [T]he *graphe* part of *autobiography*, the act of writing, the transformation of life into text, is seen by Kingston's critics as a mechanical conveyance of facts from the autobiographer's mind to the reader's via a medium in the physical world, the process pleasant or not depending on the author's literary talents. In the case of *The Woman Warrior* debate, correspondence between word and thing is deemed so perfect that a Chinese term, *kuei* [ghost], is supposed to be translatable by only one English equivalent, with all other overtones outlawed. (Wong, 1992: 258)

Wong points to the pitfall of looking at translation and representational authority too narrowly. Whereas Kingston's detractors hold her to "authentic" translation, Wong points out that Kingston actually questions the premise of translation in her text. Wong and many other critics have praised this "interrogative" modality of Kingston's work (Cheung, 1993; Schueller, 1989, 1992; Wong, 1992, 1995).

The post-modern interrogations of the authority of traditional discourses that provide a broader context for these analyses of Kingston have been thoroughly wide-reaching. There has been a persistent effort within critical evaluations of Asian-American writing to shun ethnography and translation altogether. This basis for analysis has become so ingrained that it seems any sign of ethnographic explanation or any appearance of translation in an Asian-American text automatically flags it as suspect, while those who write in a genre considered to be artistically and/or politically "progressive" might be "let off the hook" or automatically perceived as problematizing an ethnographic stance. The critical reception of Amy Tan's work is especially intriguing because so many critics seem to use the analytical apparatus developed around Kingston's texts as the prototype from which to take their cue when analysing Tan's texts. An overwhelming number of critics have read *The Joy Luck Club* as a post-modernist text (Braendlin, 1995; Heung, 1993; Ho, 1995; Schueller, 1992; Shen, 1995; Souris, 1994; Xu, 1994). The labelling of the text as post-modernist seems to have closed off the possibility of examining it for ethnographic modes of writing.

Opening up this deadlock in which post-modern writing is cast in opposition to ethnographic writing can steer us away from demonizing all ethnography. Such an opening up would make it possible to recognize and acknowledge the ways in which Tan's *The Joy Luck Club* does indeed employ the native informant ethnographic mode while Kingston's *The Woman Warrior* could be described as a critical ethnography of differential knowledge. This contrast between Tan and Kingston, however, has been obfuscated by the way that ethnography and post-modern writing have been cast as opposing genres. The interventions within feminist ethnography that highlight the intersections between fiction and ethnography, therefore, can be effectively applied in dislodging these problematics of ethnography and translation from the circumscribed niches of authenticity and generic form.

Kamala Visweswaran's *Fictions of Feminist Ethnography* (1994) is useful for an inquiry into the literary use of anthropological writing techniques because she tackles the issue of genre and elucidates how genre is defined with regard to the writings of women of colour. Her analysis of the link between fiction and ethnography provides a valuable analytical model and disentangles the mutually exclusive categories of fiction and non-fiction, or realist and post-modernist genres from their ties to diametrical poles of ethnographic versus artistic authority. Visweswaran recovers authority for Ella Cara Deloria and Zora Neale Hurston by stressing that the domains of both "serious" fiction and ethnography were reserved for White men, a reality confirmed by the fact that Hurston and Deloria have not been recognized until recently for their anthropological work (Visweswaran, 1994: 33). She argues that in addition to racist and sexist prejudices, the lack of recognition for Hurston and Deloria stemmed in part from generic prejudices. She writes: "Yet in identifying the 'literary or rhetorical dimensions of ethnography,' the 'authorizing fictions' of anthropology, ... even the ethnographers of the experimental kind stop short of considering the novel as anthropology" (Visweswaran, 1994: 2). Therefore, one way to recover their "ethnographic authority," she suggests, would be to read their novels as critical ethnographies. Visweswaran asserts that "feminist [ethnography] can make a contribution to the study of colonialism ... through a critique of the politics of representation itself" (Visweswaran, 1994: 32).

Perhaps such a disentanglement would be one step towards rectifying a practice of translation that departs from its complicit role within colonial structures of cultural domination. Tejaswini Niranjana writes in *Siting Translation: History, Post-Structuralism and the Colonial Context*:

> The rethinking of translation becomes an important task in a context where it has been used since the European Enlightenment to underwrite practices of subjectification, especially for colonized peoples. Such a rethinking – a task of great urgency for a postcolonial theory attempting to make sense of "subjects" already living "in translation," imaged and re-imaged by colonial ways of seeing – seeks to reclaim the notion of translation by deconstructing it and reinscribing its potential as a strategy of resistance. (Niranjana, 1992: 6)

Along with anthropology, many within post-colonial studies, cultural studies, feminist studies, and translation studies have initiated a critique of translation practices that overlooks power differentials between cultures and homogenizes "difference" (see Dingwaney and Maier, 1995; Venuti, 1992). Tan and Kingston provide contrasting conceptions of translation relevant to the issue of negotiating difference not only within anthropology and literature but also in feminist theory. I turn now to an initial comparison between Tan's translation practice and Kingston's. We find some compelling contrasts between the techniques they use that ultimately are emblematic of the differences in how they assert ethnographic authority.

In *The Kitchen God's Wife* (1991), Tan's use of "sugar sister" as a translation of the Chinese word for "cousin" is a mistake resulting from the confusion of the homonyms "hall" and "sugar." The native Chinese-speaking mother, Winnie, explains to her English-speaking daughter, Pearl, "[Auntie Helen] and I called each other *tang jie*, 'sugar sister,' the friendly way to refer to a girl cousin" (Tan, 1991: 154). Wong has argued that the italicized Chinese words in Tan's texts are meant to be "markers of authenticity," but that, ironically, this mistake and many others show that Tan's ethnographic authority is cultivated on the basis of a problematic authenticity (Wong, 1995: 187). Many of the authenticating Chinese phrases in Tan's texts are not even mistranslations, they are simply unidiomatic Chinese phrases. Since these appear in the narratives of both daughter and mother characters they cannot justifiably be interpreted as misunderstandings only on the part of the non-Chinese-speaking daughters. The mistakes are too numerous to list; my main purpose here is to underscore that even though Tan is obviously an unreliable mediator, she clearly uses the rhetoric of cultural authority, incorporating translations and facts about Chinese culture in her novels in order for them to be read as "authentically" Chinese.

In the way that "sugar sister" is given as a gloss in Tan's text, a similar example of mistranslation in Kingston's *Woman Warrior* is offered here as a parenthetical aside. When the narrating daughter describes the power of her mother's ghost stories, she says: "My mother relished these scare orgies. She was good at naming — Wall Ghost, Frog Spirit (frogs are 'heavenly chickens'), Eating Partner ... " (Kingston, 1989a [1976]: 65). The literal translation of frog is "field" chicken, not "heavenly" chicken, however. Like Tan's "sugar sister" mistake, it also arises from a confusion of two homonyms. But in *China Men* (1989b [1980]), Kingston seems to offer us a rejoinder by including a "heavenly chicken" rumination that is specifically explained as a pun:

> "A field chicken?" I repeated. "Field chicken," [Say Goong] said. "Sky chicken. Sky toad. Heavenly toad. Field toad." It was a pun and the words the same except for the low tone of field and the high tone of heaven or sky. He put the toad in my hands — it breathed, and its heart beat, every part of it alive — and I felt its dryness and warmth and hind feet as it sprang off. How odd that a toad could be both of the field and of the sky. It was very funny. Say Goong and I laughed. "Heavenly chicken," I called, chasing the toad. (Kingston, 1989b [1980]: 166)

Notice that Kingston does not provide the Chinese term at all. She uses the explanation of the pun to meditate on the nature of toads and the language used to represent them. In this initial comparison, we could conclude that Kingston ultimately refuses the ethnographic stance by not "explaining" or translating the pun literally, while Tan takes pains to incorporate the rhetoric of cultural explanation. However, this simple distinction does not rest on whether or not an author "translates."

Neither the strategy of insisting on a clear boundary between experimental and ethnographic writing nor that of claiming that the boundaries have been completely subverted really addresses the particular ways in which ethnographic discursive techniques are employed by *both* Kingston and Tan. Kingston's translations, generally, are not indicative of a complete rejection of ethnographic discourse, though she certainly questions it constantly. Tan's mistranslations also do not reflect a refusal to translate, or a refusal of the ethnographic paradigm. Her mistranslations, far from showing that she eschews the "native informant" stance, show that she is completely inadequate as a native informant and ethnographer. In fact, a comparison of Tan and Kingston is particularly revealing of how they use ethnographic authority to different ends. Tan actually uses realist anthropological techniques while Kingston employs an experimental mode that might be considered a critical intervention of traditional ethnographic discourse.

Tan's Ethnographic "Fiction"

The Joy Luck Club features Chinese mothers for their ability to "translate." Each mother shares her past history of hardship in China in order to give her daughter strength to cope with her American life – as a minority within the dominant culture, each daughter faces the dilemma of having low self-esteem within her relationships and career. These stories are instigated by the death of Jing-mei (June) Woo's mother, after which June is asked by the other mothers to take her mother's place in their Joy Luck Club. The "native" mother is valorized as the holder of "authentic origin." The Americanized daughters' relationships to their "mother tongue" is especially significant; maternal language guides the daughters through American life as the mothers impart feminist knowledge to them by recounting their triumphs over Chinese patriarchy. The anthropological structure of Tan's novel supports a narrative of assimilation into American culture for the daughters that casts Chinese mothers as "primitive" and "pathological," but whose linguistic power can be tapped in the process of cultural as well as feminist assimilation.

The four chapters in the section "American Translation" contain the parallel narratives of the mothers' power to translate Chinese wisdom into American life. Each daughter begins "her" chapter with complaints about her mother's pathological hold over her, but by the end each discovers that her mother indeed knows best and has imparted that wisdom through an act of translation; the daughter's original shame over being Chinese is turned into ethnic pride through the mother's lessons. Rose Hsu Jordan, for example, is going through a divorce and feeling vulnerable. A Chinese phrase turns out to be the crucial therapeutic cure for Rose, who is chastised by her mother for going to a therapist to discuss her divorce:

"Why can you talk about this with a psyche-atric and not with mother?"

"Psychiatrist."

"Psyche-atricks," she corrected herself.

"A mother is best. A mother knows what is inside you," she said .... "A psyche-atricks will only make you *hulihudu*, make you see *heimong-mong*." (Tan, 1990 [1989]: 210)

The mother's jabs in the sparring over the correct pronunciation of "psychiatrist" underscore the inappropriateness of the daughter's reliance on Western "psyche-atricks." Rose may be proficient in English, but she's supposed to realize that her psychiatrist can not compare to her mother, who of course knows what's best for her and names her problem in Chinese: she has simply become "*hulihudu*" and "*heimongmong*." The naming does the real trick: Rose takes to her mother's linguistic diagnosis and comes around:

I thought about what she said. And it was true. Lately I had been feeling *hulihudu*. And everything around me seemed to be *heimongmon*. These were words I had never thought about in English terms. I suppose the closest in meaning would be "confused" and "dark fog."

But really, the words mean much more than that. Maybe they can't be translated because they refer to a sensation that only Chinese people have, as if you were falling headfirst .... (Tan, 1990 [1989]: 210)

Rose's notion of untranslatability fixes Chinese traits and words within an essentialized Chinese identity. Nevertheless, this essentializing diagnosis serves as the cultural salve with which Rose heals her wound. Ironically, what is untranslatable does the trick. Her newly acquired Chinese self-understanding fortifies her weak self; Rose is finally able to stand up against her husband Ted. Rose, as each of the other daughters does, learns about her mother's own feminist struggle in her Chinese past and with the help of her mother applies the lesson to her own life in the U.S. *The Joy Luck Club*, then, taps anthropologically into "*the* Chinese woman" to reap benefits for Western women. This easy translation of Chinese female suffering into an American feminist context seems to appeal to a feminist solidarity that can smooth over the cultural differences between feminist struggles.

The overall novelistic structure of *The Joy Luck Club* in fact supports an "easy" anthropological "in" to Chinese female suffering that ultimately allows the reader to be "mothered" by the Chinese mothers in the way that the American-born daughters are. The novel structures itself not as a dialogue between the mothers and daughters, but as one between each narrator and the reader, which seems to position the reader as an ethnographic observer and each narrator as native informant. As novelist, Tan seems to function as "native ethnographer" who mediates between the narrating "informants" and the reading audience. At the same time she employs the "objectivity" of realist fiction techniques to render her ethnographic power transparent. Also unsettling is the way in which all of the women in the novel are written as "one" universal Asian woman despite the fact that there are eight different women. The text seems compelled to produce one replicating Chinese mother/daughter pair who open up a window into their experiences for the American readership. Consequently, they seem to be written into one master narrative, one cultural text with which to establish an ethnographic reality. This homogenization is a classical rhetorical strategy in traditional ethnography. Sally Cole writes, "A standard means of achieving ... authority in ethnography has been to homogenize the subjects (to speak of 'The Andaman Islanders' or 'The Nuer' for example) and to speak 'objectively' about them. It is this kind of ethnography that has undergone such extensive rethinking since the mid-1980s" (Cole, 1995: 190).

The appeal of being mothered by the Other is in fact one of the original ostensible purposes of anthropology, which was to study the cultural origins of the Other as "the *roots* of human behavior" for the West (Trinh, 1989: 65). James Clifford has noted, "Cultural anthropology in the twentieth century has tended to replace (though never completely) these historical allegories with humanist allegories. It has eschewed a search for origins in favor of seeking human similarities and cultural differences. But the representational process itself has not essentially changed" (Clifford, 1986: 102). Clifford traces a narrative pattern relevant to the "roots" narrative at work in *The Joy Luck Club* in his discussion of the pervasive use of the "ethnographic pastoral." This is a temporal trope that posits the notion that a present "inauthenticity" can be regenerated through the salvaging of an "authenticity" found in the past. Clifford explains that the ethnographic pastoral's story of "cultural loss and textual rescue" (Clifford, 1986: 115) is embedded in the assumptions of *writing* ethnography, in its very *textualization*: "The text is a record of something enunciated, in a *past*. The structure, if not the thematic context, of pastoral is repeated" (Clifford, 1986: 116). In *The Joy Luck Club*, each narrative is itself a textualization of the narrator's oral account of her experience, and in the case of the mothers' narratives, each is the enunciation of a *past* experience in another culture.

Tan's fiction follows the traditional rhetorical conceit of anthropology, what Trinh Minh-ha has described as the "positivist dream of a neutralized language that strips off all its singularity to become nature's exact, unmisted reflection" (Trinh, 1989: 53-54). Her fictions seek to render ethnographic power transparent in a traditional positivist anthropological manner and her translations therefore adhere to an artifice of cultural authenticity though they are ethnographically spurious. It is important to examine Tan's technique because, as Trinh Minh-ha suggests, perhaps anthropological authority can be deconstructed through a critique of its fictiveness: "Anthropological writings can ... be determined as fictions from the standpoint of language. They assume, through a system of signs, a possibility as a fact, irrespective of its actuality as sign" (Trinh, 1989: 70). Tan's ethnographic techniques and translation practices construct her novel precisely as an ethnographic fiction and therefore exemplify the problematic premises inherent within the colonialist anthropological paradigm. What *The Joy Luck Club* enacts, then, are the strategies by which Tan relies on a mode of authenticating translation to set up an elaborate ethnographic fiction.

Kingston's "Betrayal" of Ethnography

Unlike the Joy Luck mothers, the mother in *The Woman Warrior* does not step in and fix her daughter's American conflicts through translation. The narratives within Kingston's text centre on the mother's storytelling and the daughter's frustration at not being able to find direct applications of these Chinese stories of strong and undervalued women for her own life in America. Kingston problematizes the process by exploring the daughter's difficulties of translating the mother's world-view. By illustrating the specific political circumstances that dictate the necessity of translation for the narrator and her mother, Kingston emphasizes the power dynamics that marginalize the mother and the immigrant community. She also shows how the daughter interrogates the epistemology of cultural knowledge in the process of translation.

I use "betrayal" to suggest a double phenomenon: *The Woman Warrior* foils conventional ethnography and it also *reveals* itself as an ethnographic text, a critical re-visioning of ethnography. While the former phenomenon has been widely acknowledged and often emphasized as a repudiation of anthropological and sociological documentation, few have attempted to account for the latter phenomenon. Even as most critics identify *The Woman Warrior* as a mixed-genre text, hardly any have included ethnography as one of those genres.[1] The narrator reports: "I read in an anthropology book that Chinese say, 'Girls are necessary too'; I have never heard the Chinese *I know* make this concession. Perhaps it was a saying in *another* village. I refuse to shy my way anymore through *our* Chinatown, which tasks me with the old sayings and the stories" (Kingston, 1989a [1976]: 52-53; emphasis added). Kingston's narrator does not reject the anthropological account outright. She allows for the possibility that there are varying sayings and customs in different villages and Chinatowns. This concession offers a critique in its highlighting of the fact that there is no all-encompassing study that can divulge the "truth" she seeks about the value of girls in Chinese society. The reference to this other account obliquely places her own account as one ethnography within the context of anthropology. Thus *The Woman Warrior* depicts differential knowledge as a significant key to ethnographic practice.

Kamala Visweswaran suggests that "betrayal" can be read as emblematic of the practice of feminist ethnography "at a moment when feminist theory is repositioning itself along the lines of difference" (Visweswaran, 1994: 41). Visweswaran analyses the betrayals that are unavoidable because of the differential positionings of those involved within an ethnographic project. She posits "betrayal as symptomatic of an inequality and power differential between women, as well as a marker for women's agency" (ibid., 1994: 42). *The Woman Warrior* opens with a story of multiple betrayals. In the first chapter, "No Name Woman," the narrator's mother tells her about an aunt who betrayed the family by becoming pregnant out of wedlock. The story also tells of the villagers' and family's betrayal of the aunt for her transgression. The mother issues an injunction against ever speaking of the aunt and therefore the narrator's effort to avenge her aunt by sharing her story necessarily breaks the code of silence.

The opening chapter of *The Woman Warrior* is ostensibly a record of the narrator's coming to terms with the betrayals that take place in the act of writing. The narrator's urge to expose the cultural injustice enacted against her aunt implicates her within yet another betrayal. She writes: "I am telling on her" (Kingston, 1989a [1976]: 16); her own complicity is not lost on the narrator. Visweswaran recognizes that her own "agency and culpability" as ethnographic "interlocutor" has less to do with her own agency than with "the very organization of knowledge and the structure of inquiry" (Visweswaran, 1994: 47). Her analysis of betrayal and feminist ethnography provides an appropriate guide for analysing the way that Kingston allegorizes the problematics of "writing culture." In Kingston's staging of the power dynamics of anthropology through moments of translation, she also addresses questions of difference in feminist epistemology.[2]

The narrator of *The Woman Warrior* explores the epistemological parameters of knowledge in order to make sense of her own position in the world and of what that positioning forces her to negotiate. She asks, What are the betrayals I must commit in the process of coming to terms with my own truth? This opening story of betrayal immediately introduces the narrator's problem – her mother doesn't attempt to translate the significance of the aunt's story into an American context for her. The mother's injunctions are so minimal that she is left to her own devices to piece together not only her own family background, but her family's village experience, Chinese history, and the place of women in Chinese society in order to understand fully her aunt's story and thereby find a way to translate it effectively. She attempts to humanize her own aunt and to explore the nature of marriage, rape, adultery, private desires, as well as the desperation of an impoverished community, by relying on anthropological conjecture to fill in the gaps. She tests generalizations against personal knowledge: "Women in the old China did not choose"; "No one talked sex, ever"; "Imagining her free with sex doesn't fit, though. I don't know any women like that, or men either" (Kingston, 1989a [1976]: 6-8).

What's recorded is her process of solving this epistemological puzzle. Caught between Chinese and American models of womanhood, the narrator's efforts to situate the story's significance within different contexts lead her to see how the meanings depend on the understanding of differential specificities she desperately tries to master. In figuring out how the incipient danger of sexuality, about which her mother warns, must apply to her own life, she finds that the act of imagining alternative scenarios for her aunt is the way to engage her own subjectivity and cultural positioning: "Unless I see her life branching into mine, she gives me no ancestral help" (Kingston, 1989a [1976]: 8). The book proceeds steadily to meditate on the contingency of context and the differential knowledge that arises from specific positionings. The next chapter, "White Tigers," for instance, explicitly points to how inadequately the Chinese woman warrior myth translates into an American context in which the daughter must confront sexist and racist treatment from her employer.

One episode in the last chapter of *The Woman Warrior*, "Song for a Barbarian Reed Pipe," portrays the pressures the narrator negotiates as she attempts to translate her mother's world-view. This particular episode shows us how Kingston delineates the social and political effects of her own positioning and illustrates effectively Visweswaran's claim that "a feminist ethnography can consider how identities are multiple, contradictory, partial, and strategic" (Visweswaran, 1994: 50). When the delivery boy from the pharmacy accidentally brings medicine to their house by mistake, the narrator's mother demands that she seek "reparation." The daughter, however, is ashamed since she suspects the druggist will misunderstand.

"You get reparation candy," she said. "You say, 'You have tainted my house with sick medicine and must remove the curse with sweetness.' He'll understand."

"He didn't do it on purpose. And no, he won't, Mother. They don't understand stuff like that. I won't be able to say it right. He'll call us beggars."

"You just translate." (Kingston, 1989a [1976]: 170)

The mother commands her daughter to "just translate," staunchly convinced that the druggist will understand and comply to her sense of cultural propriety, even though she must rely on the daughter to communicate the transaction. Such a confident attitude contrasts with the wariness the daughter feels, especially in her helplessness to communicate the impossibility of the task to her own mother.

The daughter cannot figure out how to explain the concept of reparation candy to the pharmacist. Instead, she just blurts out,

"Mymotherseztagimmesomecandy," I said to the druggist. Be cute and small. No one hurts the cute and small.

"What? Speak up. Speak English," he said, big in his white druggist coat.

"Tatatagimmesomecandy." (Kingston, 1989a [1976]: 170)

The narrator's nervous-childish words delivered in her ultra colloquial American English effectively fail. In fact, her words are marked as foreign by the druggist. And once she is marked as foreign, the narrator tries to offer an ethnographic explanation:

"My mother says you have to give us candy. She said that is the way the Chinese do it."

"What?"

"That is the way the Chinese do it."

"Do what?"

"Do things," I felt the weight and immensity of things impossible to explain to the druggist. (Kingston, 1989a [1976]: 170-71)

The situation traps the narrator into an ethnographic stance from which she can only define her mother and the Chinese as unexplicable people: "That's what the Chinese do." Ironically, when the result is that the druggist then regularly delivers off-season candy to the family (after Valentine's

Day, Halloween, Christmas, and Easter) and therefore acts as a "Chinese" druggist would, "except [Chinese druggists] give raisins," the mother believes that she has been triumphant in a cross-cultural lesson in customer service (Kingston, 1989a [1976]: 171). The mother is even more convinced in the power of her cultural reality to be translated, while the daughter is fully aware that the druggist still has no conception of "reparation sweetness." The success of the cultural compromise depends on the mother's own unawareness of the fact that the family has become the repository for left-over candy. But the narrator knows and she bears the brunt of the difficult power relationships to be negotiated, reporting that "My mouth went permanently crooked with effort" (Kingston, 1989a [1976]: 171). The episode dramatizes effectively the power differentials of age, gender, class, and culture that the narrator confronts while translating. It does not portray resolution as easy and automatic. Translation, Kingston shows time and time again throughout the text, involves differential positions that are difficult to bridge. This particular episode shows us how traumatic – even though rendered humorously – it has been for the daughter to translate effectively, given her social, cultural, and political positioning. The druggist delimits the boundaries from within which she must attempt to fulfil her mother's request to "just translate." Kingston exposes the process by which the daughter has been inscribed by the palpable markers that position her within American society. This episode delineates the paradigmatic position of woman of colour as translator.

In its portrayal of translation, *The Woman Warrior* addresses the issue of feminist difference and epistemology by concentrating on the problematics of positioning in particular. Highlighting the prominence of her portrayal of the importance of differential positioning within the practice of translation helps us to place Kingston's work squarely within the context of work by U.S. women of colour. In "U.S. Third World Feminism: The Theory and Method of Oppositional Consciousness in the Postmodern World," Chela Sandoval (1991) identifies Kingston, along with Anzaldúa (1987), Lorde (1984), Walker (1986), and Moraga (1981), as among a group of U.S. women of colour authors who have participated in theorizing the practice of "difference" as "oppositional consciousness" within feminism (Sandoval, 1991: 5, 19 n. 18-20). This mode of differential consciousness rooted in the practice of U.S. Third World feminism as articulated by Sandoval notably complements and contextualizes Visweswaran's discussion of Donna Haraway's concept of "situated knowledge" (see Haraway, 1985, 1988) as important to feminist ethnography.[3] Visweswaran writes: "I want to advance the case for a critical feminist epistomology that finds its stakes, as with other interested and subversive epistomologies, in limited location and, as Haraway put it, 'situated knowledge.' This feminist way of knowing sees the process of positioning itself as an epistemological act" (Visweswaran, 1994: 48). Such positioning, which can productively acknowledge differences, has critical implications for conceptions of feminist solidarity and practice.

The contrast in the use of translation in the works of Tan and Kingston is emblematic of the contrast between a universalized vision of ideal feminist solidarity and one that envisions the necessity of confronting differences. Visweswaran proposes that the drawback of idealizing universal sisterhood is that a feminism "that theorized a sisterhood without attending to the divides that separated women" (ibid., 40) can easily lead to a counter-productive pessimism. Contending that Judith Stacey's conclusion in "Can There Be Feminist Ethnography?" (1988) – that "betrayal" reveals the inherent impossibility of feminist ethnography – is a result of her desire for "a feminism based upon assumed affinity and identity," Visweswaran instead posits a feminism that represents "a contested field of meanings around issues of specificity and difference" (ibid.). She affirms that "betrayal" should allow us a way to examine "power relations" within feminist ethnography rather than force us to surrender in the face of an idealistic longing for feminist sisterhood. Kingston's focus on the potential betrayals involved in the act of translation differs from Tan's focus on the idealized promise of translation. In contrast to Tan's universalizing feminist translations, in which resolutions are either impossible or are reached through homogenized universals, Kingston's work emphasizes the differences that are not so easily surmounted. The last line of *The Woman Warrior* reads, "It translated well" (Kingston, 1989a [1976]: 209), but Kingston's point is that translating well across different contexts requires serious acknowledgement of differential positioning.

Notes

I wish to acknowledge the past support of two Meg Quigley summer research fellowships in Women's Studies from Mills College. I would also like to thank Rae Bridgman, Sally Cole, and Heather Howard-Bobiwash for their helpful suggestions and overall editorial generosity.

1   I realize the danger of calling for an anthropological reading, given that so many critics have uncritically applied anthropological studies of women in Taiwan and China to *The Woman Warrior*. But I venture the risk of according Kingston "ethno-graphic authority" in my attempt to encourage a re-thinking of these para-digms. For the few references that briefly mention ethnography, see Mitchell, 1981; Hsu, 1983.

2   For other important articles that address the issue of difference within feminism, see Brah, 1992; Mohanty, 1991; Sandoval, 1991.

3   Many of the early feminist studies of *The Woman Warrior*, for instance, centre on gender much more than race and reveal the necessity of an analysis that can account for differential positioning based on race *vis à vis* gender. Many adminis-ter an application of Nancy Chodorow's theory of female development (see Chodorow, 1978) and/or French feminist theories on *écriture feminine* (for instance, Cixous, 1975; Irigaray, 1985; Kristeva, 1974) without taking race into account. See especially Barker-Nunn, 1987; Demetrakopoulos, 1980; Hunt, 1985; Juhasz, 1985; Rabine, 1987.

References

Anzaldúa, Gloria. 1987. *Borderlands, La Frontera: The New Mestiza*. San Francisco: Spin-sters/Aunt Lute.

Barker-Nunn, Jeanne. 1987. "Telling the mother's story: history and connection in the autobiographies of Maxine Hong Kingston and Kim Chernin," *Women's Studies* 14, 1: 55-63.

Behar, Ruth. 1995. "Introduction: Out of Exile," in Ruth Behar and Deborah A. Gor-don, eds., *Women Writing Culture*. Berkeley: University of California Press, 1-29.

— and Deborah A. Gordon, eds. 1995. *Women Writing Culture*. Berkeley: University of California Press.

Braendlin, Bonnie. 1995. "Mother/Daughter Dialog(ic)s in, around, and about Amy Tan's *The Joy Luck Club*," in Nancy Owen Nelson, ed. *Private Voices, Public Lives: Women Speak on the Literary Life*, Denton, Texas: University of North Texas Press, 111-24.

Brah, Avtar. 1992. "Difference, Diversity, and Differentiation," in James Donald and

Ali Rattansi, eds., *"Race," Culture and Difference*. London: Sage Publications, 126-45.

Chan, Jeffrey. 1977. "'Woman Warrior' Review Faulty," *s.f. journal*, May 4.

—, Frank Chin, Lawson Inada, and Shawn Wong, eds. 1992. *The Big Aiiieeeee! An Anthology of Chinese American and Japanese American Literature*. New York: Meridian.

Cheung, King-Kok. 1990 "*The Woman Warrior* versus *The Chinaman Pacific*: Must a Chinese American Critic Choose between Feminism and Heroism?" in Marianne Hirsch and Evelyn Fox Keller, eds., *Conflicts in Feminism*. New York: Routledge, 234-251.

—. 1993. *Articulate Silences: Hisaye Yamamoto, Maxine Hong Kingston, Joy Kogawa*. Ithaca, NY: Cornell University Press.

Chin, Frank. 1992. "Come All Ye Asian American Writers of the Real and Fake," in Jeffrey Paul Chan, Frank Chin, Lawson Inada, and Shawn Wong, eds., *The Big Aiiieeeee! An Anthology of Chinese American and Japanese American Literature*. New York: Meridian, 1-92.

—, Jeffrey Paul Chan, Lawson Inada, and Shawn Wong, eds. 1991 [1974]. *The Big Aiiieeeee! An Anthology of Asian-American Writers*. New York: Mentor.

Chodorow, Nancy. 1978. *Reproduction of Mothering: Psychoanalysis and the Sociology of Gender*. Berkeley: University of California Press.

Chung, L.A. 1991. "Chinese American Literary War." *San Francisco Chronicle* August 26.

Cixous, Hélène. 1975. *La jeune née*. Paris: Union Générale d'Editions.

Clifford, James. 1986. "On Ethnographic Allegory," in James Clifford and George E. Marcus, eds., *Writing Culture, The Poetics and Politics of Ethnography*. Berkeley: University of California Press, 98-121.

Cole, Sally. 1995. "Taming the Shrew in Anthropology: Is Feminist Ethnography 'New' Ethnography?" in Sally Cole and Lynne Phillips, eds., *Ethnographic Feminisms, Essays in Anthropology*. Ottawa: Carleton University Press, 185-205.

Demetrakopoulos, Stephanie A. 1980. "The Metaphysics of Matrilinearism in Women's Autobiography: Studies of Mead's *Blackberry Winter*, Hellman's *Pentimento*, Angelou's *I Know Why the Caged Bird Sings*, and Kingston's *The Woman Warrior*," in E.C. Jelinek, ed., *Women's Autobiography: Essays in Criticism*. Bloomington: University of Indiana Press, 180-205.

Dingwaney, Anuradha, and Carol Maier, eds. 1995. *Between Languages and Cultures: Translation and Cross-Cultural Texts*. Pittsburgh: University of Pittsburgh Press.

Finn, Janet L. 1995. "Ella Cara Deloria and Mourning Dove: Writing for Cultures, Writing Against the Grain," in Ruth Behar and Deborah A. Gordon, eds., *Women Writing Culture*. Berkeley: University of California Press, 131-147.

Haraway, Donna. 1985. "A Manifesto for Cyborgs: Science, Technology, and Socialist Feminism in the 1980s," *Socialist Review* 80 (March): 65-107.

—. 1988. "Situated Knowledges: The Science Question in Feminism and the Privilege of Partial Perspective," *Feminist Studies* 14, 3: 575-99.

Harrison, Faye V. 1995. "Writing Against the Grain: Cultural Politics of Difference in the Work of Alice Walker," in Ruth Behar and Deborah A. Gordon, eds., *Women Writing Culture*. Berkeley: University of California Press, 233-45.

Hernández, Graciela. 1995. "Multiple Subjectivities and Strategic Positionality: Zora Neale Hurston's Experimental Ethnographies," in Ruth Behar and Deborah A. Gordon, eds., *Women Writing Culture*. Berkeley: University of California Press, 148-65.

Heung, Marina. 1993. "Daughter-Text/Mother-Text: Matrilineage in Amy Tan's *Joy Luck Club*," *Feminist Studies* 9, 3: 597-616.

Ho, Wendy. 1996. "Swan-Feather Mothers and Coca-Cola Daughters: Teaching Amy Tan's *The Joy Luck Club*," in John R. Maitino and David R. Peck, eds., *Teaching American Ethnic Literatures*. Albuquerque: University of New Mexico Press, 327-45.

Homsher, Deborah. 1979. "*The Woman Warrior*, by Maxine Hong Kingston: A Bridging of Autobiography and Fiction," *Iowa Review* 10., 4: 93-98.

Hunt, Linda. 1985. "'I Could Not Figure Out What Was My Village': Gender Vs. Ethnicity in Maxine Hong Kingston's *The Woman Warrior*," *MELUS* 12, 3: 5-12.

Hsu, Vivian. 1983. "Maxine Hong Kingston as Psycho-Autobiographer and Ethnographer," *International Journal of Women's Studies* 6, 5: 429-42.

Irigaray, Luce. 1985. *This Sex Which Is Not One*, transl. Catherine Porter with Carolyn Burke. Ithaca, N.Y.: Cornell University Press.

Juhasz, Suzanne. 1985. "Narrative Technique and Female Identity," in Catherine Rainwater and William J. Scheik, eds., *Contemporary American Women Writers: Narrative Strategies*. Lexington: University of Kentucky Press, 173-89.

Kim, Elaine. 1982. *Asian American Literature: An Introduction to the Writings and Their Social Context*. Philadelphia: Temple University Press.

—. 1990. "'Such Opposite Creatures': Men and Women in Asian American Literature," *Michigan Quarterly Review* (Winter): 68-93.

Kingston, Maxine Hong. 1989a [1976]. *The Woman Warrior*. New York: Vintage.

—. 1989b [1980]. *China Men*. New York: Vintage.

Kristeva, Julia. 1974. *La révolution du langage poétique*. Paris: Editions du Seuil.

Lee, Virginia Chin-lan.1963. *The House That Tai Ming Built*. New York: Macmillan.

Lidoff, Joan. 1991. "Autobiography in a Different Voice: *The Woman Warrior* and the Question of Genre," in Shirley Geok-lin Lim, ed., *Approaches to Teaching Kingston's The Woman Warrior*. New York: MLA, 116-20.

Lim, Shirley Geok-lin. 1992. "The Tradition of Chinese American Women's Life Stories: Thematics of Race and Gender in Jade Snow Wong's *Fifth Chinese Daughter* and Maxine Hong Kingston's *The Woman Warrior*," in Margo Culley, ed., *American Women's Autobiography, Fea(s)ts of Memory*. Madison: University of Wisconsin Press, 252-67.

Lin Yutang. 1935. *My Country and My People*. New York: John Day Co.

Lorde, Audre. 1984. *Sister Outsider*. New York: Crossing Press.

Lowe, Lisa. 1996. *Immigrant Acts: On Asian American Cultural Politics*. Durham, N.C.: Duke University Press.

Mitchell, Carol. 1981. "'Talking Story' in *The Woman Warrior*: An Analysis of the Use of Folklore," *Kentucky Folklore Record* 27, 1-2: 5-12.

Mohanty, Chandra Talpade. 1991. "Under Western Eyes: Feminist Scholarship and Colonial Discourses," in Chandra Talpade Mohanty, Ann Russo, and Lourdes Torres, eds., *Third World Women and the Politics of Feminism*. Bloomington: Indiana University Press, 51-80.

Moraga, Cherríe, and Gloria Anzaldúa, eds. 1981. *This Bridge Called My Back: A Collection of Writings by Radical Women of Color*. Watertown, Mass.: Persephone Press.

Niranjana, Tejaswini. 1992. *Siting Translation*. Berkeley: University of California Press.

Rabine, Leslie W. 1987. "No Lost Paradise: Social Gender and Symbolic Gender in the Writings of Maxine Hong Kingston," *Signs: Journal of Women in Culture and Society* 12, 3: 471-92.

Sandoval, Chela. 1991. "U.S. Third World Feminism: The Theory and Method of Oppositional Consciousness in the Postmodern World," *Genders* 10: 1-24.

Schueller, Malini Johar. 1989. "Questioning Race and Gender Definitions: Dialogic Subversions in *Woman Warrior*," *Criticism* 31, 4: 421-37.

—. 1992. "Theorizing Ethnicity and Subjectivity: Maxine Hong Kingston's *Tripmaster Monkey* and Amy Tan's *The Joy Luck Club*," *Genders* 15 (Winter): 72-85.

Shen, Gloria. 1995. "Born of a Stranger: Mother-Daughter Relationships and Story-telling in Amy Tan's *The Joy Luck Club*," in Anne E. Brown and Marjanne E. Goozé, eds., *International Women's Writing: New Landscapes of Identity*. Westport, Conn.: Greenwood Press, 233-44.

Smith, Sidonie. 1987. *A Poetics of Women's Autobiography*. Bloomington: Indiana University Press.

Souris, Stephen. 1994. "Only Two Kinds of Daughters: Inter-Monologue Dialogicity in *The Joy Luck Club*," *MELUS* 19, 2: 99-123.

Stacey, Judith. 1988. "Can There Be Feminist Ethnography?" *Women's Studies International Forum* 11, 1: 21-27.

Sugimoto, Etsu. 1925. *A Daughter of the Samurai*. New York: Doubleday Page & Co.

Tan, Amy. 1990 [1989]. *The Joy Luck Club*, New York: Ivy Books.

—. 1991. *The Kitchen God's Wife*. New York: G.P. Putnam's Sons.

Tong, Benjamin. 1977. "Critic of Admirer Sees Dumb Racist," *s.f. journal*, May 11.

Trinh T. Minh-ha. 1989. *Woman, Native, Other: Writing Postcoloniality and Feminism*. Bloomington: Indiana University Press.

Venuti, Lawrence, ed. 1992. *Rethinking Translation: Discourse, Subjectivity, Ideology*. New York: Routledge.

Visweswaran, Kamala. 1994. *Fictions of Feminist Ethnography*. Minneapolis: University of Minnesota Press.

Walker, Alice. 1986. "Letter to an Afro-American Friend," *Ms. Magazine*.

Wong, Sau-ling Cynthia. 1988. "Necessity and Extravagance in Maxine Hong Kingston's *The Woman Warrior*: Art and the Ethnic Experience," *MELUS* 15, 1: 3-26.

—. 1992. "Autobiography as Guided Chinatown Tour? Maxine Hong Kingston's *The Woman Warrior* and the Chinese-American Autobiographical Controversy," in James Robert Payne, ed., *Multicultural Autobiography: American Lives*. Knoxville: University of Tennessee Press, 248-79.

—. 1995. "'Sugar Sisterhood': Situating the Amy Tan Phenomenon," in David Palumbo-Liu, ed., *The Ethnic Canon: Histories, Institutions, and Interventions*. Minneapolis: University of Minnesota Press, 174-210.

Xu, Ben. 1994. "Memory and the Ethnic Self: Reading Amy Tan's *The Joy Luck Club*," in Amritjit Singh, Joseph T. Skerrett, and Robert Hogan, eds., *Memory, Narrative, and Identity: New Essays in Ethnic Literature*. Boston: Northeastern University Press, 261-77.

Yalom, Marilyn. 1991. "*The Woman Warrior* as Postmodern Autobiography," in Shirley Geok-lin Lim, ed., *Approaches to Teaching Kingston's The Woman Warrior*. New York: MLA, 108-15.

FOUR

U.S. FEMINIST ETHNOGRAPHY AND THE
DENATIONALIZING OF "AMERICA":
A RETROSPECTIVE ON *WOMEN WRITING CULTURE*

Deborah A. Gordon

What then of the celebrated definition of the modern state as that which holds the monop-
oly of the (legitimate) use of violence? And what then of that equally celebrated defini-
tion stressing bureaucratized rationality? Are we forced to think not only of groups of
armed men and prisons, and not only of stately pyramids of filing cabinets and rules and
regulations, but also — and this is surely the whole and consuming point, where violence
and reason blend — of ghosts and images and, above all, of formless, nauseating, intangi-
bility?

— MICHAEL TAUSSIG

IN THIS paper I explore the affiliations and afflictions of the U.S. nation-
state as they played themselves out in *Women Writing Culture* (Behar and
Gordon, 1995). *Women Writing Culture* is a volume in which feminists in
North American anthropology considered women's contributions to the
discipline's purpose at the end of the century. The contributions included
new readings of women anthropologists, reclaimed the writings by women
of colour for cultural description, and proposed new visions of feminist
ethnography. As one of the book's editors, I want retrospectively to situate
the volume within what Mary John (1996)has argued in *Discrepant Dislocations*
is a persistent dominance of the West in U.S. feminist ethnography. In particular, John's insistence that the dominance of the West lies in the unacknowledged national location of the United States in feminist ethnography
has made me realize that *Women Writing Culture* enacted the "politics" of
national location without adequate understanding of the social fabric of the
United States that positioned its contributors' silences. This essay is not a *mea*
culpa but an exercise in a kind of self-reflexivity that places one's work in history.

John's "anthropology in reverse" suggests that American feminists have
"experiences and displacements of fieldwork" that "sharpen but do not fun-

damentally unsettle their partiality to and familiarity with the institutions and debates of 'home'" (John, 1996: 117). Where do we see the signs of the nation-state, unacknowledged and, thus, inflecting *Women Writing Culture*? Today, the "U.S." character of the volume appears to me to lie in its relative inarticulateness around class. It is through the nexus of unacknowledged national location and class relations that U.S. feminism continues to represent itself as born of a "placeless place." Thus, it is able to extend its influence far beyond its geographic borders.

In John's analysis, the persistence of Western imperialism exists in the fact that U.S. feminists do fieldwork among women elsewhere, while failing to study feminisms and *feminists* elsewhere. U.S. feminist ethnography has yet to formulate a fieldwork in which one would seek out a roughly equivalent feminist intelligentsia in other places. It will not be possible to do so without noticing the collapse of liberalism as national ideology, its consequences for the state, and the manifestations of this collapse in feminist ethnography written from American universities.

Corporatizing the Subject: Institutional Contexts

The literature on the corporatizing of universities in the U.S. has exploded in recent years. What has been less understood is how corporatization is a subject-producing activity and the impact it has had on U.S. feminist scholarship. Corporatizing a subject is a different kind of activity than the "hailing" of the subject that Althusser proposed and that has been expressed in feminist theory as interpolation. Corporatizing as an ideological production is fluid self-authoritarianism. It works not through alienation but disorientation. The symbolic and practical centre of this disorientation is an entrepreneurialism of the self, in which class is less a relatively stable identity than a compulsion to perform. A corporatized subject is an intensified version of Weber's *Protestant Ethic and Spirit of Capitalism*, but with a very different kind of "material" or "capital" with which to work. Performative class relations do not depend on ideologies of sexual or racial natures. On the contrary, performative class identities are not "identities" as much as they are actions whose goal is literally to produce capital in their very enactment. What counts as capital is not so much having the money to purchase a stereo system, for example. It is a "position that emerges in and through the performance of getting the system in the first place and the subsequent performances in which it continues to be deployed" (Watkins, 1995: 50). Ideologies of rising social expectations, in Watkins's analysis, get relocated from educational certification and job availability to consumption and consumer practices, and mass culture assumes a critical pedagogical role.

In this kind of social organization, where the educational function of ideology shifts increasingly from social welfare institutions like public education to mass culture, a new ideological field has emerged. The separation of the new from the obsolete is the essential template here, what Watkins calls "technoideological coding." Technoideological coding positions those of us who are faculty in U.S. institutions of higher education, not as a political threat to the state, as was the case during the "culture wars" of the 1980s, but as merely outmoded. For unlike under previous social conditions, where "others" were inferior by "nature," today they are more likely to be treated as a drag on "the new."

The production of obsolete people, technologies, and ideologies depends on teachers and professors in the heavily contested public educational institutions of the U.S. Like social workers, who are asked to "do more with less," as if this request is an outcome of some objective reality called "the market," faculty are now enlisted to buffer people between the violence involved in constructing the disposable populations of the late twentieth-century U.S. body politic and the possibility that certain narratives of change will induce rebellion and subversion rather than acquiescence. The ruling narratives of change accept deadly forms of inequality as necessary to the social transformation of globalization. In the expansion of public higher education in the U.S. during the Cold War, universities were the site of ideological work that linked explanations of social change to domestic and foreign policy. What well-financed research goes on today is as likely to occur in think-tanks whose ideological agendas are, as in *The Bell Curve* case, about demonstrating the defunct nature of social explanation for understanding discrepancies in I.Q. scores between African Americans and Anglo Americans. The emergence of think-tanks during the Reagan-Bush era of national government is one piece in the reorganization of higher education in the U.S. in which all universities but the most élite may be destined to become supply and distribution centres in what Watkins (1995) fingers as "school culture reform." School culture reform assumes that educational institutions, whether vocational or academic, do not extend their influence through a social network that connects them to industry, political parties, civic organizations, etc.

On my campus, the Women's Studies department is engaged in a fund-raising project for scholarships for students to work as teaching and research assistants for the faculty. The project also sought to finance public programming. Because the faculty's fund-raising efforts are supported by women in the community whom we appreciate as volunteers rather than as, say, taxpayers contributing to the university's funds by means other than taxes, some of these women have contested the "public" programming for Women's History Month. Fund-raising is a source of attaining funds that is hardly more politically progressive than lobbying for increases in operating budgets or spending time campaigning for legislators sympathetic to higher education funding. Under conditions of "post-civil" society (Hardt, 1995), where capital is both corporate and flexible, however, faculty labour is increasingly about publicity: the "work" of teaching and research is marketing oneself and one's department for whomever.

Thus, the research function of Wichita State University has changed since my hiring in 1992. Pressure on faculty to gain external funding and a rewards system promoting applied research and undergraduate teaching are only the most obvious signs of this shift. More damaging, however, is the top-down management of curricular changes that is sweeping the nation's education system. Greater administrative control of academic expertise places faculty in the labour-intensive position of giving hours of input with little impact on policy. I have been involved in a reading and writing group composed of faculty interested in cultural studies with an emphasis on feminist criticism and anti-colonial representation. Financial support and visibility for this activity were one possibility raised in a committee for encouraging interdisciplinary activities. That possibility was nixed for a more "social" faculty gathering. Support for specialization, which encourages faculty to identify with their profession as much as their campuses, gave way to a more administratively driven promotion of the university as a kind of culture. As Watkins has argued, the notion of school cultures works hard to derail the links between any given campus and a larger system of higher education. Assuming that each campus has its "culture" is part of an ideology that seeks to undermine what has been the main function of U.S. public education during the twentieth century – to present the illusion of upward mobility and the notion that education is a vehicle of class equalization.

Wichita State University sees itself as part of a venerated tradition of "localism," in which anxiety over the non-local professoriate revolves around its contamination of the rural populist Utopia. "Wichita," or "the community," is a trope used by and for managing faculty labour and keeping them ignorant of national trends in scholarship. In Wichita, this management of labour is tinged with a compensatory exclusivity. Based on perceived rejection by Washington, and by business people and legislators from the coasts, administrators and some faculty deploy a rhetoric of "uniqueness" to justify this prohibition on research that cannot be monitored by local interests. Ironically, the rhetoric of uniqueness obscures the centrality of places like Kansas to a version of the nation that equates it with the free market. Kansans saw themselves as the centre of the nation during the nineteenth century when the union depended on its entrance to the nation as a non-slave state. By the late twentieth century, however, Kansans see themselves as having slipped to the margins, despite the spread of what they consider their own ideology just about everywhere. The result is that Kansans tend to cling to themselves as harbingers of Truth. Thus, progressive cultural politics such as feminism, which are not local and homogeneous but diversified and different, tend to be viewed with suspicion. Liberal versions of feminism as equal rights and upward mobility for women, except in the area of reproductive rights, are accepted by administrators, local politicians, and donors. Feminist scholarship, however, has pushed beyond the liberal pluralist demand for inclusion in political representation and the economic pies. It has created tension between, on the one hand, the need for feminism as part of the academic analysis of racial inequality, economic distribution, and sexual abjection and, on the other hand, compensatory cleaving to a project of purifying "America."

Feminist faculty, thus, have to prove their membership in "the community." To return to an activity such as Women's History Month, the inevitable question emerges, although usually just below the surface of conversation, about who constitutes this "public." How fund-raising shapes the "public" of Women's Studies is a question we have yet to be able to answer. Alignment with relatively powerful and wealthy donors and higher echelon administrators is part of the emerging picture of that construct. Because Women's Studies has a history of being more entrepreneurial than other departments in gaining funding, we are now in a position to lead other departments into an alliance with those who manage the legislatively and socially created scarcity of higher education funding. In an ideological environment that values relatively privatized solutions to social and political problems of inequity in higher education, "conflict of interest" becomes a moot point. The line between research and teaching is obscured by the discourse of the market. Whether in literal fund-raising or in the more subtle demand that faculty promote their programs through activities that could constitute a conflict of interest, the conception of a department as an academic unit gives way to it being something closer to a start-up company. The temptation is ever present to mediate the conflicting demands on faculty with the notion that if women do the work of marketing Women's Studies with other women, then this constitutes a feminist challenge to business as usual. Yet, the notion of "women" as a unity cannot hold. Only when faculty have a political will that resists intellectual questioning can this operate.

One has to work hard in 1999 to excuse oneself from participating in the epistemological sea change of seeing women, not as an identity, but rather as an opening onto a field of disagreement.

Today I look back at *Women Writing Culture* with an eye towards this kind of remaking of subjectivity, faculty labour, and the refashioning of the "public" of public education in the U.S. university. Indeed, *Women Writing Culture* now appears to me as an artefact of higher education in a post-civil society, where management is supposed to somehow make research faculty look unnecessary. As part of corporatized "public" institutions, Women's Studies departments rest on a "decentred flexible form." This form is capable of managing "that which produces 'high value,' namely its intellectual capital, its skilled personnel" (Gordon, 1995a: 5).

In suppressing the lives of scholars who labour in Women's Studies in urban universities rather than in research institutions, *Women Writing Culture* misunderstood its own institutional terrain, because what is happening at urban universities is also taking place at the research institutions of the U.S. The rhetoric of anti-élitism that scholars invoke against each other in Women's Studies, often only with the purpose of shaming colleagues, misses that the multiversity has disappeared, for it was the multiversity that spawned canons. In some half-articulated sense, this disappearance is contained in Behar's gesture in her introduction to *Women Writing Culture*:

> Some are tenured and comfortable but kept by administrative burdens from doing the writing that matters. Some are untenured and struggling to do the writing that matters while juggling heavy teaching loads and the burdens of being "junior" faculty. Three are students struggling to do the writing that matters while trying to earn a doctorate (Behar, 1995a: 8).

In identifying *Women Writing Culture* with the discipline of anthropology, we missed understanding what it means to belong to Women's Studies departments and programs under conditions of multinational capital and a public university workplace where faculty are being squeezed to fit class agendas.

Women Writing Culture did not take for granted the nation-state. Some contributors, such as Aihwa Ong, sought to bring to anthropological theory and experimental writing the dialogues of anthropologists and informants who are attached to more than one nation. Ong's self-representation, as "clinging to the raft of being an overseas Chinese" (Ong, 1995: 352) rather than a Chinese American, marks a struggle not to affiliate with nationalism in the U.S. and to insist on the global and mobile contexts of gender. Nonetheless, the persistent belief that "America" is an immigrant nation remains a kind of overarching ideological underpinning of the volume. While contributors worked to counter the sense that migration means "starting over" and "settling," we did not frame the volume as writing against "culture" (Abu-Lughod, 1993) but as contesting for a nation that has mutated far beyond what we conceptualized. In that sense, we are a product of the anthropological notion of culture in which an older model of the nation as functional whole was essential. The notion of culture where one studied a theme such as middle-class adolescence to get at a deeper essence (Neiburg and Goldman, 1998) has obviously been challenged in recent years (Clifford, 1997; Kaplan, 1997). The myth of immigration so central to how U.S. nationalism has dealt historically with ethnic diversity encouraged us not to be conceptually critical enough of the liberal underpinnings of this model.

Locales, *Women Writing Culture* reminds, are hybrid and fluid, not fixed, but the volume does not thematize how cultural hybridity relates to the realignment of class relations on a global scale. As Kaplan nicely underscores, Manhattan may have more in common, "culturally," with the seventh *arrondissement* in Paris than with the Bronx (Kaplan, 1997: 158). Culture is the site of racialized, class, gendered, and sexualized conflicts. We accepted this premise, and laced it with a critique of American racial identity politics *and* White backlash. Without a more robust sense of what class as an analytic category means to this revised definition of anthropology's "object," we could not say much about the increasing class divisions in the institutions in which we worked.

Not surprisingly, it took a younger, post-doctoral scholar at Northwestern University to let off some of that steam. Kate Gilbert (1996), annoyed with the volume's introduction in which Behar recognized that women experience different kinds of marginality in the academy, but marginalized they are, would not have it. Gilbert noted that Behar framed *Women Writing Culture* within a rhetoric of marginality that obscured the fact that, from Gilbert's point of view, most of the contributors were "big hitters" in anthropology. Unaccountable to some institutional forces, like some she probably knows only too well, we were, nonetheless, cognizant of others. We knew that administrators and department chairs can coerce women into doing more service for their institutions than their male colleagues. We knew that women of colour experience the kind of marginality that comes from simply being ignored, on the one hand, then trotted out as the sign of somebody's benevolence, on the other. Finally, we knew of the institutional forces that work against women being able to publish at rates men do and with the concomitant influence.

Gilbert's review challenges the contributors to *Women Writing Culture* to recognize, from different locales in a globalized traffic in feminist scholars, that women are positioning themselves and being positioned along class lines within the U.S. academy as well as in the field. This class positioning is an underlying but unarticulated theme of her review; it has everything to do with the slipperiness of the "public" nature of universities that reproduce the social relations of advanced capitalism. Class positioning means jockeying for the new forms of citizenship being offered to an already privileged class, those "U.S." workers, technical and professional, who increasingly "reside" and get their sense of citizenship, not from the streets or the Immigration and Naturalization Service, but from within the American-owned multinationals. Analysing class and nation requires watching one block of the traffic in Women's Studies and feminist anthropology.

Anti-Racist Politics: From a Retreat to Feminist Ethnography

The anti-racist politics of radical women of colour, for Gloria Anzaldúa came from her encounter with racism among staff members at a women's retreat. Anzaldúa was the only woman actually to accept and receive a scholarship intended for three women of colour to attend a Merlin Stone workshop (Moraga and Anzaldúa, 1981a: xxiii). It was in conversation with Stone after poor treatment from the staff for being a "scholarship" attendee that she identified the need to compile the collection of writing that became *This Bridge Called My Back*. The 1981 National Women's Studies Association meeting in Storrs, Connecticut, was also a key event in forming a new identity – women of colour – to make alliances "across class, race, culture, and gender differences" (Sandoval, 1990). Chela Sandoval came to identify this model as exemplifying "oppositional consciousness." A fourfold typology of identities with varying relations to White, male, capitalist power characterized the theory of consciousness she abstracted from the meeting. White women suffered objectification by White men but came to construct a sense of "self" by objectifying people of colour, while men of colour could call on circuits of gendered power. Women of colour, Sandoval argued, were relegated to a final category against which all the others were provided their particular meanings and privileges.

However, as Sandoval noted, this typology could not be taken as frozen but rather as complicated and ever-changing. The unpacking of this moving typology is best embodied by *This Bridge* and by the textual and political space it opened up. Texts followed its lead in challenging heterosexism and homophobia in cultural terms. *This Bridge* emerged from within political and academic trajectories of the 1970s. Scholarship in Ethnic Studies programs at urban universities and the alternative presses of the 1970s had largely been ignored by academic feminists in Women's Studies during that decade. *This Bridge* played a crucial role in disseminating to feminists, first in Women's Studies and then in the disciplines, work that had a history in those sites of cultural politics. A cohort of women anthropologists, who entered the tenure track during the 1980s and around 1990, took *This Bridge* as a foundational text.

As a result, *This Bridge* marked a renaissance in feminist theory. It opened up contention and alliance among White feminists and feminists of colour in the academy, and not just in the sites of cultural production identified with independent writers and artists. *This Bridge*, like the women of colour caucus at the 1981 National Women's Studies Association meeting, was not built on the kind of identity politics that White feminists had developed in the 1970s. In that politics, in which one self-identified in a taxonomic grid of ideologies — socialist feminist, radical feminist, cultural feminist — race was the silent operator that permitted White women to ally politically in and through what became racially and age-marked ritualized disagreements (King, 1994; Haraway, 1985).

By the time *This Bridge* came into print, White feminists were already disaffected from some strains of the political imaginary they had helped to create around 1970. The message of radical women of colour was that there was no unified sisterhood; instead, women were contradictorily positioned in more than one social movement. Rather than perceiving this message as threatening, some White women found hope in it that feminism could be less about building a "home" that rested on some forms of coercion that passed as commitment. These White women, such as Judith Stacey, were themselves doing fieldwork during the 1980s and were grappling with these problems in the field (Stacey, 1988).

For feminists in anthropology, the message of *This Bridge* hit home in a technical, disciplinary way as well. By the mid-1980s the "sex" of the infamous sex/gender system, which Gayle Rubin had first proposed in 1975 and others had developed, came to seem an artefact of anthropological and biological rhetoric. In 1983, James Clifford had called "culture" an abstraction (Clifford, 1983). In 1987, Collier and Yanagisako's criticism of anthropological kinship circulated among feminist anthropologists. Collier and Yanagisako permanently undermined the anthropological notions of social organization from the 1950s and 1960s that had shaped the notion of women's universal subordination. Their introductory essay to *Gender and Kinship: Toward a*

Unified Analysis produced a powerful allegory for a new kind of feminist anthropology. This new tale struggled to get on the pages of Marjorie Shostak's *Nisa* (1983) but was limited by the text's residual counter-cultural desire for communal living habits and sexual liberation for women.

Collier and Yanagisako's figure of the "woman" of feminist anthropology was one in which women as well as men were political "actors." Liberal, somewhat Machiavellian, this figure attracted younger women because it destroyed woman's "place" and the various feminist Utopias of the 1970s that had assumed marriage or heterosexual coupling. By 1989, Collier and Yanagisako had backpedalled. They suggested that in their desire to rid anthropological kinship studies of the assumption that women's capacity for nursing or child-bearing was responsible for their social "role," they had substituted a Western liberal, self-possessed individual for the figure of Western motherhood that often undergirded anthropology's understanding of kinship and the family. Their retraction appeared in the more internationally distributed and less nationally based *Critique of Anthropology*. Less accessible to younger feminists who had read *Writing Culture* (Clifford and Marcus, 1986) and whose reading protocols were more grounded in American anthropology journals, Collier and Yanagisako's retrospective criticism of their own philosophical assumptions did not impact their academic daughters.

Overshadowing, at least initially, the question of women's agency or subjectivity was feminist ethnographic authority. More familiar with the critiques of racism by women of colour, due to the fact that they were being increasingly read in seminars on feminist theory and criticism, this younger cohort was socialized to politicize the term "ethnographic writing" for a distinctly "feminist ethnography." They were also more prepared, as newer Ph.D.s, to use modes of academic writing that would allow them to participate in a feminism accountable to racial and cultural positioning. Anti-racism became a discourse through which feminists in anthropology could borrow from and alter the notion of ethnographic dialogue that had been opened up by scholars interested in ethnographic writing.

What was lost in this shift was the way that *This Bridge* recognized how class privilege could buffer some women of colour against certain injuries. Mirtha Quintales, for example, commented that "many of us who identify as 'Third World' or 'Women of Color,' have grown up as or are fast becoming 'middle class' and highly educated, and therefore more privileged than many of our white, poor and working class sisters." She noted, "I have had opportunities, (or have known how to make them for myself), that my very white, working class American lover has never had." Cautiously, almost defensively, she said, "I'm a bit concerned when a Latina lesbian sister generalizes about/puts down the 'white woman' — especially if she herself has white skin," and "I cannot presume to know what it is really like to grow up American 'White Trash' and destitute" (Quintales, 1981: 152).

Feminist ethnography responded not only to anti-racist feminism but also to *Writing Culture* and the legacy left by the deconstruction of biology and sexual difference. The "agency" of ethnographer and informants came to define "the field" that feminist ethnography represented. This move put a conceptual spin on women of colour that was concerned with the theoretical implications of texts such as *This Bridge* through altering the generic range of ethnography. *This Bridge* allowed feminist ethnographers to claim an anti-colonialist politics in and through ethnographic writing. As it passed through the hands of faculty in Women's Studies, *This Bridge* became accessible to feminists in anthropology who were, by the late 1980s, responding as well to the criticism of Western feminist social science by Third World feminists (Mohanty, 1984, 1988; Ong, 1988; Spivak, 1985).

Initially, the feminist ethnographer was figured as a Western feminist whose desire to know other women led to non-innocent and situated knowledges. That "deconstructive" trajectory for feminist ethnography shifted, however, in light of efforts to reconstruct the field as "homework." As feminist anthropologists attempted to ground feminist ethnography in "homework," that is, the study of personal histories that bring subjects to authorship and to the discipline (Behar, 1993; Visweswaran, 1994), "the field" became mutual self-reflexivity among women (Behar, 1996). Feminist ethnography became an accounting for how scholars of colour come to design the research that they do.

The latter, most forcefully articulated by Kamala Visweswaran, took Angie Chabram's call for Chicano intellectuals to account for their pre-professional histories (1990) and broadened it to scholars of colour. In doing so, the working-class origins of Chabram's reconceptualizing of fieldwork disappeared in Visweswaran's awkward depiction of her middle-class background. Middle-classness has an under-thematized place in her account. Racism crosses class lines. This insight, however, does not do away with the textual trouble her middle-class background enacts. Feminist ethnographers' relative wealth and privilege, which we were prepared to discover in the field as a result of ethnographies such as Shostak's, made middle-classness a silent trauma when it came to accounting for our own lives. As Visweswaran points out, the Indian migrant community of California is divided by class, with Sikhs residing as farmers in the poorer agricultural valley and Hindus in San Francisco as business people. When it comes to her own account of why she became an anthropologist, however, she notes that her questions about college were not "whether but where to go" (Visweswaran, 1994). Ultimately, she bifurcates class and race with the category of generation. She insists that social class marked her father's first-generation experience as an immigrant to the U.S., thus displacing her own middle-classness onto a unified category of "White feminists."

In part, the way race is made to carry "surplus antagonism" (Ortner, 1991: 185) of other axes of power, such as class, may have been the result of the way Anzaldúa but not Moraga came to influence feminist ethnographers. Anzaldúa's book, *Borderlands*, has been read by more anthropologists than Moraga's *The Last Generation*. Anzaldúa entered the doctoral program in Literature at the University of California, Santa Cruz, in the late 1980s and edited another volume, *Making Face, Making Soul*, as a result of teaching in a Women's Studies course on women of colour at Santa Cruz. Anzaldúa decided to compile *Making Face, Making Soul* because of how White students resisted the writing of women of colour. Anzaldúa felt a need for a greater textual field on women of colour that could impact academic Women's Studies. *Making Face* included contributions by poets, writers, artists, and activists, as had *This Bridge*, but also a greater number by faculty and graduate students. In her introduction to *Making Face, Making Soul*, Anzaldúa noted the limits of White women's responses to women of colour in the course she taught. As she shifted her criticism of White women's racism from a retreat to the Women's Studies classroom, the powerful class dilemmas and injuries raised in *This Bridge* dropped away. The criticism of "theory" articulated in Anzaldúa's edited collection was powerfully appropriated by feminists in anthropology seeking to expand the ethnographic genre.

While Moraga came to revise the residual anti-capitalism of the Chicano movement in *The Last Generation* (1993), Anzaldúa criticized the way that women of colour were called on to mediate between White feminists and women of colour. She argued that "it takes too much time to explain to the downwardly mobile, white middle-class women that it's okay for us to want to own 'possessions,' never having had any nice furniture on our dirt floors or 'luxuries' like washing machines" (Anzaldúa, 1990: 384). Her argument was true enough. Moraga, however, looked to the past as a weapon against this kind of functionalist naturalizing of class envy:

> What was once a radical and working-class Latino student base on university campuses has become increasingly conservative. A generation of tokenistic affirmative-action policies and bourgeois flight from Cen-

tral America and the Caribbean has spawned a tiny Latino élite who often turn to their own racial/cultural identities not as a source of political empowerment, but of personal employment as tokens in an Anglo-dominated business world. (Moraga, 1993: 58)

Women Writing Culture thus inherited a conceptualization of race through forgetting that the state mediates racial identities so that their class contexts are left hard to name. What Moraga memorialized in 1993 had disappeared from the political memory of feminist ethnography. Decolonization has been identified with collections such as Hymes's *Reinventing Anthropology* (1969), but that volume did not capture the contentious, overlapping space of women's liberation, anti-imperialist protest, and anti-cultural politics. Because *Reinventing Anthropology* came out of Hymes's teaching experience in the Department of Anthropology at Berkeley, its sense of racial politics was heavily marked by the critique of colonialism of Native Americans. To a great extent this was a product of the work of Theodora and Alfred Kroeber, both of whom taught at Berkeley in the early decades of the twentieth century and had created a visibility for the department by bringing Ishi, a Yana Indian, to work *and live* in the Museum of Anthropology on the campus (Kroeber, 1964). Women of colour, as Sandoval argues, were the women moving in and out of positions within that political tripartite that Hymes's volume missed. Their presence within the ethnic literary politics of the 1970s was not tied to a volume of essays but to the alternative journals promoting that politics, such as *De Colores*. These journals and their institutional location begin to be gleaned from the bibliography of *This Bridge*.

Ironically, it was James Clifford who glimpsed back at that moment in his much maligned image of "co-authorship" in 1983. Not surprisingly, that image has vexed feminist ethnography. Suggesting that this image's Utopianism was irresponsible, due to the fact that the anthropologist authors her or his ethnography, feminists have nonetheless felt provoked to at least gesture towards sharing their authorship with informants.[1] Co-authorship was explicitly Utopian, in Clifford's eyes, because the ideology of Western authorship was finally what was at stake in ethnographic authority (Clifford, 1983). That Clifford could see authorship as an *ideology* in 1983 was not a result of men appropriating the critique of ethnographic authority that women really authored. It was not that men in anthropology or cultural criticism could give up authorship, subjectivity, and the rest of the humanist tradition, because they already had "their" enlightenment in what has become one standard feminist argument in any number of areas of cultural production. The experiments with anonymous or collective authorship in which writers challenged the profit-driven publishing industry in alternative presses and underground media of the late 1960s were one origin of Clifford's as well as women's liberationist distance from authorship. Not post-structuralist trendiness but the anti-capitalist cultural politics of that moment were buried alive in Clifford's image of the dispersal of ethnographic authority.

Through reading symptomatically I have tried to construct another trajectory for *Women Writing Culture* than the much celebrated one of multicultural America that graces its back cover. Instead, I want to close by underlining the absence of an anti-capitalist critique in U.S. feminist ethnography as something that is presently blocked by the reorganization of the United States I alluded to earlier in this essay. By paying attention to "our" own difficulties in articulating class in *Women Writing Culture*, I have hoped to push feminist ethnography, written from the United States, towards becoming a vehicle of class acknowledgement. For feminist ethnography to come to terms with its class moorings, neither a facile conceptual discarding of the nation-state nor attending to certain kinds of diasporic identities will do. Rather, it is the nexus of nation and class, itself possible to see from listening to the voices of feminists elsewhere, that requires feminist ethnography accounting.

Notes

1 Stacey included a chapter in her ethnographic account, *Brave New Families*, written by one of her key informants. Behar(1995b) mocks her own attempt to give a copy of her book, *Translated Woman*, to Esperanza, the Mexican marketing woman's life story. Visweswaran, as well, sent chapters of her doctoral thesis to India to be read by women with whom she worked during her fieldwork done in graduate school (personal communication).

References

Abu-Lughod, Lila. 1993. *Writing Women's Worlds: Bedouin Stories*. Berkeley: University of California Press.

Anzaldúa, Gloria, ed. 1990. *Making Face, Making Soul: Creative and Critical Perspectives by Women of Color*. San Francisco: Aunt Lute.

Behar, Ruth. 1993. *Translated Woman: Crossing the Border with Esperanza's Story*. Boston: Beacon Press.

—. and Deborah A. Gordon, eds., 1995. *Women Writing Culture*. Berkeley: University of California Press.

——. 1995a. "Introduction: Out of Exile," in Behar and Gordon eds., *Women Writing Culture*. Berkeley: University of California Press, 1-29.

——. 1995b. "Writing in My Father's Name: Diary of *Translated Woman's* First Year," in Behar and Gordon, eds., *Women Writing Culture*. Berkeley: University of California Press, 65-84.

——. 1996. *The Vulnerable Observer: Anthropology That Breaks Your Heart*. Boston: Beacon Press.

Chabram, Angie. 1990. "Chicano Studies as Oppositional Ethnography," Special Issue: Chicano Cultural Representations: Reframing Alternative Critical Discourses *Cultural Studies* 4: 237-38.

Clifford, James. 1983. "On Ethnographic Authority," *Representations* 1: 118-46.

——. 1997. *Routes: Travel and Translation in the Late Twentieth Century*. Cambridge, Mass: Harvard University Press.

Clifford, James and George Marcus, eds. 1986. *Writing Culture: The Poetics and Politics of Ethnography*. Berkeley: University of California Press.

Cole, Sally, and Lynne Phillips, eds. 1996. *Ethnographic Feminisms: Essays in Anthropology*. Ottawa: Carleton University Press.

Collier, Jane Fishburne, and Sylvia Junko Yanagisako. 1987. "Gender and Kinship: Toward a Unified Analysis," in Collier and Yanagisako, eds., *Gender and Kinship: Toward a Unified Analysis*. Stanford, Calif.: Stanford University, 14-50.

—— and ——. 1989. "Theory in Anthropology Since Feminist Practice," *Critique of Anthropology* 9, 2: 27-37.

Gilbert, Kate. 1996. "Fastening the Bonds of Womanhood," *Women's Review of Books* 13: 21-22.

Gordon, Avery. 1995. "The Work of Corporate Culture: Diversity Management," *Social Text* 13, 3: 1-30.

Haraway, Donna J. 1985. "A Manifesto for Cyborgs: Science, Technology and Socialist Feminism in the 1980s," *Socialist Review* 80: 65-107.

Hardt, Michael. 1995. "The Withering of Civil Society," *Social Text* 14, 4: 27-44.

Hurtado, Aida. 1989. "Relating to Privilege: Seduction and Rejection in the Subordination of White Women and Women of Color," *Signs* 14: 833-55.

Hymes, Dell, ed. 1969. *Reinventing Anthropology*. New York: Vintage Books.

John, Mary E. 1996. *Discrepant Dislocations: Feminism, Theory, and Postcolonial Histories*. Berkeley: University of California Press.

Kaplan, Caren. 1997. *Questions of Travel: Postmodern Discourses of Displacement*. Durham, N.C.: Duke University.

King, Katie. 1994. *Theory in its Feminist Travels: Conversations in U.S. Women's Movements*. Bloomington: Indiana University Press.

Kroeber, T. 1964. *Ishi in Two Worlds*. Berkeley: University of California Press.

Mohanty, Chandra Talpade. 1984. "Under Western Eyes: Feminist Scholarship and Colonial Discourse," *Boundary* 2, 3: 333-58.

Moraga, Cherrie. 1993. *The Last Generation*. Boston: South End.

—— and Gloria Anzaldúa, eds. 1981. *This Bridge Called My Back: Writings by Radical Women of Color*. Watertown, Mass.: Persephone.

Neiburg, Federico, and Marcio Goldman. 1998. "Anthropology and Politics in Studies of National Character," *Cultural Anthropology* 13: 56-81.

Ong, Aihwa. 1986. "Colonialism and Modernity: Feminist Representations of Women in Non-Western Societies," *Inscriptions* 3/4: 79-93.

——. 1995. "Women Out of China: Traveling Tales and Traveling Theories in Postcolonial Feminism," in Ruth Behar and Deborah A. Gordon, eds., *Women Writing Culture*. Berkeley: University of California Press, 373-89.

Ortner, Sherry B. 1991 "Reading America: Preliminary Notes on Class and Culture," in Richard G. Fox, ed., *Recapturing Anthropology: Working in the Present*. Santa Fe, N.M.: School of American Research, 163-85.

Quintales, Mirtha. 1981. "I Paid Very Hard for My Immigrant Ignorance," in Cherrie Moraga and Gloria Anzaldúa, eds., *This Bridge Called My Back*. Watertown, Mass.: Persephone, 150-56.

Rubin, Gayle. 1975. "The Traffic in Women: Notes on the 'Political Economy' of Sex," in Rayna Rapp Reiter, ed., *Toward an Anthropology of Women*. New York: Monthly Review Press, 157-210.

Sandoval, Chela. 1990. "Feminism and Racism: A Report on the 1981 National Women's Studies Association Conference," in Gloria Anzaldúa, ed., *Making Face, Making Soul: Creative and Critical Perspectives by Women of Color*. San Francisco: Aunt Lute.

——. 1991. "U.S. Third World Feminism: The Theory and the Method of Oppositional Consciousness in the Postmodern World," *Genders* 10: 1-24.

Schneider, Dorothee. 1998. "'I Know All about Emma Lazarus': Nationalism and Its Contradictions in the Congressional Rhetoric of Immigration Restriction," *Cultural Anthropology* 13: 82-99.

Shostak, Marjorie. 1983. *Nisa: The Life and Words of a !Kung Woman*. Cambridge, Mass.: Harvard University.

Spivak, Gayatri Chakravorty. 1985. "Three Women's Texts and a Critique of Imperialism," *Critical Inquiry* 12: 243-61.

Stacey, Judith. 1988. "Can There Be a Feminist Ethnography?" *Women's Studies International Forum* 11: 21-27.

——. 1990. *Brave New Families: Stories of Domestic Upheaval in Late Twentieth Century America*. New York: Basic Books.

Visweswaran, Kamala. 1994. *Fictions of Feminist Ethnography*. Minneapolis: University of Minnesota Press.

Watkins, Evan 1995. *Throwaways: Work Culture and Consumer Education*. Stanford, CA: Stanford University Press.

FIVE

BEYOND SELVES AND OTHERS: EMBODYING AND ENACTING META-NARRATIVES WITH A DIFFERENCE

Cory Silverstein

I need to understand how a place on the map is also a place in history within which as a woman, a Jew, a lesbian, a feminist I am created and trying to create. Begin, though, not with a continent or a country or a house, but with the geography closest in — the body.
— ADRIENNE RICH (1986: 212)

MANY of us live in borderline zones that have yet to be socially acknowledged or defined. Each situation demands and/or emphasizes different identity markers so that one is constantly encountering an array of possible "selves." Lila Abu-Lughod (1990) refers to this condition as "multiple selfhood." She points out that native anthropologists, and feminists in general, often find themselves simultaneously, or alternately, high and low on different scales of hierarchy. Although one may partially control the presentation of one's identity in a given situation, for the most part others ascertain who one is based on socially determined categories such as man/woman and White/ethnic. The binary hierarchical structure of these categories tends to essentialize individuals and polarize groups (Abu-Lughod, 1991; Ortiz Barillas, this volume). The inadequacy of these categories to accommodate the social mosaic produces an ambiguity that is threatening to personal and group identity. Struggles to carve out satisfactory identities inadvertently challenge those of others and lead to increasing social strife. Thus, a major challenge of our times is to imagine ways to enact a new social order that is neither ambiguous nor essentializing.

Like many feminists today, I aim to eradicate, not racism or patriarchy, but rather the structure of binary oppositions. This is necessary to develop new models of identity that acknowledge the particularities of individual and group positionings.[1] Yet, a point of concern is that identities defined by "multiple selfhood" are still locked within the existing social hierarchies. Can we be satisfied with identities constrained by these pre-defined hierarchical categories? Is it possible to maintain multiple identities within this framework without our lives becoming fragmentary bits of actions, the interrelations over which we have little control? I suggest it may be possible to develop a model for social identities and relations that embraces difference without sacrificing wholeness. To do so, it is necessary to extend our analysis of hierarchy and power to the ways in which we may *embody* sets of binary oppositions.

Feminists have had difficulty conceptualizing an identity that encompasses difference and wholeness. The role of politics in feminist theory is one reason for this obstacle. In particular, we assert that we are grounded in the "real world" of particular political events and movements. The concreteness of the political realm contrasts with the abstract and representational nature of academic concerns. But the map of politics is, unfortunately, also representational. The concrete situations we live through are steeped in, even predetermined by, the symbolism of binary oppositions and the meta-narrative of colonialism, of which patriarchy is a part. When we define our identity against this structure – by gender, race, class, nation, sexual orientation – we become "fragmented" (Ebron and Tsing, 1995: 399).

In introductory anthropology courses we often teach that culture is largely unconscious. But we seldom give any further thought to the implications of this statement, especially where it concerns how culture may be inscribed on our own bodies. As Judith Okely (1992) points out, the embodiment of cultural patterns of movement and gesture can affect one's status as an insider or outsider in relation to a given community. But the embodiment of cultural conceptions also patterns how we perceive the whole framework of "self" and "other." It is my premise that the ways in which we perceive our physical selves in relation to our surroundings form the basis of culturally specific frameworks for the ordering of social relations. While enculturation processes account for how this relationship is *maintained*, I suggest we begin an investigation of the exact processes through which orientations to social structure may be *established* or *changed*.

Zeek Cywink, an Anishnaabe storyteller with whom I share my life, observed that the overwhelming factor in the embodiment of binary oppositions in Western culture is the tendency to orient our selves according to the right and left sides of our own bodies. Thus, Westerners have embodied a binary model, in which the only fixed point on the landscape is a self to which all else relates. This egocentric and self-referential orientation to the environment sustains the hierarchical social system, and hinders the democratization of social action and discourse. This paper explores the possibility of transforming the existing scales of social hierarchy at its foundation by altering the orientation of our bodies to physical and social environments. I develop this theme first through examining an ethnography of Bali that focuses on the embodiment of spatial and social models. Then, turning to North America, I discuss various personal narratives that reflect on the narrators' own experiences of the relationships among body, space and social structure. As one strategy among many, I propose that a shift in orientation within ourselves from the binary left and right to the four cardinal directions might stimulate a model in which all persons are continually at the centre of overlapping and moving spheres that nevertheless share the same stable and horizontal points of reference.

Margaret Mead and "The Balinese"

In 1991, as an undergraduate student, I launched my first attack on the hierarchies of binary oppositions. In an analysis of Balinese Geringsing textiles, I suggested that this form of sacred cloth embodied the "mid-point between," and thus transcendence of, "complementary oppositions" in Balinese thought. Since I had neither experience in the field nor familiarity with feminist and post-modern theory, I idealistically ignored the politics of Balinese women's actual status and the problematic category of "the Balinese." Furthermore, a re-examination of my source materials casts doubt on the idea of the "complementary" nature of the oppositions, if "complementary" is taken to infer equal value. Margaret Mead and Gregory Bateson's (1942) monograph on Bali did, however, leave an indelible impression on me. What interests me now is that the monograph reflects a theoretical approach that seeks to *illustrate* the processes through which cultural conceptions are embodied within individuals.

To show how the Balinese embody cultural conceptions, Mead and Bateson used a form of presentation that was, at that time, an "experimental innovation." Mead's introduction employed her characteristically "journalistic" writing style, although it had been criticized as "so synthetic that it became fiction" (Mead and Bateson, 1942: xi-xii). Bateson wrote analytic descriptions of sequences and sets of photographs depicting Balinese engaging in everyday activities during phases of life from birth to death. In this way, the monograph provides a detailed analysis of the relation among spatial orientation, social structure, and body gestures, postures, and cultural prohibitions.[2]

One of the insights in this collaborative photographic analysis concerned how Balinese infants quickly learned the rules about using right and left hands. The former was to be used for receiving gifts, pointing, and handling food, while the latter was to be reserved for "unclean" tasks such as handling the genitals. Women and girls carried infants on their left hips so that their own right hands would be free for socially appropriate tasks. Consequently, the right hands of the infants were necessarily either behind the backs or pinned under the arms of their caregivers. When an infant was offered food or a gift, its caregiver would repress the infant's impulse to extend his or her free left hand and instead extract the right hand from its inconvenient position. By the time most Balinese children were three years of age, they were fully versed in the appropriate uses of their hands (ibid., 13, 132).

These socially prescribed uses of the hands mirrored a similarly hierarchical pattern evident in the layout of all architectural structures in relation to the four cardinal directions. While Balinese determined the east-west axis by the sun, they conceived the north-south axis in relation to a sacred mountain in central Bali. On the southern side of the island the "inland" direction was due north, whereas on the northern side of the island "inland" was due south. According to Mead (ibid., 6), "inland"/east was superior and "coastward"/west was inferior no matter where one was on the island. For example, village temples were built on the "inland"/eastern corner of the village, while cemeteries were placed just beyond the "coastward"/western limit of the village boundary. Similarly, within household compounds, the family shrine was housed towards the former, while the kitchen and latrine occupied the latter. In this spatial hierarchy, emphasis was also placed on the directions up and down, so that the mountain was valued over the coastal shore. That these directions bore relation to social status was evidenced by the fact that the superior person of the household always slept east or "inland" of his inferiors and all persons slept with their heads (up) to the "inland"/east and their feet (down) to the "coastward"/west. Mead concludes that the embodiments of these spatial orientations were integral to Balinese processes of enculturation: "The words for the cardinal points are among the first a child learns and are used even for the geography of the body. A Balinese will tell you that there is a fly on the 'west' side of your face" (ibid.).

One would surmise from Mead and Bateson's analysis that this early training in the hierarchical order of the "geography of the body" was imperative to effective functioning within a society in which each social encounter was patterned with multiple scales of social hierarchy. The Balinese at that time had age grades, castes, and various levels of social strata within village organization that were marked not only by socially prescribed physical gestures and postures, but also with various forms of language, including terms of address, personal pronouns, and vocabulary. Under these circumstances, relational ambiguity was the cause for a great deal of anxiety. For instance, one photograph shows an older lower-caste boy from a different village playing among a group of younger upper-caste boys with his back turned to them because, he explained, "he did not want them to see his drawing (which was more skilful than theirs)" (ibid., 132). The extremity of anxiety occurred when an individual was deprived of geographic, temporal, and social orientations:

> In a strange village, where he does not know the cardinal points or the local customs, and if he does not know what day it is in at least three of the intercogging weeks, nor the caste and order of birth for the person with whom he is trying to converse, the Balinese is completely disoriented. To this state they apply the term, *paling*, which is used also for those who are drunk, delirious, or in trance. (ibid., 11)

Considering how important the embodiment of these orientations was to the Balinese, it is ironic that the very contextualization that Mead and Bateson attempted to achieve through the use of sequences of photographs is at least partially defeated by the recontextualization inherent in this medium. For example, although the children depicted in the photographs are said to orient themselves to the cardinal directions at all times, the text accompanying the photographs identifies them as "the girl on the right" or "the two children on the left" (ibid., 143). The flat surface of the photograph is, of course, oriented with reference to the Western viewer's right and left. Ironic, too, is the fact that while Mead embraced the scientific "objectivity" of photographic realism to counter criticisms of her artful literary style, present trends in theory criticize the former while advocating the latter. This recontextualization of the Balinese freezes their sequences of images in a time and place beyond their sense of orientation. From a post-modern perspective, this may illuminate Westerners' embodiment of the binary oppositions of right/left and self/other, as well as the colonial context of anthropological fieldwork, more than it elucidates "the Balinese."

Four North American Location Narratives

Of lasting value in the above study is the detail with which Mead and Bateson depict the processes through which infants and youth learn to orient their bodies to geographic and social metaphors so that their cultural conceptions seem "uniquely real" (Geertz, 1966). The relationships that their study reveals among conceptions of the body, physical environment, and social structure may be fruitfully applied to an analysis of neo-colonial and neo-patriarchal social relations in North America. To explore this relationship further, I present four North American narratives representative of differences in gender, culture, sexual orientation, class, education, theoretical leaning, and geographic biographies.

The first narrative is comprised of selected portions of James Clifford's "location exercise," which he begins with a quotation from Adrienne Rich (1986: 212): "A place on the map is also a place in history." The narrative appears to be his reflections on his own historical/geographical location as an eastern United States White urbanite:

I've always felt slightly disoriented in Santa Cruz. Even after ten years. The sunsets are particularly disturbing. Here I am on the West Coast, yet the sun sinks into the ocean, off to my right, behind the land. That mountain in the view is not an offshore island but Monterey peninsula. We are looking south, across the arc of a wide bay ....

In Santa Cruz I can never quite reconcile this "cartographic" location, on the West Coast, with the evidence of my senses registering more land "out there," and with the sun going down to my right, behind the hill. There's a permanent discrepancy between the realities of the map and experience, with the first always (never quite) overriding the second. Were I one of those people who situate themselves concretely, by means of the four directions .... But I'm not. The map – the great abstract coast, the hemisphere – is more real to me than the local curve of the shore ....

Centres and borders, homes and other places, are already mapped for us. We grow, live across and through them. Locations, itineraries: helping us to know our place, our futures, while always having to ask ... "Where WE run out of continent?" (Clifford, 1989: 186-87)

Clifford has identified and eloquently expressed a conceptual world-view applicable to many Western scholars for whom "the map" determines what *is*. Specifically, the self is defined in relation to left and right sides of a representation that is permanently facing North. This childhood orientation proves more powerful than sensory experience and leads to a permanent sense of displacement. Parallels to colonialism are evident here: the explorers came, they saw, and they *re*named, according to their preconceived map – the "savage" defined in terms of the "civilized." In this light, post-modernism, in which the sign (the map) is severed from the signified (the world), may be seen as a historic progression of colonialism. In identifying text as the new territory of colonial battles, Clifford quite accurately defines the conditions of the age of information. Now that the colonialists have literally "run out of continent," what is left but to discover new, virgin territory in the representational realm of text?

Clifford's orientation may be slightly different from that of anthropologists because for him "the other is the anthropological representation of the other" (Rabinow, 1986: 242). Anthropologists, however, must undergo the initiation rite of fieldwork, which requires them to temporarily (and partially) let go of the familiar map. Thus, their plunge into "experience" results in a "loss of self" that they then reconstitute through the act of writing (Crapanzano, 1977: 71-72; Kondo, 1986: 82-85). In re-creating self through the act of writing, the author can thereby enact the meta-narrative of conquest over wilderness and uncharted seas, which are figuratively within the individual, charted onto the social landscape and mapped into the territory of text. Clifford attempts, with some success, to address the power imbalance between the studier and the studied by advocating "dialogic" textual strategies (1986, 1988 [1983]). He also challenges the binary hierarchies of identities based on static geographic locations by positing an approach to inquiry that encompasses "travelling cultures" (1992). Yet, like the idea of "multiple selves," Clifford's ideas of "partial truths" and "movement" as a signifier of identity do not get to the root of the problem. The self-referential, binary and hierarchical bodily orientation remains intact, thereby continuing to fix exclusionary identities and disintegrate the wholeness of other identities.

The second narrative is one I had heard many times *before* I read Clifford's "location exercise." The contexts of its telling range from casual social settings to public speaking engagements and discourse with academics. It is a "true" story that Zeek Cywink likes to tell as part of his mission to "educate White people." He is originally from a small reserve community in the Manitoulin Island region, but has been living in the city for more than a decade. Zeek agreed to share this story in print because, as he says, "the guy in the story is also a Clifford":

> We had been working in Toronto, you know, in construction, and my buddy, he was always getting lost — could never get his directions right. So, we'd come out of an elevator and he'd go one way and I'd go the other way. He'd start walking away, and I'd be walking to the work site, and he'd stop and realize — oops — and turn around and go, "Are you going the right way?" And I'd say, "C'mon, we have to go this way." He'd get off the elevator first because he was the boss, and he'd

start marching away and I'd laugh and wait for him to realize that I wasn't going with him, wherever he was going.

So, one day we're driving around the city – well, I was driving around the city and he was giving me directions to a job site. And he'd say, "I want you to go down to this place," and I'd ask him how to get there, and he'd say, "Well, go down to this street and third set of lights, turn right, and go two blocks and turn right again and go a street and turn left at those lights and it's the third building on your right, that's where the driveway is." We didn't always go to the same place, so he didn't always give me the same directions, but he'd always give me directions the same way.

One day I was driving around with him, and all of a sudden it struck me, and I says (he grew up in England, so I said), "You know what, mate? I figured out how come you're always getting lost." And he said, "Why's that?" 'Cause he knew he was always getting lost. "Why am I always getting lost?" I says, "Because you only have two directions – left and right. I have four." So, I have east, south, west, and north and that's how I orientate myself. And this guy was always left and right, and with only those two directions, he was always getting lost. I never get lost. (Zeek Cywink, taped interview, May 1997)

Zeek observes that, in general, Westerners move in a world that physically evolves around them. There are no fixed points of reference beyond the self. Westerners are literally what might be termed "ego-centred." Like Columbus, they are lost without knowing it. For example, he points out the absurdity of the term "Westerner" because from the point of view of the colonized *he* is truly a "Westerner" in relation to the colonizers. As an anthropologist, I note that the ego-centred Euro-Canadian orientation is reinforced by our bilateral kinship system in which "ego" is the centre of a constantly changing radius of individuals. In contrast, unilineal descent patterns, such as the traditional Anishnaabe *dodem* system, are stable structures through which the individual passes. As well as his orientation to the four directions, Zeek is oriented to his lateral and lineal relations. In Zeek's sense of place there is also a constant awareness of his home reserve as his place of origin. His concrete grounding results in a narrative form that proceeds as dialogue-in-action rather than analytic reflection. This is because for him daily experience, as opposed to a representational map, is the context out of which "truth" arises.

While Zeek's narrative refers specifically to the practical application of the four directions as geographic markers, two characteristics of Anishnaabe cosmology are pertinent to this discussion. First, Anishnaabek always refer to the four directions in clockwise order: East, South, West, and North. This circular sequence contrasts with the Western custom of following the order of a cross: North, South, East, and West. The former pattern promotes the equality of the directions while the latter emphasizes the up/down hierarchy of the North/South axis. Second, in Anishnaabe cosmology the four directions are "grandfathers" who, as the term suggests, are kin to the present Anishnaabek. Moreover, they possess equally valued powers that enable them to perform different sacred functions.[3] Although an age hierarchy places the Persons of the Four Directions above humans, they are nevertheless in intimate relation to the latter and equal among themselves.

These aspects of Anishnaabe cosmology contrast with the hierarchical orientation of the Balinese to the cardinal points. In each case, however, one can see how the presence or absence of spatial hierarchy arises directly out of the significant features of the landscape itself. The island of Bali is dominated by a central mountain range and circumscribed by the sea, whereas Anishnaabe territory is continuous land patterned by systems of inland water routes that traverse higher and lower geographic features, all of which are imbued with local and national significance. Thus, movement within Anishnaabe territory produces an egalitarian orientation to the environment. While Clifford strives towards these ideals, his and the following narratives show that Western orientations do not stem directly from the natural landscape.

The third narrative is made up of portions of an autobiographical essay by lesbian feminist Minnie Bruce Pratt (1982). I chose her story because, even though it was written over a decade ago, it presents some of the key concepts in recent feminist thought. As well, Pratt "politicizes the geography, demography and architecture" of the communities in which she lives and has lived (Martin and Mohanty, 1986: 195):

> I am speaking my small piece of truth, as best I can .... So here it is: I'm putting it down to see if our fragments match anywhere, if our pieces, together, make another larger piece of the truth that can be part of the map we are making together to show us the way to get to the longed-for world.
>
> Where does the need come from, the inner push to walk into change, if by skin colour, ethnicity, birth culture, we are women who are in a position of material advantage, where we gain at the expense of others, of other women? ... What do we have to gain? (Pratt, 1982: 16)

Pratt then tells a story of how her father took her into the courthouse at the centre of her hometown where her grandfather was a judge for over forty years. Her father wanted her to see the town from the top of the clock tower. He wanted her to see his view from the centre. She describes the buildings that she would and wouldn't have seen if she had been willing to go to the top. She feared the climb, however, because she was "a white girl, not boy."

> Yet I was shaped by my relation to those buildings and to the people in the buildings, by ideas of who should be in the bank handling money, of who should have the guns and the keys to the jail, of who should be *in* the jail; and I was shaped by what I didn't see, or didn't notice, on those streets.
>
> Not the way your town was laid out, you say? True, perhaps, but each of us carries around those growing-up places, the institutions, a sort of back-drop, a stage-set. So often we act out the present against a back-drop of the past, within a frame of perception that is so familiar, so safe that it is terrifying to risk changing it even when we know our perceptions are distorted, limited, constricted by that view. (ibid., 17)

Pratt expresses the idea that, to change the social order, we have to change the metaphor of our orientation to our environments. Her feminist "map," however, is partial, fragmented, and *in the process* of becoming only a "larger piece" because female selves cannot attain the "view from the centre." She is keenly aware of how she has embodied an orientation to the world that is defined by the architectural structures of margin and centre. Rather than the four directions, she orients to the four corners of politically charged rooms and buildings. She concludes that one thing she gains from change is a more "truthful" view of the world – a "world of overlapping circles, like movement on the millpond after a fish has jumped, instead of the courthouse square with me at the middle, even if I *am* on the ground" (ibid.). This poetic conception replaces the polarized square with the egalitarian form of the circle as the basic form of social relations. But it still reflects the egocentric Western orientation because there are no stable points of reference: the overlapping circles come and go with the movement of each individual fish that breaks the surface of the water. As well, Pratt's analogy posits the stage upon which social drama unfolds as a flat and undifferentiated surface. As her narrative shows, however, the "back-drops of the past" that we all carry with us into the present are invariably patterned in specific ways.

The final narrative I present is my own. Like Mead and Bateson's analysis, I present it as a series of snapshots. But, unlike their "objective" observation of others, my snapshots look inward and subjectively at the stages through which I formulated and reformulated orientations to my physical and social environments:

I was a four- or five-year-old child living in Saskatoon – a city within a landscape of flat space and big sky. My parents took me out canvassing for the New Democratic Party (NDP), which, I quickly learned, was "leftist" or "left-wing." The "right-wing" capitalist conservatives were the "bad guys" who caused all injustice. From these fundamental "facts" I extrapolated the general view that all things leftist, or unconventional, were good even though authorities desired conformity. Later, as a young teen, I symbolically inscribed this orientation on my body by piercing my left ear twice and my right ear not at all.

I first learned about the four directions through my childhood travels on the Toronto subway system, which at that time consisted of a North/South line crossed by an East/West line. Starting when I was about eight, I made a game of getting subway transfers from all the stations. Since I never left the train stations on the East/West axis of the transit system, the experience was largely underground where I was unaware of the sun's movement. The geography of south and north, however, was well-known to me. Travelling south from where I lived, downtown was literally *down* an ancient shoreline, under the train tracks and through the core to the lake.

Meanwhile, during the same period, my family often travelled "north" to the cottage, where I had virtually no conception of cardinal directions. It was actually northeast of the city. The fact that the shoreline was almost always shaded meant little to me in terms of direction. Standing on the shoreline, I knew that to the left was Endicott Bay and to the right was Wild Cat Island. North and south were synonymous with the dichotomy between the city and the "wilderness" characteristic of Ontario cottaging traditions.

Awareness of my relation to the cardinal directions developed during many years' residency in New York City and one year in Taos, New Mexico, as well as through extensive overland travelling. Returning to Toronto, my orientation took a radical turn as I became involved in Native communities in Ontario. Initially, the dichotomy between urban and rural was dissolved as I participated in communities that continually moved between cities and reserves, encompassing both simultaneously. Much travel increased my awareness of the four directions. I pierced my right ear so that I could wear the beaded earrings that were now a part of my everyday life. Eventually, I pierced my right ear again for balance and the number four.

Yet, while the structure of dichotomies was transforming internally, externally my social position as a White person in a Native world challenged my basic assumption of my position within the highly valued left. From the point of view of some Anishnaabek, I was another one of the "bad guys" on the right. Further complexities arose because, as partner to an Anishnaabe man and one of the teachers of a Native women's beading circle, the relative importance of the polarities of male/female versus Native/non-Native was in constant play. Finally, despite the politically and ideologically subversive nature of my background, it and the position that I now occupied as an academic conferred privileges upon me in certain contexts, while the same traits became liabilities in other situations.

Despite my parents' lifelong commitment to social justice, the structure of binary oppositions was inscribed within my body at a very early age. The significant categories pertain to politics *within* Euro-Canadian society and their values are opposite to the dominant view. Unlike race and gender, the criteria for these categories do not depend on physical traits. Displacement occurs when the physical trait of Whiteness becomes a homogenizing stereotype, thus placing me in the category of those I've always considered to be "them." It is not difficult for me to feel displaced, however, because left and right are not stable markers of place. My awareness of the cardinal directions did not begin to develop until my teenage years. Like that of Clifford, the story ends unresolved.

All of the above narratives are stories about being displaced or "lost" and the desire for a secure sense of social location. In the ethnographic example, Mead observed that the Balinese were "lost" when deprived of known indicators of social place. From this point of view, one could assume that they would become "lost" due to the influence of globalization processes. Although contemporary ethnographers would attribute more adaptability and agency to non-Western peoples than did Mead, there can be no doubt that colonization and globalization have been responsible for wide-scale displacement. The North American narratives illustrate how a sense of displacement can be common to *all* groups, although positioning on different scales of hierarchy affects the degrees and forms of alienation. In all cases, however, it seems that a sense of place is essential to satisfactory identity formation. Zeek's narrative provides a solution to the problem of how to achieve a sense of place without the necessity of a *bounded* geographic location, although as we have seen, the existence of a nationally designated land base is a key factor in the security of his identity.

Embodied Wholeness and Models of Social Relations

When we do our "location exercise," we must begin, as Adrienne Rich says, with the body. How "naturally" our bodily orientations translate into political metaphors is apparent in the language we use to describe political positions: the Right is right (the normative centre) and the left is what is "left over" (the margins, the other). In spatial terms, right is not only at the centre, but also up, where left is down. The awkward imbalance of this structure explains why it is in constant strain and requires a continuous violence to uphold. Yet, it is fundamental to the vast majority of people who grew up in the West regardless of gender, race, ethnicity, or class. Though for each of us it has different consequences, for all of us the binary oppositions begin here, embodied, enacted in our very steps. Orientation to the four directions realigns the body. The structure is actually a sphere. The centre *is* at the centre, not at the top. On a broader scale, the cardinal directions are never remote because they are embodied, while at the same time, every body is always at the centre because each is always in the same relation to the fixed cardinal points.

Everyone should try the simple exercise of becoming "one of those people who situate themselves concretely, by means of the four directions" (Clifford, 1989: 187). It may be possible that by realigning our bodies to the four cardinal points, preferably as determined by the sun's course, we become more secure in our place in the world, thus reducing the threat of social displacement. We also become accustomed to a certain way of thought and being in the world that if consciously applied to social relations, may facilitate egalitarianism. But how might this internal transformation translate into an identity politics that promotes equalization of access to textual and political territory?

In our daily interactions and our representations of those relationships, we should strive to *enact* and *inscribe* a meta-narrative, not of difference but with a difference. Many kinds of re-imaginings are possible and actually occurring. I follow those feminists who insist that, as individuals, we cannot be reduced to fragmented sets of categories (Abu-Lughod, 1990: 18-19; Hastrup, 1992: 121-22, 124; Strathern, 1987: 264). In the model I am suggesting, we work with the centrifugal force of our environment. Presently, the imagined centre is not the centre. What is holding up the top is what is down below: our own complicity (Mohanty, 1988: 81). Those to the left should not fear the wholeness of a unified self because such hegemonic selves as we have known are only possible within the system of binary oppositions. Rather, we should quietly embody a wholeness of a kind where every person and place is at the centre of overlapping and moving spheres. By broadening the context of reference points from two within self to four beyond self, it is possible to undercut the ego-centred conceptual "map" at the base, thereby establishing a pattern in which selves are not fragmented by social categories. Although still representational, this orientation provides a literal "grounding" outside textual and political bearings.

To translate a personal orientation to the environment from an individual perception to a social structure, the new perspective must *inform* political action rather than replace it. Whether inscribing or enacting, this strategy demands a rigorous recognition and validation of *multiple* personal and collective selves and centres, as well as their *movement* and *overlap*. Negotiation of new criteria for value between and among overlapping selves is an urgent agenda. Simultaneously, new criteria for flexible boundaries (and ultimately borders) must be established according to the expressed needs of existing and emergent centres. For example, of foremost importance in this regard is the speedy and just settlement of Canadian First Nations and Métis land claims. In this process, these new criteria will in turn *inform* the construction of alternative histories that are based on the premise of inclusion rather than exclusion.

By starting with our bodies in relation to our physical environments we arrive at very similar principles to those that underlie the post-modern movement in academia. The difference, however, is that the former "grounds" personal and social identity in flexible wholenesses that maintain social categories of equally valued difference, whereas the latter leads inevitably to fragmentation, dislocation, and the elimination of differences that are crucial to political identity. Representational and physical territory *is* being reclaimed and making a difference. The question is: what kind of difference do we want to make?

Notes

1 Among whom are: Abu-Lughod, 1990: 25-26, 1991: 144-45; Behar, 1995: 22; Callaway, 1992: 29,38-39; Cole, 1995: 199; de Laurentis 1986: 11-13; Ebron and Tsing 1995: 390-91; Mascia-Lees *et al.* 1989: 22; Martin and Mohanty 1986: 193; Mohanty, 1988: 79; Phelan, 1991: 138-40; Rich, 1986: 221; Tedlock, 1991: 81-82.

2 My discussion of Mead and Bateson's findings is presented in the past tense because I am dealing only with their 1936-38 study. I do not attempt to evaluate their findings in light of more recent studies of Bali nor to present Balinese perceptions.

3 See Benton-Banai (1979: 24-25) for an introduction to the Grandfathers of the Four Directions and an explanation of their powers.

References

Abu-Lughod, Lila. 1990. "Can There Be a Feminist Ethnography?" *Women and Performance: A Journal of Feminist Theory* 5: 7-27.

——. 1991. "Writing Against Culture," in Richard Fox, ed., *Recapturing Anthropology: Working in the Present*. Santa Fe, New Mexico: School for American Research Press, 137-62.

Behar, Ruth. 1995. "Introduction: Out of Exile," in Ruth Behar and Deborah Gordon, eds., *Women Writing Culture*. Berkeley: University of California Press, 1-29.

Benton-Banai, Edward. 1979. *The Mishomis Book: The Voice of the Ojibwa*. St. Paul, Minn.: Indian Country Press.

Callaway, Helen. 1992. "Ethnography and Experience: Gender Implications in Fieldwork and Text," in Judith Okely and Helen Callaway, eds., *Anthropology and Autobiography*. London: Routledge, 29-49.

Clifford, James. 1986. "Partial Truths," in James Clifford and George Marcus, eds., *Writing Culture: The Poetics and Politics of Ethnography*. Berkeley: University of California Press, 1-26.

——. 1988 [1983]. "On Ethnographic Authority," in James Clifford, *The Predicament of Culture*. Cambridge, Mass.: Harvard University Press, 21-53.

——. 1989. "Notes on Theory and Travel," *Inscriptions* 5: 177-88.

——. 1992. "Travelling Cultures," in Lawrence Grossberg, Cary Nelson, and Paula Treichler, eds., *Cultural Studies*. New York: Routledge, 96-116.

Cole, Sally. 1995. "Taming the Shrew in Anthropology: Is Feminist Ethnography 'New' Ethnography?" in Sally Cole and Lynne Phillips, eds., *Ethnographic Feminisms: Essays in Anthropology*. Ottawa: Carleton University Press, 185-205.

Crapanzano, Vincent. 1977. "On the Writing of Ethnography," *Dialectical Anthropology* 2, 1: 69-73.

de Laurentis, Teresa. 1986. "Feminist Studies/Critical Studies: Issues, Terms, and Contexts," in Teresa de Laurentis, ed., *Feminist Studies/Critical Studies*. Bloomington: Indiana University Press, 1-19.

Ebron, Paula and Anna Lowenhaupt Tsing. 1995. "In Dialogue? Reading Across Minority Discourses," in Ruth Behar and Deborah Gordon, eds., *Women Writing Culture*. Berkeley: University of California Press, 390-411.

Geertz, Clifford. 1966. "Religion as a Cultural System," in Michael Banton, ed., *Anthropological Approaches to the Study of Religion*. London: Tavistock, 1-44.

Hastrup, Kirsten. 1992. "Writing Ethnography: State of the Art," in Judith Okely and Helen Callaway, eds., *Anthropology and Autobiography*. London: Routledge, 116-33.

Kondo, Dorinne. 1986. "Dissolution and Reconstitution of Self: Implications for Anthropological Epistemology," *Cultural Anthropology* 1, 1: 74-88.

Martin, Biddy and Chandra Mohanty. 1986. "Feminist Politics: What's Home Got to Do With It?" in T. de Laurentis, ed., *Feminist Studies/Critical Studies*. Bloomington: Indiana University Press, 191-212.

Mascia-Lees, Frances E., Patricia Sharpe, and Colleen Ballerino Cohen. 1989. "The Postmodern Turn in Anthropology: Cautions from a Feminist Perspective," *Signs* 15, 1: 7-33.

Mead, Margaret, and Gregory Bateson. 1942. *Balinese Character: A Photographic Analysis*. New York: New York Academy of Sciences.

Mohanty, Chandra. 1988. "Under Western Eyes: Feminist Scholarship and Colonial Discourses," *Feminist Review* 30: 61-88.

Okely, Judith. 1992. "Anthropology and Autobiography: Participatory Experience and Embodied Knowledge," in Judith Okely and Helen Callaway, eds., *Anthropology and Autobiography*. London: Routledge, 1-28.

Phelan, Shane. 1991. "Specificity: Beyond Equality and Difference," *Differences* 3, 1: 128-43.

Pratt, Minnie Bruce. 1982. "Identity: Skin Blood Heart," in E. Bulkin, M.B. Pratt and B. Smith, *Yours in Struggle: Three Feminist Perspectives on Anti-Semitism and Racism*. Brooklyn, N.Y.: Long Haul Press, 11-63.

Rabinow, Paul. 1986. "Representations Are Social Facts: Modernity and Post-Modernity in Anthropology," in J. Clifford and G. Marcus, eds., *Writing Culture: The Poetics and Politics of Ethnography*. Berkeley: University of California Press, 234-61.

Rich, Adrienne. 1986. "Notes Towards a Politics of Location," in *Blood, Bread and Poetry: Selected Prose, 1979-1985*. New York: W. W. Norton, 210-31.

Strathern, Marilyn. 1987. "Out of Context: The Pervasive Fictions of Anthropology," *Current Anthropology* 28, 3: 251-70.

Tedlock, Barbara. 1991. "From Participant Observation to Observation of Participation: The Emergence of Narrative Ethnography," *Journal of Anthropological Research* 47, 1: 69-94.

SIX

"HOME HAS ALWAYS BEEN HARD FOR ME": SINGLE MOTHERS' NARRATIVES OF IDENTITY, HOME AND LOSS

Susan Frohlick

Introduction: "Being in Space Is Not Easy"

THIS essay is both a critique and a recognition of the significance of "home" and its multiple meanings and practices in the context of single mothers' life stories. Feminist anthropologists and geographers argue that home (or the lack there of) is a crucial spatiality of women's everyday lives, a diagnostic of power and gendered subjectivity that should not be taken for granted (Rose, 1993; Massey, 1994; Moore, 1994). Home is neither a neutral container nor an essential place but rather a lived, felt, and highly mediated experience and social space in which subjects are defined and determined (Kirby, 1996). Home as a corporeal, discursive, social, and imagined space is examined here for the specific ways it affects women's lives and identities and for the ways in which "it is not an easy space to occupy" (Rose, 1993). Answers are sought to the questions Kathleen Kirby (1996: 5, 124) has posed: "In what ways are subjects the effects of spaces?" and "How is subjectivity lived as a space by people, and lived differently by different kinds of subjects?"

More specifically, the everyday spatialities of home are critical experiences from which we can gain a better understanding of "single mother" subjectivities. Linda McDowell (1996: 41) has suggested, "The sense of oneself as a certain sort of woman, defined by class, 'race,' religion, age, and so forth, is given meaning by the actualities of everyday experience. And this experience itself is a complex series of cross-cutting locations in which the significance of different aspects of the self varies." I aim to show how the "sense of oneself" as a single mother comes to the fore within the located, embodied experiences of home. Of particular importance is how discourses of "home," naturalized as a stable and fixed place, can produce experiences of loss, dislocation, and marginality for some women.

Recently, I collected and analysed narratives from women in Vancouver in terms of the meanings they gave to their identities as single mothers.[1] While the narratives in this essay tell important cultural stories, it is significantly my own story as well as parts of theirs that I present here. At the time of writing up my research, I lamented the lack of opportunity to be able to follow more centrally a spatially oriented analysis. As I explained then, "Although I wanted to put much more ethnographic emphasis on their homes as sites of identity-making and contests over social space, the women's insistence on telling stories of struggle, survival, hardship, and marginality did not allow me to stray as far as I would have liked in that theoretical direction" (Krygsveld, 1996: 32). This essay provides the opportunity for me to "stray" in ways that I hope are fruitful both ethnographically and theoretically and that do not betray too much the senses of self that the women attempted to share with me.

One of the feminist goals underpinning my analysis is that of critiquing nostalgic notions of "home" as a safe, secure, familiar place of belonging (see John, 1996; George, 1996; Martin and Mohanty, 1987; Visweswaren, 1994). A second feminist goal is that of revealing the myriad processes of "othering" that occur in specific times, locations, and social spaces for particular categories of women (see Frankenberg and Lati, 1993; Grewal, 1994). More than anything else, my earlier research involved an attempt to understand single mothers' complex experiences of being made to feel different "against the horizon of 'normalized' motherhood and family images" (Polakow, 1993: 3). This essay focuses on specific ways that "home" is implicated in the multiple dislocations that women who are single mothers, including myself, experience.

I draw here on the life stories of two women.[2] Raine is a young, White, lesbian single mother on social assistance living in an east side neighbourhood in Vancouver. Her narrative demonstrates the politicized connection she sees between her social location and her uneasy experiences of home. Home, as a place of healing and meaningfulness, increasingly recedes for her as her circumstances continue to constrain this idea and fantasy. Rose, a single mother in her forties, lives in a largely White, middle-class neighbourhood and copes with the "hidden" disabilities of multiple sclerosis. Her narration demonstrates a complex relationship among body, space, and self as she struggles to renegotiate her sense of identity and bodily abilities in more positive terms within constraining physical and social spaces.

Home is used in this essay as a critical site for examining issues of single motherhood and identity for a number of reasons. First, single motherhood is a social category produced by discourses that mark women living outside the naturalized nuclear home as deviant and pathological, and their homes and families as incomplete and "broken" by virtue of the "missing male" (Fineman, 1995; Moore, 1994; Mullings, 1995). Home in this sense is a code for family "order" that impinged directly on the everyday lives of the women in my study. Second, "home" was a common predicament for them in that they had to deal with the practices of home on an everyday basis, yet on terms not of their own making. It was not exactly their "choice" to become single mothers, nor did they always have control over the terms of child custody or support payments, for example. In other words, home was not an easy space for the women to occupy as they negotiated its material dimensions (such as locating affordable housing; arranging adequate child care; unpacking boxes). Nor were the strongly felt symbolic dimensions easily dealt with (such as reconstructing home as the "place in our mind"). Third, home was the locale of lived experience. This included the negotiations I have just described that were often framed in terms of survival, hard work, struggle, and isolation, as well as personal transformation and well-being. Their homes are "lived bodily practices of incorporated knowledge [that] bind the material and the symbolic indissolubly" (Moore, 1994: 81). They were spaces in which the women came to know discrimination and oppression intimately.

Homework as Fieldwork

> Why is it that despite recent critiques of place and voice in anthropology, we have yet to turn to our own neighborhoods and growing-up places? (Visweswaren, 1994: 104)

Writing as a feminist means considering the implications of the analytical and editorial decisions that I make for the women I interviewed and being loyal to their "own words." Before presenting the women's narratives, it is important to discuss the issue of intersubjectivity, that is, my own role in the creation of these women's "selves and identities" in the context of "the ethnographic encounter" (Probyn, 1993). My own "arrival story," imbued with upheaval, dislocation, and struggle towards consciousness, is an important element to this creation. I recount it briefly as a resource and tool for reflexivity, although this is not in any way straightforward. Elspeth Probyn (1993: 142) has cogently pointed out that while the importance of specifying one's position cannot be doubted, "how to do justice to all its instances is far from self-evident."

Part of the impetus for interpreting the women's narratives as testimonies to struggle and dislocation was a response to assertions like Raine's, "I want my unique story to be out there, my reality, because I think it is often overlooked in discussions about single parenthood ... I feel like I'm a real survivor." I used their stories as they wanted me to, to qualify the countless negative images they have faced and to interject complexity into the diverse ways that single mothers negotiate their identities through marginalizing discourses. My own ordering of the category "single mother" was one fraught with difficulties stemming from my own experience, and so I was an empathetic listener. However, while my project is about uncovering how "single mother" is "colonized" (Fineman, 1995) by wider public and legal discourses, for example, it is important that the reader is aware of how I, too, have reinscribed the women in a particular way.

I became a single mother five years ago when my son was three and I left my marriage of ten years. A child of White, Catholic, working-class, second-generation Canadian parents, I was the only daughter to be divorced. Following my divorce, I returned to Canada and to university as a full-time student after a ten-year absence, during which time I had been living and working in the Caribbean under conditions of considerable financial security. I did not find my new social dis/location to be an easy one and experienced it as a moment of multiple loss: of "family," home, income, dreams, identity. I found myself marked in a new way. Up until that point, as a relatively privileged White woman I had moved through life with an "unmarked and unnamed status" (Frankenberg, 1993: 1). After years of being a married mother I experienced a discordance in being repositioned a *single* mother. For many reasons this strongly affected me. Looking back, I see that my own rather negative image of a "single mother" had been mediated by classist, racist, and sexist discourses that cast divorced and unmarried mothers as default and undesirable positions. When growing up it was assumed that I, along with my sisters, would marry and have children and remain married to my husband until "death do us part." Blind and naïve to those women living in what Valerie Polakow (1993) has described as the "zone of deviance and moral suspicion," I knew of no single mother living in our neighbourhood. When "they" were alluded to, it was in terms of misfortune or pity.

These growing-up places are important sites from which to examine my own "blind spots and privilege" (Visweswaren, 1994). Kamala Visweswaren has argued that a feminist ethnography based on "homework" (as a kind of "fieldwork"), in which we as anthropologists interrogate our own roles in the constitution of "home," can "form the basis of an accountable positioning that seeks to locate itself in and against the master discourses of race, class and sexuality that inscribe it" (ibid., 104). This gaze homeward allows me to ask what my own background has to do with my emphasis on single motherhood as "loss" (and I invite the reader to do the same). What cross-cutting axes of race, class, and gender connect Raine's and Rose's stories of home with my own? I cannot assume, as Raine glibly pointed out for me, that the women's realities are the same as mine. "I never hear lesbian single mothers mentioned .... I've often felt marginalized by the whole scene.[3] They assume that everyone was married and then divorced, that we were married and living some kind of middle class lifestyle. That's not my reality at all." At the same time, however, I cannot assume "difference" either. Critically, there is commonality between us as women marked by the "missing male." I use the narratives that follow to draw out the specific ways in which this mark seems to matter in the women's everyday lives and spaces.

Refusing the Givenness of Home

Raine lives with her young son in a co-op apartment. She became a single mother when she was a teenager living in and out of foster homes. Raine was suicidal at the time of her pregnancy, receiving very little support from anyone. Nevertheless, after the birth of Michael she managed to rent a base-ment suite and finish high school while working full-time and taking care of him on her own. When Michael was a baby, Raine came out as a lesbian and subsequently experienced discrimination while looking for housing and as a tenant. After hospitalization for mental exhaustion, she tried living with roommates to ease her workload, but this was not very successful. When I interviewed Raine she had just moved into the co-op after breaking up with her partner, and her story demonstrated a refusal of the "givenness" of home. Home – as a space of comfort, security, and peacefulness – was some-thing Raine felt she has not had equal nor automatic access to, in ways that others do.

> I've always had a hard time with home, it's always been a hard one for me .... I moved here three months ago and I'm not unpacked yet. It's pretty sad. It's always been a struggle with me and I guess that goes right back to my childhood. It has always just seemed like work, and never fun, and never good just to be at home. It is always overwhelm-ing ... all these boxes and papers that I have to deal with. Living in poverty, there is always bureaucracy to deal with – papers to fill out, people to contact.
>   The home thing is also hard because I moved a lot. No home has

been perfect for me. That's why I moved so often. I moved nineteen times by the time I was fourteen. I move so often I always have a closet full of boxes – always. I'm always having stuff that I need to find that I can't find because it's buried in the box in the closet.

But it's not just that. It's about always having my work around me .... I always feel overwhelmed by my home .... I'm always just so exhausted. I've been at school all day, made dinner, dealt with Michael, I just don't have the energy to unpack at night!

The unpacked boxes that litter Raine's apartment signify a series of forced dislocations for her. They also signify the physical labour involved in maintaining a home by a woman who single-handedly carries out the household duties. The boxes represent being made to move by circumstances that must be seen in contrast to my own "mobility." I have moved a lot, too (but growing up I lived in the same house for eighteen years), and my belongings are scattered between my parents' attic and various other places. But my mobility has been propelled by "choice" – to travel, and to return to university, for example – whereas Raine has been unfairly evicted and otherwise been forced to move since early adolescence. Our different readings of the unpacked boxes derive from our different social locations and experiences of home, although certainly not entirely.

Raine did not take home for granted. She politicized home as an impossible space wherein she has had an ongoing struggle to find and make a place for herself and her son against barriers of poverty, abuse, homophobic and sexist discrimination, and her own inability to overcome the politics and weightiness of "home" work. When Raine said that "home has always been hard for me," she was referring to much more than daily household chores. "Home" work can be distinguished here from housework in that Raine used it to denote the expansive range of symbolic and material practices involved in her work *at* and *for* home. This included entertaining her son, finding affordable, decent housing, and making a comfortable living space where she and her son could do meaningful activities and find peace.

Crucially, when Raine talked to me about this home work she could not separate her identity as a poor, young, lesbian single mother from the implications this held for her with regard to the everyday burden of chores and child care. "I find that I'm just a little too aware of how unjust it is .... So I sit around analysing, theorizing, about how I shouldn't have to do this ... and meanwhile it still has to be done. I'm so bitter about the hand I've been dealt that it keeps me from getting the work done." Home was a difficult space for Raine to occupy in that she struggled on a daily basis with coming to terms with "the hand that I've been dealt." Raine escaped home at the same time that she desired it. Her age, class, and sexuality are inextricably connected to this experience. As she put it, "there is a part of me that just wants to go out because I have missed out on so much." Raine's subjectivity, then, as a teenage mom, a lesbian mom, and someone who has few resources, has much to do with the way that her particular home space is produced and practised.

This awareness of who she is and its implications carry through to Raine's insistence that even as home has clearly been difficult for her, she does not embody in any fashion a "broken home."

> No, I don't feel like it's a broken home. I do feel like I have a love/hate relationship with my home. But in terms of the enigma of home ... I do feel strongly that it is me and Michael and I'm really proud of that. We are not waiting for somebody else to come along and complete our home and family. This is our home and I have no illusions about anybody else coming into make it anything else.

Underpinning Raine's insistence that she and her son are a complete family unit is the politics to which many single mothers must submit – the ubiquitous possibility of having children taken away through courts of law that strive to reinscribe hegemonic nuclear family/household arrangements (Fineman, 1995; Lewin, 1990). Not only was she making a claim to an identity as a person with stakes in reconfiguring "family," but she was demonstrating to me an acute awareness of the power relations and potential danger in considering herself anything less than "intact." Through her vulnerability as a lesbian, as well as through her poverty, Raine mediates her understanding of home – as a secure place of belonging – as a reality she has never been able to "afford," symbolically or materially, nor likely will in the future.

Her recent breakup with a childless, educated, middle-class woman served to accentuate the "enigma of home" for Raine in an ironic way, an irony that underscores the conflicting desires Raine held for home as a two-parent family space *and* as a Utopian space of social transformation.

> We had this ideal home image together .... She had more resources, more ability to make money, she was going to buy land and women could come live on the land and build farmhouses and work on the land. It would be like a land trust, there for women who need land .... We were going to do this together as a family, and now that's broken

down, too. So, I'm feeling pretty bitter, that she can leave me and make off with the resources.

It's also about future stability and financial stability. The direction that this country and province is going I don't see that I'm going to be able to live on welfare much longer. I don't have any more than one year of post-secondary education. I don't have resources. I don't have child care. How am I going to get enough money to buy land?

Home is a dream about ultimate belonging-to places, and here a contestation surfaces: how will Raine secure a place of belonging in a landscape that privileges and enables particular household forms over others? "Who has the power to make places out of spaces?" (Gupta and Ferguson, 1992: 11). Home has "never been perfect" for Raine, and this must be linked to what she described as her "thrice-marginalized self."

As a single mother who is also lesbian and also poor, she has been made to move from one place to another in search of a place that "fits" and is not substandard, by others as well as by her own discontent with the quality of housing afforded by someone in her social position. Home as a consonant space is not a possibility for her in that her material life, as a single mother on social assistance with no support from family, keeps her from it. "Single mother" is usefully seen, then, as a spatial as well as a discursive construction bound by the social, material possibilities of what constitutes "home."

One other thing about home ... is that so many of our homes have been substandard in so many ways. In the last place, Michael's bedroom was really tiny .... The place before that I didn't have a bedroom. He had the bedroom and I slept in the living room. It's about poverty, about not having the resources to have a nice, big place, and I have a lot of resentment about that. I feel like I've been targeted in so many ways, around home, trying to find a home. It has been so hard when I've been apartment hunting trying to find homes, because I'm a single mother – because I'm single, I'm a mother, and because I'm poor, never mind the fact that I'm also a dyke! That has made it really hard to feel like I want to put my roots down and stay awhile. I haven't put up anything that requires nails .... This is so impermanent. Home for me has always been hard. It is really hard. I just want to feel really comfortable somewhere.

Unlearning the Nostalgic Rememberings of Home

Rose lives with her two teenage children in a house she owns. She immigrated to Canada from England when she was eighteen in order to transcend her working-class parents' social status. Rose became business partners with her husband. They separated when she could no longer tolerate his arduous work-oriented lifestyle. At that time, Rose had just had her second child and was diagnosed with multiple sclerosis. She managed to keep making the mortgage payments on her house and has remained in the same house for eighteen years, a marker of "stability" she is notably proud of.

While it has been difficult for Rose as a disabled single mother to keep up with the physical demands of home, she spoke gravely of its symbolic significance. A devout Christian, Rose has struggled with the loss of her husband's presence in the home, coded by Rose as the container of "the natural union of man and woman." This has been a strongly felt loss for her but more crucially, she thinks, for her children. Rose has remade her home as an appropriate moral space of "proper" family and motherhood, mediated through her religious beliefs and her identity as a disabled woman, as well as through her class position. Rose's narrative reveals a complex relationship between her struggle to renegotiate the multiple strands of her identity and the reconstitution of space through this renegotiation, which has been "subjectively lived but also defined by others" (Dyck, 1998).

Rose's story of single motherhood indicates how crucially "home" has been part of a *process* for her, a process in which she has struggled to reconstitute it as a space reflective of a positive image of herself.

> One of the things that used to really bug me was that you always ended up telling people about your woes and never telling them about the good things. All people ever heard was how broken you were, and what a mess you were. You would just have to apologize for it .... I didn't have anything but tears and sorrow to share with them, because it was really hard! [pause] I had to find my own memories and that was hard.

Rose had not wanted to be a single parent. She wanted to have a husband, and still found it difficult to accept that she was forced to take on the task of raising her two children alone. The man she had married had forsaken this joint commitment, and they were now permanently separated. Her desire to tell others "the good things" and the "joys rather than the sorrows" about herself can be traced in part to her strongly held beliefs in dominant social imagery of "marriage, house, and family." Within the spatial contexts of a religious community Rose struggled with renegotiating her identity as a "good mother." Her "broken home" became a marker of her new status as incomplete mother/woman – a marker of struggle rather than joy – within a social space that particularly valorizes nuclear families. This "marking" by others is a central obstacle for Rose that she repeatedly tried to resist. In admonishing me, "do not cast me in stone," she implied that her subjectivity is much more complex than a stereotypical reading of her home space as "broken" might produce. She insisted that while she regarded her home in one sense as "broken," by virtue of her husband's absence, it is short-sighted to render her in these terms.

Rose's story reveals an exemplar romantic plot in which the gendered physical labour and fatigue of "home" work were hidden beneath her strong desire for love and marriage. It was through a new reading of her self as disabled that she was able to "let go of the dream and the lies."

> I was living with my husband and had my children before I was diagnosed with multiple sclerosis. My husband is a workaholic and is in denial about the fact of what that has done to his life. The choices he was making, I couldn't live with him, it was too stressful for me, with my illness. I just couldn't deal with it. I didn't have the energy, and I just had to concentrate on the kids, and myself. He wasn't helping me. He was just using it as a stopping place ... and that was adding me more stress. I couldn't live in that lifestyle any more. It had to be slower [pause] I had to get him out of my life ... realized that the greatest good was in myself and the two children .... So, even though I still love the person, it's not about love .... It's been a number of years ... but I finally realized that I was doing everything on my own anyway.

Isabel Dyck has commented on how the reconfiguring of home space is often one strategy for women diagnosed with multiple sclerosis to accommodate their declining abilities. This reconfiguration is "not confined to a simple equation between physical experience and environment," but rather is closely interwoven with women's renegotiation of their identities, and as such extends to the social as well as material aspects of home (ibid., 13). As Rose explained it, her disability was best accommodated by reconfiguring her home as a space without her husband's presence because he was physically and mentally draining for her. Although he had contributed very little to the household or parenting duties, and thus appears in Rose's story as a symbolic and romanticized male head of household, it was only after the diagnosis of her illness that she clearly recognized this. The house was an arena in which she could exert considerable control in managing her illness and life, and thus she did so.

Rose's home was a source of power for her in a way that stands in contrast to Raine's (and my own). This is linked to the ownership of her home and the "stability" this represents for her in terms of financial security and sociogeographical continuity.

> Fortunately, by some great miracle, the day before I had my daughter I signed the papers on this house ... we managed to put a deposit down and that's where we still live. It's only because I was fortunate enough to keep it. It was a miracle that it all worked out [pause] I am very very fortunate to live in this house, because it stabilized me, to stay in one place, otherwise it would have been very difficult to have a stable life. I am really really blessed.

Rose did not have to negotiate her sense of self in the context of landlords or other rental agents. Thus, she was not "buffeted and bruised" (Rose, 1993: 145) and made to feel self-conscious, for example, under the public surveillance of a rental housing market that was exacerbated for Raine by her welfare status. Rose's power is also linked to her heterosexuality, which allowed her to "fit in to" a heterosexualized landscape in a way that Raine could not. Yet, the marker, "missing male," is not static and matters in different ways and must be negotiated differently depending on the social space.

That Rose's ability to "stay in one place" was central to her renegotiation of identity as a single mother lays open tenacious developmental narratives about the pathology of uprootedness. Even though she had begun to re-remember in a less romantic way her husband's contribution as notably absent even before they separated, Rose nevertheless struggled gravely with the implications of his absence on her children's emotional well-being. At the same time that her home had become a healthier space for her in her illness and to raise her children as she saw fit, Rose could not help but see it as a loss because of the "missing male."

> I feel like my children missed out on having a father. That's a terrible thing. It's sad. They have to deal with that themselves. I can't cry for them any more. They don't yet know the loss. I understand the loss more than they do, but even then ... I know it has ramifications ....
> I know what they've missed, and I've tried to replace it with people

in the church, but that's impossible .... I hoped that was enough. We had lots of things happening in my house, lots of other people invited in, and I thought it was enough but the fact is it probably was not .... My children will be affected by the circumstances. [pause] It cannot be helped.

Rose's renegotiation of a more positive self and a sense of being a competent mother, as a single mother and a disabled woman – what she calls "a double whammy" – was mediated through her own readings of her body's physical performance and, again, what this meant for her children. Trying to remake home in terms of a "proper" and "complete" space was especially hard for her because her illness was invisible.

It was hard for me to ask for help .... I was finding it difficult to understand the illness because I was still walking around. It didn't look like I had anything. I didn't have a leg off or an arm off .... So, when people looked they would think there was nothing wrong. I didn't want to admit it to myself ....

I'm trying to find things to do with them outside of the home, because that's really hard. I can't go on a walk ... playing ball, playing tennis, that's the hardest area, being active with them, because I'm not active .... They don't have a parent that participates in sports. Because their father doesn't participate.

Rose's sense of self was affected by a script that pathologizes and constructs as a "risk" the "missing father" in single mother-headed homes (Febbraro, 1994; Mullings, 1995). Much time and energy was put into trying to find people in her community to replace what the children have "missed" by his absence, an absence that carries contradictory and ambivalent meanings for her. Her attempts at re-creating a "proper environment" for her children initially extended to the church she belonged to. But this proved unsuccessful for Rose in that the people whose lives she wanted to be part of did not accept her new status. Who Rose was, then, was socially defined through a spatial context that expanded any fixed parameters of where and how "home" is constituted. Who she was in the eyes of the church community was crucial, and there *his* presence was irrevocable and irreplaceable.

I found that being a single parent with two children, you don't fit into some lifestyles. They were afraid of you because you weren't like them and they didn't know what to say. I wanted to be with the married couples and families that I liked .... I wanted to be with them ... like them! I didn't really understand at the time that I craved for things that I wasn't able to ... they became my family but they still didn't let me into their families the way that I wanted ....

I didn't want to be with other single folks, I wanted to be with married couples. [pause] I could pretend that I was still married ... but that was part of the refusal, of wanting your husband back and having this perfect thing. I was in denial about that.

Although Rose attempted resolutely to narrate her life in terms of the joy rather than the sorrows of single motherhood, it was impossible for her to forget the deleterious consequences of her identity marked by an indelible loss. While Rose struggled to remember her experiences in more honest, less nostalgic terms so that she could ultimately reconstitute a less fractured self, her narrative is punctuated by references to a home space symbolically and materially fractured.

Conclusion: Returning Home to a Place We Have Never Been Before

Am I also saying that anthropologists, once they do their homework, will have "nowhere to go"? Yes, but not entirely. Home once interrogated is a place we have never been before. (Visweswaren, 1994: 113)

My own narration of home and identity has changed considerably during the course of my fieldwork in Vancouver. Through the ethnographic dialogue between theory and practice, the women's words and my interpretations of their words, and the refraction of all this back onto the daily pulse of my own life and selfhood, I "return" home a different person. I have a different sense of myself as a "certain sort of woman" (McDowell, 1996: 41) and, certainly, a different view of what constitutes home for me and how and why. Perhaps most importantly, I have come to view my own "predicament" in much more social and political rather than personal (and pathological) terms.

As I write this I am packing up our rented apartment, after moving to Toronto to attend university, and am preparing to move once again – the fourth time in five years – this time to a cheaper place. This move is a consequence of who I am – a full-time student trying to survive on limited funding, for one thing. But I also see that my choice to move *here*, this neighbourhood rather than another, is inextricably related to my middle-class desires and imaginings. Take one example: the backyard of this spacious Victorian house seemed extremely important to me when I signed the lease. But my son has hardly used it; he prefers to play in the park down the street. "The backyard," then, is a residual idea from my own earlier years in the late 1960s growing up in suburban Vancouver and from my married life. It reflects my stubbornness to re-create those memories and to make up for the loss of something intangible in spite of the different time and space I now occupy.

Kathleen Stewart (1996: 65) has described home as "a vibrant space of intensity, where things happened and left their mark. Home is sweet not despite loss ... but because of it. A place made present by an absence ... it grows tactile with the longing emergent in the memory of a violent loss." For me, remaking home as a single mother has been very much about holding onto those vibrant spaces and markings, not only of my childhood but of my married life, for they are important to the negotiation of my identity as a "certain sort of woman," past, present, and future. In other words, "single mother" is a significant spatializing experience for me in that it has been about lamenting lost girlhood fantasies about home, making up for what I do not have now, and dreaming of home-to-be in new ways. The realization of home "depends on the ideas that persons are carrying inside their heads about their lives in space and time" (Douglas, 1991: 290).

But at the same time that I hold onto these markings, through my research I have come to be critical of these nostalgic longings. We must find a new way in which we can "return" to a different "home." Dorinne Kondo (1996: 97) has urged, "We must ask who is creating this nostalgic 'home,' for whom, and for what purpose?" Of particular interest to me is the way that home was narrated by Raine and Rose as a paradoxical, contradictory space – a space that each of them desired and imagined in a particular image but an image they were unable to make real. Their narrations enable us to see more clearly the complexity of how subjectivities are lived spatially. Their longings for an idealized image of home produces multiple losses for them in the course of their everyday lives. Both women search for a putative "lost" stability and completeness of their identity, family, and home life, in various ways, at the same time that they remind themselves that it has never actually existed for them. Stability and completeness are myths, hopeful memories, imagined geographies. Yet these myths and memories of "stability" underscore the meaningfulness of home in very poignant ways: they are "broken" and yet they are not broken.

This is the paradox I want to draw out. It is not that these women's lives and households were incomplete by virtue of their single motherness, because that would be to reinscribe them narrowly and categorically.

Rather, their narrations of themselves as "broken" and "incomplete" are mediated through tenacious cultural scripts about what exactly constitutes (proper) home, regardless of the fiction of these scripts (George, 1996). While Kathleen Stewart's claim that home is a place made present and tactile by an absence and longing certainly rings true here, her notion that "home is sweet *because* of this loss" is more questionable. I have tried to show ethnographically how this "loss" is actually part of the difficulty of home. Home is a difficult space for Raine, Rose, and myself to occupy because, as gendered subjects, we are inserted into "a network of pre-existing positions" (Kirby, 1996) and must deal with the tensions that occur between our bodies, spaces, and "culture."

Notes

I would like to thank Margaret Rodman for her helpful comments on an earlier version of this paper. I would also like to thank the co-editors of this volume, Rae Bridgman, Heather Howard-Bobiwash, and Sally Cole, for organizing the conference panel "Feminist Interrogations in Text and Practice" at the Canadian Anthropology Society meeting in June 1997 in St. John's, Newfoundland, in which a version of this paper was first presented. I owe an additional debt of thanks to Rae Bridgman for her encouragement along the way, as well as to my committee members, Dara Culhane and Noel Dyck, for their expertise and support. It is to the women who participated so generously in my study that I wish to give my deepest acknowledgement.

1 The stories to which I refer are the personal narratives I collected from July 1995 through August 1996 for my Master's thesis. In total, I interviewed fourteen women who were single mothers living in the Vancouver area and from various backgrounds, although the majority of the women were White. Most of the women were solicited through a notice printed in the summer 1995 issue of the Single Mothers' Services newsletter published and distributed through the Vancouver Young Women's Christian Association (YWCA). The rest were solicited through word of mouth. The interviews lasted from two to three hours and were semi-structured in format. For a more detailed account of the research methods, see Krygsveld 1996.

2 The women's names have been changed and other identifying features omitted to assure their anonymity. It is a difficult balance to both protect and represent a woman's "voice," using as we must some degree of reduction and decontextualization (Said in Behar, 1993: 271).

3 "The whole scene" refers to a wide array of single mothers' services provided by the Young Women's Christian Association.

References

Behar, Ruth. 1993. *Translated Woman*. Boston: Beacon Press.

Douglas, Mary. 1991. "The Idea of a Home: A Kind of Space," *Social Research* 58, 1: 287-307.

Dyck, Isabel. 1998. "Women with Disabilities and Everyday Geographies: Home Space and the Contested Body," in R.A. Kearns and W. M. Gesler, eds., *Putting Health into Place: Landscape, Identity and Well-being*. Syracuse, N.Y.: Syracuse University Press, 102-19.

Febbraro, Angela. 1994. "Deconstructing Single Motherhood: In Search of Stable Categories or Social Change?" paper presented at the annual meeting of the Canadian Psychological Association, Penticton, B.C.

Fineman, Martha. 1995. *The Neutered Mother, the Sexual Family, and Other Twentieth Century Tragedies*. New York: Routledge.

Frankenberg, Ruth. 1993. *White Women, Race Matters: Social Construction of Whiteness*. Minneapolis: University of Minnesota Press.

— and Lati Mani. 1993. "Crosscurrents, Crosstalk: Race, 'Postcoloniality,' and the Politics of Location," *Cultural Studies* 7, 2: 292-310.

George, Rosemary Marangoly. 1996. *The Politics of Home: Postcolonial Relocations and Twentieth-Century Fiction*. Cambridge: Cambridge University Press.

Gupta, Akhil, and James Ferguson. 1992. "Beyond 'Culture': Space, Identity, and the Politics of Difference," *Cultural Anthropology* 7, 1: 6-23.

Grewal, Inderpal. 1994. "Autobiographic Subjects and Diasporic Locations: Meatless Days and Borderlands," in I. Grewal and C. Kaplan, eds., *Scattered Hegemonies: Postmodernity and Transnational Feminist Practices*. Minneapolis: University of Minnesota Press, 231-54.

John, Mary. 1996. *Discrepant Dislocations: Feminism, Theory, and Postcolonial Histories*. Berkeley: University of California Press.

Kaplan, Caren. 1996. *Questions of Travel: Postmodern Discourses of Displacement*. Durham, N.C.: Duke University Press.

Kirby, Kathleen. 1996. *Indifferent Boundaries: Spatial Concepts of Human Subjectivity*. New York: Guildford Press.

Kondo, Dorinne. 1996. "The Narrative Production of 'Home,' Community, and Political Identity in Asian American Theater," in S. Lavie and T. Swedenburg, eds., *Displacement, Diaspora, and Geographies of Identity*. Durham, N.C.: Duke University Press, 97-118.

Krygsveld, Susan (a.k.a. Susan Frohlick). 1996. "Telling Tales of Survival and Dislocation: An Ethnography of Single Mothers, Identity, and Social Space," M.A. thesis (Simon Fraser University, Burnaby, B.C.).

Lewin, Ellen. 1990. "Claims to Motherhood: Custody Disputes and Maternal Strategies," in F. Ginsburg and A. Tsing, eds., *Uncertain Terms: Negotiating Gender in American Culture*. Boston: Beacon Press, 190-214.

Martin, Biddy, and Chandra Mohanty. 1986. "Feminist Politics: What's Home Got To Do with It?" in T. deLauretis, ed., *Feminist Studies/Critical Studies*. Bloomington: Indiana University Press, 191-212.

Massey, Doreen. 1994. *Space, Place, and Gender*. Minneapolis: University of Minnesota Press.

McDowell, Linda. 1996. "Spatializing Feminism: Geographic Perspectives," in Nancy Duncan, ed., *Body Space*. New York: Routledge, 28-44.

Moore, Henrietta. 1994. *A Passion for Difference*. Bloomington: Indiana University Press.

Mullings, Leith. 1995. "Households Headed by Women: The Politics of Race, Class, and Gender," in F. Ginsburg and R. Rapp, eds., *Conceiving the New World Order: The Global Politics of Reproduction*. Berkeley: University of California Press, 122-39.

Polakow, Valerie. 1993. *Lives on the Edge: Single Mothers and Their Children in the Other America*. Chicago: University of Chicago Press.

Probyn, Elspeth. 1993. *Sexing the Self: Gendered Positions in Cultural Studies*. New York: Routledge.

Rose, Gillian. 1993. *Feminism and Geography: The Limits of Geographical Knowledge*. New York: Routledge.

Said, Edward. 1985. "In the Shadow of the West," *Wedge* 7/8: 4-5.

Stewart, Kathleen. 1996. *A Space on the Side of the Road: Cultural Poetics in an "Other" America*. Princeton N.J.: Princeton University Press.

Visweswaren, Kamala. 1994. *Fictions of Feminist Ethnography*. Minneapolis: University of Minnesota Press.

SEVEN

"OH, SO YOU HAVE A HOME TO GO TO?": EMPOWERMENT AND RESISTANCE IN WORK WITH CHRONICALLY HOMELESS WOMEN

Rae Bridgman

I HOPPED on my bicycle and prepared to make the trek home from one of the first days I visited Savard's, a shelter for homeless women. A woman who was living there asked me, "Where are you going?" I answered gaily, casually, "I'm going home." "Oh, so you have a home to go to?" she asked, followed by, "Do you have furniture?" I was startled. Yes, I had a home to go to. But now, the questions gnawed at me. Her assumption had been that I did not have a home to go to. In her mind, I had somehow automatically belonged to the category "homeless." The questions were disturbing because the boundary between "home" and "homeless" clearly demarcated our positions of "roofless" and "with roof," "without furniture" and "with furnishings."

Her questions also reminded me of how the nature of ethnographic fieldwork has changed as more anthropologists have stayed home to conduct research "in their own backyard." For many anthropologists, fieldwork away from home or the "journey elsewhere" has been and remains one of the key identifying markers of the discipline. Fieldwork assumes arriving and leaving, isolation, a lengthy stay, and layers of difficulty in obtaining information (Jackson, 1990: 12). Not consciously articulated enough has been the continued privileging in anthropology of research "away," with a parallel questioning or downplaying of the strength of urban research in one's "home town." Caputo expresses the conundrum eloquently: "in my own experience I have felt that my 'field' has been viewed variously as inauthentic or as an impoverished version in certain anthropological circles precisely because the element of distancing oneself geographically was 'missing'" (Caputo, forthcoming: 9).

"Oh, so you have a home to go to?" The question continues to haunt me for it lays bare the very basis upon which most anthropologists conduct research, entering and departing "from the field," never wholly "in the field" or "of the field" whether they are doing their research close to home or far away. My passage of "separation" is condensed by a bicycle ride, and even on the way "home" I greet some of the street people I have come to know through my research. The boundaries of the relationship between the researcher and the researched become all the more intimate within a context where "they [potentially can and in fact do] read what we write" (Brettell, 1996).

This essay draws on research begun in January 1995 to document several innovative shelter and housing initiatives in Toronto for the chronically homeless (Anderson, 1997; Bridgman, 1998a, 1998b). The greatest part of the discussion is inspired by the design and development of one of the projects — Savard's, a small pilot "safe haven" shelter project for women street survivors. The essay is based on research that is very much in progress as Savard's had been open only six months at the time of writing (Bridgman, forthcoming). Savard's has been developed by an advisory resource group comprised mostly of front-line workers together with a non-profit organization, the Homes First Society. I want to explore Savard's as a site for understanding in very concrete ways, "on the ground," from "street level" issues around empowerment and resistance. The words "empowerment" and "resistance" have preoccupied a large part of general feminist theorizing, community practice and pedagogical debates, and have occupied attention in general anthropological discourse. Discussed are some of the methodological problems that are palpable in research involving the chronically homeless and those who provide supportive housing for them. These include issues around access and trust, ethical issues, and questions around representation and "voice." The essay also considers the extent to which conventional boundaries between "home" and "homeless" are potentially disrupted in research of this nature.

Savard's accommodates a maximum of ten women and is staffed twenty-four hours a day by two community housing workers. It was named by staff after Diane Savard, a woman many of the staff at Savard's knew. She had survived the streets of Toronto to become a community worker who in turn helped many others. She died in 1993 at the age of thirty-seven. The women street survivors' project was originally inspired by news of a project, named Women of Hope, started in 1987 by a group of nuns in Philadelphia (see Culhane 1992). The project was reputed to have had great success in helping chronically homeless mentally ill women, many of whom had spent years living on the streets, come "inside." There were no expectations for treatment or medication placed on the women. In early 1995 a group of front-line workers, municipal housing officials and staff from Homes First visited Philadelphia to learn firsthand what was being done at Women of Hope. They found a project that had substantially changed from its beginnings. Many of the residents were medicated and participation in programming had become mandatory. The group returned to Toronto disappointed in what they had seen, and resolute that they would not repeat the Philadelphia experience.

Rules at Savard's are few. Violence is not permitted. There are no weapons. Consumption of alcohol or use of illegal drugs on the premises is not permitted. There is no rent or other fee charged. There are no curfews, and women may come and go as they please. No one will be barred, although a resident may be asked to "go for a walk" for a period of hours or days should there be some provocation. There is no time-limit on how long someone may stay. Should a woman decide to leave Savard's her bed will be held for her for a period of two weeks after last contact which can include a phone call. Under a special funding arrangement with the city's Hostel Services, a per diem (daily service fee) is still charged for those two weeks after last contact, even if the bed is not literally occupied (shelters generally receive a fixed rate of funding from the municipal government per person sheltered). HOP (the Hostel Outreach Program) provides referrals to Savard's and does street outreach to chronically homeless women. Women are not required to take medication unless they so choose, and referrals are made only when a woman has indicated interest. A key word explored in this article is *non-intervention*, a stance that is in profound contrast to the working philosophy of many social service providers.

My research has been undertaken with the idea that it is important to document innovative projects that seem to be working, that seem to be helping alleviate the plights of those who are chronically homeless, that build on their strengths, especially when so much of the literature on homelessness seems to focus on the homeless as the "walking wounded." We need to understand the potential inherent in experimental or pilot projects that have actively identified as their mandate, as Savard's has, that it "will evolve and change as the women involved teach, educate and inform us about their strengths, abilities, issues, needs, wants and perspectives" (excerpted from Savard's Founding Principles).

By chronically homeless, I am referring to those who have been unable to maintain stable housing for any length of time. They may spend much of their time living outdoors on the street. The numbers of the chronically homeless also include people living from hostel to hostel, people on the barred lists of existing shelters, people released from institutions, such as consumers/survivors of the mental health system or those who have served extended jail sentences, and people who may have been severely debilitated by the conditions of homelessness. For some, their behaviour (talking or laughing to themselves, gesturing in ways that may be perceived as threatening), hygiene or health issues (mental health or substance addiction issues), and inability or unwillingness to communicate with others may intersect with a chronic cycle of homelessness.

Resistance and Empowerment

Analyses focusing on resistance link individual so-called subversive action, often characterized as the "struggles of the downtrodden" (Brown, 1996: 730), to broader politically saturated agendas that challenge dominant, hegemonic forces. Feminist ethnography, which scrutinizes the comparative and political dimensions of gender and the everyday survival strategies of those we study at home and elsewhere, scrubs the face of the personal to reveal the political and reconstitutes "subtle forms of subaltern rebellion" as resistance (ibid.,: 729).

Within the literature on chronically homeless women suffering from mental illness, words such as "non-compliant" feature. They are also labelled as "resistant" to treatment. These women are identified as having "problems," as being social "problems," and their homelessness is a "problem." It may be useful, however, to turn the telescope the other way to ask, what is it that these women are resisting? What is it about the provision of shelter or services that is not working for them? In their exercising of what Breton (1994) characterizes as "negative power," that is, the ability to withhold their support, participation, consent, and involvement in programs designed by 'expert others' for them, these women communicate their need to step outside the bounds of structures and limits set by others. Jean Calterone Williams (1996) has documented the institutional control and surveillance that are generally part of shelter life and staff world-views, and juxtaposed these next to the small acts of resistance by homeless shelter residents and residents' evaluations of shelter and staff practices in the Southwestern United States. This vestige, for so it appears to be, of control has been taken by women who in some cases have remarkable urban survival skills, and are understood by society at large to be marginalized, to be powerless, to have relatively speaking, little control over the state of their lives.

Colette Browne provides an excellent review of varying definitions of empowerment, clarifying how empowerment in conventional meanings of the word comes to stand for individual control over rights, resources, or other persons.[1] It is a concept associated with force, strength, command, coercion, domination and personal advancement. In social work, empowerment has come to be associated with the processes by which service providers assist "clients," particularly those who have been historically oppressed, to help themselves. A specifically feminist conceptualization of empowerment, according to Browne (1995: 360) requires a "process of liberation of self and others, as a life force, a potential, a capacity, growth, and energy, where one works towards community and connection responsibly as opposed to working primarily toward one's individual good."

Linking these two concepts, resistance and empowerment, offers a fruitful avenue for exploring the perceptions and experiences of the women who live at Savard's and the women who work there. The specific question I am posing here is: What is the nature of the relationship between empowerment and resistance in work with chronically homeless mentally ill women, as illuminated through the lens of Savard's?

Homelessness in Toronto

In Canada, the numbers of those who are homeless are growing. This is apparent from counts at shelters and even from anecdotal evidence (for example, the growing numbers of visibly homeless people sleeping on the streets of Toronto in doorways of shops on Yonge Street and of those sleeping on grates beneath the bank towers at Bay and King Streets). There was no attempt made in the most recent 1996 census to count the homeless, as has been attempted in the United States. At the time of that census-taking, however, a three-phase study sponsored by the Canada Mortgage and Housing Corporation was under way to develop a reliable service-based way of counting the homeless population (Peressini, McDonald, and Hulchanski, 1996; Aubry, Currie, and Pinsent, 1996).

In Toronto as of October 1995, approximately 20,000 households were on waiting lists for subsidized housing. The vacancy rate in the city was at a five-year low of 0.8 per cent, and 16 per cent of City of Toronto residents (representing 75,555 people) had their social assistance benefits cut by 21.6 per cent as a provincial budgetary cost-saving measure. The November 12, 1995, count of occupied shelter and hostel beds in Metropolitan Toronto indicated that 3,627 people were being sheltered, roughly 23 per cent more than the previous year's count (Patychuk, Phillips, and McKeown, 1996). In 1980, there were 1,025 hostel beds in Metro Toronto, 141 for single women and mothers with children. In 1996, sixteen years later, there were 3,902 beds (1,446 for single women and women with children) – a 335 per cent increase over a sixteen-year period and a tenfold increase for single women and women with children.

Women and Homelessness

The first comprehensive analysis of women's experiences of homelessness was by Sophie Watson with Helen Austerberry in 1986, *Housing and Homelessness: A Feminist Perspective*. They documented the experiences of 160 single homeless women in London, England, and analysed social policies favouring nuclear families. They proposed that these policies accounted for single women's vulnerability to homelessness within a market-dominated housing system.

The connections between homelessness and domestic violence have been increasingly recognized in the research on homeless women. For women who have been abused by their partners, "home" may be a place of fear rather than a sanctuary of "domestic bliss." Lily, one of the women with a history of homelessness I have met in the course of my research, tells a story of domestic abuse that is not uncommon. She was born in Hong Kong, but moved to Canada with her parents when she was a child. She was diagnosed with schizophrenia when she was thirteen and was hospitalized for more than a year, then stabilized on medication for a period of time. She eventually married and had three children, whom she left when they were young: two years old, one year old, and newborn. Since that time she has kept in touch with her ex-husband and has been able to visit the children occasionally. She speaks still with a lilt, as English is her second language:

> The children are with their dad. I don't got a place when I left. I don't have a place to keep them when I left. I got no place to go. I was homeless. I had to leave because he was beating me up. I left, I had to, to save my own self. My eye was bleeding. I don't know how to lay charges. I don't know anything about the law. I could have laid charges. No, I was sick with schizophrenia. I didn't know how to take care of my legal rights. No friends. My parents – couldn't talk to them. They know, but nothing they can do. *Nothing.* I was helpless.
>
> I stayed out on the street for a while. People give me money, and buy me food, see me sitting out by the street. There are nice people out there. It's true. I stay up at night, I don't sleep. Not with traffic going by, I can't sleep. Just maybe sleep when I go to one of the drop-in centres, maybe have a few hours during the day. At night I would just sit, sitting down by the sidewalk. Nobody bothers me. I always keep to myself. I don't bother anyone, and they don't bother me. A

long time, months, I don't remember, probably close to year I was on the street. Just one day at a time. I had to dress up warm in the wintertime. You have to survive.

My research suggests that homelessness may not be quite the problem that we as a society have formulated. Instead, *housing may be the problem and homelessness a solution*, as Annabel Tomas and Helga Dittmar (1995) have suggested from their sample of twelve in-depth interviews with homeless women in Great Britain. By turning to the streets, women like Lily have escaped the confines of unseeing, unhearing walls, doors, and roofs. However, even as women may not be safe in their own homes, once on the street they are also at great risk of violence.

Shelters for women in Canada have historically taken on a different face from those built for men. Hostels for men developed in the late nineteenth century in response to a growing migrant workforce of single males moving from rural areas to urban centres to work on the railroad or in industry. Churches were the first to provide shelter, using a "charity model." Stays were short and were for men who were ill or between jobs. Once employed, men preferred to move to rooming houses. Within this legacy, men's hostels generally offer minimal services with dormitory accommodation (bunk beds), limited hours of operation, and an emphasis on men going out to work or at the very least seeking work. In Toronto, Seaton House, a shelter for men built in 1931, represents the epitome of this kind of facility and accommodates 650, although at times in the past it was used to shelter as many as 900 men.

Women's hostels in Toronto began to open in the late 1970s and early 1980s (within a context of growing awareness of the needs of abused women). Between 1970 and 1993 a total of 371 residential facilities for abused women opened in Canada (more than half of these are concentrated in Quebec and Ontario). The typical period for staying is 11 to 20 days. In 1992-93 yearly admissions were over 86,000 (with almost half of these being children) (Novac, Brown, and Bourbonnais, 1996: 38).

A number of the shelter facilities are based on feminist principles with the goal of empowering women. Usually situated in large houses, women's shelters have a more supportive atmosphere than most men's shelters (supportive counselling, referrals, and child care may be part of services provided). They generally accommodate a smaller number of women (the average is around 30) than are "warehoused" in men's shelters. Shelters in general (both women's and men's) operate on rules of behaviour, strict hours of operation, first-come-first-serve policies, and limits on duration of stay;

these conditions of use may pose barriers to those who are unable or unwilling to respect such limits.

A "Safe Haven"

Savard's founding principles are challenged on a daily basis as staff attempt collectively to work through ideas about various aspects of life at the shelter:

- flexibility
- being non-judgemental
- dealing with violence
- whether to have a television or not
- whether to keep non-prescription drugs (aspirin) on hand or not
- how to support women's interest in enjoying or using the kitchen facilities without losing too much food, cooking ware, or cutlery in the process
- how to deal with theft or "borrowing"
- whether or not to give out cigarettes if asked
- confidentiality and record-keeping
- countless small and not-so-small questions that all revolve around how to help the women regain control of their lives.

The keyword in all this, which arises in staff meetings and in casual conversations, is *non-intervention*. According to one of the staff members, the belief in non-intervention "arises from a distinct analysis of women's anger, that women will react in angry ways or abusive ways or violent ways, [but] not [really] socially unacceptable ways for very real reasons related to their oppression." Non-intervention requires that staff not intervene in interactions between residents, unless to defuse the threat of what is termed a "critical incident" of physical violence. To call police is a measure of absolute last resort.

One particular instance of racist verbal abuse by Teresa, one of the women living at Savard's, was aimed at Donna, another resident. This incident highlights contradictions that can arise in working through issues of non-intervention, on a daily basis at Savard's. In this instance, which I did not witness, I am relying on interviews with staff, discussions at several staff meetings, and an unsolicited conversation with Donna that lasted almost an hour. Missing among these perspectives is the voice of Teresa.

There had been ongoing confrontations between Teresa and Donna. Two of Teresa's relatives suffer from severe mental illness, according to Savard's staff, and live in the hostel system. Teresa, herself, has been barred from every hostel.

Donna admits she's depressed. Her ever-reeling soliloquy is querulous. "Why am I here? Why am I living like this?" (I think to myself, are these not the existential questions we all at some level ask ourselves?) One of the staff, somewhat testily to my mind (for these questions are indeed posed over and over), responds, "I can't answer why, Donna. I can't answer that question for you." To my eye, she looks physically healthy. I know she eats well at meals, although she is picking distractedly, nervously, at the fabric of her clothes. Donna turns to me and says, almost in a whisper, "I was living 'on the street.'" She reverts back almost as a mantra to life on the street. "Life on the street is full of death. The street is full of death. There are bad people out there. Someone said to me, 'Even a dog has a place to go home to.'" She repeats, "Even a dog has a place to go home to."

One evening Teresa was on a rant, and for an hour harangued Donna. Teresa, subject to violent outbursts more than once, several weeks later assaulted one of the staff members. After this, she was asked to leave for a period of two weeks, but it was made clear that she could return to live at Savard's if she wished.

Donna told me that Teresa had called her "nigger" and "Aunt Jemima." She went on, "And staff did nothing. They say, she can't help herself, she can't help it. Now that's a judgement call. I told her you're Black like me. But you know, she thinks she's White." She continued:

This place isn't safe. Why do I keep running? I don't drink. I don't do drugs like some of the women here. I've told staff I want to live here forever. This place isn't safe either. Some of the people who live here aren't very nice. Teresa, she's not a nice person. She hit one of the staff, you know. Is that what you call safe? I'm asking you. And now she's going to be coming back here? Why are they letting her come back? Now that's not right. I left before because she was here. And notice she picked on the one staff who's not White? You see, I've got that all figured out. I put all these pieces together.

Donna expects a system of reward and punishment. The ultimate punishment shelters generally hold as ransom over residents, is that "you will not be able to return, if …." Within the rules that Savard's has set for itself, there is no such ultimate punishment, even for such a transgressive act of verbal racist abuse as Teresa has committed against Donna. In seeking to accommodate those who cannot be accommodated elsewhere, where is the line drawn between individual rights and collective security and protection from fear? At what point intervention?

One of the staff I interviewed was very concerned about the seeming lack of clarity around such instances of racism. "I don't think we do deal with it, and I think we have to deal with it .... I think this is something we have to talk about more, and I think we're, I don't think we've worked it out yet. I think we're a little immobilized still by our policy of non-intervention .... We're feeling immobilized." In her words,

> We don't do anything .... I have heard Teresa say some things that made me sick, physically feel sick, just awful stuff .... Teresa seems to deny [her Black heritage]. She does not acknowledge that in any of her self-talk. She completely externalizes, it's the other that's the person of colour. She never [pause] I find that really fascinating.

Another question is provoked by this incident. What barriers to service provision may there be for someone who is perceived by others as belonging to a particular category of identity (and therefore may be "eligible" for services offered by a particular agency), and yet thinks of herself as belonging to another? In not recognizing or by active denial of her Black heritage, Teresa challenges the physical basis upon which we as a society judge racial or ethnic identity.[2]

Not in Conclusion: Questions Arising

Access and trust-building have been palpable issues in this research. During staff meetings or advisory meetings with other front-line workers, I have been careful to clarify at times whether it is appropriate for me to be recording contents of the meeting. At other times, I have been explicitly told, "Please do not take notes, but you are welcome to stay." In this way, control of the documentation process for Savard's remains with those staff I have been working with. Copies of drafts of publications arising, including this article, have been given to administrators and staff of Savard's for their review and suggestions.[3] Those who provide shelter and housing for the homeless do not own the homeless, but they do take on the roles of advocate and gatekeeper. Inherent in my research is a conflict between the founding ideas about Savard's as a *safe haven* and interviewing or conducting research, which can be construed as an *intrusive act* that contradicts the terms of what a safe haven is or should be. This requires ongoing consultation with staff.

"What are you writing? Why are you writing? I don't want you writing here!" These words were stated directly and angrily. I was actually jotting down a few reminders of things I needed to do on the way home. Since that reprimand I have never again brought out pencil and paper when I was "hanging out" with residents at the housing projects I've been documenting. Writing up the contents of conversations and insights happens after leaving the site, or in a pinch, a visit to the washroom can allow for a few hurried notes.

The conventional action of interviewing someone assumes that there is an ongoing process of asking questions and receiving answers. The research challenges become quite different when some may not be able to respond to questions, or when any questions are perceived as threatening. Even to greet a person by name may challenge that person's ownership of self and sense of control. I heard these words one day uttered in rising crescendos:

Don't you use my name.
Who gave you permission to use my name?
It's my name, and I don't want you using it.

A name becomes one of the last possessions.

How can I tell the stories of those women I have met without betraying their confidences? The issue of anonymity, particularly for individuals, is, as Mary Carol Hopkins (1996) points out, elemental to the practice of anthropology and to most social science research. Yes, I can change names and identifying details, but the circles we move in are very small sometimes. The story of Lily is not a true story. Lily does not exist. She represents the stories of many of the women with whom I have spoken, and her words were spoken, but by another. Should I not use the name of Savard's to identify the site? Not to do so in some ways discounts the ground-breaking work that those who have worked so hard to bring Savard's into being have given to the project. It also denies the contributions that Diane Savard made during her lifetime.

As this essay represents research in progress, it feels premature to draw conclusions about the lessons that Savard's can offer us that may help other chronically homeless women come off the streets, or that may help in the designing of programs and training of staff to help this population. What does seem clear at this point is that the hopes and ideals driving a project of this nature may require a shift when the project is actually implemented. Indeed, the original founding principles for Savard's articulate the need to evolve and change. Rather than a static model, the vision accounts for needing to learn and making changes based on that learning. This appreciation of the need to evaluate and change represents a fundamental part of the approach to the provision of housing and social services for a population that has been notoriously difficult to help. The difficulties in assessing appropriate strategies are echoed in some of the difficulties I have experienced in conducting research.

I end this essay by posing a number of questions to emphasize the nature of research as a never-ending endeavour. While the discussion has been framed by concepts of empowerment and resistance, a number of other questions arise from this research. Many of these questions can only be answered by the passage of time. How will Savard's measure its "success" in reaching its target population? Will the project "gentrify" over time, as some women may decide to stay? Will this become a "home" for them rather than a temporary way station, and how may this affect Savard's way of operating? Can the conceptualization of empowerment as active non-intervention function as useful currency in other contexts? Will the principles upon which Savard's presently operates change? Will there, for instance, be a shift towards encouraging women to accept referrals or to enter treatment programs? How will the wisdom garnered from this pilot project, which seeks to "listen" to women who come to live there, be shared with other organizations?

Notes

This essay represents a revised and expanded version of two conference papers: "'Oh, you have a home to go to?': learnings from extended ethnographic research among women street survivors and those who help them," delivered at the annual Canadian Anthropology Society meeting, Memorial University, St. John's, Newfoundland, June 1997; and "Conducting research on homelessness: lessons from extended ethnographic research on the development of housing for the chronically homeless," delivered at the annual Qualitative Research Conference, University of Toronto, August 1997. The support of the Social Sciences and Humanities Research Council of Canada is gratefully acknowledged. The research upon which this essay is based has been funded through a Strategic Grant [Women and Change] (1998-2001).

RAE BRIDGMAN

1   Elizabeth Rocha (1997) provides an excellent review of the many and varied conceptions of empowerment within different disciplines and represents its manifestations as steps in a ladder.

2   Over the last several years there has been considerable debate within the discipline of anthropology over the utility of "race" as a system of human classification. Representative of this debate is J. Anthony Paredes' cogent commentary, "Race Is Not Something You Can See," in which he comments on the ambiguities inherent in his own physical appearance and his visual misidentifications by others (Paredes, 1997).

3   Although I would have liked to have been able to give copies to the women living at Savard's, this was not possible as it was not part of the research arrangements negotiated with the Homes First Society.

References

Anderson, Rae (a.k.a. Rae Bridgman). 1997. "Street as Metaphor in Housing for the Homeless," *Journal of Social Distress and Homelessness* 6, 1: 1-12.

Aubry, Tim, Shawn Currie and Celine Pinsent. 1996. *Development of a Homeless Data Collection and Management System: Phase One*. Ottawa: Social and Economic Policy and Research Division, Canada Mortgage and Housing Corporation.

Brettell, Caroline B., ed. 1996. *When They Read What We Write: The Politics of Ethnography*. Westport, Conn.: Bergin & Garvey.

Breton, Margot. 1994. "On the Meaning of Empowerment and Empowerment-Oriented Social Work Practice," *Social Work with Groups* 17, 3: 23-37.

Bridgman, Rae (a.k.a. Rae Anderson). 1998a. "The Architecture of Homelessness and Utopian Pragmatics," *Utopian Studies* 9, 1: 50-67.

——. 1998b. "A 'City' Within the City: A Canadian Housing Model for the Homeless," *Open House International* 23, 1: 12-21.

——. Forthcoming. "Women Street Survivors: A Safe Haven for Chronically Homeless Women," in Susan Frohlick, Jacquelyne Luce, and Margaret MacDonald, eds., *Women Bodies Space*. Ann Arbor: University of Michigan Press.

Brown, Michael F. 1996. "On Resisting Resistance," *American Anthropologist* 98, 4: 729-49.

Browne, Colette. 1995. "Empowerment in Social Work Practice with Older Women," *Social Work* 40, 3: 358-64.

Caputo, Virginia. Forthcoming. "'At Home and Away': Reconfiguring the Field for Late Twentieth-Century Anthropology," in Vered Amit-Talai, ed., *Constructing the Field in the Contemporary World*." New York: Routledge.

Culhane, Dennis. 1992. "Ending Homelessness Among Women with Severe Mental

Illness: A Model Program from Philadelphia," *Psychosocial Rehabilitation Journal* 16, 1: 73-76.

Hopkins, Mary Carol. 1996. "Is Anonymity Possible? Writing about Refugees in the United States," in Caroline B. Brettell, ed., *When They Read What We Write: The Politics of Ethnography*. Westport, Connecticut: Bergin & Garvey. 121-29.

Jackson, Jean E. 1990. "'Déjà Entendu': The Liminal Qualities of Anthropological Fieldnotes," *Journal of Contemporary Ethnography* 19, 1: 8-43.

Novac, Sylvia, Joyce Brown, and Carmen Bourbonnais. 1996. *No Room of Her Own: A Literature Review on Women and Homelessness*. Ottawa: Canada Mortgage and Housing Corporation.

Paredes, J. Anthony. 1997. "Race Is Not Something You See," *Anthropology Newsletter* (of the American Anthropological Association) 38, 9 (December): 1, 6.

Patychuk, Dianne, Janet Phillips and David McKeown. 1996. *Excerpts of Draft Report: Deaths among the Homeless in the City of Toronto, 1979 to 1993*. Toronto: Department of Public Health July 1996.

Peressini, Tracy, Lynn McDonald and David Hulchanski. 1996. *Estimating Homelessness: Towards a Methodology for Counting the Homeless in Canada*, Background Report prepared for Research Division, Canada Mortgage and Housing Corporation. Ottawa.

Rocha, Elizabeth M. 1997. "A Ladder of Empowerment," *Journal of Planning Education and Research* 17: 31-44.

Tomas, Annabel Tomas and Helga Dittmar. 1995. "The Experience of Homeless Women: An Exploration of Housing Histories and the Meaning of Home," *Housing Studies* 10, 4: 493-515.

Watson, Sophie, with Helen Austerberry. 1986. *Housing and Homelessness: A Feminist Perspective*. London: Routledge & Kegan Paul.

Williams, Jean Calterone. 1996. "Geography of the Homeless Shelter: Staff Surveillance and Resident Resistance," *Urban Anthropology and Studies of Cultural Systems and World Economic Development* 25: 75-113.

EIGHT

"LIKE HER LIPS TO MY EAR":
READING ANISHNAABEKWEG LIVES AND
ABORIGINAL CULTURAL CONTINUITY IN THE CITY

Heather Howard-Bobiwash

Introduction

Much anthropological attention has focused on issues of representation and interpretation in textual production. There has been
less discussion of the reception of or process of reading our texts
in the communities of practice from which they have originated (Brettell,
1996; Wolf, 1992). As Ruth Behar (1995) found, efforts to discover how our
work is received may meet with indifference. For those of us who work in
urban contexts the boundaries between personal, field, and academic circles
may overlap and flow into each other, collapsing bases of knowledge and
forming new sites from which creative and innovative anthropology may
emerge. In this essay, I examine a reading of Native women's personal narratives by an audience of three Native women and one anthropologist. The
research reported here takes a feminist "grounded theory" approach (Stanley and Wise, 1990: 22-24) in which "feminist theory emerges from and
responds to the lives of women" (Personal Narratives Group, 1989: 4).

The theories and methods of the personal narrative have been applied
and debated in anthropology for some time. In North America especially,
anthropologists and others recorded the life stories of Native men and some
Native women before and following the turn of the twentieth century.
These biographers sought to either "salvage" elements of "disappearing
races" (Krupat, 1985; Brumble, 1990) or to add a "human" dimension to
anthropological science by presenting the individual "informant's" perspectives on his/her "worldview" or "culture" (Langness, 1965: 8). By the middle
of the century, the debates in anthropology centred primarily on the verifia-
bility of the life story, or on the validity of an individual's perspective against
the ethnographer's "objective" observations from a range of other sources
(Kluckhohn, 1945; Langness, 1965). At the "periphery" of the discipline,
women practitioners have found that personal narratives provide insights

into culture and society not afforded by conventional anthropological methods (Personal Narratives Group, 1989: 3-6; Cole, 1992; Golde, 1970; Myerhoff, 1979). Some feminist scholars have reflected critically on how personal narratives invert power structures by validating the experiences of the subaltern (Frieden, 1989), and show how individuals contribute to historical processes (Behar, 1990). Others have examined ways in which personal narratives may blur the boundaries of dichotomies between the personal and the political, or between the individual and the collective (Sommer, 1991; Salazar, 1991). Yet others have highlighted how personal narratives shape subjectivities and interpretations through the dynamics of the relationship between the researcher and the "subject" (Cole, 1997; Borland, 1991).

This paper explores how biographical material was received by a small reading circle of three Native women and myself. I formed the reading circle by asking women with whom I come into contact on a daily basis through my work with the Native Canadian Centre of Toronto (the Centre), if they would be interested in participating in this research, which also presented an occasion for gathering and socializing. Mary Fox, Frances Sanderson, Pat Turner, and I met regularly over a three-month period and read two Anishnaabekweg (trans. "Ojibway women") life stories. The first, *I Am Nokomis, Too: The Biography of Verna Patronella Johnston*, was written by anthropologist Rosamond Vanderburgh in 1977. The second book, *Moose to Moccasins*, was the autobiography of Madeline Katt Theriault, written in the early 1980s and first published in 1992. Before discussing the books, we had two sessions during which I answered questions about feminism and anthropology and about my own role in the urban Aboriginal community and my aspirations as a graduate student in anthropology. Subsequent sessions were spent enjoying snacks, and even dinner in two of the participants' homes. Usually, I initiated discussions by setting my small tape recorder in view and reading passages from the books. The "book club," as it came to be known, continued to meet after the research was completed.

The purpose of this paper is not to review the books, nor is it to make claims about the validity of Native versus non-Native biographical representations of Native people. Rather, I present an "ethnography of reading" (Boyarin, 1993) from a feminist perspective in that I highlight the collective analysis generated by women actively engaging the texts, and I explore the transformative dynamics of reading in groups. Elizabeth Long (1993: 194) describes these dynamics as follows:

> Reading in groups not only offers occasions for explicitly collective textual interpretation, but encourages new forms of association, and

nurtures new ideas that are developed in conversation with other people as well as with the books .... In such groups, reading becomes more communal than our image of the scholar-anchorite would have it, and more active than the picture of reading as a leisured feminine pastime. [They] offer forums for critical reflection that have been crucial in negotiating the moral and ideological dimensions of social identity.

This form of research is clearly experimental. The reading circle's interpretations, reactions, and reflections on the Anishnaabekweg life stories and the discussions they stimulated attest to the possibilities of methodological innovations in group interviewing. As well, they contribute to new theoretical perspectives on the textualization of Native women's verbal art. In particular, I examine contrasting perspectives on the issue of the emotional quality of Aboriginal women's biography. I also present ideas expressed in the reading circles concerning the (dis)continuity of the structures of oral traditions in Native women's life history texts and the roles of Native women in the continuity of Aboriginal culture in the urban context.

Grandmothers' Words: Verna's and Madeline's Stories

I selected the two life stories read by the group primarily because the subjects, Verna Patronella Johnston and Madeline Katt Theriault, were already known to the participants and because they had made the transition from "bush," or reserve life, to life in an urban centre. This was an experience that the women in the reading circle could relate to personally. The reading circle began with "Verna's book," as it was always referred to. *I Am Nokomis, Too*, which means "I am Grandmother, too," describes Verna's struggle to sort out her identity as an Aboriginal woman. She was the daughter of an Anishnaabe father and an English mother, and the wife in an unsatisfactory marriage. She grew up and raised her own family within the economic and social injustices of life on the Cape Croker reserve (250 km northwest of Toronto) during times of massive change from the 1910s to the 1950s. Unusual for many women at the time, she left her husband in 1945 and came to Toronto, where she worked for a while before returning to the reserve to try to work out her marriage and set up a foster home for Native children. In 1965, Verna returned to Toronto and opened a boarding home for young Native women while they attended technical schools so that they could become "career women" — more independent and not confined to what Verna felt was the limited option of marriage. In the environment of "Indian consciousness-raising" of the 1960s and 1970s, Verna became acutely aware that the younger generations of urbanizing Aboriginal people needed the help of "Nokomis" (which also has the meaning of a knowledgeable respected elder) to ensure the continuity of cultural identity and traditions in the city. She taught crafts, spoke on Native culture, and published the book, *Tales of Nokomis*, in 1970, a collection of stories she learned from her "Grandma Jones." Verna Johnston died in 1996.

I Am Nokomis, Too is also interesting for the way the anthropologist, Vanderburgh, chose to present the work. In the introduction, Vanderburgh makes clear her objective of privileging Verna's own voice throughout the text, while also emphasizing that the book is meant to be a "popular account" and not an ethnographic or "scholarly" text (1977: 11-15). In addition, an unedited transcript of a taped interview with Verna that took place in 1977 follows the main body of the book. Vanderburgh concludes with a chapter entitled "Reflections," which she says is needed "in order to give the reader a broader view of the story of Verna Johnston's life. The narrative itself offers an extremely subjective view of that story, but here a more objective approach is shown" (Vanderburgh, 1977: 195). The book accentuates the ideals of the North American mainstream women's movement of the 1970s. Vanderburgh portrays Verna as an exceptional and determined woman who breaks free from what are described as oppressive Anishnaabe gender role expectations. Vanderburgh's emphasis on including Verna's voice, the unedited interview, and her portrayal of Verna as someone actively challenging societal norms and creating spaces for other young women to do the same foreshadow feminist life history research undertaken a decade later (Geiger, 1986; Personal Narratives Group, 1989; Wolf, 1996).

Madeline Katt Theriault's *Moose to Moccasins* is a much shorter book and the published version contains many extraordinary photographs. This book is the personal account of Madeline's life growing up, marrying, and facing hardships in the Bear Island, Lake Temagami region in northern Ontario. She was born on her grandfather's trap-line and grew up learning and working on the land. At the age of fifteen, her grandparents arranged her marriage to a seventeen-year-old boy from the Temagami village. She continued to work on her husband's trap-line and helped to raise her younger sister and brother. Most of the book recalls what life on the trap-line was like and is set out in short, practical chapters, each describing a particular activity such as making rabbit-skin blankets, food preparation, and, of course, the process of turning moose into moccasins. These chapters are loosely connected to form the narrative.[1] Madeline's life had some tragic and surprising turns, including the loss of her husband and her brother to tuberculosis and her own bout with the disease, which led to her two daughters being taken away from her. Madeline's life documents the relationship between Native trappers and the Hudson's Bay Company from the point of view of a wife and mother trying to survive under increasingly difficult circumstances as hunting grounds were settled, turned into beaver parks, or lost to logging. Coping with these imposing changes, Madeline worked at a hunting lodge cooking for tourists, and she travelled to sportsmen's shows in the United States to staff booths promoting the hunting lodge.

The Temagami region was also the site of the filming of *Silent Enemy* in 1928, meant to capture Ojibway life "disappearing to civilization." Madeline played a cameo role in the film, worked on making most of the costumes, and cooked for all the crew and actors for virtually no pay. Faced with no longer being able to live off the land, Madeline married again and worked as a cleaner in a doctor's office and as a matron in a jail in Haileybury, Ontario. Though this marks only the first half of Madeline's life, the book ends in the mid-1950s when Madeline went to live in the city of North Bay, Ontario, where she still resides in a home for the elderly. Madeline was saddened by the loss of her eyesight and thus by her inability to write down more about her later life (personal communication).

Madeline worked hard to put this book together and to make it available to younger people, who she worried would have a limited understanding of what the traditional way of life was like. She describes in the book her difficulty in writing and translating her thoughts into the English language. She first had the manuscript typed and copied for distribution. It was later published by Natural Heritage Books, which maintained the integrity of the original manuscript and added more than fifty photographs. Madeline was born one year before Verna Johnston, and reading the two books together brings to life the bigger picture of the effects of colonialism, the nature of Native-White relations, and changing gender and cultural adaptations.

The Narratives of the Circle

A by-product of the reading circle was that snippets of the personal narratives of the women in the circle also surfaced during our discussions of the two published narratives. Invariably, the stories of Verna and Madeline aroused memories from all of us in the group, and in our discussions we pieced together both our separate journeys and where our paths converged.

Pat (Salter) Turner is Tuscarora/Onondaga of the Six Nations of the Grand River. Born in the late 1930s, she has spent most of her life in Toronto.

Her mother had been a member of the first "Indian Club" in Toronto in 1950 (the forerunner of the Centre), so Pat came early in life to "Indian organizing" in the city. She has consistently toiled to recruit Native people in the city to participate in the establishment of institutions and to bring their resources and volunteer skills to building the Native community in Toronto. She met her late husband, Jim Turner, an Anishnaabe from Bear Island, Lake Temagami, through their work together in the community and she is the mother of three children and grandmother to three more.

Mary Fox, now retired, came to Toronto as a teenager from Wikwemikong Unceded Territory on Manitoulin Island. When she arrived in Toronto in the 1940s she spoke almost exclusively her Anishnaabe language. She worked as a domestic in private homes for room and board when she first moved to the city, and she married and worked in an office job for another part of her life. Mary is a skilled craftsperson and has spent many years volunteering with the Centre's Ladies Auxiliary and Seniors Club doing and teaching bead-work, quilting, sewing, and other crafts, mainly for fund-raising for the Centre.

Frances Sanderson is currently the executive director of Nishnawbe Homes, a non-profit Native housing agency. In her capacity as a centre board member, she and I collaborated on a community-based publication celebrating the Centre's 35th anniversary (Sanderson and Howard-Bobiwash, 1997). Frances's mother came to Toronto from the Whitefish First Nation (Anishnaabe), Birch Island, Ontario, in the early 1940s to work as a nanny. She married a man of Spanish origin and Frances was born in Toronto. Like Pat, Frances's mother had also been active in the early Native organizations in the city. Growing up, Frances visited her mother's family on Birch Island as often as her family could afford to. Frances has been captain of the Canadian women's bowling team and still maintains unbroken international records. She met her husband in the bowling alley where she worked when she was seventeen. They have been married thirty years and have two daughters and two grandsons.

Having "married into" the Native community in Toronto in 1995, on a daily basis I find myself in the strange (but not necessarily awkward) locations between the two worlds of the ethnographer and the "ethnographee," between my paid and volunteer work at the Centre, and my status as a graduate student at the university down the street, between researcher and friend, and between being an "oddball feminist" in my White world and an active non-Native member of this urban Aboriginal community. The questions guiding my research thus have emerged from these experiences, from my own interest in Native women's life histories in relation to the politics of identity and self-determination, and from my desire to begin my research by making it of value to this community in which I have the privilege to live. Some of these questions included: How can the written accounts of Aboriginal women's lives contribute in a practical way to the urban Native community? How are women's personal narratives tied to the lives of urban Aboriginal institutions? And, how have women been instrumental, from within an Aboriginal framework, to creating cultural continuity in the city?

While these questions played a central role in the reading circle, an important feature of this method of collecting data was the flexibility it offered the women to ask their own questions which stimulated fruitful exchange. These included our conversations about anthropology and feminism, the association between higher education and the loss of a sense of cultural identity, and the role of women and family in ensuring cultural continuity not just in terms of traditional practices but especially in relation to traditional forms of socialization and interaction. These questions kindled ideas about the economic welfare of Aboriginal people in Toronto, homelessness, youth concerns, leadership, and self-determination.

Aboriginal Women's Life Histories and Aboriginal Women Audiences

After only a few of the reading circle sessions, two interesting aspects surfaced that add to understanding the processes of transforming Aboriginal women's verbal art into written words. These aspects, I believe, only become apparent during the reading process – from the engagement of Aboriginal women readers with the Aboriginal women's life history texts. The first of these relates to perceptions about the emotional quality of Aboriginal women's biography, and the second to the (dis)continuity of the structures of oral traditions in Native women's life history texts.

Reading and Feeling Aboriginal Women's Verbal Art

Some Eurocentric readings of Native women's autobiography note their "lack" of emotional content but do not provide analyses of this claim (Bataille and Sands, 1984: 17; Carr, 1988: 141, 143). Native women's life histories have been discussed most often in terms of their ethnographic content rather than their literary quality, and in terms of methodology rather than as a genre. In *American Indian Women Telling Their Lives* (1984), literary scholars Gretchen Bataille and Kathleen Sands attempt a systematic analysis of Native women's personal narratives. They explain the "conservative" emotion in Native women's autobiography as the result of cultural norms that call for women to be emotionally restrained. They also suggest that emotional expression often appears absent in Native women's autobiography because the narrator may assume that the emotional quality of what she is describing is a given and doesn't require "cues" to trigger readers' emotional response:

> American Indian women's autobiographies tend to be retrospective rather than introspective, and thus may seem understated to those unaccustomed to the emotional reserve of Indian people. There is little self-indulgence on the part of Indian women narrators; events occur and are articulated in words conservative in emotional connotation. Even moments of crisis are likely to be described without much intensity of language, or emotional pitch may be implied or stated metaphorically rather than directly. Such understatement is not an indication of repression or absence of emotional states but often evidence that the narrator simply takes the state for granted. (Bataille and Sands, 1984: 17)

While Bataille and Sands recognize the diversity of Native women and their expressions of individuality in their autobiographies, they nonetheless rely on an over-generalized High Plains (Lakota/Sioux) model for what they say are "characteristics that stand out as central to the identity of Indian women"(Bataille and Sands, 1984: 18). Discussions in the reading circle add needed depth to Bataille and Sands's observations. First, the Anishnaabekweg autobiographies do contain emotional signals and superlatives, and even a frequent use of exclamation marks! What is noticeable about these enlivened moments, perhaps more so to the non-Native reader, is the seemingly mundane nature of the event being described. For example, in *Moose to Moccasins*, exclamations and lengthy descriptions were often related to the preparation and eating of various foods or to the hard work involved in tanning hides and making clothing. One incident Madeline recalled vividly was when she and another woman inadvertently caused the death of a horse. After they discovered their husbands' liquor still hidden in the woods, they dumped the fermenting fruit out onto the ground, which the horse then ate and consequently died (Theriault, 1992: 49-51).

Stories like these were filled with lessons for the women in the reading circle and aroused long discussions of the women's own memories, of their mothers, of hard work, and of many types of foods and medicines and their preparation. More importantly, especially in relation to the urban context of the readers' lives, these discussions inevitably turned to how their memories were intrinsic to Aboriginal cultural socialization and to building a sense of community, for example, through participation in the preparation and eating of food. They pointed to the pivotal role of women in these processes and attributed the disruption of Native families to the undermining of Native women in their roles as the custodians of traditional culture. In addition to the well-known attacks on Native families such as the removal of children to residential schools and foster care and the subsequent loss of Native languages, the introduction of various technologies and the growth of dependence on non-Native government funding were also cited by Mary, Pat, and Frances as contributing factors to the breakdown of social relations. The following dialogue, inspired by a passage on food preparation in "Verna's book," illustrates this point:

Frances: If you look at the society now, very few women do the work they did together before. They cook but they pick food up at the grocery store on the way home, and they have to hand the kids over to day care in order to go to work. I think this is a big distinction with back then, and that's where kids got all their good family values because the mother was there all the time and they didn't have too much chance to get in trouble.

Mary: Okay, you had the occasional person who was mean and you would see that in public with a man arguing with his wife or whatever, but most people lived side by side and lived together and worked together with respect for each other. As I'm sitting here listening to this you can just see the progression where changes are made as years go by. The respect among people – this is what I don't see today, but back then there was so much of it, even from the kids. But today it is so awful, not only in the Native community but in all nations.

Frances: It's not the same when you don't have to work to put a meal together and eat together. Back home on Birch Island when there is a wedding or other party, turkeys are bought but they are sent all over the community and in every house people are preparing it all, and they all march it up the hill to the community hall, everyone is involved in it.

Mary: Women were the main focal point, okay, a guy might be a chief but it's still the woman who is behind it. It is, what do you call that, a matri ...

Frances: A matriarchal society. As far back as I can remember, it has always been women – they organized the weddings, they organized the family, they organized everything going on at the church, they did all that organization.

Mary: Even today, who is running all the organizations? And who started them up?

Frances: And who thought they were necessary?

Mary: That's not to discredit the men, they had their jobs, too. I think women have options depending on which era you were born. Are you being bound by a rope or what? I think you are bound by your way of thinking. It's like those kids at the Centre, you have to have that drive within yourself, or it has to be instilled in you.

At another session, Pat recalled:

Well, Millie Redmond used to have people over to her home and that's where the Indian Club started because of those women sitting around and saying maybe we should be having something where other Native people will come out to. A lot of people did that. My mother said when she first came to Toronto, everyone would go to the Jamiesons' because there would always be a lot of socializing. So, I think, as long as there were Native people in the city, people from the reserve or other people in town would always congregate there, and that would have been in the 1920s. I remember when the Centre was on Beverley Street we talked about getting grants. But we could have earned it ourselves, we didn't have to go and get a grant to do all that, we could have done it ourselves. My mom used to say that all those women who were in the Native women's auxiliary really worked very hard. There would be six or seven of them cooking and catering to different events and people don't do that so much any more.[2]

The reading circle's emotional responses to Verna's and Madeline's expressions of delight as they recounted family food preparation went beyond a simple identification with, or nostalgia for, the circumstances described. The women in the reading circle made analytical associations between the stories and the issues they feel are problems in the Native community in which they live today. They are active in the community and are thinking about how they can draw on their cultural experiences to contribute to the life of the community and to the rebuilding of the Native family and its culturally specific socialization structures. They are also keenly aware of the role of women in shaping those structures.

Following somewhat on what Bataille and Sands (1984) suggest, some tragic, despairing, or frustrating events in Verna's and Madeline's narratives do appear to be described without much emotion because it may be expected that the reader would respond emotionally automatically. However, incidents that are specific to the lives of Aboriginal women, such as those resulting from institutional racism and injustice, may invoke the emotions of only those readers who can identify with the experiences, no matter how sympathetic or anti-racist non-Native readers may think themselves to be. Although some accounts in the two books of incidents of racism, poverty, displacement, and the destruction of their communities are not necessarily illustrated with a great deal of emotional characterization, or because in Verna's case the story is told through a third party, they certainly aroused sometimes overwhelming and frustrating responses from the reading circle. A powerful conversation was stirred up after I read some passages from Verna's biography that related her experience with Catholic education through which she was made to feel ashamed of being "Indian" and, as Vanderburgh put it, "the transformation from savagery to responsibility was made more sure" (1977: 61). Of the three women, only Mary had directly experienced the impact of Christianity on her reserve community through the educational system. Pat and Frances had, however, been raised in the Christian faith by converted parents. The focus of the conversation did not dwell on the impact of these experiences in their lives, however, as much as on the ways in which the women had resisted them:

Pat: Well, they've been down home for years [evangelists at Six Nations] and we went to the Baptist Church and we would always hear them talk about how everyone else was going to hell except the Baptists. I think that's one thing that has really bothered me. I also went to this woman's group here in Toronto. I think it was a group of the Orange Lodge, and I was so mad – you go there and they say you'll never marry a Catholic, and I thought I might not be Catholic myself but who the heck are these people who are going to tell me who I am going to marry and how to raise my children!

Frances: And all those churches preached to love your brother and sister and everything else. I think the younger generation now is viewing things differently and asking questions where for me it was like blind faith. You took it, you didn't question it. Now, they don't take everything as law and they are realizing the values of being more traditional and that is more spiritual to them. I think there is a shift that way. I see that a lot with the kids coming into Nishnawbe Homes. They don't practice religion but they practice their own culture.

Mary: I wanted to go to high school and the priest and the Native agent wouldn't let me. My dad was very outspoken and my dad fought for things that he believed in. As a result of that he would get into hot water and they wouldn't speak to you for a while. My dad approached them to let me go to school in Spanish [a residential school in the town of Spanish west of Sudbury, Ontario] because my aunt was working there, and he was shuffled back and forth between the priest and the Indian agent and finally he said, "One of you guys tell me what is going on here?" And they said it was only the orphans who go there [which was false]. So finally he said, "Well, Mr. Fox, you have a farm and cows, you don't need your kids to go to school." Anyway, I told my parents, just forget about it and I was thinking I was going to leave anyway and start looking after myself. So, I came to the big city with one of my girlfriends, and I was one of the first girls to leave Wiky [Wikwemikong] in those days. So, I was almost like a star when I went home because I earned my own money. And this priest who stopped my schooling comes over, too. [She took on a high sarcastic tone to imitate the priest, and a low monotonous one for herself.] "Oh, hi Mary! How are you?!" Fine. "I hear you are living in Toronto!" Yes. "How do you like it?" Fine. "Do you ever think of coming back to school?" I just had that lump in my throat, eh? It was like I had a knife being turned in me! So that is why I don't have to think twice to tell a priest to go to hell or whatever.

In "Verna's book" in the unedited interview, Vanderburgh asked Verna what it means to be "Indian" and Verna responded that knowing and preserving Native heritage was important (Vanderburgh, 1977: 185). When I put this question to the reading circle, Mary noted:

I don't think you ever get any respect until you are Anishnaabe – not just "Indian." That is just from my own observations and the way I see it. It is difficult to be a Native person but a lot of it has to do with your way of thinking. It is very hard to go out there with an open mind.

There is still that mind-set from the non-Native that is there all the time. And I don't know how many generations it's going to take to erase that. If you look through history the White people have survived by robbing other people and erasing other nationalities. There is still a lot of discrimination there, some people let it run off their backs, and others are bothered by it. But if you stand up for yourself and say something then you are labelled a militant. I don't know how many generations it will take to change that, it will have to change, and it will change, I just don't think I will be around to see it.

The reading circle's "reading" thus warns against culturally deterministic explanations for the image of the stoic, emotionless Native woman in written life histories, and instead suggests that the continued colonization of Native women — of their bodies, their words, and their relationships — perpetuates and institutionalizes their subjugation and prescribes their passivity.[3] Lee Maracle (1996: 17) writes:

Whereas Native men have been victims of the age-old racist remark "lazy drunken Indian," about Native women white folks ask, "Do they have feelings?" How many times do you hear from our brothers, "Indian women don't whine and cry around, nag or complain." At least not "real" or "true" Indian women. Embodied in that kind of language is the negation of our femininity — the denial of our womanhood. And, let us admit it, beneath such a remark isn't there just a little coercion to behave and take without complaint whatever our brothers think "we have comin'?"

The women in the reading circle demonstrated how the emotional yardstick in Native women's autobiography needs to be balanced with those of Native women readers and measured from the perspective that Native women's lives are, de facto, frustratingly politicized. This is particularly so in terms of how the women assessed Verna's, Madeline's, and their own life experiences in relation to how they could teach or lead to lessons about finding culturally based practical solutions to Native community problems, and how women play a role in those solutions.

Aboriginal Women's Life History Texts and Oral Tradition

The second issue that emerged from the reading circle related to the (dis)continuity of the structures of oral traditions noted in Aboriginal women's life history texts. The issue of the structural persistence and transformation of oral traditions has been debated considerably by scholars concerned with the processes of translating Aboriginal verbal arts into literary arts (see Krupat, 1985; Blaeser, 1996; Cruikshank, 1994; Brumble, 1990; Evers, 1997 for some varied examples). I will not go into detail here about these debates but rather want to add some of the observations made on this issue by the women in the reading circle.

The written accounts of women's lives cannot or should not in any way replace oral traditions. Certainly the emphasis shared by the women in the reading circle on building a sense of community contradicts this prospect; that is, they stress the value of physically working together in environments conducive to traditional direct communication and face-to-face socialization. However, the reading circle suggested ways in which written life histories can also fit into strategies for cultural continuity in the city. For instance, the women quickly recognized the reproduction of Aboriginal structures of oral communication in Madeline's autobiography that they felt could not be as easily detected in Verna's account, which had been rewritten by a non-Native anthropologist. Pat, who has known Madeline for many years, said she enjoyed the book because it really sounded like her:

Pat: It is written the way she speaks, they didn't change her writing in the book at all. It's her words that are in here. [Mary: Which is nice, really nice.] They didn't fix it up and put into proper English. And I love listening to old people talk, I am fascinated to hear them.

Frances: I found this book fun to read because it is such short little glimpses and it is just like when you talk to someone who is older, who has been around for a long time and they are talking and they say, "Oh that reminds me of this," and they tell you a little story and then they are reminded of another thing and they tell you another story. They're not all pieced together in a real flowing story, it's all little bits and pieces.

Mary: Yeah, but you can grasp that much better than the structured one because you lose the meaning in that.

Frances: Verna's book is not the way we talk. It is the European way of doing things. Madeline's is more like family writing. Madeline wanted to leave a legacy. Verna was just relaying information, it was more like an interview, but Madeline's is more like a life. This really triggers all little remembrances. This one is like her lips to my ear, whereas Verna's has been homogenized a couple of times for a general public. One is rough but real, the other one is homogenized.

Indeed, the published version of an autobiography without the hand of a non-Native editor is very rare, as Alice Kehoe has noted: "American Indian women's biography has always been a juggling of the two influences of the Euro-american literary tradition, and the American Indian oral traditions" (Kehoe, 1985: 585). Vanderburgh did address the issue of writing Native women's biography by publishing the unedited interview. Verna, too, had discussed the preservation of Native culture and heritage in response to the question of what the meaning of being "Indian" is. In fact, she stated that Native people from different cultural backgrounds are united mentally, and that this "Indian culture" can be kept alive through recording. However, she asserted that "there are things we don't do and one of them is writing biographies" (Vanderburgh, 1977: 190). She explained that the idea of completing the story of one's life and fixing it on the page also fixed the person in a stasis – if the story had ended in the book, would not her life end, too? If not, then why write an incomplete life history? (Vanderburgh, 1977: 14, 191).

The reading circle has perhaps provided the suggestion of a compromise or "adaptation" that would begin to address this quandary. In our first sessions, Frances had talked about how, historically, in her Birch Island community, and, she deduced, in others as well, there would be at least two people responsible for retaining and passing on the knowledge of the community; they attended weddings, births, funerals, and other community events and took on "apprentice" storytellers to learn the art of mentally recording the community knowledge. What the women in the reading circle contemplated was that an Aboriginal life history, free to flow in a "natural" way, far more resembled the "talk" of oral traditional communication and would therefore be received more enthusiastically by Aboriginal people than that which is "bottled" for mass or academic consumption. What seemed to be most important to this process of integrating written history into Aboriginal life was making sure the mechanisms would be in place to ensure continuity between the past, present, and future generations. This connection was powerfully illustrated when Frances described her strong feelings after reading Vanderburgh's concluding statement, that "Verna's generation is the last at Cape Croker to have touched the hands of 'free' Indians, people who actually began their lives free from intervention and domination by whites, but who ended up as wards of an indifferent government" (1977: 209). This, Frances related, was perhaps the most profound contention made in the book:

> I felt very, very strange. I felt so bad. I felt terrible. And I started think-
> ing about them, "free Indians" – what a strange concept – not a reser-
> vation Indian, not a treaty Indian, not a status Indian, just a person,
> and we'll never see that again. And that was what she saw – the
> extinction of the free Indian. That is really sad. I was really upset by
> that. Just the term, *free*. I thought that is weird. We use this wonderful
> language about the land of the free and the brave, and yet we are not.
> She grew up talking to them. They were the Elders when she was a lit-
> tle girl. I would be so thrilled to go back there for a little while, and lis-
> ten – not even talk to them, just sit in the corner and listen to them
> talk.

> *Mary* (from the kitchen): Why do you say that? Sit in the corner and
> just listen to them?

> *Frances*: Because they have so much to say, I don't want to interrupt
> them with my stupid questions, I just want to let them tell me about
> things.

> *Mary*: Because this is what we did as kids growing up. When people
> came to visit, you didn't interrupt, the kids just sat there and listened
> while two or three people talked.

> *Frances*: I would listen to my mother and her sisters talk like that
> because on top of entertainment, it is history. It is a part of my history.
> And that is why I would like to go back and listen to that group of old
> women sitting around quilting and having a cup of tea – that last
> group of free women, free Native women. This was the last of the free
> generation and Verna had a chance. At least she had a chance, and I
> think in a strange kind of way she may have passed that on. I think it is
> a perfect kind of anthropology book because it passes on what life was
> like, then. We aren't going to see it and we can't guess what it was like.

Conclusion: Feminism, Aboriginal Women, Cultural Continuity, and Urban Lives

The interpretation of Native women's life history by non-Native feminists
has met with limited satisfaction, particularly among Native women

activists and scholars, in part because of the vast chasm that separates our different experiences and objectives. Rather than call for radical changes to gender systems, Native women have struggled for a "retraditionalization of complementary male and female roles ... [and speak] of women's concerns within the context of political issues most vital to American Indian communities: the land, resources, treaty rights, and the survival of Indians as Indians," as Teresa Laframboise has deftly noted (Laframboise, 1985: 782-83). According to Guerrero (1997) feminism needs to examine the underlying problems entangled in patriarchal and colonialist (as well as capitalist) structures in order to have a role in Native women's resistance and emancipation. As Monture-Angus (1995) tells us, in the struggles for self-determination, Native women figure centrally in the education and cultural continuity of Aboriginal peoples, particularly in relation to their positions in defining and strengthening the family.

Patriarchy is one form of domination in the lives of Aboriginal people; it is only one aspect of being colonized. In this chapter, I have presented an ethnographic account of reading Native women's life history that is grounded in these understandings of Native women's collective experience and in the individual perspectives expressed by the women in the reading circle. The analyses extrapolated by the women from reading about the lives of other Native women illustrate how Native culture may be simultaneously preserved and transformed in light of their objectives as Aboriginal people and as women. This included reflecting and acting on how to adapt traditions to new circumstances, a position that expands on Bataille and Sands' observation that Native women's autobiographies "attest to the endurance of the tradition of Indian storytelling as it is transformed into a new literary form" (1984: 24). Also, in keeping with Long's (1993) assessment of the value of the grassroots social analysis that emerges from women's reading groups, the reading circle engaged in a creative process to generate ideas about contributing to the building of a sense of community and identity for urban Aboriginal people. Native women's biography has tended to be read in terms of ethnographic content where the focus has been largely on the subjects' success in maintaining a traditional way of life or in assimilating into non-Native society. As a researcher working within an urban Aboriginal community, I find this binary opposition particularly ineffectual. I am arguing against such a reductive dichotomization and the assumption that because Native women (and Native people in general) migrated to cities and chose so-called "non-traditional" options on their life paths they have assimilated and sacrificed traditions. On the contrary, this research with a small reading circle provides an indication of the creative cultural processes at work in Aboriginal urbanization as Native women proactively participate in cultural continuity and are developing new forms of consciousness in the urban context.

Notes

I am very grateful to Mary Fox, Frances Sanderson, and Pat Turner for their friendship and their work in this research. They are all wonderful Grand-mothers, balancing the experiences and knowledge they carry with the integrity of insight that understanding is a life-long learning process. This research was made possible with the help of a Fonds FCAR (Formation des Chercheurs et Aide à la Recherche, Quebec) doctoral scholarship. I am also grateful for the support of the University of Toronto Department of Anthropology Melissa Knauer Award for Research in Feminist Anthropolo-gy, 1997. Finally, I appreciate the insightful comments and unwavering men-torship of my co-editors to this volume, Rae Bridgman and Sally Cole.

1   Brumble (1990) discusses this form of autobiographical style, which tells "one brief story after another," and attempts to reproduce oral storytelling in the written form as particular to some Native American writings; he refers specifi-cally to Scott Momaday's "staccato-like narrative" or strategic choice to "write autobiography after the fashion of the nonliterate, oral Indian storytellers" (1990: 166-67).

2   The group interview does not lend itself easily to the shears of the anthropolo-gist or the editor. The conversation goes back and forth between several people with questions and ideas bouncing off one another. To maintain the integrity of what is said, I have tried, wherever possible, to reproduce sections of dialogue with the relays intact rather than incomplete sound bites.

3   Helen Carr (1988: 142) has also discussed the subjugated imagery of Native women created in their "as-told-to" autobiographies, particularly in terms of their con-struction as the "Indian Other," characterized by an association between danger and women's sexuality, as "part of the discourse of dispossession of the seven-teenth century."

References

Bataille, Gretchen M. and Kathleen Mullen Sands. 1984. *American Indian Women Telling Their Lives*. Lincoln: University of Nebraska Press.
Behar, Ruth. 1990. "Rage and Redemption: The Life Story of a Mexican Marketing Woman," *Feminist Studies* 16, 2: 223-58.

HEATHER HOWARD-BOBIWASH

—. 1995. "Writing in My Father's Name: A Diary of Translated Woman's First Year," in Ruth Behar and Deborah A. Gordon, eds., *Women Writing Culture*. Berkeley: University of California Press, 65-82.

Blaeser, Kimberly M. 1996. *Gerald Vizenor: Writing in the Oral Tradition*. Norman: University of Oklahoma Press.

Borland, Katherine. 1991. "'That's Not What I Said': Interpretive Conflict in Oral Narrative Research," in Sherna Berger Gluck and Daphne Patai, eds., *Women's Words: The Feminist Practice of Oral History*. New York: Routledge, 63-75.

Boyarin, Jonathan, ed. 1993. *The Ethnography of Reading*. Berkeley: University of California Press.

Brettell, Caroline, ed. 1996. *When They Read What We Write: The Politics of Ethnography*. Westport, Conn.: Bergin & Garvey.

Brumble, H. David. 1990. *American Indian Autobiography*. Berkeley: University of California Press.

Carr, Helen. 1988. "In Other Words: Native American Women's Autobiography," in Bella Brodzki and Celeste Schenck, eds., *Life/Lines, Theorizing Women's Autobiography*. Ithaca, N.Y.: Cornell University Press, 131-53.

Cole, Sally. 1992. "Anthropological Lives: The Reflexive Tradition in a Social Science," in Marlene Kadar, ed., *Essays on Life Writing: From Genre to Critical Practice*. Toronto: University of Toronto Press, 113-51.

—. 1997. "Dear Ruth: This is the Story of Maggie Wilson, Ojibwa Ethnologist," in Elspeth Cameron and Janice Dickin, eds., *Great Dames*. Toronto: University of Toronto Press, 75-96.

Cruikshank, Julie. 1994. "Claiming Legitimacy: Prophecy Narratives From Northern Aboriginal Women," *American Indian Quarterly* 18, 2: 147-67.

Evers, Lawrence J. 1997. "A Conversation with N. Scott Momaday," in Matthias Schubnell, ed., *Conversations with N. Scott Momaday*. Jackson: University Press of Mississippi, 36-44.

Frieden, Sandra. 1989. "Transformative Subjectivity in the Writings of Christa Wolf," in Personal Narratives Group, ed., *Interpreting Women's Lives: Feminist Theory and Personal Narratives*. Bloomington: Indiana University Press, 172-88.

Geiger, Susan. 1986. "Women's Life Histories: Method and Content," *Signs: Journal of Women in Culture and Society* 11, 21 (Winter): 334-51.

Golde Peggy, ed. 1970. *Women in the Field: Anthropological Experiences*. Chicago: Aldine.

Guerrero, Marie Anna Jaimes. 1997. "Civil Rights vs. Sovereignty: Native American Women in Life and Land Struggles," in M. Jaqui Alexander and Chandra Talpade Mohanty, eds., *Feminist Genealogies, Colonial Legacies, Democratic Futures*. New York: Routledge, 101-21.

Kehoe, Alice B. 1985. Reviews in *American Ethnologist* 12, 3 (August): 584-86.

Kluckhohn, Clyde. 1945. "The Personal Document in Anthropological Science," in

Louis Gottschalk, Clyde Kluckhohn, and Robert Angell, eds., *The Use of Personal Documents in History, Anthropology, and Sociology*. New York: Social Science Research Council Bulletin 53, 78-173.

Krupat, Arnold. 1985. *For Those Who Come After: A Study of Native American Autobiography*. Berkeley: University of California Press.

Laframboise, Teresa. 1985. "Book Review," *Signs: Journal of Women in Culture and Society* 10, 4 (Summer): 782-85.

Langness, L. L. 1965. *The Life History in Anthropological Science*. Studies in Anthropological Method. George and Louise Spindler, gen. eds. New York: Holt, Rinehart and Winston.

Long, Elizabeth. 1993. "Textual Interpretation as Collective Action," in Jonathan Boyarin, ed., *The Ethnography of Reading*. Berkeley: University of California Press, 180-211.

Maracle, Lee. 1996. *I Am Woman*. Vancouver: Press Gang Publishers.

Myerhoff, Barbara. 1979. *Number Our Days: Culture and Community Among Elderly Jews in an American Ghetto*. New York: Dutton.

Monture-Angus, Patricia. 1995. *Thunder in My Soul: A Mohawk Woman Speaks*. Halifax: Fernwood.

Personal Narratives Group. 1989. "Origins," in Personal Narratives Group, ed., *Interpreting Women's Lives: Feminist Theory and Personal Narratives*. Bloomington: Indiana University Press, 3-15.

Salazar, Claudia. 1991. "A Third World Woman's Text: Between the Politics of Criticism and Cultural Politics," in Sherna Berger Gluck and Daphne Patai, eds., *Women's Words: The Feminist Practice of Oral History*. New York: Routledge, 93-106.

Sanderson, Frances, and Heather Howard-Bobiwash, eds. 1997. *The Meeting Place: Aboriginal Life in Toronto*. Toronto: Native Canadian Centre of Toronto.

Sommer, Doris. 1991. "No Secrets: Rigoberta's Guarded Truth," *Women's Studies* 20: 51-72.

Stanley, Liz, and Sue Wise. 1990. "Method, Methodology and Epistemology in Feminist Research Processes," in Liz Stanley, ed., *Feminist Praxis: Research, Theory and Epistemology in Feminist Sociology*. London: Routledge, 20-60.

Theriault, Madeline Katt. 1992. *Moose To Moccasins: The Story of Ka Kita Wa Pa No Kwe*. Toronto: Natural Heritage Books/Natural History Inc.

Vanderburgh, Rosamond M. 1977. *I Am Nokomis, Too: The Biography of Verna Patronella Johnson*. Don Mills, Ont.: General Publishing.

Wolf, Diane L. 1996. "Situating Feminist Dilemmas in Fieldwork," in Diane L. Wolf, ed., *Feminist Dilemmas in Fieldwork*. Boulder, Colo.: Westview Press, 1-55.

Wolf, Margery. 1992. *A Thrice Told Story*. Stanford, Calif.: Stanford University Press.

NINE

WHO ARE WE FOR THEM?
ON DOING RESEARCH IN THE PALESTINIAN
WEST BANK

Celia Rothenberg

Pat Caplan (1993: 78) argues that as anthropologists we should ask about ourselves and the people with whom we work: "Who are we for them? Who are they for us?" The latter question generally receives far more attention than the former. But asking and taking seriously who we are for them can lead us to more sensitive and appropriate research practices and questions than a singular focus on who they are for us. Further, when asked and answered together, these questions may also begin to break down the dichotomy of Us and Them and allow us instead to develop a continuum of experience and identification with those with whom we do research. Indeed, it was through learning the answers to "Who are we for them?" that I came to understand my experience of being an American researcher in a Palestinian village in the West Bank who was told by villagers that she is related to both Finnish anthropologist Hilma Granqvist and Louise Baldensperger, the daughter of French missionaries. Further, this experience shaped the way I approached my research while in the village. This paper explores these processes, demonstrating aspects of reflexivity in fieldwork that, while often overlooked, may be important to other feminist anthropologists while in the field.

I carried out my fieldwork in Artas, a village of approximately 3,000 Palestinians two kilometres south of Bethlehem in the Israeli-occupied West Bank between July 1995 and August 1996. From the 1930s until the present, Artas has been known to the small circle of readers of Hilma Granqvist's ethnographies (1925, 1931, 1947, 1950, 1965) on life in the village based on her research there. I chose Artas as the site for my doctoral research because I had read Granqvist's ethnographic works, found them inspiring, and was intrigued to see the site of her research. Here, I briefly introduce Granqvist, aspects of her work, her host in the village, Louise Baldensperger, and the concept of reflexivity in fieldwork as it is generally defined and used; I then examine the memories some elderly villagers have of Granqvist and the influence of these tales on my research and villagers' perceptions of my identity. Through this examination the question "Who are we for them?" remains central.

Hilma Granqvist and Louise Baldensperger

Hilma Granqvist, a Finn of Swedish descent, was born in 1891 and died in 1972. She graduated from Helsinki University in 1921, where she studied pedagogy, history, and philosophy, after which she went to the University of Berlin to study the Old Testament. In 1925 she obtained a grant from a Finnish student union to study the lives of village women in Palestine, and in October 1925 she began her research in Artas. For this first period of fieldwork she stayed in Artas for twenty months; she returned in March 1930 for another fifteen months (her trip was financed this time by an American foundation); and in 1959 she obtained the necessary funding from a Swedish foundation to return to Artas for a final four months of research. Granqvist, or Helima as she was called by the villagers, chose Artas in part because it was located conveniently close to Jerusalem, but primarily because she had heard that Louise Baldensperger lived in the village (Weir, 1981: 9). Between the first two periods of her fieldwork she studied anthropology under Westermarck at the London School of Economics and in 1938 she studied anthropology under Firth and Malinowski (Weir, 1981: 10).

Granqvist's host in the village, fondly called Sitt (Miss) Louise by villagers, was the daughter of missionary parents from Alsace, France. By the time Granqvist first joined Baldensperger in Artas in 1925, Baldensperger had been living in Artas for more than thirty years. Baldensperger's father had come to Artas in 1848, bought land there, and built a house (Baldensperger, 1913: 111). Although her parents and brother eventually moved away from the village, Louise returned to the house to live, and left the village to live in Jerusalem only when she became quite elderly. She was widely known for her knowledge of plants and village folklore, and over the years she assisted numerous scholars – linguists, botanists, and biblical scholars – who came to Artas.

Grace Crowfoot, a botanist who had collaborated with Baldensperger on the book, *From Cedar to Hyssop: A Study in the Folklore of Plants in Palestine*, published in 1932, describes Sitt Louise:

When I first knew her, in 1927, she was already an old inhabitant of the village affectionately known there as "Sitt Louise." She was indicated to me as one who knew and loved the village folk, and who had a rare understanding of their language, manners and customs, and who further knew much about the flowers of the district. To the Palestinian village came Bible students, linguists, botanists and others in search of information who went away with packed note books, part obtained from her and part through her, for, because of her friendship with the people of the village, studies of serious scientific value could be carried forward there. (quoted in Barghouti, 1987: 23)

Sitt Louise's help and knowledge was immensely valuable to Granqvist's research. Granqvist (1931: 19) wrote of Sitt Louise:

It was of inestimable help and value to me that my colleague in Artas, Louise Baldensperger, had actually lived in the village more than 30 years and knew the people thoroughly. With the great interest in folklore which seems to be a family trait [this comment refers to Sitt Louise's brother, Philip, author of *The Immovable East*], she has collected a rich experience of fellahin [peasant] customs and habits and life, especially in her own village. Through her my eyes were opened to much that was characteristic in the village life and through her I won almost immediately the trust and sympathy of the people, so that they were willing to allow me to take part in everything and to give me all the information I desired.

When I first read Granqvist's works, I was struck by the uniqueness of her style and by her relatively unknown status in mainstream anthropology. It is clear that Granqvist's works stand as a model for feminist researchers committed to pursuing innovative textual styles in their research and as a model for collaborative works that give credit where credit is due (i.e., to Baldensperger and her key informants, Hamidya and Alya). Indeed, Granqvist's work can be read as a precursor to the well-known call by Abu-Lughod (1993) for "writing against culture." For example, Granqvist (1931: 17-18) wrote of her method:

I obtained a whole series of facts relating to individuals and their fates. To me such pictures from reality appear of specially great value for the view they give of the life of a people as individuals, of whom we are so very incompletely informed and find it difficult to imagine what they are like .... By reports of actual cases one obtains an interesting insight into how the different ways of looking at things clash, how by changes and complications one rule is substituted for another or how compromises are made when necessity arises.

Individuals' stories are told by Granqvist with great clarity and insight, at times making her ethnography read more as a dramatic play, as she generally cited her informants by name and verbatim. For example, when describing the "marriage policy of the women" – the preference of women who have come to Artas from another village for their sons to marry a girl from their own village – Granqvist (1931: 95) wrote:

> Let us hear some of these women express themselves on the matter. Fatme Sahtur, a Bethlehem woman declared: "I take no other as daughter-in-law to help me in my old age than the daughter of my brother." And the reason for Ibrahim Ayes having his first wife from Nuba is due to the influence of his mother Fadda who said: "I will not have any woman of Artas as a daughter-in-law, but a maiden from my family who will help me in my old age; I will have a maiden from Nuba." And Sa'da Ahmad from el-Walaje praised her good fortune: "O Lord, be thou praised that the daughter of my brother came into the house as my daughter-in-law."

The words of her key informants are heard throughout the text, as are Sitt Louise's. It is evident that Granqvist took the words and knowledge of village women seriously and hesitated to make sweeping theoretical statements about their lives, respectful of the diversity of choices and life paths that exist in the village. She also warned her readers of the "biblical danger," the "temptation to identify without criticism customs and habits and views of life of the present day with those of the Bible, especially of the Old Testament" (1931: 9). She further argued – in distinct contrast to the majority of her colleagues – that the focus on the oppression of Arab women must not be seen in isolation from other social facts; one must understand the position of women with respect to the norms of family life that affect both men and women (1931: 57).

Those who did read her work were usually impressed. Evans-Pritchard (1937: 20) wrote in a review of Granqvist's first two volumes, *Marriage Conditions in a Palestinian Village*: in *Man: The Journal of the Royal Anthropological Institute*:

> It is not easy to praise too highly Miss Granqvist's book. Her descriptive powers and use of texts are excellent. Her statistical material is

well arranged. Her fieldwork methods have not been bettered by any anthropologist. In recording her material she brings out clearly the way in which formal rules and actual practice affect each other and the relations between individual behaviour and social structure. Social inter-relationships are defined and illustrated with a great deal of detail. Social rules are explained both in the words of informants and by citing an abundance of real situations in which they are evoked. It is, moreover, not simply a study confined to marriage ceremonial, or even to marriage relationships, but treats of the conditions of family and kinship in general. The author is to be congratulated on an excellent piece of work.

In a review in *American Anthropologist*, Margaret Mead (1951: 254-55) described Granqvist's later works, *Birth and Childhood among the Arabs* and *Child Problems among the Arabs*, in the following way:

These volumes are essentially ethnological descriptions of birth and childhood, seen from the standpoint of a woman ethnologist with the wise women of the village as her informants. They provide an exceedingly rich record of folk usage, proverb and song, interwoven with vivid descriptions of actual events, verbatim explanations from informants, queries raised by the ethnographer, and carefully organized formal treatment of census material and proper names .... The material is approached and organized simply in terms of the importance of understanding something about the life of women and children without any psychological apparatus ... the fidelity of the ethnologist to her material and the wealth of example and verbatim comment makes this a record which can be used in the interpretation of other types of material on Arab culture. It illustrates particularly well the value and irreplaceability of carefully recorded detail.

In spite of the excellent reviews Granqvist's work received, the social science citations index reveals the citation most common from Granqvist's works is her statistics on the occurrence of different types of marriages in the village; I have also occasionally run across a note of comparison on a specific ritual or belief. Eickelman (1989), in his comprehensive review of the anthropological literature on the Middle East, gives Granqvist's five ethnographies a footnote. It seems that Granqvist's work is difficult to summarize or even grasp quickly. Ironically, perhaps there is too much detail in her work, too much consideration of conflicting stories.

While many feminists are now trying to recover anthropology's lost female voices (for example, Behar and Gordon, 1995), Granqvist remains marginalized within the discipline. Perhaps this is in large part due to the fact that Granqvist was writing as both a woman and from the European periphery, Finland. No matter the reason, Granqvist was unable in her lifetime to locate herself more centrally in British or American anthropology circles, despite the fact that she wrote her works in English. My fascination and respect for Granqvist's work, however, led me to Artas to pursue what I originally envisioned as a follow-up study to some of Granqvist's areas of inquiry, including village marriage patterns, child-rearing customs, and women's work. My proposed methodology included recognizing the need for self-reflexivity in fieldwork, or, in other words, situating my identity for both my informants and the future readers of my own work. Initially, I believed that this simply meant telling villagers who I was and trying to the best of my ability to be aware of the biases that informed the way I would look at their world.

The term "reflexivity" in fieldwork has many connotations, but it may be defined here as "the tendency of feminists to reflect upon, examine critically, and explore analytically the nature of the research process" (Fonow and Cook, 1991: 2). Self-reflexivity, also sometimes referred to as positionality, is understood by many anthropologists to refer to the revelation of the researcher's identity to both informants and readers and the exploration of how that identity affects her/his research (Wolf, 1996: 35). Feminist anthropologists in particular have argued that when the identity of the researcher and the researched are placed "in the same critical plane" (Harding, 1987: 9) the entire research process becomes clearer and more readily scrutinized for the biases that informed the research process (see also, Cole and Phillips 1995). For example, Harding writes:

> That is, the class, race, culture, and gender assumptions, beliefs, and behaviors of the researcher her/himself must be placed within the frame of the picture that she/he attempts to paint .... Thus the researcher appears to us not as an invisible, anonymous voice of authority, but as a real, historical individual with concrete, specific desires and interests. (ibid.)

Indeed, feminist anthropologists have often asked themselves and others how they should "locate themselves in their research, in the process of doing research and writing texts" (Wolf, 1996: 34).

When I arrived in Artas I was committed to the goals of self-reflexivity as

I then understood them and have described them here. Yet I quickly confronted the questions: What should I do when many of my claims about my identity are interpreted as largely meaningless or irrelevant to the people I had chosen to study? What happens when the observed tell the observer fairly exactly who she is (or should be) — as they see her? "Who are we for them" must be taken seriously in these cases, just as seriously as revealing aspects of our identity as we perceive it. It became clear to me that I should privilege villagers' claims about who I was for them in the context of their lives and social world over my own. Indeed, this also helped me to establish a research agenda that was more responsive to what villagers see as important and meaningful about their lives.

Remembering Sitt Louise and Helima

While the academic world has in large part forgotten Granqvist, some elderly villagers nonetheless remember not only Helima, but also Sitt Louise. In the early days of my fieldwork, despite my knowledge of Granqvist's presence in the village, I was surprised to find myself introduced as, "Celia, who is here just like Helima." I had assumed memories of Granqvist would be all but entirely lost (as they are in mainstream anthropology) or would have little influence on contemporary villagers. While surprised by the omnipresent comparison between myself and Granqvist, I found this common introduction was a way to begin my research during my first few months in Artas, initially pursuing the relatively straightforward question of what I could learn about the work of Helima and Sitt Louise when they had lived in the village.

The ongoing importance of Granqvist's and Baldensperger's past presence in the village is seen most obviously in Mr. Musa Sanad's Centre for Folklore Research, found on the west side of Artas. Mr. Sanad powerfully feels his genealogical and intellectual connection to his aunt Hamdiye — who had been one of Granqvist's and Baldensperger's two key informants — and, thus, also to Helima and Sitt Louise. He considers himself to be the village and family heir to the intellectual wealth of Helima's and Sitt Louise's works, which relied so heavily on the words of his aunt. Continuing the work of these women, Mr. Sanad has kept detailed records of village births, deaths, and marriages since 1967. It is a remarkable fact that his work was never damaged or taken by the Israelis. It is Mr. Sanad's dream to rebuild the ruined remains of the small stone house in which Sitt Louise and later Helima lived. Mr. Sanad's own modest home has hosted scholars, journalists, and reporters in their quests for information. Mr. Sanad has one tattered copy of Granqvist's first ethnography, *Marriage Conditions in a Palestinian Village*; the other four he cannot obtain in the West Bank, despite the fact they are easily obtainable inside Israel (when I returned to Canada I sent him bound photocopies of the other four ethnographies).

Thus, Mr. Sanad's Folklore Centre is a tribute to and acknowledgement of Helima's and Sitt Louise's presence in the village and the most obvious symbol of the contemporary legacy of the two women in the village. The one-room centre is on the first floor of a deserted home. Mr. Sanad has hung on the walls pictures of Granqvist, letters from her nephew, articles written by journalists about her from around the world, examples of traditional Palestinian embroidery, and numerous pictures of his family – in short, those things he believes represent Helima, Sitt Louise, and Artas today. In Mr. Sanad's autograph book are the signatures of numerous students, scholars, reporters, interested lay people, and most recently, intrigued (or maybe lost) international election observers, many of whom visited the village to see the site of Granqvist's work.

I wandered into Mr. Sanad's Centre one hot sunny day and found Mr. Sanad there, making some of his endless notes for the book on Artas he envisions writing someday. He showed me artefacts from Sitt Louise's and Helima's sojourns in the village and his own records of village life. After I told him about my research plans, we immediately decided that I would live in the village with members of a family he knew well. The arrangement was easily made, the result of Mr. Sanad's sense of relatedness to Helima and, therefore, consequent sense of responsibility to a researcher following in her path. I returned a few weeks later and took up residence – the first foreigner to live in Artas since Granqvist's departure in 1959.

Fortuitously, two of my neighbours in the village were (nearly seventy years ago) the children standing with Helima in the photo on the front page of *Portrait of a Palestinian Village* (Seger, 1981; see page 145), a published collection of a fraction of Granqvist's photos. Unfortunately, I never learned the identity of the woman partially cut off by the frame of the picture. The picture provided an obvious starting point for my interview with Abu Ra'id (a pseudonym), the now grown-up little boy standing with Granqvist. This first interview about Sitt Louise and Helima not only set the pattern for many of my early interviews but also was one of the most striking examples of the narratives of reminiscence I collected.

I began the interview by mentioning that I had seen Abu Ra'id as a little boy in the photo with Helima on the first page of "The Book," as it is known in Artas. While I expected that mentioning the photo would help spark conversation, I did not expect the degree of lively and lengthy responses that

Himla Granqvist dressed for a wedding in the village of Artas, circa 1930. From Karen Seger, ed., *Portrait of a Palestinian Village* (London: Third World Centre for Research and Publishing, 1981). Reproduced with the permission of the Palestine Exploration Fund.

followed. Explanations of who was in the photo and how the people in the photo were related to the numerous people in the room sprang forth: that is, this same elderly gentleman, Abu Ra'id, whom I was interviewing was married to Im Ra'id, who is (somewhat convolutedly) related through marriage to Mr. Sanad, whose aunt (Hamidye) had been one of Granqvist's key informants. In the same photo with Helima and Abu Ra'id (my research assistant's[1] grandfather, by the way), but on her other side, stands a little girl, Mr. Sanad's mother. The multiple types of links connecting the two children in the photo with Helima to the children and adults in the room were then pointed out to me. Clearly, if I wanted to know about Helima, I needed to know the genealogies of those who still feel a connection to the two women. Then, someone ("related to whom???" I remember thinking) commented, "And now you are here just like Helima," drawing me into the genealogy.

Trying to ignore both my suspicion that Helima had been far more efficient, brave, and competent than I (indeed, my suspicion at that moment was that any fieldworker anywhere had these qualities) and my spinning head, I tried to get to what I thought we had not yet reached: memories of Sitt Louise and Helima. Abu Ra'id seemed taken aback at my request for a "real memory" and was suddenly quiet at my promptings. But then he told me the following story:

> When Helima was staying with Louise there was a dog who had puppies. One day a child broke the leg of one of the puppies. So Helima took the puppy all the way to Jerusalem to treat it. Can you believe that? She had to walk the whole way there and the whole way back. That same day when I went out of the house to bring the cow in, I saw a white shape shining on the mountain, so I took my younger brother to see what it was. We heard the shape yell, "Sitt Looouiisse!!" We knew that it was Helima and that she was lost in the dark. So we brought her to our house; it was very dark and very cold and it was raining. We made a fire and then we brought a long stick and wrapped a cloth around its top to make a torch to take Helima back to Sitt Louise's house. When we got to the house, Helima hugged Sitt Louise and thanked me over and over. She called me "*ibn achui*" [literally, son of my brother; used here as a term of endearment]. Can you believe that? Me — *ibn achui*! [I wrote in my notebook: "My research assistant Muhammed sighs impatiently and comments that he's heard this story of his grandfather's a hundred times."]

Ah, I thought – a "real" memory of Sitt Louise and Helima after nearly an hour of sorting out the genealogies of the kids in the picture (and the room)!

A few days later I interviewed an elderly couple in the neighbourhood of Sitt Louise's and Helima's home. The woman told me, "We knew Sitt Louise. She and Helima would come to our house. Sitt Louise used to bring her dog. I used to collect special flowers for Sitt Louise and in return she gave me sweets. I would go to the spring and bring water for them, too. Sitt Louise grew old here. We loved her." A different older couple told me nearly the same story a week later still; they, too, had gathered flowers for Sitt Louise and brought water for her and Helima. Sitt Louise's collaborative work with Grace Crowfoot, *From Cedar to Hyssop* (1932: vii), confirms that she often paid small sums to children in the village to bring her flowers and plants; she used these specimens to add to her own collection of plants mentioned in the Bible as well as to make "herbariums for schools, and little card souvenirs of the Holy Land."

Villagers also remembered that Helima went everywhere in the village with her camera. At the conclusion of one woman's scant recollections of Helima and Sitt Louise, she told me the following:

> I think it was Sitt Louise's brother's son who came back here to visit once. Or, no, it was Helima's sister's niece who wrote letters to Artas. Yes, that's right. I think perhaps Sitt Louise and Helima were relatives. Cousins. Yes, cousins. And their cousins' children came back here once. But then they all stopped coming. We don't know what happened to them. We worry about them sometimes. [Who exactly do you worry about? I asked.] I mean, we worry what became of them. What happened to them all. It's strange to never come back and visit, isn't it? I mean, they lived here with us.

Indeed, it was rare for me to do an interview about Sitt Louise and Helima without hearing an attempt to remember which of their relatives had returned to Artas to visit and re-establish ties with the villagers. Predictably, I would then be asked if I was not in fact a relative of the two.

The above quotations represent some of the most succinct and typical recollections of Helima and Sitt Louise. First, villagers would relate the necessary family tree, which began with the person who knew Helima or Sitt Louise and stretched to the present relatives of that person. Next, there would be some tale or anecdote concerning the two, emphasizing their normal functioning in everyday life in the village, and, often, a comment on the two women's relation to one another. Finally, the elderly teller of the tale would be reminded that the unknown fate of the two is both puzzling and strange, and he or she would frequently make some attempt to connect the two women to the present, through me or a through a cloudy memory of a relative of the two who may once have visited the village.

Shaping My Research Questions

I decided to record memories of Sitt Louise and Helima as a pathway into my own research questions, particularly in light of the fact that my original research plan aimed to follow up some of the questions pursued by Granqvist. What I soon realized, however, was that the importance of recording villagers' memories of the two women went far beyond gathering a small if precious package of stories about their lives in the village or providing a pathway into my preformulated research questions. Rather, this process both reshaped many of my research questions and allowed me to learn how villagers understood my identity in important ways.

I found that I was able to follow clues about what is important in women's lives by listening to what the villagers, through their memories of Sitt Louise and Helima, were telling me to explore. As can be seen above, "memories" of Sitt Louise and Helima are formulaic in their composition; they are best appreciated as condensed statements of some of the key social themes in village life. These memories thus became a kind of metaphor for my research questions. Indeed, a Palestinian filmmaker from Jerusalem accompanied me one day to the village, anxious to capture villagers' recollections of the two women on film. He was thoroughly disappointed by what he found and told me it was nothing but old people's ramblings. In my view, he was wrong in his belief that these stories lack meaning (and in his assessment of the appeal of telling such memories at least for a feminist filmmaker). Yet it is true that the stories of the two women do require some careful deciphering.

I had originally overlooked those parts of my interviews that did not have to do directly with anecdotes of Sitt Louise and Helima, despite the fact that these discussions generally took more time and effort on the part of my interviewees than any other. I now understand, however, that implicit in the act of remembering Sitt Louise and Helima are a definition of family and a comment on the nature of personhood – indeed, to be more specific, on womanhood – which are especially meaningful for Palestinian village women today and for my presence in the field. In my search for what I thought were more substantive memories of the two women in the form of anecdotes about their lives, I believe now that I initially missed some of the points that members of Artas's oldest living generation were trying to tell me: Sitt Louise and Helima had become genealogically linked to the village(rs), or, more simply, they were family. As I read and reread my translations of villagers' stories of Sitt Louise and Helima while in Artas, I began to understand and use these stories as a vehicle for understanding three main aspects of my research.

First, the ways in which villagers understand Sitt Louise and Helima to have been related to one another gave me some idea of the importance village women place on their relationships to one another. Recognizing this led me to explore in detail the practice of relationships and roles of women as neighbours, extended family members, and even close family members – relationships left largely unexplored in the literature on Palestinian women (Granqvist is the notable exception). As Rema Hammami (1995: 20) points out in a recent review of this literature, Western writers have focused on women's prescribed roles in the patriarchal extended family or *hamula*, while local Palestinian writers have focused on women as symbols of "family honor." In both approaches described by Hammami, concepts such as "patriarchy" and "traditional family norms" are relied on but not problematized, and consequently the texture of women's relationships and women's own perspectives on those relationships are overlooked. In short, women have been objects in research, rather than subjects and actors in their own right.

Yet from listening to memories of Sitt Louise and Helima for what they can tell us about village life, we are led to consider how women live together and take care of one another, and that they sometimes do so without male kin. Further, Granqvist's own work points to a similar sense of the necessity of describing women's lives, as mentioned above. This insight led me to recount aspects of the lives of the women I knew best, with as little intrusion of theoretical terms as possible, in one chapter of my thesis. This approach allows me to put forward a woman-centred perspective on the events of daily life, understanding how it is that women shape, confine, and change each other's lives. Understanding women's relationships is key to appreciating a range of issues, including how marriages come to be arranged or how a woman may experience her most harsh criticism or, even outright oppression, from other women.

Second, stemming from this focus on women's relationships, I was further led to examine some of the requirements for "family" identity or, at least, "the kind of family that matters" (to paraphrase my informants) from the point of view of the women whom I knew best in the village. For women, the "kind of family that matters" is developed and maintained through what I have called the logic of social geography (Rothenberg, 1998), a concept that recognizes physical proximity and women's individual preferences as allowing for the development of reciprocal relationships and friendships that are most important to the workings of women's daily lives. This concept works to deepen and broaden perspectives on the *hamula* that reflect the dominant male discourse on relations in the village. While women may, like men, use the idiom of the *hamula* to describe their relationships to one another – indeed, neighbours are often family members – they combine this perspective with the implicit logic of social geography. Women may explicitly recite genealogies (such as those stretching to Helima and Sitt Louise in which they are enmeshed) as men do; yet the practices of women's daily relationships are centrally shaped (although not wholly encapsulated) by the limitations and allowances of social geography.

The concept of social geography thus creates space for recognizing the variety of ways an individual may experience ties to others: while some people may have (and emphasize) a genealogical link stretching back in time to a certain group of people from the moment of their birth into the community, others, like Sitt Louise and Helima, can establish meaningful ties and the potential for future ties by first becoming neighbours. Women are particularly key in creating the latter type of ties based on their preferences for some neighbours over others. The long-term residence of Sitt Louise and Helima cemented and built on the obligations, rights, and duties inherent in the discourse of family ties. Importantly, not only did Sitt Louise and Helima become neighbours, linked to those around them and, consequently, their descendants, but, in the language of the present-day Palestinian resistance, they showed that they were steadfast, or *sumud*. Sitt Louise and Helima, demonstrated their steadfastness through years of residence in the community, by becoming close to their neighbours, participating in their festivals, mourning their deaths, entertaining their children, recording their stories, and, of course, taking their pictures. This argument builds directly on the ethnographic data I gathered; while I venture into more theoretical terrain than Granqvist ever chose to do in her work, I remain cognizant of her implicit warnings about sweeping statements describing village life.

Yet one simple fact remains about Sitt Louise and Helima (and here was a third clue for my research): they did what good family should never do – they left and they did not come back. Attempts to remember just who it was from their families who returned to Artas is a way of trying to restore the two women's good reputation as steadfast villagers/family members. At a moment in time when many Palestinians from the diaspora are returning to Artas, rebuilding their old family homes, or buying land near Artas to build new homes, the absence of Sitt Louise and Helima is a kind of desertion, a shameful shirking of their family responsibilities.

The centrality of social geography in women's lives thus has important implications for their relationships with villagers from Artas who left the village before 1967 and found themselves unable (or, indeed, unwilling in some cases) to return after the Israeli occupation. Many of these villagers now live in Amman, Jordan. As part of my research, I interviewed these families. How these women experience the unravelling of family/neighbour ties is central here, for it has forced them to articulate their previously implicit understandings that both family and neighbours are those to whom one is "close." Villagers in Artas are often deeply disappointed, emotionally and financially, by those who leave, never return, and/or make few efforts to maintain their emotional ties to the village; this often strengthens their sense of emotional attachment to others as stemming centrally from the possibility of being closely located to one another.

Significantly, after recording a family genealogy with Mr. Sanad I would find he had omitted all the members of a family who had left the village and not returned, or who had not sent a child of theirs back to the village. Mr. Sanad, historian and village genealogist, is widely held to be the most responsible recorder of such kinds of village history (when a villager did not know his or her family tree I would invariably be sent back to Mr. Sanad, who often sent me back to the family again to verify or fill in certain parts of his own archival records). His careful records speak to his dedication to his village's history and future. Leaving the village without sending back a child means certain erasure from his family trees, an omission that symbolizes the importance of proximity. Yet sending a daughter back to the village means that Mr. Sanad's records, which have in the past recorded only men's names, now include female names, as a young woman may be the sole representative in the village of a particular branch of a family that has left. This may suggest that while women and men have often traced their genealogies in informal ways through women – as seen in the oral genealogies relating back to Helima and Sitt Louise – the political situation is now forcing a change in even the dominant paradigm of male-traced genealogies.

Who Are We for Them?

In addition to shaping my research questions by directing me to the importance of women's relationships to one another, the requirements for the "kind of family that matters," and villagers' relations with those who are far away, memories of Sitt Louise and Helima also shaped perceptions of my identity. Before I arrived in Artas I argued in my dissertation proposal for the need for self-reflexivity in fieldwork, or, as I described above, situating my identity for both my informants and the future readers of my work. Once in Artas, however, I found that rather than locating myself as a researcher through my own claims about my identity, the villagers in large part located me through their understanding of the history of other female researchers in the village: I was genealogically (if metaphorically) linked to these women. Further, I soon learned that some of my specific claims about my identity (e.g., being from a particular part of the United States) often lacked meaning or importance for villagers; I had to be responsive to their views of what constituted aspects of a meaningful identity. Thus, they taught me who, in the context of village life, I was. This is another strand of the concept of reflexivity: not only situating ourselves through our own identity claims, but recognizing, and at times giving precedence to, exactly how we are situated by others.

Helima, Sitt Louise, and I shared a common goal: we recorded the ways of village life, an endeavour that every villager I met thought to be worthwhile and important in light of the history of political and military occupation in the area. Indeed, my work was carried out in a political climate that has dictated such an endeavour to be of greater importance than ever before, as the Israeli government has tried to minimize the importance of Palestinian culture and history in the region. We also shared a common background from the perspective of many villagers. Despite the fact we were not biological family, for many villagers the parallels of our situations — I, like the two of them, am a single, female researcher from the West — are close enough.

For me, the villagers' knowledge of the two women and my follow-up presence were often enough to open doors. Particularly striking was when I was in Amman, led from house to house in one of the city's Palestinian refugee camps where most Artasis live. I was guided from door to door by the son of a man who had left Artas more than thirty years earlier. When my guide knocked on the doors of people he knew only by name, he would introduce himself as Abu Ra'id's grandson, drawing on his most immediate link to the village as the place of his extended family's residence, and me as a member/scholar of the village just like Sitt Louise and Helima. Without fail, such introductions elicited long and drawn out attempts to find links to both Abu Ra'id and the two women; once found, no matter how remote the connection, we settled into rather more intimate discussions, I believe, than would have been possible had we lacked a genealogical connection to the people of Artas. As I had been in Artas for nearly half a year by the time

I went to Amman and was by then known simply as Celia, I was quite vividly reminded of Sitt Louise and Helima and their ongoing role in my research. It was tempting to believe that I had struck out on my own, which in part I had, but I was not at any time – and should not have been – freed of my identification with, and debt to, the two women.

The historical precedent of Sitt Louise and Helima's research in the village was thus extraordinarily important for my research questions and for villagers' impression of my identity. Yet, the fact remains that I am not Finnish or Christian, but American and in part (and who can say which part?) Jewish; here I must also take seriously the feminist insight that aspects of our identity – as we know it – should be known to both our informants and those who read our work. My father's family is Jewish, my mother's, Lutheran Swedes. According to Israeli civil law (based on an orthodox interpretation of Jewish law), I was thus not Jewish, as Judaism is inherited matrilineally, although I am in many ways intimately tied to Jewish people. I told my hosts this information at the outset of my research. While they were surprised, they asked me if I actually believe that they think all Jews are the same. In turn, I was (albeit naïvely) surprised by the implicit sophistication of their question. In practical terms, my hosts agreed that they knew best whom to tell or not about the sum total of my background and I left the matter in their hands. (I must say, however, that it was actually quite rare for anyone to ask if I was Jewish; I believe the general assumption was that a Jewish woman would not come live in a Palestinian village.)

The sophistication of my hosts' reaction to my decision to reveal this aspect of my identity was as important to my research as the influence of Sitt Louise and Helima, if in a slightly more subtle and somewhat more personal way. I was intrigued by the complexity of the relations between Jews and Palestinians, a complexity both reflected in that initial conversation about my Jewish identity and lived by myself and many villagers in our daily lives. Slurs, taunts, and derisive comments are without a doubt part of the daily vocabulary of many villagers. Indeed, I often heard women, when a child was misbehaving, call the child "a little Jew." Yet an analysis of insults is limited in terms of what it can tell us of life in the West Bank and the range of feelings that women may also harbour towards Jews. As my research unfolded, I drew out analyses of village women's feelings towards and relationships with Jewish Israelis, which are complicated, subtle, and often conflicted. I did so in part, undoubtedly, due to the nature of my identity, which may have led me to look past derisive comments and towards what I believe is a more fruitful and thought-provoking discussion; yet this focus is also in part a result of what is able to be found by any researcher in the West

Bank who rejects the simple dichotomy of Jewish victimizer versus Arab victim as evidence of the sum total of experiences, thoughts, and feelings on either side of the Israeli-Arab conflict. Indeed, we should recall Granqvist's insistence on refusing to homogenize the lives of villagers. There is a great deal of political diversity in the West Bank among villages, towns, and refugee camps. For a variety of historical, political, and economic reasons, Artasis are not generally considered politically radical by either their fellow Palestinians or Israelis with whom I spoke (who generally knew the area, but not the village itself). The politically moderate atmosphere of Artas compared to some villages in the West Bank and many in the Gaza Strip may allow for the development of the complex relations and feelings towards Jewish Israelis upon which I later focused.

While the knowledge of my Jewish identity is thus important for both my readers and many villagers, I firmly assert that my link to Helima and, consequently, to Sitt Louise was not only the most explicit in daily discourse but also the most pertinent aspect of my identity for many villagers. While the question of whether or not I am Jewish rarely arose (not many thought to ask), my relation to the two women always came up. Indeed, my presence in the village, I would like to think, in part repaired Sitt Louise and Helima's reputations as village deserters.

The fact that my research was in large part directed by the villagers, and that my identity was largely defined by them, created a flexible approach to my research. Villagers guided me towards what they believed to be important, directing me towards more fruitful paths of inquiry than my original research plan envisioned. I appreciate the debt I owe to the work and presence of the women researchers who preceded me not only for their historical precedence but also for their real and living influence on my work. I further grew to appreciate the political and emotional sophistication of the villagers with whom I became close.

Who Can We Become?

I often wonder if my presence in the village will be offered as a genealogy to other researchers who may find themselves in the village in the future. Partly confirming my suspicion that this may come to be true (and personally quite touching), a postcard arrived in my mailbox a short time ago from a young married couple in the village to whom I had been quite close. It reads: "If you don't remember we do. We will not forget you forever. The people who loved you, Adil and Amina." Muhammed and I exchange electronic mail, so I receive news from the village almost daily. I also occasionally call his family, as they have the only phone in the neighbourhood. With the availability of relatively easy electronic communications technology, I will not disappear from their lives. Unlike Sitt Louise and Helima, I can now maintain at least a virtual presence in Artas! Who I will become for them – and them for me – remains to be seen; but by looking at the various dimensions of these questions I may be lead to even more interesting answers in the years to come.

Notes

I gratefully acknowledge the support for this research and its writing from the Research Institute for the Study of Man (Landes Award), University of Toronto (Open Fellowship, Melissa J. Knauer Award, and Lorna Marshall Award), and the Harry Frank Guggenheim Foundation (Dissertation Award). I would like to thank Professors Janice Boddy, who oversaw this research, Michael Lambek, who introduced me to the works of Hilma Granqvist, and Sally Cole, who patiently helped me through the editing process. Finally, without the good humour and immense support of the villagers of Artas this research would not have been possible. I especially thank Mr. Sanad and Muhammed.

1 My research assistant, whom I will call here Muhammed, has asked that his identity be protected. I respect and agree with his wish. I am unable, therefore, to provide any detail about his identity.

References

Abu-Lughod, Lila. 1993. *Writing Women's Worlds*. Berkeley: University of California Press.

Baldensperger, Philip. 1913. *The Immovable East*. London: Sir Isaac Pitman and Sons.

Behar, Ruth, and Deborah A. Gordon, eds. 1995. *Women Writing Culture*. Berkeley: University of California Press.

Barghouti, Abdullatif, comp. 1987. *Arab Folk Stories from Artas: Miss Crowfoot and Miss Baldensperger*. Bir Zeit: Bir Zeit University.

Caplan Pat. 1993 "Learning gender: Fieldwork in a Tanzanian coastal village, 1965-1985," in D. Bell, P. Caplan, and W. Jahan Karim, eds., *Gendered Fields: Women, Men and Ethnography*. London: Routledge, 168-81.

Cole, Sally, and Lynne Phillips, eds. 1995. *Ethnographic Feminisms: Essays in Anthropology*. Ottawa: Carleton University Press.

Crowfoot, Grace, and Louise Baldenperger. 1932. *From Cedar to Hyssop: A Study in the Folklore of Plants in Palestine.* London: Sheldon Press.

Eickelman, Dale. 1989. *The Middle East: An Anthropological Approach.* 2nd ed. Englewood Cliffs, N.J.: Prentice-Hall.

Evans-Pritchard, E. 1937. "Review of Marriage Conditions in a Palestinian Village," *Man: The Journal of the Royal Anthropological Institute* 36, 20-24: 20.

Fonow, Mary, and Judith Cook. 1991 Back to the future: A look at the second wave of feminist epistemology and methodology," in Mary Fonow and Judith Cook, eds., *Beyond Methodology: Feminist Scholarship as Lived Research.* Bloomington: Indiana University Press, 1-15.

Granqvist, Hilma. 1931, 1935. *Marriage Conditions in a Palestinian Village.* 2 vols. Helsingfors: Societas Scieniarum Fennica. Commentationes Humanarum Litterarum III. 8, VI. 8.

_____. 1947. *Birth and Childhood among the Arabs.* Helsingfors: Soderstrom.

———. 1950. *Child Problems among the Arabs: Studies in a Muhammadan Village in Palestine.* Helsingfors: Soderstrom.

———. 1965. *Muslim Death and Burial: Arab Customs and Traditions Studied in a Village in Jordan.* Helsingfors: Helsinki.

Hammami, Rema. 1995. "Commentary: Feminist scholarship and the literature on Palestinian women," *Gender and Society: Working Papers.* Bir Zeit: Women's Studies Program.

Harding, Sandra. 1987. "Introduction: Is there a feminist method?" in Harding, ed., *Feminism and Methodology.* Bloomington: Indiana University Press, 1-15.

Mead, Margaret. 1953. "Review of Birth and Childhood among the Arabs and Child Problems among the Arabs," *American Anthropologist* 53: 254-55.

Rothenberg, Celia E. 1998. "Spirits of Palestine: Palestinian village women and stories of the jinn," Ph.D. dissertation, University of Toronto.

Seger, Karen, ed. 1981. *Portrait of a Palestinian Village.* London: Third World Centre for Research and Publishing.

Weir, Shelagh. 1981. "Foreword," in Karen Seger, ed., *Portrait of a Palestinian Village.* London: Third World Centre for Research and Publishing, 9-15.

Wolf, Diane. 1996. "Situating feminist dilemmas in fieldwork," in Wolf, ed., *Feminist Dilemmas in Fieldwork.* Boulder Colo.: Westview Press, 1-56.

TEN

NARRATING EMBODIED LIVES: MUSLIM WOMEN ON THE COAST OF KENYA

Parin A. Dossa

In her 1992 essay, "Experience," Joan Scott argues that what we count as experience is not self-evident but is always contested and therefore political. In this paper, I employ the paradigm of "embodiment" to foreground unexamined bodily/lived experiences of Swahili Muslim women on the island town of Lamu (Kenya). By the paradigm of embodiment, I mean experiential understanding of life situations. The paradigm of embodiment locates the roots of human experiences in the body as the existential ground of culture and self (Csordas, 1994), where the body is understood as a thinking, feeling, and acting entity. As a non-positivist strategy, it complements the genre of life narratives where verbally articulated discourse is the norm. My purpose is to suggest a frame that goes beyond the listening-telling paradigm of life narratives (Ong, 1995) that seek to address the "crisis of representation" in feminist/subalternist anthropology, but ultimately, remain confined to capturing "words."

For some time, I have used the narrative genre to foreground the lived reality of ethnographic subjects (Dossa, 1994, 1997, 1999). I adopted the use of narrative because it "nurtures trust and increases the informant's power to influence the ethnographic product" (Ong, 1995: 355). Following feminist work on life narratives (Personal Narratives Group, 1989; Behar, 1993; Ong, 1995; Abu Lughod, 1993), I have sought to let women relate their life experiences in their own way. After careful recording of six of fifteen narratives, I noticed a recurring statement: *Shisi hapa na faya kazi ya makono* ("Here, we work with our hands"). In listening to this statement I began to appreciate finally that, despite my painstaking efforts to listen to women's stories, I was missing out on a critical element: images of women's bodies at work, engaged in aesthetic and creative endeavours, on the move and in positions of repose. The telling and listening paradigm became inadequate, echoing Minh-ha's (1989: 36) observation that:

we do not *have* bodies, we *are* our bodies, and we are ourselves while being in the world. Who can endure constant openendness? Who can keep on living completely exposed? We write–think and feel – (with) our entire bodies rather than only (with) our minds or hearts. It is a perversion to consider thought the product of one specialized organ, the brain, and feeling, that of the heart.

In this essay I explore the life narrative of Zeinub (pseudonym). Zeinub's life encapsulates broad principles that inform the narratives and embodied knowledge of other Lamu women of similar status, that is women of Arab ancestry and of the middle class. Her narrative spans historical and emergent roles and identities of Lamu women, including their negotiation of the "veil." As a person who has covered similar experiential terrain, I am cognizant of women negotiating varied, subtle, and ambiguous gender-segregated spaces: both my grandmother and my mother, in her early life, wore the veil, and they explained its riddance through the discourse that veiled women cannot work outside the home or get an education. By attending to negotiation of spaces both by myself as an insider/outsider and by Zeinub in her deliberate blurring of public/domestic worlds, I reveal how everyday experiences and practices of ordinary women can contribute to developing critical theory. Zeinub's life is presented here in the form of a narrative that foregrounds her embodied experiences acquired in the course of living. This focus is akin to the spirit captured by Minh-ha (ibid., 119): "The story depends upon every one of us to come into being. It needs us all, needs our remembering, understanding, and creating what we have heard together to keep on coming into being. The story of a people. Of us, peoples."

Lamu Town: Introducing a Gendered Perspective

Lamu is the oldest Muslim town in Kenya and the only Swahili settlement that has retained a pre-industrial town centre while sustaining a growing urban community. Lamu was saved from the disruptive effects of colonization and Western capitalism around the turn of the century when it was bypassed for Mombasa during the construction of the Ugandan railway. Contrary to common interpretation that the town drifted into obscurity in the 1920s (Mbote, 1986; Ngari, 1986; Siravo and Pulver, 1981), Lamu's obscurity was that of not being enveloped in the exploitative modes of rapid and uncontrolled development. For the local people – stratified into groups of "Arab," Bajuni from the mainland, Hadramout from Oman, and others – its compact townscape, ecological adaptation to the tropical climate, over a thousand-year-old heritage, practice of Islam, and reconfiguration of its social life in response to changing circumstances were conducive to maintaining a commercial as well as a subsistence base of agriculture, livestock, trade, fishing, mangroves, and crafts. Women's sociocultural and economic contributions in this gender-segregated town, however, have not been foregrounded. As Strobel (1979: 4) observes: "To write about women on the Swahili coast is to probe the history of the inarticulate and invisible."

Over the last two decades, Lamu has been subject to rapid state-initiated interventions of industrial development and market economy growth. Two visible expressions of this change are tourists and an influx of new residents from mainland Kenya. On average, 8,000 tourists visit the town each year. To outsiders, Lamu appears untouched by the disruptions of urban capitalism. Its unspoiled environment of sand beaches, its historical architecture of narrow streets and alleys, and its town life with no automobiles are considered ideal for tourists. Growth of the tourist trade has attracted people from the mainland looking for economic opportunities in a developing town. The population of Lamu has risen rapidly, from 7,406 in 1975 to 18,291 in 1996. Lamu has been the site of Kenyan economic development projects that have been of minimal benefit to the local people, who have been bypassed on the grounds that they do not have the necessary "expertise." The attempt to modernize Lamu has undermined local people's subsistence base to the extent that the majority now live in poverty.

Recognizing the need to act in a situation where many face starvation, women are engaged in multiple income-generating endeavours. In a gender-segregated town where males socially occupy the public sphere (*inje*) and women's space is designated as *dani ya jumbani* (literally, inside the house), women's engagement in earning a living requires a considerable amount of social negotiation. As women are expected to remain covered outside the house, these negotiations take place through women's bodies. Zeinub's narrative reveals dynamics of embodied (that is, experiential) knowledge, reconstructed in relation to the two locally recognized categories, *dani* (inside) and *inje* (outside). As a person whose early years of life were immersed in experiential understanding of the world, familiar to women in Lamu, I first present my own story to highlight our shared experiences.

Border Ethnographer: Doing Fieldwork; (Re)Visiting Home

My research in the predominantly Sunni Muslim town of Lamu does not constitute a field site in the conventional sense. My three trips between 1990 and 1997 to Lamu formed part of (re)visiting home. I was born and grew up as a Shi'a/Asian Ismaili Muslim in Uganda (East Africa) and lived there until the Asian exodus in 1972. The expulsion of 60,000 Asians by Ugandan President Idi Amin has its roots in the colonial period. Vincent (1994) documents the colonial hierarchy of three constituencies: Europeans and Asians (non-native of Ugandan Protectorate), chiefs and landowners (natives), and peasants (natives), an order she describes as reified through "law-related hegemonic constructions." As non-natives of the Ugandan Protectorate, the hegemonically constructed position of Asians as "above" that of native Africans led to hostility that persists to this day.

My life history is linked to the cohort of Ismaili women who experienced a rupturing of embodied knowledge through colonial and diasporic experiences. When I migrated to Canada and was homogeneously categorized as "Indo-Canadian," I began to realize my own loss. I did not have the opportunity to appreciate the diversity of cultural traditions that exist in my natal country: Asian, Muslim, African, and also European. The hegemony of the latter forestalled an experiential understanding of the first three, insidiously suppressed under colonial rule. It was partially a search for identity and the need to rediscover forms of embodied knowledge that informed my decision to (re)visit home, a move reinforced by affinal ties: I am married to an Ismaili Kenyan from Mombasa, a coastal Muslim town closely allied to Lamu.

Despite my roots in East Africa and knowledge of indigenous languages of Kiswahili and Gujerati, I do not claim to be an indigenous anthropologist. A "native" stance would be pretentious as my advanced education in the West and my profession as an academic have created cultural and class differences that need to be taken into account. As Wolf (1996: 17) has rightly stated, the insider-outsider paradigm does not have much value since most of us belong to bicultural or multicultural worlds. For myself, living in between spaces of Africa and Canada is a vital and rejuvenating force as it gives me space to explore my cultural losses. In not being subjected to allegiance to any one home country, one can achieve freedom from the "conflation of identity and location" (Ong, 1995: 352). Border positions can then be used as vantage points to explore other possibilities and other ways of being. In my case, it has given me the opportunity to retell narratives of women with whom I share a similar story: patriarchal/colonial forms of domination as well as (re)configurations of embodied learning. Our very different experiences required negotiation and recognition of the fact that there cannot be total empathy and bridging of differences. Shared stories have to remain open – they do not require an ending or a sense of closure.

Life narratives formed one medium through which I negotiated my border position, for there existed an element of reciprocity: women narrated their lives for themselves as a way of achieving consciousness in order to reinterpret and remake their worlds and with the full knowledge that I would share their stories with others. Narayan's (1993) problematization of whether an indigenous anthropologist can become "native" and Wolf's (1996) observations on power dynamics in fieldwork make me wary of assuming a native stance. Both our common histories and our differences – especially of class – framed our relationships. The status and position of Muslim women in Lamu centre on the subject of dress. The latter is appropriated by women to convey their own embodied understanding. Zeinub's life narrative provides an illustrative example.

Retelling Life Narratives: Recapturing Meaning

I met Zeinub through a women-in-development (*madeleyo ya wanawake*) project. She had called me into her craft store and said: "There is going to be a *harambe* for women. Can you sign this form and donate some money?" I was slightly taken aback because she did not ask me if I wanted to donate. While I was struggling with the issue of location and positionality, Zeinub had already decided that as a "privileged" Muslim, I was expected to give. When I asked Zeinub what her role was in the project, she replied: "None. I am just helping this organization to obtain funds. I myself do not believe in this kind of development. Women would do well to take their own initiative, *locally*."

This incident brought home to me Zeinub's multiple locations in the town. With the increase in poverty, women in Lamu have begun to look towards development projects to ameliorate their situation and work towards a more sustainable way of life. According to the local women, there has been a lot of talk and very few practical benefits. This aspect was emphasized by a man from the élite:

> It will take a long time before these projects are implemented – if ever they are. If they are implemented, not all women will benefit from them. The "big" ones [those in the upper socio-economic strata] will get the money. Myself, I have to think of what we are going to eat today and I have to think of how I can send my children to school. I have to act today. I have to act now.

Some of the development projects, such as sewing and embroidery classes, poultry farming, and basket and mat weaving, have resulted in frustrations and even led to divisions among women. For example, a six-month course on sewing and embroidery set up by an international donor agency serves very few women. Six machines are set up in two rooms and close to thirty women are taught at a time. Others are on a waiting list. Those who finish the course discover that their skills are not marketable because, as one woman explained, "it is only in Lamu that women wear handmade clothes. Everywhere else, they wear ready-made clothes." Likewise, women who learn embroidery and produce beautiful local designs on ladies' belts and blouses and on tablecloths and napkins find that there is no market for such products. No infrastructure exists for export and the local people have no purchasing power. Only a handful of the products are sold to the tourists. The limited market leads to stiff competition among women. A symbol of illusory development is a broken sewing machine that has been lying around for about six months. A sewing instructor remarked: "It will sit here until I can find someone who can get a part from Mombasa. It was better in the olden days. I had a simple machine and if it broke down it was fixed within twenty-four hours. I did not have to worry about parts."

Zeinub is fully aware of the dynamics and contradictions of development projects. She represents a particular sector of indigenous Lamu women who have made a conscious choice not to be part of the development endeavour. She knows that the projects only help a few women. At the same time, she is fully cognizant of the need to support other women and this explains her involvement with the fund-raising activity to which she herself contributed a reasonable sum. What I perceived to be a contradiction may indeed be understood as embodied knowledge acquired situationally in the context of an intricate web of female-centred networks. Hence, women in Lamu are loyal to many groups with differing interests. Zeinub's support of the project amounted to supporting women who were working in this area. People precede projects. Her statement about local initiatives revealed her grounding in the local culture and the political implications of outside interventions via development projects. The question that arises is: How is embodied knowledge acquired in Lamu where the conventional position of women has been overtly articulated in terms of "staying at home and covering bodies?" A glimpse of Zeinub's early life helps us to acquire some understanding of this complex process.

Mila athu na ka kua jumbani: "Our culture is to stay at home." This phrase, reiterated by women on various occasions, encapsulates Zeinub's early years. Zeinub is a twenty-eight-year-old woman with four children. She identifies herself as an Arab — a group that considers itself to be superior owing to its upper-class affiliation and linkage to the birthplace of Prophet Muhammed *vis-à-vis* other Muslims: Bajuni, Hadramout, Bohras, among other subgroups. Zeinub's upbringing was typical for women in Arab families. She studied up to grade seven and attended Madrasa (Quranic school) until the time she reached puberty, after which her father made her stay at home. As Zeinub explained:

> My father said: "Young girls of twelve to thirteen years old should stay at home." That was final. I did not mind being at home. I helped my mother cook food and learned how to sew. It was really fine. Three years went by and after that my marriage was arranged to a man in Mombasa. My husband was a relative from my father's side. I had a big wedding [harusi] at Kanu Hall. It was grand. My husband gave me a dowry of money, Swahili furniture, jewellery and clothes. I flew to Mombasa where I lived for four years. I had two children. Then my marriage came to an end. I could not continue staying with my husband. He was chewing mira [an intoxicating substance] and then he started taking drugs. He lost everything as he could not work. I phoned my father. My father said: "I am sending you a plane ticket. Come home." Upon my return to Lamu, I practiced ada [female seclusion of three months and ten days following divorce or being widowed].
>
> After two months, I remarried. Someone had mentioned to my father that there was a suitable man for me. They came with a proposal. My father asked me and I accepted. He was a good man. My second wedding was small – just family. I had two more children from my second husband. He is presently in Nairobi working for a transport company. My youngest child is one and a half years old.

Until the time of her second marriage, Zeinub's life can be read as typical of her class and origins. The period between puberty and first marriage is the only time when young girls are strictly secluded. Owing to the practice of early marriages, this period is quite brief – usually young women marry between thirteen and sixteen years of age. Thus, "real" seclusion, mistakenly understood by outsiders as a homogenized practice followed by women throughout their lives, is only practised at one particular period, and that also for the purpose of ensuring women's virginity. In Zeinub's words:

> It is very important that during the time of her first marriage, a woman is a virgin. If she is not a virgin, no man will give her the dowry. It is shameful for the family. A man does not want to touch a woman who is not a virgin. Evidence has to be produced to show that

a woman is a virgin. After the marriage is consummated, the blood-stained sheet must be shown to the families of the bride and the groom.

Purity of a woman and its association with the honour-shame complex (Abu-Lughod, 1986; Mernissi, 1987) inform the practice of female seclusion among Muslim women in the Middle East and most parts of Africa, among other places. Seclusion, however, does not translate into inactivity or social confinement. In Lamu, for example, it is rare to come across a woman who is totally isolated. Thus there are other layered aspects that come to light as Zeinub's life unfolds situationally, with veiling forming a medium through which experiential knowledge is acquired over time and in varied spaces.

Through her first marriage, Zeinub secured a handsome dowry that belonged exclusively to her. That Zeinub's wedding took place at Kanu Hall (rented for the purpose), not at her parents' large stone house, and that she flew to Mombasa (as opposed to making an eight-hour bus ride) symbolized her middle-class status. Very few women in Lamu have these privileges, as the town's poverty has not spared the formerly wealthy Arabs.

One culturally specific value represented in Zeinub's narrative is the close ties that women continue to maintain with their natal families. Typically, a woman marries two or more times, maintaining her father's name at all times. It is not uncommon for a woman to initiate divorce on the grounds of infidelity or lack of provision. For Zeinub, loss of her husband's capacity to support her was a strong basis for divorce.

Zeinub's second marriage did not change her life a great deal, other than the fact that she had two more children. She continued to live with her parents, a practice not uncommon among Arab women of Lamu. So far, Zeinub's profile is that of a wife, a mother, and a daughter. She stayed home, looked after her children, and cooked and stitched with other women in the house. Learning through observation constitutes an integral part of women's lives in Lamu. Activities of meal preparation, sewing, applying henna, hairstyling and numerous beauty techniques, and making of *kofia* (the embroidered cap worn by males during prayers) take place in groups. This form of unstructured learning becomes part of the repertoire of embodied understanding of life situations, evident in the performance of *salat* (daily prayers). During this time, women's bodies are in repose, accompanied by ritualized movements of standing, sitting, and kneeling.

While these activities made Zeinub skilful in housework, domestic roles constituted only a part of her social space. In Lamu, intricate connections exist between households. This has partly to do with the architecture and spatial organization of the town. Its compact townscape contains alleys that structurally connect rather than separate households. With no automobiles, and only two main streets, mobility is not an issue. Gender segregation has prompted women to form strong kinship, neighbourly and peer ties. Thus, female-centred networks are activated in different contexts: everyday life situations, times of crisis and ritual occasions. Zeinub's explanation was echoed by other women:

> We women are perceived to be at home. People don't know what we do at home. We have our way of life that other people can't understand. We women support each other. When there is a wedding in town, we get involved. If there is a funeral we make it a point to go. We always visit people who are sick. You must have seen women walking to the hospital.

In the course of these interactions, women cultivate vital social relationships. In Zeinub's case, exposure to different households enabled her to gain knowledge of beauty care, expressed primarily through skin care and the application of henna on hands and feet and in hairstyles. Women are also exposed to sewing and cooking on a daily basis. These skills are not acquired in the context of structured time and space. They are developed in the course of relations with specific individuals. Knowing about other women's lives is in itself a process of exploration and learning that ultimately becomes part of embodied knowledge. Thus, being at home does not translate into constricted space.

Lamu women's recognition of restricted norms and modes is associated with an exploration of the possibilities embedded in female as well as in-between spaces. Negotiation of these spaces is informed by specific strategies. One woman spoke with me while washing dishes (woman's uncovered body at work) outside her house. When she said that she is at home and she likes it, I asked her: "How will you meet your marriage partner." She replied: "Right here. There are many men who pass by this alley." Other strategies include loosening of the veil after marriage, detours from female visiting when discreet interactions with males occur, greater leeway in moving around during weddings, and so on. These forms of negotiations amount to blurring of gendered boundaries. In this light, women's hospital visiting is strategic: although there are two gender-segregated wards, men and women often meet when visiting a common uncle or grandmother.

It is important to note that women's perception of change and negotiation spans a period of time as established traditions are reworked in such a manner as to cause the least disruption. Change and reconstruction of life, as Zeinub's narrative illustrates, require placing female bodies into spaces, activated and given meaning in relation to women's concerns. In other words, women's reinterpretation and reconstruction of cultural norms occur through the varied use of their bodies in space and in time: through work and through words; in repose and in movement; in its beautified and non-beautified forms. We continue with Zeinub's narrative for further insights.

Embodying Male Spaces: Working Outside the Home

> Since I was young, I used to observe how my mother would cut cloth and have a dress ready for me to wear in one day. Every Idd [Islamic festival], I would get a new dress – my sisters, too. I used to watch other women apply henna and do their hair. I even used to watch my brother do craft work at our shop. I did not even know that I was good with my hands until one day I decorated my sister's hands and legs (with henna). The design was beautiful. My brother saw it and said: "You are the person I am looking for. I want someone to run our crafts shop. How do you feel working outside the home." I thought, let me give it a try. The next thing I knew, I was working full time in the shop. My husband does not mind that I am working outside home – well, he can't object, he is not even here. It is all right so far as I keep myself covered.

Zeinub has been running her brother's store for the last two years. She earns a salary that she keeps in a bank account in her name. The store sells Swahili furniture and hand-carved crafts. Zeinub can carve intricate designs and make crafts herself, an age-old practice reserved primarily for men. Her knowledge of furniture is extensive enough to make her a good sales-woman. She is one of the handful of businesswomen in Lamu. Zeinub informed me that she enjoys her work and likes being out of the house: "There are too many women in our house. There is no point in my staying at home, too. My mother looks after the children and my sisters and sister-in-law do the cooking." In a place where the idea of upper-class Muslim women working outside the home was unthinkable a decade ago, Zeinub's relatively smooth entry into the labour force is of interest. The fact that she is able to apply home-based skills to the workplace shows that staying at home does not translate into idleness, an image associated with veiled women. The issue is availability of resources and not lack of skills.

Zeinub's family business caters primarily to tourists. This makes the craft industry seasonal, with little activity during the low tourist season from April to June. Unlike her brother, Zeinub does not organize her life solely around the craft shop. Introduction of varied pursuits has allowed her to redefine gender-segregated boundaries. To begin with, Zeinub has maintained the practice of female visiting. She receives guests while doing other work – an enactment of the domestic scene. Occasionally, she treats them to soft drinks. While Zeinub cannot leave the shop for "visits," she does not miss out on female-centred rituals: funerals, birth ceremonies, weddings, and homage paid on the occasion of women returning from *Haj* (pilgrimage) in Mecca. As noted above, these activities are crucial for the establishment and sustenance of women's networks.

Zeinub has been innovative in other ways. She sells seasonal fruits from her family *shamba* (farm) which is run by hired help, mostly by people of non-Arab origins. For example, during the mango season (April to June), she fills a large locally made basket with the fruit and keeps it at the entrance. Passersby cannot miss seeing it and the carefully selected large mangoes are sold quickly. Zeinub also caters to the female market by selling henna, *halud* (perfume), henna hair dye, and home-made coconut hair oil. These items are not displayed. They are kept in an inner shelf of the shop and women come to know about their availability through word of mouth, an example of female centred flow of information.

The extra cash is necessary, according to Zeinub: "In this day and age we all need money. Things are expensive and needs are many. Say you want to send your child to school. You need extra things: raincoat, backpack, lunchbox, pens, books – the list has no end." Families must travel to Mombasa to purchase imported items. The trip takes eight hours by bus and forty minutes by plane. The need to purchase school items has arisen as more and more Muslim boys and girls are acquiring formal secular education, introduced and run by the state. While school fees are subsidized, supplies and uniforms are not covered. Responsibility for these purchases falls on women.

School items, like other imported goods, are produced in the international market, which has penetrated Lamu in recent years. Lunch-boxes may come with labels: "Made in Korea"; "Made in China"; "Made in India." Very few items come from Europe or North America for the obvious reason that they are more expensive and beyond the reach of almost 90 per cent of the inhabitants. Zeinub's initiative, then, forms part of women's efforts to earn extra cash in an attempt to deal with additional demands placed on women to educate their children for a global economic market. Men feel increasingly trapped as tourism has undermined the development of the local economy to the extent that there are very few jobs outside the tourist sector. Hence, women's waged work is an important source of income.

Zeinub presents an image of the few women visibly present in the labour force. What is of special interest is that Zeinub has redefined and embodied the male public space. Her shop is not exclusively for tourists. It is a place where the vital gendered activity of female visiting takes place and where non-craft items catering to the local market are sold. Zeinub's innovative strategy of introducing local items constitutes resistance to the total and absolute encompassment of the shop into the fluctuating and unreliable tourist (foreign) industry. Furthermore, cash earned from the local products makes a difference. In Zeinub's words, "It means that my children do not have to walk back from school soaking wet. I have bought good raincoats for them. It means that my children are properly clothed; it means that they do not run out of books."

It is important to note that cash earned is converted into use value to cater to vital needs. For other women from the lower-class sector, cash earnings make a difference as to whether their families eat one, two, or three times a day. Veiled women of Lamu are creating a buffer zone during a time when the tourist industry has not met even a quarter of the expectations of the local people and when local trade in mangroves, fishing, and agriculture has all been appropriated by the state. Gaps and fissures caused by external control of the local economy are filled in by women. Zeinub's case is one example of women's initiatives in holding families together for daily survival. Ten years ago, women were not visible working outside home. It was unthinkable, a consensus expressed by both men and women: women's place is in the *zumbani* (house). In a subtle and a significant way, Zeinub has blurred what is ideologically constructed as a sharply demarcated boundary between male and female spheres. On slow days, she brings her younger children to the store for a short while. This is practical owing to the short distance between homes and shops. Given the compact nature of the town, an average distance between the two would be a ten-minute walk. Zeinub also brings "house work" to the store. Once, while cutting a piece of plain blue cloth spread on her office table, she said, "My daughter has outgrown her Madrasa school uniform. I am going to cut it here and when I go home, I will stitch it at night. It takes me one day to make a dress." Zeinub is very fond of stitching, which she learned through observation:

I just watched my mother. I never really tried it too much. My mother used to say: "You must learn stitching. It will be useful one day." I told my mother: "We will see when the time comes." When I started stitching, it just came naturally to me. I think I am good at stitching.

Continuity and change observed in Zeinub's life narrative reveal women's bodies at work, on the move, in silent posture and selectively engaged in the aesthetics of "dressing up." The underlying principle at work is embodied knowledge. As Zeinub explained it: "Not only do we women know how much to hold on to, what changes to bring, but also when, where, and in what manner."

Embodied /Disembodied Self

The importance of embodied understanding acquired in the process of "coming into being" was brought home to me following the death of a sister of Zeinub's friend, Farida. Zeinub informed me that it was necessary to provide financial help to Farida's family. I offered my donation to Zeinub upon which she said, "This is not the way to do it. We should go to her house and give it there." She did not say anything else. Like other women in Lamu, I was expected to learn by observation and make this knowledge part of my experience.

When we arrived at Farida's house, a couple of women were sitting out on mats that had been arranged in a circle. During such gatherings, the sitting place of women is an enclosed space created by mats strung between poles that are arranged in a circle. This space is activated through women's bodies engaged in reciting the Qur'an, saying prayers, and sitting silently in repose. Zeinub and I took our places among the women. When it was time to leave, Zeinub got up and hugged Farida and discreetly placed some money in her hands. I followed suit and did the same. It then dawned on me that this form of ritualized giving to a friend or a relative is not mere charity. It is an obligation informed by the principle of collective reciprocity that people fulfil towards each other. Assistance given varies according to class, ethnicity, status, and relationship. Whatever the case may be, a recipient invariably gives back in kind. When I gave a donation to Farida, she responded by holding my hand and saying a prayer. She prayed for *barakat* (prosperity and well-being) and peace. This form of reciprocity is critically important, as a person is never put into an absolute position of dependency. It is when one's presence is established culturally and ritually (Zeinub and I had first participated in the "ceremony") that the reciprocal act of giving occurs as part of an embodied experience.

The second incident of not being grounded in Lamu women's experiential understanding of situations occurred through my own initiative. I had made contact with a prominent male leader in Lamu by the name of Ali. I decided to listen to the *khutba* (lecture) on cleanliness that he was going to deliver on *Juma*, a special day of Friday prayer. As a woman, I knew that I would not be able to enter the mosque. Women in Lamu pray at home and have *dharasa* meetings at Madrasas or private homes. Ali suggested that I stand outside the mosque to hear what he had to say. As streets in Lamu are busy places, I could not catch all the words. I also found it frustrating that I could not see the face of the speaker and bodily gestures that complement verbal discourse. As I stood outside the mosque, I wondered whether women in Lamu felt excluded and "oppressed" in not being able to participate in male-centred activities. It was only after I shared my experiences with women that it occurred to me that I had attempted to participate in a "disembodied" activity. I did not have the cultural knowledge of the "body" to explore other possibilities of when, where and how women speak. Women did not feel that they were missing out on what I regarded as mainstream activity. Lamu women were content to participate in the relatively informal atmosphere of *dharasa* meetings when they engage in discussions – an activity that does not happen in a mosque. Thus, women in Lamu exercise agency and negotiate gendered and in-between spaces in the form of embodiment, individually as well as collectively.

Conclusion: Living Through Women's Bodies

Feminist/subalternist discourse on Muslim women posits two positions: (1) they cannot speak owing to their entrenchment in the double shadow of patriarchal and colonizing culture; (2) they reach a stature of "speaking subject" if they resort to subversive devices, activated at the margins. Their speaking status, in this view, only comes to light if feminist/subalternist scholarship can accommodate their agency through innovative strategies and special sensitivities. Zeinub's narrative, together with those of other Muslim women in Lamu, cannot be contained within this frame. The double patriarchal/colonizing gaze is not Zeinub's total experience. Her perception of colonizing culture is that it has affected and undermined Lamu society as a whole, a manifest expression of which is poverty. Women in Lamu do not consider themselves to be engaged in female-centred subversive activities. To view them in this light would be to impose outside perceptions on their lives and to assume that occurrences in the public male sphere are more important than private, female-centred activities.

PARIN A. DOSSA

As we have noted, women acquire multivalent knowledge through their bodies in specific spaces: home, visiting, participation in rituals, and, recently, engaging in waged work. The veiled cloak, a bodily attire, cannot be simply equated with women's "oppression." One may argue that gender-segregated societies, such as Lamu, are informed by asymmetrical relationships of power and that women do articulate their position as being lower (*chini*) than men. This form of discourse is embedded in complexities as it is continually reworked through the culture-specific practices of embodiment. And in this context women acquire culture-specific knowledge on how, when, and where to "speak." In the course of this essay, I have attempted to show that there is no simple equation between veiling/seclusion and women's oppression and lack of opportunities. Zeinub's narrative has shown that the veil is one means through which women occupy multiple spaces.

Beyond discourse and beyond practice, "subalternist feminism" calls for understanding women's positions that take into account women's embodied experiences in multiple spaces, reworked and reconstructed over time and as informed by culturally specific as well as in-between strategies. It is in this context that experiences of women in Lamu can best be understood.

Note

I would like to acknowledge my gratitude to the Social Sciences and Humanities Research Council of Canada for sponsoring this research. My special thanks to Sally Cole for her valuable comments.

References

Abu-Lughod, Lila. 1986 *Veiled Sentiments: Honor and Poetry in a Bedouin Society*. Berkeley: University of California Press.

—. 1993. *Writing Women's Worlds: Bedouin Stories*. Berkeley: University of California Press.

Behar, Ruth. 1993. *Translated Woman: Crossing the Border with Esperanza's Story*. Boston: Beacon Press.

Csordas, Thomas, ed. 1994. *Embodiment and Experience: The Existential Ground of Culture and Self*. Cambridge: Cambridge University Press.

Dossa, Parin. 1994. "Critical Anthropology and Life Stories: Case Study of Elderly Ismaili Canadians," *Journal of Cross-Cultural Gerontology* 9: 335-54.

—. 1997. "Reconstruction of the Ethnographic Field Site: Mediating Identities, Case Study of a Bohra Muslim Woman in Lamu (Kenya)," *Women's Studies International Forum* 20, 4: 505-15.

—. 1999. "On Law and Hegemonic Moments: Looking Beyond the Law Towards Subjectivities of Subaltern Women," in D. Lacombe and D. Chunn, eds., *Law as Gendering Practice: Canadian Perspectives*. Cambridge: Cambridge University Press.

Emberley, Julia V. 1993. *Thresholds of Difference: Feminist Critique, Native Women's Writings, Postcolonial Theory*. Toronto: University of Toronto Press.

Enslin, Elizabeth. 1994. "Beyond Writing: Feminist Practice and the Limitations of Ethnography," *Cultural Anthropology* 9, 4: 537-68.

Mbote, William N. 1986. "Planning for Conservation of Historic Towns and Monuments," workshop/conference. Nairobi: Office of the President, Kenya.

Mernissi, Fatima, 1987 [1975]. *Beyond the Veil: Male-Female Dynamics in Modern Muslim Society*. Bloomington: Indiana University Press.

Minh-ha, Trinh T. 1989. *Woman Native Other*. Bloomington: Indiana University Press.

Nagari, John. 1986. *Conservation, Regional Planning and Development*. Nairobi: Physical Planning Development.

Nagata, Judith. 1995. "Modern Malay Women and the Message of the Veil," in W. J. Karim ed., *'Male' and 'Female' in Developing Southeast Asia*. Oxford: Berg Publishers, 101-20.

Narayan, Kirin. 1993. "How Native is a 'Native' Anthropologist?" *American Anthropologist* 95: 671-86.

Ong, Aihwa. 1995. "Women Out of China: Traveling Tales and Traveling Theories in Postcolonial Feminism," in R. Behar and D. Gordon, eds., *Women Writing Culture*. Berkeley: University of California Press, 350-72.

Personal Narratives Group, ed. 1989. *Interpreting Women's Lives: Feminist Theory and Personal Narratives*. Bloomington: Indiana University Press.

Scott, Joan W. 1992. "Experience," in J. Butler and J. Scott, eds., *Feminists Theorize the Political*. New York: Routledge, 22-40.

Siravo, F. and A. Pulver. 1981. *Planning Lamu: Conservation of an East African Seaport*. Nairobi: National Museums of Kenya.

Stacey, Judith. 1988. "Can There Be a Feminist Ethnography?" *Women's Studies International Forum* 11, 1: 21-27.

Strobel, Margaret. 1979. *Muslim Women in Mombasa: 1890-1975*. New Haven: Yale University Press.

Vincent, Joan. 1994. "On Law and Hegemonic Moments: Looking Behind the Law in Early Modern Uganda," in M. Lazarus-Black and S.F. Hirch, eds., *Contested States: Law, Hegemony and Resistance*. New York: Routledge, 118-37.

Visweswaran, Kamala. 1994. *Fictions of Feminist Ethnography*. Minneapolis: University of Minnesota Press.

Wolf, Diane, ed. 1996. *Feminist Dilemmas in Fieldwork*. Boulder, Colo: Westview Press.

ELEVEN

OFF THE FEMINIST PLATFORM IN TURKEY:
CHERKESS GENDER RELATIONS

Gönül Ertem

I N an essay written for International Women's Day, a Cherkess intellectual suggests that

> the Cherkess woman cannot be thought of in isolation *vis-à-vis* the new concepts and trends in the world concerning "the woman." The Cherkess woman also experiences all the problems that women in the culture of the country in which she lives do, and [she] struggles. She carries on her struggle functionally sometimes in the family, other times, if she works outside, in her work environment. (Bir, 1995)

Bir emphasizes that Cherkess women realize they must work and be economically independent if they are to reap the benefits of contemporary Turkish society as much as men do. She asserts that Cherkess women share this awareness with other women in Turkey; however, she observes, "among Cherkess women this awareness has formed *very early*" (ibid., emphasis added). With such an asserted temporal lag, she turns to the status of women in general. Such vagueness is characteristic of the few published opinions written by Cherkess women on women's position in Cherkess society. My project in this paper is to seek culturally and historically specific answers to Cherkess women's approach to women's issues. I draw on my field research to examine Cherkess gender relations and to discuss the ways in which Cherkess and Turkish agendas have historically been constituted.

Since the 1980s Turkish feminists have been determined to reform the terms of women's participation in public as fully autonomous beings who are entitled to their own bodies and lives. Despite the universal premise and effects of feminist politics, women's mobilization around the cause of female autonomy is limited. The Turkish feminist platform propagating the reformation of public and private spheres has been disputed by the Cherkess and used to confirm ethnic difference. The asserted difference deems the Turkish feminist agenda irrelevant for Cherkess women and legitimizes their disengagement from it. Divergences between trajectories of women who share the same public/national space are not new. The rich international feminist literature produced since the 1980s by groups of women, such as women of colour, Third World women, and lesbians, as a response to the universalist formulation of feminism is hard to miss. My concern, then, is not to lament the improbability of a "universal sisterhood" in the Turkish context but to rethink, or simply to ponder, the implications of sisterly non-alignments for the success of women's specific and separate agendas. My descriptions in the following pages will situate the divergent trajectories of Turkish and Cherkess women *vis-à-vis* the modernist project of nationalism and the post-Cold War ethnic revivalism in Turkey. The gendered tension embedded in the Turkish context will, I hope, lead us to highlight, once again, the significance of feminist politics as an obligation, just as we acknowledge feminism as a culturally specific experience. It is with this contention that I will make the soft-spoken struggle of Cherkess women public.

My ethnographic example comes from the Cherkess of Eskişehir, a city of approximately 500,000 people in central-western Turkey, where I conducted my doctoral research between 1992 and 1994.[1] During this period, I also travelled with the Cherkess to other towns in Turkey, such as Istanbul, Ankara, and Kütahya, to attend events of cultural and political significance and to interview various leaders of the Cherkess national organizations or publications. My interest in Cherkess community politics and my ties with them have continued through research, visits (in 1995, 1997, and 1998), and correspondence.

The historical process that has re-formed the social and cultural identities of ethnic groups in Turkey and constituted modern Turkish identity is complex. During the past 130 years of their participation in the Ottoman imperial and Turkish nation-building processes, the Cherkess have been impacted by Islamist, socialist and ethno-nationalist discursive movements while contending for their distinct identity overtly or covertly. Like the majority of Turkish nationals, they are Muslims. They helped shape and became integrated into the modern Turkish state. However, since the Turkish nation was imagined to unify around a "Turkish" identity, as with other ethnic groups, Cherkess participation has had no such name. In addition, due to the restructuring of the political and legal system in the Turkish nation-state in the 1920s and the increasing hegemony of the national institutional framework, the foundation of Cherkess *Xabze* (tradition) has gradually eroded. By the 1990s the unintended consequences of the community's historical blending with Turkish society had created strong feelings of unease and a strong desire to preserve distinct Cherkess social relations (Ertem, 1999). I was repeatedly told that Cherkess ethnicity is "intent to resist cultural assimilation."

Nonetheless, whereas the national political arena in Turkey has, since the early 1980s, become a site of ongoing struggle for various politics of identity led by the Kurds, Alevis, and Islamists, ethnic Cherkess mobilization is tenuous. Especially in gendered politics Cherkess women are visibly absent, despite their negotiations against gender asymmetry within their communities. The ethnically undifferentiated national identity at the foundation of the Turkish nation has undeniably silenced Cherkess women and limited their participation in women's movements in Turkey. However, Cherkess women's non-alignment in the politics of gender in the national arena is not only an effect of their "muted" ethnic position (E. Ardener, 1975; S. Ardener, 1975). Ethnic loyalty no doubt requires Cherkess women, along with men, to remain distant from or even to react against feminist agendas by publicly advocating an essentializing discourse of identity, often at the cost of expediting assimilation among younger generations, particularly women.

In the 1990s, modernity is the hegemonic discourse of *liberty* in Turkey. Many Cherkess are critical of the contaminating effects of "Western-oriented" modernity, which is at the foundation of contemporary Turkish society. However, the national will for modernity has pressured the Cherkess to re-evaluate Cherkess social relations through the idiom of modernity. Cherkess women's distance from gendered national struggles is thus grounded in a cultural concept of modernity, which states that "the Cherkess culture is already modern." A non-segregated Cherkess public sphere constitutes the foundation of Cherkess modernity. Cherkess *Xabze* (tradition) has codified *the style of* and *places at which* gender tension is enacted without segregating men and women, as is customary in many patriarchal or Islamic societies. This distinct cultural feature provides a firm discursive ground for the Cherkess to subvert relations of power embedded in ethnically diverse but ideologically homogeneous national contexts such as Turkey. This reversed hierarchy has generated Cherkess women's non-alignment *vis-à-vis* the feminist platform in Turkey. How Cherkess gender relations are lived in cultural *and* national publics in modern Turkey must be understood, but first I turn to the development of Turkish women's trajectory.

The Modernist Public Sphere of Turkey

The Turkish nation is a classic case of modernist desire and its transformative power. The nation-state was founded in 1923, following the defeat of the Ottoman Empire in World War I, on the constructive premise of modernization (Bozdoğan and Kasaba, 1997; Lewis, 1979; Shaw and Shaw, 1977). Central to modernization was gender equality. As the leader of the nationalist revolution, Mustafa Kemal's reasoning with custom exemplifies this vividly:

> In some places I see women throwing a cloth or a towel or something of the sort over their heads, covering their faces and their eyes. When a man passes by, they turn away, or sit huddled on the ground. What is the sense of this behavior? Gentlemen, do the mothers and daughters of a civilized nation assume this curious attitude, this barbarous posture? It makes the nation look ridiculous: it must be rectified immediately! (in Abadan, 1967: 83)

The rectification was initiated by Civil Code reforms (1926) and suffrage, which gave women the right to participate in regional (1930) and national (1934) elections. These republican reforms were considered "a landmark of progressive reform" since they "liberated women from an Islamic order based on patriarchal norms" (Tekeli, 1990: 270). They undeniably changed the social fabric most by granting legitimacy to women's public presence and participation. Prior to these reforms, women's public presence in the Ottoman Empire was restricted by imperial edicts, which enforced gender segregation and reinforced gender avoidance by regulating women's clothing according to their religious affiliation, as well as the times and terms of their visibility in public spaces with men (Göle, 1996; Şeni, 1995). Thus, Ottoman women's means of participation in the public sphere was primarily informal.

The Kemalist public sphere, on the other hand, was designed to be egalitarian and gender-blind. Early reformers actively encouraged women to participate in public life. As long as women shared the will to modernize – themselves and, by extension, the nation – they were encouraged to further their education and pursue a professional career with equal pay. Early on, a critical number of women "endorsed the modernist reforms earnestly" and took the opportunity to become professionals (Arat, 1997: 100). Following suffrage, eighteen women parliamentarians (4.5 per cent of the total) joined the parliament in 1935 (Abadan, 1967). Jayawardena (1986: 38) emphasizes that this was "the highest number of women deputies in Europe at that time, when many European countries, including France and Italy, did not even have [a] female franchise" (see Tekeli, 1981: 299). Over time, the proportional representation of women parliamentarians declined, however, remaining at 2 per cent since 1946 (Arat, 1996: 30).

To modernize the private sphere, modernist Kemalists reformed the Ottoman Civil Code of 1917, basing their reforms on the Swiss model. The 1926 Civil Code abolished polygamy and marriage by proxy and granted all women of Turkey equal rights in divorce and inheritance. Kemalists also gave civil marriage precedence over religious marriage, which was thus stripped of all but its symbolic power. Such secularization of the Civil Code was a first for the people of Turkey in three respects: (1) it categorically delegitimized any conjugal union that might have been based on Islamic custom or scripture; (2) it brought a previously private communal and familial affair such as marriage under the jurisdiction of the state (Starr, 1992); and (3) it firmly recognized the conjugal family as a seat of modern power within which spousal authority was granted to men (Sirman, 1989).

Presumably "the newest in continental Europe and the one which exhibited the highest degree of respect for equality of men and women" (Şener, 1985: 416), the Swiss law adopted by the Kemalist reformers nonetheless gave legitimacy to a gendered power hierarchy within the conjugal union by constituting the male (husband) as the head of the family. By law, the husband is the provider, whereas the woman's primary duty is domestic. As "the head of the family," a man has the right to choose the family's place of residence. "The husband does not have to reside in the house belonging to his wife. It is his lawful right to have a house of his own, even if he resides in his wife's house at the beginning. His weak financial condition cannot be an excuse to deprive him of this right" (Şener, 1985: 409). Women's work *outside* the home is contingent upon her husband's consent. Parental authority over children is shared; however, "where the parents do not agree, the father's decision prevails" (Şener, 1985: 415).

Granting each and every man in a marital union the title of "family head," the new law thus paved the way for *the breakup of hierarchies among men* in a patriarchal order. It gave younger men autonomy *vis-à-vis* their fathers or uncles who traditionally oversaw, along with their spouses, the economic and social well-being of younger couples in their families or lineage. This legal coming of age endowed young married men (over eighteen years of age) of patriarchal households with the authority to become family heads themselves (cf. Sirman, 1990). Such legal subjugation of women and children in the family to their husband-father signals the creation of the modernist private sphere (Sirman, 1989).

The effects of this legal restructuring of Turkish society have been varied. Increasing ethnographic evidence indicates the various ways in which women of different ethnicities and classes gain awareness of legal rights that the Kemalist reforms have granted them (e.g., Ertürk, 1995; Öncü, 1981; Starr, 1997). On the other hand, the frequency with which men appropriate or evoke their legal advantages in family disputes has not been ascertained. However, the tension between modernist national principles, which compel men to condemn gender discrimination, and their dominant *pederşahi* (patriarchal) values has been well documented. For instance, Arat's *The Patriarchal Paradox* (1989) indicates that women's aspirations for a political career have largely been due to the encouragement or support of their fathers, husbands, or brothers. Their success also requires the support of male colleagues.

Kemalist emancipation has often been predicated on loyalty to hierarchies of the private sphere. In order to steer honourably away from the "potential spouse" or "loose woman" status, women and men who partake in public life domesticate it by evoking kinship ties, by conjuring up images of brothers and sisters, mothers and sons, uncles and aunts (Arat, 1989; Kandiyoti, 1991; Kandiyoti, 1997). The transference of kinship relations to formal, professional relations suggests a societal unease with sexual tension and its potential. And the alleviation of this through a tender reinforcement of the hierarchies of the private sphere can be debilitating for women who seek to exert their potential in public life. Women politicians whom Arat interviewed were indignant that they were either treated as *bacı* or *abla* (sister and older sister, respectively), regardless of the age difference between the speakers, or were masculinized with the title "Mr. Politician" (Arat, 1989: 106). Women in activist groups of the 1960s and 1970s were similarly domesticated and desexualized by male activists as either *bacı*, which evokes gendered sibling hierarchies, or *yoldaş* (comrade), which strips partisans of their sexual identities (Berktay, 1995). During the heat of Kemalist modernization, as people from all walks of life and traditions encountered each other in ever-expanding urban publics, metaphors of kinship permeated the society from the marketplace to the parliament. Such *domestication* has had considerable impact on women's exertion of power in public.

For educated urban women – primarily college professors, students, and professionals – who were growing up or active participants in the politically charged atmosphere of the 1960s and 1970s, the Kemalist public sphere was increasingly stifling. In the aftermath of the 1980 military coup, when all forms of extra-parliamentary political activity were banned, these women started gathering at homes for seemingly traditional tea parties (Sirman,

1989; Tekeli, 1990). Here they would create a forum where they could discuss gendered concerns that had been muffled in their respective political and professional organizations. A feminist discourse was soon carried into the public sphere to address these concerns independently of their now defunct organizations. The domesticated and desexualizing public sphere and the hierarchical private sphere became targets of the nascent feminist discourse.

An Emerging Feminist Public Sphere

The public emergence of an autonomous feminist discourse initiated the post-1980 democratization process (Sirman, 1989; Tekeli, 1990). Post-1980s Turkish feminism has carved itself a political space in opposition to the women's rights discourse of the previous decades, called "state feminism" (Tekeli, 1990), and its offshoots exemplified by the Turkish left (Berktay, 1995). The civic rights that women of Turkey gained through the process of nation-formation had emancipated them; however, by privileging the advancement of the society and the nation, they kept women's liberation at bay (Kandiyoti, 1987). Kemalist women are considered to be complicit with the gendered legal and social order for their enthusiastic participation in the modernization project, for, as mothers, they sacrificed their daughters' aspirations. For post-1980s Turkish feminists, an autonomous female personhood, a woman in control of her identity, including her sexuality, is fundamental.

In Tekeli's words, "In contrast to their mothers who were socialised into Kemalism," these women had participated "in the leftist movements before 1980, where they learned politics and where they acquired a sense of solidarity, but where they were unable to politicise the women's question" (Tekeli, 1990: 276). They worked hard to be equal partners in their political and professional organizations; however, women's issues were consistently considered "subordinate to questions of class and revolution .... [S]ince they were going to be disappearing of their own accord in the future, burdening the agenda with such secondary issues could only have served to distract attention from the main tasks at hand" (Berktay, 1995: 250). In her critical essay, "Has Anything Changed in the Outlook of the Turkish Left on Women?", Berktay exemplifies the ways in which women themselves, while participating side by side with their male counterparts, were both sidestepped in the decision-making processes and subjected to partisan men's paternalistic desire to mould them into colourless and mute comrades. Women's marginalization in the leftist organizations was often justified with a rhetoric that depicted women as inherently vulnerable to the attractions of a "bourgeois" order, thus possessing a "natural" tendency to betray the cause of socialism. At other times, women's criticisms were dismissed by blaming individual revolutionaries for being patriarchal due to their upbringing (Berktay, 1995).

After a year of meetings disguised as tea gatherings and a few public forums, the nascent feminist discourse went public through a page in a weekly magazine, *Somut*, where, 'according to assertively feminist principles,' every woman could write and be published. In *Somut*

> more than twenty different authors covered such topics as abortion, Women's Day, molestation, women and advertising, the ideology inimical to women in folk proverbs. There were also film reviews, stories, testimonies by women about their experiences and news items. Both from readers' letters and from the strong reactions of articles that appeared in other publications, it became clear that page four of *Somut* attracted more attention than the rest of the magazine. (Tekeli, 1990: 279)

This first feminist platform survived only four months, until May 1983, after which the unsympathetic new management of the writers' collective that owned the magazine withdrew their support. This short-lived public visibility of feminists met with strong reactions from all the competing ideologies in the national political arena – Kemalists, leftists, and conservatives alike – who shared an anti-feminist platform in spite of their political differences. Despite their small numbers (Tekeli estimates it to be in the hundreds), throughout the 1980s feminists continued taking public issue with the subjection of female identity to the well-being of the nation and its patriarchies. After a year of gestation, they re-emerged in public through a foundation called *Kadın Çevresi* (Women's Circle). *Kadın Çevresi's* goals were to promote research and original and translated publications, to develop feminist understanding and thought in Turkey, to address women's concerns and to initiate campaigns to improve structural conditions for gender equity. In the meantime, an increasingly feminist monthly magazine, *Kadınca* (Womanly), was enjoying tremendous popular support among middle-class women.

Kadınca's playful style was in stark contrast to the radical and rebellious style of feminists. For instance, on a special page, *Kadınca* "put hot pepper" on the lips of public figures to show their disapproval of discriminating remarks, attitudes, or behaviour or "kissed" those whose behaviour or words deserved feminist approval. In *Kadınca* editor Duygu Asena's words, the magazine's approach to feminism was *egalitarian*, rather than *radical* or *socialist*. *Kadınca* depicted men as "fellow victims" who suffered as much as women within male-dominated Turkish society: "Our men are blind with customs and morals. They never raise their heads to see the truth. Once they [are] awakened, we will probably be liberated all together" (Öztürkmen, 1998: 281).

Nascent radical feminists and academics were initially critical of *Kadınca's* tender approach to feminism and "its consumerist advertisements and occasional use of sexuality on its covers" (ibid., 275). Gradually, however, its role in popularizing women's issues and circulating them "to circles beyond the reach of the feminist groups" was recognized (ibid., 285). Feminists discussed various aspects of male domination, feminist theory, and politics in journals such as *Feminist* and *Kaktus*, and translated books about feminist experiences in other countries. Asena's books, *Kadının Adı Yok* (The Woman Has No Name) and *Aslında Aşk da Yok* (And Love Does Not Exist, Either), became bestsellers. These accounts "showed that ignorance in sexual matters serves to ensure female virtue and innocence, and thereby to preserve woman's social inferiority, and her compliance to male authority" (Erol, 1992: 115).

Thus, a proliferating feminist platform steadily put numerous feminist issues on the public agenda. Feminists were able to mobilize significant numbers of women to protest in rallies or sign petitions in order to expose and protest against the inequalities of the Civil Code and contradictions with which the national public sphere was saturated. By the 1990s, many women's reticence to speak up publicly about inviolably private issues such as domestic violence and sexuality was broken. Also, many women had put aside their "symbolic shield," donned for fear that they would be publicly perceived as seductive and inviting, and which consisted of dark dresses, modestly cropped hair, faces without make-up, and a solemn disposition (Tekeli, cited in Erol, 1992: 15). The new professional woman was smart, attractive, and sexy. A magazine portrayed a sociology professor on its cover. In between the discussion of her comments on current issues, the reporter commented on her fiery red long hair and lipstick, remarking how different this new type of professor was from those of his college days.

Feminists succeeded in opening up a discursive space in the national sphere for women. As Arat has recently suggested, "in their search for autonomy," along with their strong devotion to "universal human rights that go beyond local traditions and provincial moralities," they furthered the Kemalist project of modernity (Arat, 1997: 109). Cherkess women, however, repudiate the effects of the feminist platform as a component of Western-oriented Turkish modernity, which, for them, is contaminating and undesirable. While they publicly emphasize the contemporary value of authentic Cherkess relations, a strong gender negotiation continues in mixed-gender gatherings between men and women. "Mute" by ethnic positioning but remarkably vocal within the community, this soft-spoken struggle focuses on the private sphere and intimacy between husbands and wives. The latter in particular is at the heart of the feminist concerns among Cherkess women of Turkey, to whose struggle we now turn.

Turkish Modernity and Cherkess Ethnicity

In 1995, I attended a meeting of the women's group at the cultural association for the Cherkess community in Eskişehir. A year had passed since my fieldwork, and now I was back primarily to discuss with various people in the community how I was beginning to interpret what I had learned and experienced during my fieldwork in 1993-94. My inquisitive attempts to understand the meaning of Cherkess modernity, and *the elevated position* and *freedom* of the Cherkess women of which I was constantly told during my fieldwork, in contrast to traditional Turkish women, must have disturbed one of the women in the room. Her sudden shrill utterance pierced the restrained analytical tone of our chat: "*We have* our (many) cousins and brothers, isn't this liberating?"[2] Nermin hanım's outburst begs contemplation for a number of reasons. Since the sudden accessibility of ancestral lands following the breakup of the Soviet Union (1989), the Cherkess community had been excited about the prospect of establishing Cherkess sovereign states in the North Caucasus. This was a historic opportunity for the Cherkess to end their "muted" existence in diaspora (E. Ardener, 1975). Many Cherkess increasingly felt their fundamental values erode due to the prevalent effects of modernist structures and ideologies in Turkey as well as the politicized Islamism that has, in the last decade, reached young Cherkess minds.

High hopes of Cherkess nationalists for a mass repatriation movement, however, were soon dashed. Visits to ancestral lands and encounters with long-lost kin indicated that the 130 years of separation since their forced exodus had "dismantled" Cherkess ethnicity "beyond recognition" (Shami, 1995). It seemed clear that Cherkess sovereignty, which had been imagined for so long to provide a secure link to the future, was much too complicated to make real. Complications were not limited to economic, social, and ideological disparities between the scattered communities in diaspora and those in the Caucasus. In addition, many young Cherkess women in Turkey were particularly reluctant to repatriate. Patriotic feelings towards the Caucasus became an issue in romantic courtship. Young adult males wanted to see at least traces of a historical consciousness of the *Sürgün* (the Cherkess exodus) in their female counterparts. Men walked away from their *kashens*, sweethearts, disheartened due to the women's determination to stay and build their future in Turkey. Cherkess women increasingly married out of their ethnic group. Social relations promulgated in contemporary Turkish society constituted strong competition for the *Xabze*, the corpus of Cherkess tradition that carefully coded interpersonal relations and the spatial and social boundaries and styles through which power and authority (by age, gender, lineage, or merit) are exerted. Without the structural support of traditional institutions, Cherkessness was now primarily defined with respect to its non-segregated public sphere and its coded rules of respect and restraint.

This is the context in which I understood Nermin hanım's outburst. Yet I was momentarily puzzled since the relations she listed (all males) to indicate the liberated status of Cherkess women were based on kin ties. They were not relations established by the free will of women but as members of an extended family or lineage. How did the Cherkess embody gender equality? How did my presumed modernity, or my liberated personhood as a Turkish urbanite who has long lived in the United States, intersect with Cherkess gendered images of personhood or invoke this Cherkess woman's outburst? Most importantly, in what aspects of their gendered lives did Cherkess women feel most distanced from nationally expressed feminist concerns? The remaining sections of this paper seek locally situated answers to these questions.

Peer Publics and Sexualized Subjects

Cherkess cultural spaces and publics illustrate a distinct approach to gendered relations. A key principle in all interpersonal relations among the Cherkess is *resmiyet* (formality), the prevalent and highly cherished style in which *saygı* (respect) for an individual is expressed. *Resmiyet* is particularly noticeable in public relations between generations and sexes. Intricate cultural practices of romance and avoidance constitute Cherkess individuals primarily as sexual beings driven by mutual attraction. Sexual tension is regulated through ritualized romance practices of *kashenlik* (courtship) that reinforce sexual aspects of male and female identities among *unrelated* people.[3] Among sexually mature *and related* people, on the other hand, there is a strict observance of formality, which is traditionally reinforced through *avoidance practices*, called *adet* (custom).

In the Kemalist public spaces of the wider Turkish society, however, interpersonal relations, as we have seen, are grounded in the sexual identities of individuals whose ties are then reframed in terms of the desexualized, kin-based relations of the domestic sphere. Due to such an extension of the idiom of domestic relations to embrace the presumably formal and impersonal relations of the public sphere, the modern Turkish public sphere provides a protective shield for Cherkess women to participate in society and fulfil their economic and political aspirations. It also validates the asexual aspects of a Cherkess woman's identity that in the Cherkess public sphere is constrained. The desexualized modern public sphere in Turkey thus accommodates Cherkess women, who are raised to be independent and strong, as many Cherkess assert with pride, and yet who are, paradoxically, expected to devote their post-marital energies to the domestic sphere within their ethnic group. Cherkess women's "feminist" trajectory diverges from Turkish feminism in this regard. Whereas the gender-blind and domesticated Kemalist public sphere is accommodating for the Cherkess *Xabze*, the autonomous and sexually conscious feminist woman threatens its gendered internal order.

Semerkho: Joking Courtship

A Cherkess woman's primary feminist concern is to redefine her identity beyond sexuality, which is reinforced and simultaneously regulated through the highly coded cultural institution of courtship. Cherkess courtship is a stylized form of socialization that primarily takes place at mixed-gender gatherings called *zexes*. The most cited occasion for *zexes* is "a visiting girl" from outside the community. The young people gather as soon as they hear of such a "guest girl's" presence in town and visit her at the host family's house. An older member of the group is seated at the head of the room and takes the role of the *thamade*, the wise one. The conversation and interactions are guided by the *thamade*. *Zexes* may last all night, with games, dances, and music, during which the *thamade* mediates and maintains the cultural boundaries if propriety is breached. He opens the floor for the youth to express "feelings" and "thoughts" about the guest girl and officiates a publicly performed courtship. Men use their poetic prowess to steal women's attention. Women respond accordingly. Such informality, or verbal intimacy, is described as *semerkho*, in Turkish *şaka*, or joking. Outside the particular settings at which *semerkho* is performed, formality prevails. In public, say in the morning following a *zexes*, there can be no clear indication that a particular young woman and man flirted the night before. The two people resume a respectful and formal relationship. As a cultural practice, through which heterosexual desire and its expression are legitimized and reinforced, *semerkho* is a joking courtship and flirtation. In English, "flirting" elucidates this practice; however, the Cherkess vehemently argue against the use of the Turkish term *flört* to describe it. In Turkish *flört* implies dating – a one-on-one romantic relationship between two people – and may include physical intimacy, whereas the Cherkess in Eskişehir do not approve of physical intimacy.

Zexes are commonly for people between the ages of sixteen and twenty-two; however, since there is no stigma attached to unmarried people, and since members of Cherkess society stay unmarried at least until their mid-twenties, people of widely ranging ages can get together for such "fun." Since I was, for practical purposes, single during my fieldwork, I became a subject of *semerkho* at my own farewell party. My departure set the theme for the *semerkho*, which was directed to me by the older men in the group. This was a cross-generational *zexes*, since the Cherkess youth in their twenties were there along with my thirty-something friends. While my two eligible male friends were jokingly commenting on my sad departure, the younger male guests participated by muffled laughs. At one point a younger female guest asked my permission to respond in my name to Kanbek's lamenting song. In addition to my unfamiliarity with such public courtship, due to long years spent in the U.S., my song repertoire was also considerably impoverished. So I happily let my young friend sing for me a song that inquired why the beloved has not come forward until this moment if his feelings are real. With this song the evening turned into an interactive teaching session for me, the anthropologist, as mediated by *semerkho* and laughter. Younger participants thus found the means to participate without being disrespectful. Giving me their farewell gifts, my guests then departed, leaving me pondering. The next day I described my evening to another age-mate of mine. He relished my story, then jovially disapproved of my being the subject of *semerkho* at my own house. This was not right.

Zexes are an opportunity for culturally prescribed courtship during which formality is temporarily removed. The removal of formality is mediated by the cultural construct of *semerkho*, joking. Under the rubric of *semerkho*, unmarried Cherkess men and women, and to a certain extent married men, are allowed to verbalize cross-gender attraction within cultural propriety. *Semerkho* operates in the emotional borderlands of interest, attraction, and desire through ritualized simulations that foster gender ideals among the Cherkess. It is the medium through which a young person expresses emotions and thoughts, dares to cross boundaries or builds walls around his

At a Cherkess wedding, 1959. Courtesy of Saime hanım.

or her inner self.

Semerkho constitutes Cherkess men and women as sexual subjects whose potential union is cherished and jokingly negotiated at *zexes*. Women who are astute and exhibit strong will in *semerkho* negotiations are valued; however, in Eskişehir their success may not go beyond prominence at *zexes* gatherings. A woman who in the 1970s was an active and engaging participant at *zexes*, and who wanted to marry into the Cherkess community, said "Perhaps we became too familiar for each other. None of my relations went beyond *semerkho*." She then agreed to marry someone whose father was Cherkess but who had been raised in a Turkish cultural context. Another woman of the same generation remembered her own verbal skills to challenge men by repeatedly saying, with a mischievous smile, "I was good!" She could not find her heart's desire either, and prefers to remain unmarried.

The public representation of gender attraction is highlighted most distinctly in Cherkess dances. Cherkess dances are couple dances and simulate heterosexual unions in which chastity, elegance, pride, and respect prevail. Women smoothly glide over the dance floor, like pheasants, approaching and guiding the men with their eyes, heads, and hands. Men, like eagles, turn around the women, always following them attentively with, again, their eyes and heads. Men's arms guard and attempt to redirect women, while their stomping and kicking feet express feelings of passionate interest. Dances also allude to the boundaries of a couple's relationship. "Do whatever you like around the girl," a young friend's father had advised him while growing up, "but never fall down on your knees for her." Since socio-economic cleavages among the youth have increased, due especially to women's education and work, dance floors are frequently not the place where women lay eyes on their potential spouses. Dances have increasingly become competitive performances – "just fun," as many women state. Women often resent, however, that in dancing men go off on their own, turning their backs to women and performing for the community instead of harmonizing with them. Older women criticize younger ones for dancing like men by jumping and kicking around instead of gliding with subtle steps on their toes. Regardless, non-segregated gender relations, as in *zexes*, *semerkho*, and couple dances, are the backbone of Cherkess culture. They publicly signify and authenticate ethnic difference. On every occasion, even while resting on road trips, the ever-ready accordion comes out of its box and the dancing and *semerkho* begin.

Public Privacy *and* Autonomy

For the Cherkess, romance, as subtly expressed in dances, verbalized by way of *semerkho*, and lived among one's peer group, is a cherished and essential aspect of personhood. Nonetheless, sexuality beyond chaste romance is publicly repressed and completely private. This privacy is expected from the time of a couple's initial courtship. Once a couple commits to one another, they are expected to maintain a complete physical and emotional distance in public. *Semerkho* continues with others, especially for males whose culturally prescribed identity is to bring gender attraction to the fore.

Among all people whose relations entail sexual intimacy, respect is expressed as formality through practices of avoidance. Avoidance keeps the existence of sexual intimacy out of the "public" eye.[4] This "public," however, is kin, primarily the lineage of the husband. According to *Xabze*, couples are expected to refrain from interactions with each other as well as with their children while in the presence of the husband's lineage, particularly of its male members. Strict regulations of social interactions, especially verbal communication, between fathers-in-law and daughters-in-law are vivid in the collective memory, and at least symbolically observed. Younger women are increasingly critical of this familial formality. A woman in her twenties sadly observed her newly married uncle and his bride during their short visit before their honeymoon. "They acted as if they were strangers," she commented.

It is also *yemuko* (immodest) to interact with one's child or spouse in a way that suggests parental intimacy while in-laws are in the vicinity. Although urban public spaces provide considerable flexibility to a family in this regard, chance encounters with a person who needs to be avoided are not improbable. A young man remembered in tears of laughter such an encounter from his childhood. His father had taken him to the hospital due to small injuries from a bike accident. He and his father were walking to their car, he in his father's arms, enjoying the special attention from his father and the care that he had just received from the hospital staff. Suddenly, he said, his father dropped him upon seeing his uncle come around the block. The uncle then reprimanded his father for dropping an injured child in order to observe respect, but the deed was done.

Brothers and sisters avoid participating in the same social events that bring their sexual identities to the fore. However, modern public spaces do not always accommodate avoidance between siblings, who in the past would live their sexualized identities exclusively at *zexes* or in private rooms where Cherkess young women received their male guests. A Cherkess friend and I once ran into his sister while looking for a shady table in a café on the river. She was sitting with a young man, one of her *kashens*, at one of the tables. We awkwardly exchanged greetings due to physical proximity and moved to a table further down the strip. They soon left.

Such a web of restrained relations among members of the nuclear family has created an *effect* of public autonomy for all its female members since, in the ethnically blind Turkish public sphere, they can interact with others as autonomous individuals, personally and professionally (cf. Olson, 1982). Cherkess residential units in urban Eskişehir are commonly for nuclear families, sometimes with an additional senior parent. This enables Cherkess women who work in the domestic sphere to weave through neighbour-hoods to visit various family members and friends. Given such freedom of movement, for most Cherkess women individual autonomy has not emerged as an aspiration. For them, the asexual public sphere of the Turkish national context is accommodating, if not liberating. Cherkess women's struggle, in contrast, resides in matters of the private sphere.

As noted earlier, after they get married, Cherkess women are expected to devote themselves to the domestic sphere and the well-being of their new extended families. While married men continue to participate in weddings by accordion-playing or dancing; newlywed women join the ranks of mar-ried women whose participation in such occasions is peripheral and definite-ly off the dance floor. Many Cherkess couples observe codes of avoidance, which conceal displays of spousal affinity in the presence of lineage elders. It is difficult to discern the ways in which the Civil Code reform of 1926 has affected this aspect of Cherkess family life. The breaking away of conjugal families from the rural homesteads of extended families may have intensi-fied *resmiyet* or formality in order to assure a respectful relationship between young Cherkess husbands and wives. On the other hand, it may have creat-ed an opportunity for the young couple to have a more relaxed relation-ship. The favourable opinions young men express regarding the practice of formality between spouses and with children, the diversity of personal accounts, and women's highly critical opinions about men's emotional dis-tance in the family make it difficult to account for historical change. An old woman's one unfulfilled wish in life was to have a meal together with her late husband, which he had firmly refused. Was this particular to their com-munity? How strong and widespread is avoidance within the nuclear family? These are difficult questions to answer; however, women's will to redefine their relationship with their husbands is hard to miss.

In the 1990s, while feminists' search for an autonomous female subjectivi-ty was heatedly debated in Turkish society, Cherkess women were engaged in a soft-spoken struggle to recast their "private relations" in accord with their public independent selves. In urban Eskişehir, men's distance from the conjugal family and its private space, as well as the gender-blind egalitarianism of the Kemalist public sphere, has allowed Cherkess women, especially those who work outside the home, greater autonomy and freedom as individuals. However, Cherkess women's struggle for more intimate relations within the domestic sphere has been intensifying. Women are not willing to compromise, even if it means marrying out.

Transforming Conjugal Relations?

Speaking through the idiom of modernity, both Cherkess men and women of Turkey proudly point out the mixed-gender relations, courtship practices, and lack of domestic violence in their communities. However, in smaller *zexes*, gender tension is an ongoing issue. Women constantly challenge men's inadequacies and reluctance to share life in heterosexual unions beyond *semerkho*. They refer to old books, to stories of conjugal intimacy they have heard from previous generations, and seek rational explanations to bring the issue to men's awareness. In their frustration with Cherkess men's avoidance of intimacy, younger women often marry out.

Married men feel pressured by their peers and other community members to maintain distance from their families. A Cherkess man apologetically explained to his teasing friends at the Cherkess cultural association his reasons for spending evenings at home with his family: he had to be there so that *the* children would feel his authority and keep on task.[5] Another man was embarrassed while talking about the special warmth he felt towards his younger child. The first child was born and raised while the couple lived with his family, which would often require the father to stay away from his child and home, especially considering the close living quarters of urban living. Yet another man recalled the cold sweat that chilled his back while he danced *with his wife* to Western music at a party that was organized for the Cherkess community in Eskişehir. At the time he was the president of the Cherkess cultural association and was afraid – unnecessarily – that no other Cherkess couple would follow them to the dance floor. These are a few of the men who expressed their ambiguities and fears while treasuring their new power as heads of conjugal families. In contrast, women are more comfortable with practices that allow for the expression of sexual attraction, whether in the private sphere or in public. In the latter case, which violates both Cherkess and Turkish norms, *semerkho* offers a potential foil.

With the wisdom of her three marriages to a Cherkess, a Tartar, and now a Turk, a charming forty-five-year-old Cherkess woman, Candan hanım, whispered to me at a wedding: "They [men] are made of the same shit!" A little later, when an old *kashens* of hers visited our table, flirting by showering her with compliments, she asserted her Cherkessness and responded in kind. As her Turkish husband sat awkwardly through this flirtation, she commented to me that "he does not understand our ways, our close relations with men. But it is all a joke."

Reflections: Where To?

A post-1980 feminist public discourse, emerging out of the long-standing experience of Turkish women as genderless participants in the egalitarian public sphere, shook the nation with its continuing impact on the social order. Cherkess women, however, maintained a distance from feminist activism and its concerns for an autonomous female subjectivity. It is important to identify what specifically distances women in various segments of the society from feminist agendas (Johnson-Odim, 1991). Obviously, Cherkess women's distance from the Turkish feminist movement is, first of all, a question of power defined by ethnicity, which is constrained by the hegemony of the unitary nationalist ideology in Turkey. What Cherkess and Turkish women share is a strong will for "modernity." Nonetheless, their diverging definitions of modernity have limited Cherkess women's ability to participate in the Turkish feminist discourse or to speak up about their concerns. Consequently, Cherkess women's "feminist mobilization" is confined to the public sphere of Cherkess ethnicity and is bound by cultural notions of privacy.

To elucidate the growing differences between the trajectories and feminist agendas of Turkish and Cherkess women in Turkey, I have juxtaposed a description of Kemalist Western-oriented *modern* gender relations with ethnic Cherkess gender relations, presumed to be "already modern." Having lived as equal participants in the same national space, women in Turkey are now engaged in a struggle to restructure or redefine gender power. I have argued that Turkish feminism set out to increase women's autonomy by alleviating the structural inequities of the modernist public sphere and by exposing the contradictions of customary gendered roles and expectations. On the other hand, Cherkess women's primary struggle, a "soft-spoken feminism," remained concerned with redefining the private sphere and was carried out within the Cherkess public sphere. Cherkess women's choice not to engage in post-1980 Turkish feminist politics poses intriguing questions for feminist transformations in the public sphere of modern Turkey (cf. Broaten, 1991; Meehan, 1995). Its implications for the future of Cherkess ethnic identity in Turkey are of even greater significance. Cherkess women's public voice is important for the feminist public platform to expand and is a prerequisite for Cherkess ethnic identity to flourish in Turkey.

Notes

Funding for my doctoral research was provided by National Science Foundation, Social Science Research Council, and Middle East Research Competition. I am grateful for their generous support. My special thanks go to the editorial collective for their incisive comments, particularly Sally Cole. I also appreciate the encouraging input of Elizabeth Fernea, Kathleen Murphy, Kate Sullivan, and Kumru Toktamiş. De Ann Pendry's editorial suggestions have been especially helpful.

1   The Cherkess are an indigenous people of the North Caucasus. Most commonly, in English they are known as Circassians, which historically is the attributed name of one of the "tribal" groups (Adyge) I discuss in this paper. Cherkess people were scattered in waves into diaspora during the nineteenth century upon the colonization of the Caucasus by the Russian Empire. A large group of them resettled in the Ottoman Empire. The largest population of Cherkess is currently in Turkey, even taking into account populations still residing in the Caucasus. Those who remained in the Caucasus are administered in the form of various autonomous regions or independent republics within the Russian Federation or Republic of Georgia, such as the Adyge Republic and the recent (internationally unrecognized) Republic of Abkhazia.

2   In Turkish, the relations that I here translate as "cousins" and "brothers" correspond to at least four kin relations, since each maternal and paternal relative has a designated term, as well as to fictive kin relations that are strongly valued among the Cherkess.

3   Cherkess people are strictly exogamous (Aslan, 1992; Colarusso, forthcoming). According to the Cherkess rule of exogamy, spouses are chosen from outside one's lineage, sometimes of both parents, as well as outside one's intimate social network. Considering such a rule of exogamy, by lineage and social intimacy, interactions in mixed-gender gatherings represent also the young Cherkess's search to reach the eligible "non-kin."

4   Cherkess avoidance practices are very complex and vary tribally. I here discuss them as they are predominantly lived and discussed in the 1990s Eskişehir Cherkess community, which represents a more unified group with a longer history than elsewhere in Turkey (Ertem, 1999).

5   Observing the custom, he avoided publicly referring to his son and daughter as
    his own.

References

Abadan, Nermin. 1967. "Turkey," in R. Patai, ed., *Women in the Modern World*. New York:
    Free Press,82-105.

Arat, Yesim. 1989. *The Patriarchal Paradox: Women Politicians in Turkey*. London: Associated
    University Press.

——. 1996. "On Gender and Citizenship in Turkey," *Middle East Report* 26, 1: 28-31.

——. 1997. "The Project of Modernity and Women in Turkey," in S. Bozdoğan and R.
    Kasaba, eds., *Rethinking Modernity and Turkish National Identity in Turkey*. Seattle: Uni-
    versity of Washington Press, 95-113.

Ardener, Edwin. 1975. "The 'Problem' Revisited," in S. Ardener, ed., *Perceiving Women*.
    New York: John Wiley and Sons, 19-27.

Ardener, Shirley. 1975. "Introduction," in S. Ardener, ed., Perceiving Women. New
    York: John Wiley and Sons, vii-xxiii.

Aslan, Simha Cahit. 1992. *Sosyo-Kültürel Değişim ve Kuzey Kafkasyalilar* (Socio-Cultural
    Change and Northern Caucasians). Adana: Özden Matbaasi.

Berktay, Fatmagül. 1995. "Has Anything Changed in the Outlook of the Turkish Left
    on Women?" in Şirin Tekeli, ed., *Women in Modern Turkish Society*. London: Zed
    Books, 250-62.

Bir, Berat B. 1995. "Türkiye Gerçeğinde Kadın" (Woman in the Context of Turkey),
    Alaşara 1: 15.

Bozdoğan, Sibel, and Reşat Kasaba, eds. 1997. *Rethinking Modernity and National Identity in
    Turkey*. Seattle: University of Washington Press.

Broaten, Jane. 1991. *Habermas's Critical Theory of Society*. Albany: State University of New
    York Press.

Colarusso, John. Forthcoming. "Peoples of the Caucasus," in P. Pike, ed., *Encyclopedia
    of Cultures and Daily Life*. Eastward Publications.

Erol, Sibel. 1992. "Feminism in Turkey," *New Perspectives on Turkey* 8: 109-20.

Ertem, B. Gönül. 1999. "Dancing to Modernity: Cultural Politics of Cherkess
    Nationhood in the Heartland of Turkey," Ph.D. dissertation, University of
    Texas.

Ertürk, Yakın. 1995. "Rural Women and Modernization in Southeastern Anatolia,"
    in Şirin Tekeli. ed., *Women in Modern Turkish Society*. London: Zed Books, 141-52.

Göle, Nilüfer. 1996. U. Ann Arbor: The University of Michigan Press.

Jayawardena, Kumari. 1986. *Feminism and Nationalism in the Third World*. London: Zed
    Books.

Johnson-Odim, Cheryl. 1991. "Common Themes, Different Contexts: Third World

Women and Feminism," in C.T. Mohanty, A. Russo, and L. Torres, eds., *Third World Women and the Politics of Feminism*. Bloomington: Indiana University Press, 314-27.

Kadıoglu, Ayse. 1994. "Women's Subordination in Turkey: Is Islam Really the Villain?" *Middle East Journal* 48, 4:645-60.

Kandiyoti, Deniz. 1987. "Emancipated but Unliberated? Reflections on the Turkish Case," *Feminist Studies* 13: 317-38.

——. 1989. "Women and the Turkish State: Political Actors or Symbolic Pawns?" in N. Yuval-Davis and F. Anthias, eds., *Woman-Nation-State*. New York: St. Martin's Press, 126-50.

——. 1991. "End of Empire: Islam, Nationalism and Women in Turkey," in D. Kandiyoti, ed., *Women, Islam and the State*. London: Macmillan, 22-48.

——. 1997. "Gendering the Modern: On Missing Dimensions in the Study of Turkish Modernity," in S. Bozdoğan and R. Kasaba eds., *Rethinking Modernity and National Identity in Turkey*. Seattle: University of Washington Press, 113-32.

Lewis, Bernard. 1979. *The Emergence of Modern Turkey*. London: Oxford University Press.

Meehan, Johanna, ed. 1995. *Feminists Read Habermas: Gendering the Subject of Discourse*. New York: Routledge.

Olson, E.A. 1982. "Duofocal Family Structure and an Alternative Model of Husband-Wife Relationships," in Ç. Kağitçibasi, ed., *Sex Roles, Family and Community in Turkey*. Turkish Studies Series 3. Bloomington: Indiana University Press.

——. 1985. "Muslim identity and secularism in contemporary Turkey: 'The headscarf dispute'," *Anthropological Quarterly* 58, 4: 161-71.

Öncü, Ayse. 1981. "Turkish Women in the Professions: Why So Many?" in N. Abadan-Unat, ed., *Women in Turkish Society*. Leiden: E.J. Brill.

Öztürkmen, Arzu. 1998. "A Short History of *Kadınca* Magazine and Its Feminism," in Z.A. Arat, ed., *Deconstructing Images of "the Turkish Woman"*. New York: St. Martin's Press, 275-93.

Şener, Esat. 1985. "Change in the Family as Reflected in the Jurisprudence of the Republican Era," in T. Erder, ed., *Family in Turkish Society*. Ankara: Turkish Social Science Association, 401-16.

Şeni, Nora. 1995. "Fashion and Women's Clothing in the Satirical Press of Istanbul at the End of the 19th Century," in S. Tekeli, ed., *Women in Modern Turkish Society*. London: Zed Books, 25-45.

Shami, Seteney. 1995. "Disjuncture in Ethnicity: Negotiating Circassian Identity in Jordan, Turkey and the Caucasus," *New Perspectives on Turkey*.

Shaw, Stanford J., and Ezel Kural Shaw. 1977. *History of the Ottoman Empire and Modern Turkey*. Volume II: *Reform, Revolution, and Republic: The Rise of Modern Turkey, 1808-1975*. Cambridge: Cambridge University Press.

Sirman, Nükhet. 1989. "Feminism in Turkey: A Short History," *New Perspectives on*

Turkey 3, 1: 1-34.

—. 1990. "State, Village and Gender in Western Turkey," in A. Finkel and N. Sirman, eds., *Turkish State, Turkish Society*. Centre of Near and Middle Eastern Studies: Contemporary Studies. New York: Routledge, 21-51.

Starr, June. 1992. *Law as Metaphor: From Islamic Courts to the Palace of Justice*. Albany: State University of New York Press.

—. 1997. "The Legal and Social Transformation of Rural Women in Aegean Turkey," in C.Brettel and C. Sargent, eds., *Gender in Cross-Cultural Perspectives*. Englewood Cliffs, N.J.: Prentice Hall, 280-98.

Tekeli, Şirin. 1990. "Women in the Changing Political Associations of the 1980s," in A. Finkel and N. Sirman, eds., *Turkish State, Turkish Society*. New York: Routledge, 259-89.

TWELVE

COLONIAL AND POST-REVOLUTIONARY DISCOURSES AND NICARAGUAN FEMINIST CONSTRUCTIONS OF *MESTIZA*: REFLECTIONS OF A CULTURAL TRAVELLER

Milagros Ortiz Barillas

How does she name herself in her own narratives?
How does she find meaning in her own experiences,
and how does she understand the role of language
in her effort to name these experiences?

(Lionnet, 1995: 3)

Revolution as a Context for the Analysis of Constructions of *Mestiza* Identity

Revolutionaries were shocked and surprised by their defeat in the 1990 elections in Nicaragua. Having been in power since they successfully overthrew the Somoza dictatorship government in 1979, the revolutionary political party, the Sandinista Front, was confident its anti-bourgeois and anti-American platforms still held wide popular appeal. Revolutionaries were now compelled to reconsider perspectives on the historical, social, and cultural transformations taking place in Nicaragua. In this process, debates were opened about women's issues in relation to the context of revolution. Women constituted the majority of the electorate, yet in 1990 their voices were not heard during the elections and some began to ask why. Chinchilla (1995: 243) argues that although the Nicaraguan feminist movement had gained strength through the revolutionary experience, it lost momentum after the overthrow of the dictatorship because of an inadequate understanding of the roots of women's oppression and because of a "lack of models for revolutionary women's organizations in the Third World context." While these structural interpretations are valid, an examination of the complexities and subjectivities of identity formation is also important to understanding Nicaraguan political processes. We need to interrogate the homogenizing effects of the internalization, particularly by Nicaraguan women, of labels and identity markers originating in European minds to name the Other. "Third World," "Latin American," and in particular, "Mestiza" are labels that need to be problematized and unravelled to reveal the ways in which they disguise the diversity and multiple positions of "Nicaraguan" female identities, obscure the specificities of our experiences, and come to bear on the formulation of identity.

One of the numerous lessons we can learn from the Nicaraguan revolution is how complex and different our experiences have been. We can challenge the authority of "truth" based on undisputed Western perspectives that have glossed over the particularities of local Aboriginal experience and the daily lives of women. Molyneux (1985: 235) notes that discrimination on the basis of gender is experienced differentially by women according to their social class. Diverse historical, political, and cultural circumstances also shape gendered experiences of oppression, and these are especially highlighted by the revolutionary context in Nicaragua where a range of dynamics mark the relationships between specific populations and different colonial strategies in history. For example, populations of the Pacific coast were oppressed by Spanish conquerors from the early sixteenth century, and subsequently by the historical continuum of the post-colonial state[1] formed in 1821. Even at this early date, the relatively newly formed United States was focusing its interests on Nicaragua. In competition with Britain, the U.S. considered it a possible site for a canal connecting the Atlantic and Pacific Oceans. U.S. Marines were expelled from Nicaragua in the 1930s after Augusto Sandino came to power. But he was assassinated in 1934, and by 1937 the U.S. had imposed Anastasio Somoza Garcia to the presidency of Nicaragua, marking the beginning of the Somoza dynasty that maintained a dictatorship in the country for forty-two years. These political circumstances have shaped the current forms of female oppression for the majority of *Mestiza*, as well as for the indigenous Monimbo and Subtiava women of the west coast. Under the Somoza regime in the 1970s, repression worsened and many *Mestiza* women, mostly from the Pacific coast, participated extensively in revolutionary activities (Jaquette, 1990; Molyneux, 1985: 227).

On the other hand, peoples on the Atlantic coast were not conquered by the Spanish early on and Miskito, Sumo, Rama, and Creole women experienced living under an English protectorate. Consequently, they did not perceive the revolution as *their* triumph and had other expectations. It is also difficult for these women to recognize themselves within the parameters of post-colonial *Mestiza* identity, ideologically defined in terms of a so-called "improved" Aboriginal race – in fact, born of the rape of Native women (considered inferior and vanquished) by Spanish males (seen as the superior victors). *Mestizo* identity is composed of these two sources, but one, colonized by the other, is subordinated and reconstituted into a singular form. Women, their bodies acting as passive receptacles for a homogenized and statically constructed Aboriginal culture, are central to the ideology that underpins this identity.

In turn, this ideology sustained the Napoleonic ideal of a unilingual, uni-cultural Spanish Nicaraguan nation-state in the post-colonial context, still steeped in a colonial vision of conquest, which came to be challenged by Miskito fighters. When the revolutionaries gained power they made wide-sweeping constitutional changes in 1987 that redefined Nicaraguan identity in terms of a "multi-ethnic identity ... firmly rooted in the heroic actions of such 'Indo-American' heroes as Diriangen, Cuauhtemoc, Caupolicán and Tupac Amaru, who never gave up" (La Gaceta, 1987). It has also been noted by some that the revolutionaries tried to transform colonial structures through the deployment of a "moderate socialism," taking their lessons from the revolutions of others and learning to apply a form of "flexible Marxism" (Chinchilla, 1995: 244; Molyneux, 1985: 236). In addition, what is often left out of the debate about Nicaraguan political processes is the role played by the United States in delegitimizing the revolutionary agenda *internally* within Nicaragua, using the media and other sources of control and influence. U.S. imperial interests acted to accent divisive elements, such as the differences between Atlantic and Pacific coast experiences, in order to wear away at the relevance of revolutionary agendas. These examples illustrate how competing discourses within the revolutionary context shape understandings of identity. The diversity of the Nicaraguan people and their resistance to oppressive structures of power have always been there, but they became emphasized, locally and internationally, with the revolution and subsequently in their electoral politics.

Naming *Mestiza* from the Perspective of a Cultural Traveller

My intention here is not to discuss all the complexities of women and revolution in Nicaragua or to elaborate on the extensive literature on this topic. Rather, I wish to explore the ways in which colonial constructions of women, emerging from and shifting through colonial, post-colonial, and post-revolutionary Nicaragua, have given meaning to the label *Mestiza* and continue to inform Nicaraguan feminism. To do so, I must begin by acknowledging the diversity of the category "Nicaraguan women," which is constituted of a majority who identify themselves as *Mestiza* but also includes many groups of Indigenous people (Subtiava, Monimbo, Miskito, Sumo, Rama, as well as Creoles), and a minority of women of European descent. All of these women share a history of Spanish, English, and American colonialism, but have lived it from very different positions. Their choices, languages, and religious beliefs are also varied, and this wide diversity can often manifest itself within one family.

To reply to Lionnet's question – "How does she name herself?" – is personally a difficult and painful task for the majority of *Mestiza* women survivors of imperial invasions. This task cannot be separated from the structures of power within Nicaragua, which are permeated with the "vision of conquest." I will, "in my own narratives, in my own experiences," which I feel are most aptly described as those of a "cultural traveller," convey my reflections on this question. I have never been involved in any form of military action, although many men in my family have. I have not been a member of any political organization, with the exception of my participation in a literacy campaign organized by the revolutionary government in 1980. I, along with a group of other *Mestiza* girls from the city, went to the countryside to spread the written word among other *Mestiza* who we expected to be "just like us." We learned, however, that not only were all *Mestiza* not alike, but that in stark contrast to our experience, these women were struggling to continue to live by their ancestral ways and were paying the price as they experienced oppression in its most cruel forms. As a seventeen-year-old, I had set out to share my knowledge, but upon my return I realized that it was I who had been educated by these women who worked the land, made pottery, and still broke their corn with the traditional *metate*.

It was at this age that, with a degree of horror, I first asked myself Cherríe Moraga's question, "How have I oppressed?" (1981: 30). The Miskito, in particular, were challenging the legitimacy of the Nicaraguan state, and I was especially influenced by this questioning as the revolution took shape. I attempted to grasp the paradox of the great distance that separated *Mestiza* women and the colonial constructions of class, racism, literacy, and "Western" knowledge that also inextricably linked us. It is from this position that I began and continue to try to untangle and understand the naming of *Mestiza* experience.

Colonial and Post-Colonial Constructions of Mestiza

In Nicaragua, massive miscegenation did not take place in the early years of invasion because the Spaniards did not find gold and therefore did not stay in the area in large numbers. Unlike the French term Métis, also used in English to describe the offspring of European and Amerindian parents,[2] *Mestiza* carries with it connotations of rape, violence, conquest, and imposed identity. Even the naming of the post-colonial state "Nicaragua" is symbolically charged with negative "feminine" meaning. *Nicarao*, the Aboriginal leader who first welcomed the invaders, has been reconstructed and distorted in our history as passive and stupid, as well as appearing as a coward before the conquistadors by "letting" them enslave men and rape women.

Physical or even cultural indicators are inadequate in explaining the ideology of *Mestisaje*. *Mestiza* identity emerges from social relations in an ongoing process of repression (Klor de Alva, 1995; Bonfil Batalla, 1994). For some, like Nicaraguan *Mestiza* anthropologist Milagros Palma, the shame contained within this identity arises from the misogynism inherent in the original story of the *Mestizo* man (the son of a mythic conqueror father and a hated indigenous mother), which has generated a universal gendered symbolic order (Palma, 1991: 29). Behar has cautioned, however, that anthropologists have mistakenly used the term *Mestizo* to refer to non-Native people (1993: 8-9). In Nicaragua, women living in the countryside are perceived as "passive" and "ignorant," and are seen as *Mestiza* under the terms of the overarching colonial ideology.

Further evidence of how gendered colonial discourse has carried over through pre-revolutionary, revolutionary, and post-revolutionary life is reflected in the differential treatment of our historical "heroes." In the 1987 constitution, the military resistance of our male indigenous ancestors against the invasion is highlighted, but no heroism is accorded to the struggles carried out by our female ancestors who maintained Aboriginal technologies and economic systems and ensured the basic survival of families. *Malitzin*, better known as *Malinche*, who was an active, intelligent Aboriginal woman in Mesoamerican history, has been reconstructed as a traitor who helped Cortés in the war against, and conquest of, her people.[3] In post-revolutionary Nicaragua, her voice as a woman and an Aboriginal person living during the time of conquest has been silenced. Current constructions of Aboriginal female identity, and Aboriginal cultures more generally, are folded in and reinterpreted with those that originated with the representations of Mesoamerica made by colonial Spanish chroniclers.

In the early post-colonial years, Central America was briefly united to Mexico. But soon it became necessary to formulate and impose national identities on citizens in the context of the growth of nation-states. The diverse Nicaraguan people were expected to acquiesce to and internalize the dominant ideology of *Mestisaje*, a concept still very much infused with notions of victory and conquest – of Whites over Indigenous people, and of men over women. This process was more effective on the Pacific coast, where Indigenous people were most repressed and their lands extensively expropriated. The imposition of a collective *Mestizo* identity over everyone was a strategy designed to obscure inequalities and differences within the new nation-state. The claim was that, as *Mestizo*, everyone shared a common history, culture, and future – Somoza Debayle (president, 1967-79) and the woman breaking corn in the *metate*, while her children may be working for a rich landowner, were both *Mestizos*. For several reasons, however, the promotion of nationalism was not very successful. Since the colonial period, the country had operated as a peripheral province and was plagued by a history of dictatorship and puppet governments. In addition, the state had difficulties gaining control over its Atlantic coast, which remained under English Protectorate until the mid-nineteenth century. Finally, the denigration of Aboriginal cultures, placed at the bottom of the heap under the "great civilizations" of the Maya and Aztec, furthered a sense of alienation of Nicaragua from the people who lived within its borders. From this context, two contradictory stereotypes of *Mestiza* have emerged: one that is "passive" and artless, and the other a "traitor." The "passive" image of *Mestiza* is associated with the countryside and is linked to Indigenous traditions practised by those who know little of the "Western" world. The "traitor" image is associated with life in the city, where there is access to "Western" education and lifestyles, and thus where *Mestizas* may "betray" their own history and identity.

Nicaraguan Feminism and Constructions of Mestiza

Other images of *Mestiza* have emerged in the post-colonial era, propelled by the national Nicaraguan feminist movement. In particular, feminists first attempted to popularize the image of the independent woman, mirroring Western (European and American) feminist values. Later, they glorified the "fighter" based on a female appropriation of guerrilla/military imagery.

Beginning with the participation of élite women in the anti-colonial independence movements of the nineteenth century, women such as Rafaela Herrera, a "Criollo" (people of Spanish descent born in America), continue to be presented in the school system as symbols of patriotism and as heroines. In 1923, a current of feminism took form that intended to liberate educated middle-class and upper-class women. The goal of economic independence was primary, as illustrated by Josefa Toledo de Aguerri, a well-known educator and a key figure in feminist writing, "The ideal woman finds within herself her own means and her own end. She can live independently from a man, if she chooses, and is capable of making a living" (quoted in Wood, 1996: 6). But for the majority of Nicaraguan women, who worked as labourers and peasants supporting the agro-export economy, Herrera's image and Aguerri's words did not mean much. In both the colonial and post-colonial periods, their experience has been one of intensive labour and sexual exploitation, violence, crime, and dispossession of their lands. The independence of Nicaragua did not mean liberation for them. The concerns expressed by the mainstream feminist movement were, and still are, irrelevant to the majority of peasant and working class women who work and live in harsh conditions, and who are also often single-parent heads of households. For them, economic independence from men does not carry the meaning of liberation and empowerment, but rather signifies the destruction of the family and leaves them subject to exploitation.

To compound the oppression of Indigenous peoples further, the dominant sector of society rationalizes domestic violence, alcoholism, the absence of fathers, and homicide as either integral to Indigenous cultures or the result of "ignorance" and "underdevelopment." In defence of the status quo, all of this discrimination is encapsulated within the concept of *Indio* (Ortiz, 1995). In the revolutionary period, shame for one's "Indianness" diminished, although some of the "naïve" and "noble" characteristics of the colonial and post-colonial construction of "Indian" and *Mestizo* identity were reproduced in revolutionary discourse. In school, we were taught about the "Indigenous world view." In the late 1980s, leader Daniel Ortega went so far as to say that the country did not need intellectuals, but he later retracted this statement. Indigenous groups sought further autonomy and demanded greater valorization of their languages and cultures – the Miskitos demanded that their literacy campaign be in Miskito rather than Spanish – all bringing about challenges to the racist, exploitative hierarchy of Nicaraguan society. Furthermore, the U.S. economic and political attacks on Nicaragua (1981-90) ended up, ironically, serving to revitalize Aboriginal cultures, as people had to turn to traditional forms of technology, subsistence and production to be less dependent on Western goods and consumption. This was also accompanied by the revalorization of our very humble traditional indigenous dress. Only through the combination of these issues and transformations has there been a growth in the valorization of the experiences of the majority of Nicaraguan women.

Nicaragua's history of invasions, dictatorships, and American intervention shaped heroism and militarism into valued ideals, and the development of Nicaraguan feminism did not escape this influence. The critique that women's interests were not represented in the formation of the revolutionary state is legitimate (Molyneux, 1985) yet incomplete. Another important element in the analysis of the relationship between women's experience and the Nicaraguan state is the value of the militarization of women internationally, and within the feminist movement. Women's "equality" with men was measured in terms of their military participation. This position was strongly advocated by female leaders in the revolution, and the AMLAE (Asociación de Mujeres Nicaragüenses Luisa Amanda Espinoza), a feminist organization created upon the success of the revolution. As articulated by one of its members, Magda Enriquez: "We never said that we were equal. We simply demonstrated it in the battlefields" (quoted in Collison, 1990: 140), the main focus of this feminist platform was the military inclusion of women and their full participation in combat (Collison, 1990: 155; Murguialday Martinez, 1990: 52; Macintosh and Angel, 1987; Randall, 1994).

The dehumanizing effects of war were downplayed and transferred into personal sexual politics: "We all are friends and have a good laugh, joking about how when our men come home from fighting, it's just another battle in bed" (Macintosh and Angel, 1987: 89). Local and international media images of women with guns were very powerful. Symbolically, women who replaced their skirts and dresses with combat uniforms, and who handled guns, the phallic objects of war, were viewed as breaking the chains of sexual and class oppression. The warrior image was held up against the "passive" attributes of those who openly stated their opposition to armed struggle and military service, seen as synonymous with not being a good revolutionary. Although there was no direct "reign of terror," being suspected of anti-revolutionary sentiment was dangerous. This affected women in particular because, for the majority, militarization did not translate into liberation from patriarchy, but rather was yet another form of imposed order, whether the call to arms emanated from the United States and the Contras or from the revolutionaries and Miskito leaders. Women who opposed military service were also interpreted as "choosing" male and foreign domination. Macintosh and Angel document how feminist revolutionaries went to peasant women to recruit them to join the military. However, when the peasant women asked why they should join, when some joined the Contras instead, or when some did not join at all, feminists put the peasant women's response down to their illiteracy, which was perceived as equivalent to "ignorance" (Macintosh and Angel, 1987: 88-89). Again, women who did not wish to participate in combat were portrayed as lacking both gender and revolutionary consciousness (Wood, 1997: 59-60; Collison, 1990: 137; Murguialday Martinez, 1990: 118).

A further result of this development in Nicaraguan gender and revolutionary discourse was the erasure of the experiences of those women who tried to help their male relatives leave the country or who hid them so that they could escape military service (often they were young people who did not want to kill or be killed by American-trained armed forces). Mothers, sisters, daughters, cousins, aunts, lovers, wives, friends, and neighbours of all ethnic and religious backgrounds and political and sexual orientations experienced deep pain in seeing men forced to go to war to die, or to return traumatized and/or with their bodies mutilated. Thus, the association of feminism with militarization was, on numerous fronts, alienating for many women.

A third current of feminism, focused on women's sexuality, emerged in the late 1980s. It too proved to be exclusionary and also fuelled negative stereotypes about Indigenous women. This movement, which originated among women closely associated with the high-ranking spheres of military and revolutionary power, yet was independent of the AMLAE, was known as the "Erotic Left" (Partido de la izquierola erótica – PIE). The sexual liberation of women was juxtaposed against the "ignorant" or inhibited attitudes towards women's sexuality that were believed to be exhibited particularly among the "peasant" population. Palma, who conducted her fieldwork in the 1980s, concluded that sexual pleasure was perceived as a "fault" by Latin American women and that women paid the price of pain and suffering for it. As an example of female sexual repression and inhibition, Palma said that, "Among the 'peasants' in Nicaragua, girls always wear at least a panty while the boys will only cover at puberty to hide pubic hair" (1991: 72). Generalizations about "peasant" sexuality led to condescending interpretations by élites of the sexual life of "peasants." From a widely diffused story about a nurse's aide who worked with "peasants," the concept of the "Virgin Mary complex" emerged in reference to the idea that "peasant" women were "embarrassed to talk about the sex act" (Murguialday Martinez, 1990: 96; Collison, 1990: 21). Women were also denigrated for not knowing the word "orgasm." Sofia Montenegro, one of the PIE founders, states that one of the party's goals was to promote sensual pleasures among individuals that were felt to have been repressed by the Native culture as well as by the political context (Montenegro, 1991-2: 9).

Finally, the unevenness of the influence of the Catholic Church is also an important element contributing to the schisms in Mestiza identity based on race, class, and cultural differences. Feminist criticism of the Church has often been directed at the idea that Latin American women have been victims of the ideological domination of Catholicism. However, the power of the Church over women's behaviour was not applied evenly throughout the socio-economic classes. Catholic norms of conduct were actually most stringently applied to women of the privileged classes, with particular emphasis placed on virginity and obedience. This served to sustain the Spanish patriarchal system, and contrasted with Aboriginal beliefs. The Church prepared élite women for their role within the dominant class, especially in terms of subjugating other women.

These influences in national feminist movements in Nicaragua help to explain why peasant women were silent during a time in the revolution when their participation was most needed to assist in the transformation of society. The feminist movement in Nicaragua has been limiting for most women with, at one extreme, the élitist wave begun in the 1920s, and at the other extreme, a form of feminism that, while sensitive to class oppression, narrowly espoused emancipation through militarist action. In some cases, the same women who actively promoted female military service also helped their male relatives to escape to other countries and avoid army recruitment. However, unlike the majority of women from both the cities and the countryside who were hiding their male friends and family, élite women were not also struggling for basic daily survival. In the end, only those affiliated with the élite were truly able to avoid military service, and with the incredible disruptions of family and loss of life, feminist ideals of "equality" in Nicaragua soon lost all credibility.

Feminist leaders in Nicaragua seem to have been very unfamiliar with the daily reality of the majority of women, and even less aware of the vitality and significance of Aboriginal culture in their lives. As Gioconda Belli, a member of the élite circle of Sandinista power, founder of the PIE, and one of the most famous *Mestiza* poets of revolutionary times admitted, "I read Shakespeare and the world classics, but I didn't know about Latin American literature at all. I wasn't familiar with my own people's culture" (quoted in Randall, 1994: 172). Klor de Alva's (1995) and Behar's (1993) observations about the confusing nature of the word *Mestizo* are relevant here, for this further critique of Nicaraguan feminist constructions of *Mestiza* accentuates how colonial, post-colonial, and finally revolutionary discourses have served to distance and alienate peoples along class and cultural lines. The majority of women, variously labelled *Mestiza*, "peasants," "Indians," have borne the impact of this process in the formation of visions of Nicaraguan culture. Like the revolutionaries who ignored the concerns of the Miskitos, Nicaraguan feminists also failed to question the ideology of conquest that permeates identity discourses and dismisses Aboriginal experience. The homogenization of *Mestiza* identity, grounded in a perspective that viewed "peasants" as "backward" and "ignorant," was dominant among those women who were in powerful positions to direct the future of the people of Nicaragua. Understandably, the feminist movement has been rejected by the majority of women who had been defined "by nature" as inferior.

In light of this deconstruction of feminism in relation to the revolutionary movement in Nicaragua, it is possible to understand better why there was a turn to conservatism, and a gain in the power of the closely affiliated Church, after the elections that brought a woman, Violeta Chamorro, to power as the president on February 25, 1990. While President Chamorro has been popularly portrayed in association with the Virgin Mary and as a "motherly" figure to all Nicaraguans, it is not this imagery that influenced the vote in her favour, but rather a combination of considerations by the very politically aware population. First, the majority of people had become disillusioned with the revolutionaries, who were viewed as being too concerned with securing their power and who had lost touch with the majority. Second, the conservative right, supported by Americans with powerful weapons and dollars, promised a stop to military service and armed conflicts, which appealed to the devastated population. Finally, the Church had opposed the conscription of women into military service, and with that stance had gained favour among the many who had been alienated by the feminist movement.

Women could no longer live with the death, destruction, hunger, orphans, mutilations, and physical and moral exhaustion. People had come to believe that these could be alleviated only by a government that satisfied the demands of the Americans. It is difficult to explain the feelings of horror when one fears loved ones may be reduced to pieces of flesh, their entrails out. Or worse, the thought of how long it would take to die, how painful it would be in a place where there are few hospitals, little medicine and equipment – and no peace. This situation worsened with the economic embargo and bombing of agricultural co-operatives, leaving so many to the fate of becoming orphans in a place where there are no orphanages, no social welfare, and where the resources of extended families have been stretched to unbearable limits. It has been cruel beyond words. The feelings of loss cannot be described. How free have we been?

Mestiza as Cultural Traveller

The year 1992 was very significant for me as a woman and as a *Mestiza*. I was learning the Nahualt language – understanding for the first time that words I had been using all my life were in fact Nahualt. I was finishing my Master's degree at the University of Montreal, and it was the 500th anniversary of Columbus's accidental arrival in the "New World." This left me with a bitter taste of war and broken hopes. I wondered about the human and cultural devastation of European invasion in the Americas. I wondered whether it could be said that any Aboriginal group now possessed a pre-Columbian version of their culture that did not contain the elements of what Rosaldo called "imperialist nostalgia" or "mourning the passing of traditional society" (1989: 68-69). Stepping outside of the direct experiences of the Nicaraguan context, I now began to question much about the formulations of my own identity against the backdrop of the constructions of *Mestiza* I have described here. Rather than feeling as if I were living two competing processes of identity forged between feminist and nationalist discourses, as in the case highlighted by Visweswaran (1994: 69), I wondered how I might resist and disentangle myself from the static visions I had of Aboriginal cultures that I, too, had internalized as a *Mestiza* from Nicaragua. How could I dissolve the binary oppositions that had supported structures of repression and my own actions within these structures: rationality/irrationality, savagery/civilization, inferior/superior, white/brown, man/woman, and, in addition, as a woman: warrior/passive, pure/impure, countryside/city, acculturated/traditional, and traitor/victim.

My father grew up in the "countryside" in Rivas, where the Nicarao established themselves a few centuries before the time of the Spanish invasion. I inherited from him not only my physical "Indian" features, but a great attachment to his Indigenous world. In the last years of his life, when I was between ten and fifteen years old, he had fallen very ill and remained very much at home. During this time, as we became very close even as I was losing him, he had the opportunity to communicate to me the oral history and traditional teachings of his people.

My mother, identified as a *Mestiza*, was lighter-skinned and grew up with her "Criollas" grandmother and mother in the city. She belonged very much to the "White" world. However, both my parents were "Nicaraguan *Mestizos*" under state ideology. Consequently, I grew up travelling not between different states or languages but between different cultural worlds. I cross many broken borders: "peasant," "traditional," "Indigenous," Nahualt, middle-class, Spanish, and even, with their ubiquitous presence, American, as well as "oppressor," "Other," "minority," and "woman of colour." Spanish is "mine" – the language in which I learned to love and be loved – but it is also the invader's tongue, which has erased Aboriginal languages by delegitimizing them and which represents imposed visions. Nahualt is also "mine" in the dearest way and is associated with love, too.

Assimilation has been greatly defeated by Indigenous peoples in Nicaragua, as well as in other parts of the North and South American continents. Roosens (1989) argues that both European and Aboriginal heritages are claimed in processes of collective and individual identity formation, or "ethnogenesis" as he calls it. However, interpretations of ethnic groups as pressure forces are not enough to explain the will of Aboriginal survival. In Mesoamerica, the conceptualization of *Mestizo* has clouded the fact that it gathers up within itself the experiences of Aboriginal peoples who under unbearable repression have sacrificed markers of their identity in a process that has taken place over centuries (Klor de Alva, 1995: 256; Bonfil Batalla, 1989: 79). Political expectations of history compel us to take sides (Visweswaran, 1994: 132). In my case this led me to view constructions of *Mestiza* identity not in terms of the formulations of national identities alone, but as part of processes of "de-Indianization," aptly described as ethnocide by Bonfil Batalla (1989: 79). Rosaldo (1989) explains how he only understood what the Ilongot meant by "rage" upon losing their loved ones after he went through such an experience himself. Similarly, I understand the feelings of the women of Nicaragua who were neither warriors nor passively apathetic; "personal experience serves as a vehicle for making the quality and intensity of the rage" most salient (Rosaldo, 1989: 11).

My experience of education and learning different languages represents a form of cultural travelling. Often, an Aboriginal person who undertakes this travel may never "return," given the structures of power contained in Western knowledge, but the travel may also lead one to an understanding of one's own processes of "ethnogenesis" (Roosens, 1989). Weir (1996) notes that affirming a state of "non-identity" within a mythic sense of freedom becomes a way for challenging imposed identities and binary categories. She remarks, though, that some kind of repression is probably inherent in the development of a sense of self in any society. Instead of denying physical, biological, sexual, and cultural differences, we may begin to accept them as a point of departure for social solidarity, even as bodies are differently affected by structures of oppression according to class, colour, sex, and individual choices and forms of resistance. I have chosen to affirm rather than deny the Indigenous heritage received as a gift from my father, a gift also from the humble yet proud people I come from. This heritage defies binary classifications because we travel between them all. Instead, I draw upon personal experiences and relate these, as well, to what Weir has distinguished as repressive, sacrificial forms of feminist identity and other possible forms. I do this in order to shift to a sort of self-identity that allows for engagement and participation in a social world (Weir, 1996: 8). Required is a vision of culture that is fluid, full of ambiguity, spontaneity, and, as Rosaldo (1989) has suggested, "improvisations."

In 1979, my mother's house was taken by revolutionaries and used as a stronghold that soon came under military attack. I saw women and men as fighters and as victims, all within the walls of my home. I was horrified by the power of guns for human destruction, and learned about the vulnerability of all human beings regardless of gender and biological characteristics. I also learned that intelligence, abilities, capacity to deal with pain, fear, death, strength, revolt, victimization, feelings of powerlessness and aggression – all have no sex and no age. Now, as a mother, my own children have also greatly influenced my world vision. My first child was born with black eyes and a head full of black hair – an "Indian" and a boy; my second child was born with fair skin and almost no hair – "White" and a girl. For me, the body is a container of flesh and blood, of intellect and a heart to learn, to remember, and to love. We take pleasure through all our senses and can listen to those who are not heard. The body is like a continent of precious, fragile life. Colonialism has killed many bodies in violent and insidious ways, and in our context as *Mestiza*, we have had to focus on survival – on life first. My hope is for a better world for both my children.

I live in the "Western world," have a European partner, have the experience of a university education, and have learned to speak several languages. During these cultural travellings, I have come to see how incompatible all of these are with the confines of the constructions of *Mestiza* in Nicaragua, in particular the limited construction of "Indians." I am not irrational because I am an Aboriginal woman or rational because I went to university. I am both. So are we all products of both our cultural and historical legacies, and our individual experiences. I am a woman and value my own biological differences. These do not necessarily determine my choices or my vulnerability or strengths. The label *Mestiza* means for me, as for Anzaldúa (1997), the coexistence of several worlds. Instead of a sort of feminine "ethnic treatise" symbolized by *Malinche*, or an identity constructed by either negative or the absence of positive elements, I chose to see myself as a cultural traveller. I have come to see my identity, then, as a complex process of negotiations in which Nahualt is a dynamic force that deals with Spanish and Anglo domination in a world that is interconnected with many others. Finally, anthropology is for me something that I do, as was making pottery for my female ancestors: innovating, creating and preserving in a hard form, women's resistance against the odds of the last 500 years of dealing with military superpowers that have shaped our forms of female repression and silenced our voices.

Notes

I am indebted to Rae Bridgman, Sally Cole, and Heather Howard-Bobiwash for their encouragement to use my own narrative in this essay and to focus on the content of what I have to say rather than on my mastery of the English language.

1 The term "post-colonial" can be used imprecisely, sometimes having the connotation of a Utopian condition that denies the reality of neo-colonialism (Lionnet, 1995: 3). Jorge Klor De Alba (1995) offers a critique specifically within the Latin American context.
2 In Canada the term Métis is used in two specific ways: (1) people who are of French and Aboriginal descent in Saskatchewan/Manitoba (Métis Nation), and (2) other people in Canada of Native and non-Native mixed heritage.
3 *Malinche* was an Aztec princess who was given as a gift to Hernán Cortés, conqueror of Mexico. Considered the "original mother" of the first "mixed blood," or *Mestizo*, son of Cortés, she has been constructed in Mesoamerica more generally as a traitor.

References

Anzaldúa, Gloria. 1997. "La conciencia de la mestiza: Towards a New Consciousness," in Soyini Madison, ed, *The Woman That I Am: The Literature and Culture of Contemporary Women of Color*. New York: St. Marten's Griffen, 560-72.

Behar, Ruth. 1993. *Translated Woman: Crossing the Border with Esperanza's Story*. Boston: Beacon Press.

Bonfil Batalla, Guillermo. 1994 [1987]. *Mexico Profundo, Una Civilización Negada*. México City: Grijalbo.

Chinchilla, Norma. 1995. "Revolutionary Popular Feminism in Nicaragua," in Christine E. Bose and Edna Acosta Belín, eds., *Women in the Latin America Development Process*. Philadelphia:Temple University Press, 242-70.

Collison, H., et al. 1990. *Women and Revolution in Nicaragua*. London: Zed Books.

Klor de Alva, Jorge. 1995. "The Postcolonization of the (Latin) America Experience: A Reconsideration of 'Colonialism,' 'Postcolonialism,' and 'Mestizaje'," in Gyan Prakash, ed., *After Colonialism: Imperial Histories and Postcolonial Displacements*. Princeton, N.J.: Princeton University Press, 181-202.

García, Alma. 1990. "The Development of Chicana Feminist Discourse 1970-1980," in Ellen Carol DuBois and Vicki L. Ruiz, eds., *Unequal Sisters: A Multicultural Reader in U.S. Women's History*. New York: Routledge, 418-31.

Jaquette, Jane. 1989. "Introduction," in Jane Jaquette, ed., *The Women's Movement in Latin*

America: Feminism and the Transition to Democracy. Boston: Unwin Hyman Press, 1-17.

La Gaceta. 1987. October 30. Managua: Imprenta Nacional.

Lionnet, Françoise. 1995. *Postcolonial Representations: Women, Literature and Identity*.Ithaca, N.Y.: Cornell University Press.

Macintosh, Fiona, and Adriana Angel. 1987. *The Tiger's Milk: Women of Nicaragua*. London: Virago Press.

Molyneux, Maxine. 1985. "Mobilization without Emancipation? Women's Interests, the State and Revolution in Nicaragua," Feminist Studies 11, 2: 227-54.

Montenegro, Sofía. 1991-92. "When You're a Woman and a Rebel Things Get a Little Complicated," in *Latin America Connexions* 5, 6 (Dec.-Jan): 9-12.

Moraga, Cherríe. 1981. "La Güera," in Cherríe Moraga and Gloria Anzaldúa,eds., *This Bridge Called My Back: Writings By Radical Women of Colour*. New York: Kitchen Table Women of Colour Press, 27-34.

Murguialday Martinez, Clara. 1990. *Nicaragua, Revolución y Feminismo (1977-89)*. Madrid: Editorial Revolucìòn.

Ortiz, Milagros. 1995. "L'expression d'une identité à travers la poésie et les chansons au Nicaragua," in Alvina Ruprecht and Cecilia Taiana, eds., *The Reordering of Culture: Latin America, the Caribbean and Canada in the Hood*. Ottawa: Carleton University Press, 499-517.

Palma, Milagros. 1991. *Le ver et le fruit: L'apprentissage de la féminité en Amérique Latine*. Paris: Cité-femmes/Unesco.

Randall, Margaret. 1994. *Sandino's Daughters Revisited: Feminism in Nicaragua*. Vancouver: New Star Books.

Rosaldo, Renato. 1989. *Culture and Truth: The Remaking of Social Analysis*. Boston: Beacon Press.

Roosens, Eugene E. 1989. *Creating Ethnicity: The Process of Ethnogenesis*. Newbury Park, Calif.: Sage.

Weir, Allison. 1996. *Sacrificial Logics: Feminist Theory and the Critique of Identity*. New York: Routledge.

Visweswaran, Kamala. 1994. *Fictions of Feminist Ethnography*. Minneapolis: University of Minnesota Press.

Wood, Barbara. 1996. "Transforming Reality: Women and Human Rights in Nicaragua," Master's thesis, Simon Fraser University.

THIRTEEN

"*FIXO BEN*" (SHE DID THE RIGHT THING): WOMEN AND SOCIAL DISRUPTION IN RURAL GALICIA

Sharon R. Roseman

Introduction

In this essay, I use a feminist practice approach to explore the significance of the social disruptions performed by women in Galician villages in northwestern Spain. By the word "disruptions" I am referring to those "critical" narratives (Khare, 1996: 28) and actions that stand out in a society because their content and style interrupts the "logical flow" of everyday conversation and behaviours (Church, 1995). Capturing the attention of onlookers, these interruptions can comprise explicit commentary on the structural frameworks of unequal social relations and/or the socially constructed nature of cultural categories. Others might call such disruptions examples of "native" ethnography or indigenous deconstruction (for examples, see Tsing, 1993).

The disruptions that particularly interest me here are those occasions during which women publicly criticize, analyse, and attempt to control the behaviour of men living in their communities. I detail two main cases involving (1) a woman's public beating of her husband and the subsequent widespread public censure of this man, who had been drinking heavily and physically abusing his wife for several months previously, and (2) three women's public analysis – with his participation – of a young man's decline into alcoholism, unemployment, and the social status of unmarriageability. Additional examples of women's discourse on male neighbours' drinking behaviour, lack of industriousness, and belligerence all demonstrate that, on these occasions, they are involved in defining the limitations of married men's expressions of dominance.[1] These definitions are socially productive given that their public elaboration appears to aid women's attempts to control their husbands; significantly, they draw on a dense history of women publicly defining which local men are appropriate choices for mates and which are to be perpetual bachelors – a social status that has been linked with relative economic marginalization within the worker-peasant economy in this part of Atlantic Spain.

I have two reasons for highlighting the disruptions articulated by women who are members of rural Galician households: (1) The ethnographic insights that emerge from these experiences illustrate that "feminist ethnography" converges with a practice approach that emphasizes structures of economic and political inequality yet also accounts for the social agency of individuals who live within structural constraints. (2) These verbal commentaries allow me to explore one source of contemporary ethnographic anxiety: the contrast between such disruptions and the occasions of ethical conflict and personal paralysis that feminist and other critical anthropologists can experience while doing fieldwork that is not explicitly "activist" or interventionist – a variation of what Marilyn Strathern (1987) termed the "awkward relationship" between feminism and anthropology (on feminist "paralysis," also see Bordo, 1990: 142).

Feminist Practice Approaches to Women's "Disruptions"

The critical theorizing of feminist anthropologists has emerged out of their particular focus on the intersections of class, ethnic, and other hierarchical sets of relationships with relationships of gendered inequality. Like other critical anthropologists and perhaps more so than feminist scholars in other fields, feminist anthropologists have also contributed important ethnographic examples of *gendered practice* by both women and men (Collier and Yanagisako 1989; Ortner, 1984: 145).

Theorists employing a practice framework are interested in a range of topics: charting how, on the "ground level," it is the interactions between individuals that reflect and sometimes reconstitute structured relationships of inequality (Bourdieu, 1977); examining particular incidents in which individuals act to further oppress their cohorts and those who are structurally weaker than themselves (e.g., Behar, 1993; Bourgois, 1995; Scheper-Hughes, 1992); and accounting for cases ranging from organized social movements to ubiquitous forms of everyday resistance, whereby subordinated individuals oppose the status quo (Abu-Lughod, 1990; Ong, 1987; Scott, 1985). Another concern has been to distinguish between the actions and articulated understandings of individuals. Through paying close attention to what people say about their situations and about their limited possibilities for action, ethnographers have been able to contribute in crucial ways to a broader comprehension of indigenous theorizing (as in Behar, 1993; Marcus, 1992; Reed-Danahay, 1995; Roseman, 1996; Tsing, 1993). Just like elites, some of those who are dispossessed may describe their predicament in structural terms and even understand that they may exacerbate their own situations by acting in ways that are self-destructive (e.g., see Bourgois, 1995). Moreover, ethnographers who have adopted a practice approach have been able to demonstrate that having the ability to analyse one's situation does not often translate into organized political action. Indigenous theorizing can, however, have an important impact on individuals' negotiations of their immediate social relationships.

In this chapter, I demonstrate that seemingly isolated incidents involving disruptive commentaries can be viewed as examples of women's gender practices and indigenous theorizing in three ways. First, middle-aged and older women who live in rural villages in the Spanish Galician province of A Coruña perform these disruptions, like they do related speech acts such as gossip, as social control mechanisms to support other women's attempts to renegotiate their relationships with male partners (cf. Wolf, 1972:40; also see Ginsburg and Tsing, 1990). A second aspect of these disruptions is that they are didactic devices used to teach younger, unmarried women about men and marriage. On a third level of analysis, these conversations are also examples of indigenous theorizing since the women who initiate and dominate such discussions demonstrate that they have a subtle understanding of the fact that individuals of both genders are socially constructed at an early age as being (among other things) desirable or undesirable choices for marital partners.

In the remainder of the essay, I present two ethnographic examples of women's verbal disruptions. These accounts are followed by further analysis of how these disruptions constitute a female-dominated activity of inscribing the behaviour of men in their communities. I also address how this Galician ethnography demonstrates the salience of a feminist practice approach. Finally, I discuss how anthropological paralysis is itself transformed into practice when fieldworkers are enjoined to participate in the public elaboration of critical narratives.

Rosalía and Paco

> "*Hai homes que lle mallan ben a mullere.*"
> (Some men beat their wives badly.)
> — MARTA

As is the case in several municipalities in A Coruña, I have strong ties with many of the inhabitants of the community where Rosalía and Paco live. In addition, as was true of other rural locales in Galicia, much of what I knew about the dynamics among and within families was learned through observation and through my participation in the winding, intense, microscopically detailed conversations in which neighbours were engaged daily.

On a chilly fall evening, a fire was burning in Marta and Enrique's woodstove. Within five minutes of my arrival, their neighbours Estevan and Ana dropped by. It struck me at once that my four middle-aged friends were upset about something. My sense of dramatic expectancy was confirmed within minutes of our greeting each other. Adding details in turn, but mainly following a core narrative recounted by Marta, they told me that the previous afternoon their neighbour Rosalía had been seen by several passersby in her yard hitting her husband Luís on his arms, back, and neck with a broom while simultaneously screaming at him. Some witnesses were reportedly jarred not only by the violence and the public display but also by the fact that she was joined in her endeavours by their teenage daughter Anxeles.

According to Marta and Enrique, the two women's fury had been propelled both by a long-standing pattern and also by a more immediate, yet related, cause. In the past, and increasingly during the last few years when wage work had become difficult to attain, Paco had been known to beat his wife Rosalía. Like some other men in this and neighbouring villages, Paco usually attacked her in the confines of their home late at night, after returning home from an evening of drinking in one of the local taverns. However, on the previous day Rosalía had reversed that situation. She had announced her husband's brutality to the whole village, not by telling others about it but rather through explicit enactment: in broad daylight in the yard outside their house, Marta returned Paco's past blows.

The four adults reacted differently to the story of what Rosalía had done. The men chuckled nervously and made jokes about Paco having been publicly humiliated. However, both Marta and Ana (who was normally quiet and shy) forcefully emphasized the justice of Rosalía's behaviour. The men stopped smiling and listened to their wives. Finally, Enrique agreed, saying to his wife "*Tes razón* (You're right)."

Marta and Ana became even more animated and began quickly to tell me more about why Rosalía had taken action. They did not dwell on the physical abuse Paco had inflicted on his wife over the years, but immediately began to talk about the fact that he was irresponsible and had begun to leave the entire management and support of their economically precarious household to his wife. The final straw had been when he cashed a government cheque and used the money to go on a three-day drinking binge.

Marta and Ana were appalled at this behaviour, having been told by Rosalía that she intended to use that money to buy bags of feed necessary to support the couple's livestock over the winter months. Unlike most other families, Rosalía and Paco did not own land and had been unable to gain access that year to a sufficient number of fields in which to plant fodder. This aspect of the story was the one that was most emphasized to me over the next few days, by both Marta and Ana and also by other groups of women who were talking about Paco's behaviour and Rosalía's response. Again and again, I heard listeners punctuate narrators' accounts of Paco's irresponsible behaviour and the public incident with the phrase "*Fixo ben* (She did the right thing)" (cf. Burbank, 1994: 155-67).

Moreover, the public discussions of the personal difficulties the couple was experiencing did not remain restricted to these events. Rosalía took further action to attempt to control Paco's brutality and irresponsibility: she forbade him to go out in the evenings for the next two months and made this punishment well known among her female neighbours. The women, in turn, confronted their husbands and sons with this information and again asserted among themselves the correctness of her action. Although I knew a few women who intermittently marched into village taverns to tell their husbands to come home or who sometimes asked children or other men to pass on the same message, I had never before heard of a woman infantilizing her husband to the extent that Rosalía had done by imposing a curfew on him. A week later, on another rainy day, I stopped into a nearby village tavern/store late in the afternoon and ended up chatting with the woman who owned the tavern and one of her female neighbours. They asked me if I had heard about Rosalía's restriction of her husband's *vicios* (or vices) and I replied that I had. In rural Galicia, older and middle-aged women frequently say that women have to be the frugal managers and that it is mainly men who have the "vices" of spending money on alcohol and cigarettes. Like others, the two women affirmed that Rosalía had had no choice in the matter: "What else could she do?" the tavernkeeper commented to me, and I found myself agreeing.

It seemed, then, that the entire community knew about not only Rosalía's interdictions but also the details of Paco's behaviour that led up to them. The women loudly censured him. Some of the men agreed with their comments, as Enrique and Estevan had on the evening when I was told about Paco having been assaulted by his wife and daughter in public. Other men nervously chuckled about his predicament, even as they agreed that he deserved to be humiliated in this fashion. I did not hear anyone, male or female, censure Rosalía or her daughter Anxeles for their actions. Paco himself walked around the village quietly and avoided making eye contact.

A few weeks after the widespread broadcasting of this household's problems, I had further occasion to discuss the situation in a private conversation with Marta. I asked her whether Paco was listening to his wife and remaining at home during the evenings. She told me that he was not only doing so but that he had also given over complete control of the couple's finances to Rosalía. Marta also explained that Paco was reportedly spending his days working under his wife's direction, doing especially heavy physical labour around the cowshed, yard, and fields. I had been living in rural Galicia long enough for this last detail to have a strong resonance for me, a resonance that related to two different patterns. When they were being disciplined, errant children and adolescents were often assigned heavy tasks. Moreover, I had come to understand that a related procedure was used, by both family members and neighbours, in attempts to arrest the physical and social decline of the clusters of underemployed, undernourished, alcoholic men who lived in the rural parishes with which I was familiar. Like Paco, many of these men had spent some time in their youth working as migrant labourers abroad. Unlike Paco, however, very few of those men, whose excessive drinking and public displays of drunkenness had resulted in their being socially defined as "drinkers," were married household heads.

In each village, several of the more prosperous families frequently endeavoured to hire these alcoholic men to do agricultural day labour for a wage that usually included two or three meals. I had sat at numerous tables observing the women who had hired these workers trying to cajole them to eat heartily, to drink coffee in addition to wine and the Galician liqueur *aguardiente*, and to go home to sleep after a late supper instead of passing by the tavern. One of these women, a close friend of mine named Concepción, would sit chatting with these men after most of the other family members had left the table after supper. For example, she would ask one of her employees, a man in his fifties whom I will call Manolo, to tell her about his experiences in his youth as a migrant labourer in England, France, and the Netherlands. After having been present on a few of these evenings, I sensed that Concepción appreciated it when I led the late-night conversation with Manolo, allowing her to wash the supper dishes while we sat at the table behind the sink entertaining her.

My interpretation of this consistently emotionally charged hosting behaviour on the part of Concepción and other women was that they had developed the strategy of attempting to provide an alternative late-night companionship to that which these men encountered in the taverns. When men such as Manolo would leave the house, Concepción would cheerfully remark to them that she hoped they were going home to sleep because she expected to see them early the next morning for breakfast. When I would stop by on subsequent days, Concepción would sometimes be frustrated about the fact that the men had not appeared for work. In the first few months of our acquaintance, my initial, naive interpretation was that Concepción was upset on these occasions because she and her husband Alberto needed the work done that the men were hired to do. I soon came to understand that, in many cases, they were creating jobs for these men and were upset when they did not appear because the main intent had been to exert some social control over the men's alcoholism. Interestingly, in opposition to the strategy of self-help groups such as Alcoholics Anonymous, individuals like Concepción did not ask their neighbours to stop drinking. In contrast, they made a point of offering them wine first during meals —a hospitality gesture indicating respect for equals or social superiors. The emphasis seemed to be on providing them with meaningful employment for as many hours of the day as possible, making sure that they ate well, and controlling their intake of alcoholic beverages.

As I describe in the next section, similar tactics were being operationalized (after de Certeau, 1984) by members of the community in the case of the young man I have called Pepe. In addition, however, on the surprising occasion of a parish *festa*, a group of his older female neighbours decided to undertake a collective analysis (what I am calling a "disruption") of why, at only nineteen years of age, he was experiencing so much personal suffering and loss of social status. I also describe how this community attempt of a partial rescue of Pepe was limited. Like Manolo and other older men who drank excessively in rural villages in A Coruña, Pepe had already been firmly defined as unmarriageable and as someone who would never head a landed household.

Pepe

> "¿*Recordas cando empezaches a bebir, home?*"
> (Do you remember when you began to drink, man?)
> — MARÍA

I had returned to Spain for the summer and was very pleased when several friends invited me to attend an outdoor festival. Late in the afternoon, as people lingered over steaming cups of coffee, I was catching up on family news with Matilda, a woman in her thirties. While we were chatting, a thin, young man named Pepe passed by. He was grinning widely and calling out greetings to people at nearby tables. When Matilda asked Pepe to sit down and join us, he proceeded to tell us how much he was enjoying the day and to explain that he had helped to build the stage that now held the performers. While talking, Pepe used the slurring, jocular tones he and other men in the area used when drunk. He lit a cigarette, narrowed his eyes, and swayed back and forth. It bothered me to see reflected in nineteen-year-old Pepe the early signs of the middle-aged men I knew in Galicia who appeared to be almost perpetually drunk.[2]

Although I knew many of his neighbours, from previous field trips to the area, I had only remembered Pepe as one of many quiet adolescents in the area who had difficulties in school. As Matilda and Pepe laughingly compared notes on how much they had eaten that day, I recalled that several women (such as my friend Minya) had recently told me that they had been employing Pepe as a day labourer. Pepe suddenly stopped clowning around and switched to a sober, low tone of voice, asserting that he had only had two beers all day long.

Minya herself showed up at our table and then her sister Susana squeezed in beside me and touched my hand affectionately. All three women then turned to look at Pepe and Susana asked him how he was faring. "Have you been drinking much?" she demanded with a tone that I had only heard her use with her own children.

I was surprised to hear the direct question being posed in public during a festival. The other two women and myself were silent. I glanced at Pepe's face and saw it transform from the light-hearted, joking demeanour of the previous few minutes to a quiet, serious aspect. He looked up at Susana and explained that he had been working for her sister and was trying to save up the money he was earning to buy a cassette player. As she got up to go, Minya aggressively hammered at him: "And you'd better be at my place at eight sharp tomorrow morning." Like that of her sister, Minya's stern, angry-sounding tone was also familiar to me; she used it when she was concerned about one of her own children, godchildren, nieces, or nephews. Minya was replaced by María, who owned a village tavern. María, too, clearly wanted to discuss Pepe's situation and had chosen to sit with us because she heard what was being said at our table.

Over the next forty-five minutes, Susana, María, and Matilda charged Pepe to restrict how much he drank. At times, he responded seriously; in other moments, he tried to make a joke out of their intensity. For example, he remarked, "Fine. I won't drink any more Coca-Cola," after hearing Susana turn around and instruct her young son to switch to orange Fanta.[3]

The most interesting part of this disruption of the mellow and light-

"*FIXO BEN*" (SHE DID THE RIGHT THING)

hearted atmosphere of the *festa* on this day, however, came near the end of the conversation at our table. María asked Pepe to explain to me how he began drinking.

"*¿Recordas cando empezaches a bebir, home?* (Do you remember when you began to drink, man?)," she asked him.

Pepe explained to us that it had begun when, at fifteen years of age, he stopped going to school and began to work for a man who delivered beer to taverns and restaurants in the region. "We would stop and have a drink," he said. "And I was young (*Era novo*)."

It now appeared that what was becoming a collective analysis by Pepe and the three women was being undertaken with the pretext of explaining something to me. "That's right, *Saron*. That's when the trouble started," Susana said.

Pepe then described very fluidly how he had controlled his drinking until, approximately a year later, he lost his job and became depressed.

"*Que cousa. Hai que traballar* (What a blow. Everyone has to work)," Susana said next, this time in a soft voice filled with understanding as opposed to her earlier tones of rebuke.

Up until that point, I had known that this conversation was unusual. However, I was shocked when Minya asked Pepe what his parents had done about his problems. Although there was much gossip about individual families behind their backs, it was very odd to hear Pepe being asked to discuss his own parents' behaviour in front of neighbours. "*¿Qúe dixeron os teus pais?* (What did your parents have to say?)," she inquired.

Pepe mumbled an incoherent reply and seemed to me to retreat into a shell reminiscent of his younger self.

A former high school teacher of Pepe's passed by our table and demanded to know whether he was working. Matilda and Susana answered for Pepe, telling this teacher that he had been working for Minya and her husband Luís and that he was not going to spend late nights in the taverns any more.

Pepe asked a friend of mine to take a photograph of him and me, sitting together on the bench. The women watching this scene laughed and laughed, telling Pepe that, not only was I married and a "professor," but that he could not really expect to have a *novia* (girlfriend) given the "state" he was in.

As had been the case with Paco and Rosalía's situation in a nearby community a few years previously, I discovered that Pepe's story was the focus of a significant number of conversations I had with women over the next few weeks. Minya and Susana emphasized that his father also drank and that Pepe had been *perdido* (lost) when he began to work for the man who delivered beer. I also had occasion to talk with him when he ate his meals at Minya and Luís's home. One warm evening, when Pepe came into the kitchen to wash up for supper after digging fence-post holes all afternoon under an unusually hot sun, I barely recognized him. He looked healthier than I had ever seen him, having gained some weight and sporting a sun-tanned face, neck and forearms and an easy grin. He also spoke in a coherent and serious fashion about the necessity of his remaining occupied in productive work during the daytime.

"You have to understand, I'm not lazy," he said to me. Then Pepe switched to a smile, and in a self-mocking manner described how the tavern-owner María had asked another man to take him home at eleven o'clock the previous evening.

"Good!" Minya remarked, and told him to make sure not to detour too long on his way home on the present evening.

When Pepe had left, thinking back to the ridicule the young man suffered when he "played" at being photographed as my boyfriend, I asked Minya if she thought that he might now be of more interest to the unmarried, young women living in the area. Her young daughter Encarna and teenage goddaughter Sofía laughed. Minya seemed to be incredulous at my naivety; however, she took the time to explain to me that Pepe would clearly never have a girlfriend, let alone marry anyone. She then simply named some older bachelors who lived in the village, all of them alcoholics who worked under the authority of parents or married siblings and also periodically as day labourers for other households. Encarna chirped up, "Yes, *Saron*, you see Pepe is like *o noso* (our) Chuchu [nickname for Jesús]," referring to one of those middle-aged, unmarried men who periodically worked as a day labourer for her parents.

Conclusions: Women's Disruptions in Practice versus Academic Paralysis?[4]

> It was so weird this morning because I unconsciously grabbed the littlest boy in [a] ... family in ... and sat him down. His mother was hitting him because he hadn't sat down. She laughed and said: "Sharon doesn't want me to hit you but I'll hit you anyway."
> — LETTER FROM THE FIELD TO A FRIEND IN CANADA

I have included these accounts of women's critical commentaries on Paco's and Pepe's behaviour because they allow me to demonstrate the value of a feminist practice approach to anthropological research. I chose examples of

"*FIXO BEN*" (SHE DID THE RIGHT THING)

uncomfortable incidents on purpose. A practice approach not only allows researchers to do comparative research on the everyday gender practices of women and men, it also provides us with a way to contrast the practices we observe and analyse with our own discomfort in conducting those observations and analyses.

The situations I describe are likely familiar to many women and men who have undertaken intensive fieldwork in closely interwoven communities of related households. Anthropologists such as Dorothy Ayers Counts have described feeling both guilty and disempowered by their inability to intervene in, or comment on, men's regular physical abuse of their spouses in long-term field sites (Counts, Brown, and Campbell, 1992: ii-ix; Counts, personal communication). For a variety of reasons, these feelings were maintained in silence or restricted to oral discussion with trusted colleagues for many decades (also see Moreno, 1995). Although we have numerous ethnographic accounts and explanations of male-to-male violence, particularly between men of distinct settlements (e.g., Chagnon, 1983), we have few anthropological accounts of the high global incidence of men's violent acts toward women and children, or of physical attacks by adults of both genders on children and the infirm (for an exception, see Gutmann, 1996: 196-220). As Counts points out (1992), anthropologists have tended to be reluctant to criticize the members of the economically and politically marginalized communities they often study. Bourgois (1995) also mentions the dangers of unintentionally sensationalizing and thus exoticizing people's violent actions – a reading that distracts from important analyses of the social processes underlying these behaviours.

How, then, does a feminist ethnographer experience and write about her knowledge that Paco had been hitting his wife Rosalía and that Pepe could apparently not stop drinking? Is the feminist "paralysis" of the anthropologist working in a community in which she is a short-term guest more or less difficult to surmount than that of a feminist living in her home town who does not act to discover whether her subdued neighbour is being abused by her male partner? In this essay, my aim has been to provide narrative ethnographic accounts that demonstrate the processes whereby Galician women such as Minya intervene to lessen the extent of men's dominating and self-destructive behaviours, but, at the same time, show their understanding of the structural circumstances that underlie these patterns of interaction. When Susana, Matilda, and María asked Pepe to remember when and why he began to drink, they led him through a discussion of how he had become used not only to drinking but also to earning money in lieu of attending secondary school. They went further, exploring the root of his experiences of disempowerment when he lost his job. When Susana heard Pepe talk about his unemployment, she stopped playing the chastising parent and remarked, "*Que cousa. Hai que traballar* (Everyone has to work)." However, I do not assume that women's criticisms of Pepe's alcoholism will necessarily help him stop drinking. They themselves surprised me by indicating that he could not reverse the social trajectory he had begun as an adolescent. Their recognition of Pepe's *habitus* (after Bourdieu, 1977) is another aspect of a social practice approach I wish to highlight.

Similarly, I do not pretend that women's heavier criticisms of Paco's brutality and irresponsibility are equivalent to their physically entering his home and intervening in his conflicts with his wife Rosalía. If he did attack her in public, however, I am certain other men and women would intervene. In addition, I feel that if she did tell him to leave, she would be supported by her neighbours in this demand.[5] And their insistence that other men in the community publicly accept the correctness of Rosalía's reactions might aid other women in negotiating relationships with male partners in the future.

A feminist practice approach, therefore, allows me to highlight the link between political and economic inequality and the active engagement of rural Galician women in the limited disruption of particular relationships of gender dominance and gendered subjectivities. However, such an approach erases some of the apparent distinctions between my positioning as a non-interfering, outside observer and the women whose lives I study.

Without labelling me as a "feminist" or a "critical anthropologist," the women who befriended me in rural Galician communities quickly ascertained that I had firm views on classism, sexism, and racism. They frequently asked me what I thought about reports on the news and events portrayed in television programs; they also asked me to talk about what it was like to be a woman raised in Canada. In contrast to my readiness in responding to most of these inquiries about events and relationships that were distanced from "the field," I found that I was initially reluctant to talk about my impressions of life going on around us in rural Galicia; in fact, I often felt paralysed from talking and acting as I thought I did in my home community in Canada (see papers in Wolf, 1996). However, by inviting me to participate in conversations held mainly for social control and didactic purposes, my Galician neighbours and friends enjoined me to do more than observe their lives.

A practice approach demonstrates not only how productive women's disruptive commentaries can be but also how these public discussions can draw anthropologists into local analyses. The women I know in rural

Galician villages do not invite me to participate in their intense deliberations about the actions of men like Paco and Pepe simply as a welcoming gesture. They are enjoining me to participate in the local politics of gender consciousness. And it is clear that women like myself, or Aihwa Ong (1995), who describes a similar process in a recent essay, are regarded to be important voices in these discussions; unlike most of the women whose lives we study, we are relatively economically independent, well educated, and socially mobile (also see Abu-Lughod, 1993).

When I wrote the letter from which I quote at the beginning of this section, I was a neophyte fieldworker. As is common, I poured out my feelings of frustration, hypocrisy, and sadness in a letter to my friend. Sara, the woman who told her child that she knew I wanted to stop her from hitting him, is one of my long-standing interlocutors who frequently asks me to say what I think about difficult situations such as abortion and the class snobbery of some individuals who treat rural dwellers badly. My almost reflex reaction in attempting to protect Sara's son from further physical punishment, at the time it occurred, seemed to me to symbolize the absurdity of pretending that one could do politically engaged, yet non-interventionist, fieldwork. However, a few weeks later Sara initiated with me and some of her neighbours a lengthy four-woman discussion of child-rearing methods in the past and present. Furthermore, she also confided in me that she was suffering from *nervios* (debilitating anxiety attacks) and found it difficult to be patient with her children. After introducing the topic, we would return to it when I visited her and we found ourselves alone. In subsequent years, I was relieved to discover that Sara was feeling calmer and actually seemed to have an unusually relaxed relationship with her children.

A practice approach can be central to feminist ethnographers' attempts to account for women's agency, the structures that constrain that agency, and their awareness of these constraints. It can also be used to analyse not only how women's practices are socially disruptive within their local communities but also how we, as feminist anthropologists, can be similarly disruptive in subtle ways in both their and our own communities and in our writings. In my case, I realize now that there is a close coincidence between these two sets of activities. Moreover, neither constitutes feminist paralysis. I was asked to be "active" in participating in the censure of Paco and the chastising of Pepe. In this essay, with particular care to disguise the communities and individuals being described, I have chosen to recount these instances of human difficulty. My aim is to join other anthropologists who have begun to bring everyday events of both interpersonal brutality and attempts at rescue into the ethnographic literature so that they can be both de-exoticized and de-marginalized. A feminist practice approach allows me to do so in two ways. First, by demonstrating how Paco and Pepe's female neighbours disrupt the daily flow of public discourse to minutely examine and react to these men's personal circumstances and social failings, I record their practices of struggling to define these men's reputations and control their behaviours. This account of women's social disruptions in rural Galicia thus adds several dimensions to debates about gender and power in this region of Europe by linking considerations of inter- and intra-household interactions between women and men. The key to my illustration of gender practices is achieved as I juxtapose my own *reportage* of events and conversations with the way in which women reflect and act on the social processes they experience and observe. Finally, I demonstrate that these interventions productively disrupt and alter my own practices as a feminist fieldworker and ethnographer. My participation in Galician women's public and private conversations accents and consistently reminds me of some of the cross-cultural commonalities between us and the possibilities for collective action. To complement this insight, however, their perceptive analyses of the structural constraints that shape men's (and women's) behaviour also starkly highlight how, over time, my own disruptions must ultimately constitute a personal practice that emerges out of my shifting positionings as an *outsider*, friend, *visitor*, confidante, *university professor*, married woman, *producer of ethnographic texts*, rather incompetent but eager helper with the work of agriculture, *scribe and translator of the lives and words of others*, emotional participant in the life cycle events of various families and communities, and intermittently both *a quiet listener* and a perhaps not so reluctant speaker.

Notes

A total of nineteen months of fieldwork in various locales in the province of A Coruña during 1990-91 and in 1989, 1994, and 1995 were generously funded by the Social Sciences and Humanities Research Council of Canada, the Council for European Studies, the Wenner-Gren Foundation for Anthropological Research, the Universidade de Santiago de Compostela, the Xunta de Galicia, and McMaster University. The names of individuals used in this paper are pseudonyms. In addition, in order to disguise the identity of the various locales portrayed here, no nomenclative indicators are used. My sincere thanks to Heather Howard-Bobiwash, Wayne Fife, Sally Cole, Rae Bridgman, and Jean Briggs for their perceptive suggestions on how I might best formulate and revise drafts of this essay.

1   Despite the fact that some parts of rural Galicia can be described as having relative gender equality, it is not accurate to indicate an absence of social discourses supporting male dominance that characterize marriages and other relationships elsewhere in Europe (see Kelley, 1994).

2   I had observed young boys imitating this behaviour when drinking Coca-Cola during *festas*. Although the majority of my Galician male acquaintances drink alcoholic beverages daily, they control their intake and behaviours carefully; individuals who act drunk are socially censored and marginalized.

3   Many of the Galician women I know are concerned about the way in which male children in particular are affected by the sugar and caffeine in Coke, and by other *vicios* (or vices) such as gambling. In the early to mid-1990s, Coke and other soft drinks were served only on festive occasions. However, in imitation of the encouragement of overeating and adults' own consumption of alcoholic drinks during weddings, summer festivals, and other similar events, the children often drank excessive amounts of Coke. It was only when Pepe made this remark that I drew an association between the women's concern about men's alcoholism and their anxiety about young boys' uncontrolled indulgence of Coke during *festas*.

4   I have come to the realization that the tensions between non-elite and academic thinking and action (or non-action) that I explore here have a parallel in university classrooms. In response to the texts that we read and the lectures that I give, many of my students contribute their own significant series of intellectual "disruptions." I have come to realize that many of these often precise critics of academe openly identify not with us but instead with the people about whom we write. This will be the subject of a future paper.

5   Although this couple did not own land, many women in the area have inherited more property (including houses) than their husbands. If one of these men was excessively abusive and his wife insisted on their separating, he rather than she would be expected to leave the dwelling. An important and understandably unstudied topic for research in this area would be to determine whether there is less physical and other abuse by men who are economically more vulnerable than their wives who have remained in their natal households. See, however, Kelley's (1991) discussion of single mothers in coastal Galicia. It is also important to note that some of the men who I was told deserted wives in past decades may have left in part as a result of difficult marriages.

References

Abu-Lughod, Lila. 1990. "The Romance of Resistance: Tracing Transformations of Power Through Bedouin Women," *American Ethnologist* 17, 1: 41-55.

—. 1993. *Writing Women's Worlds: Bedouin Stories.* Berkeley: University of California Press.

SHARON R. ROSEMAN

Behar, Ruth. 1993. *Translated Woman: Crossing the Border with Esperanza's Story*. Boston: Beacon Press.

Bordo, Susan. 1990. "Feminism, Postmodernism, and Gender Scepticism," in L. Nicholson, ed., *Feminism/Postmodernism*. New York: Routledge, 133-56.

Bourdieu, Pierre. 1977. *Outline of a Theory of Practice*. London: Cambridge University Press.

Bourgois, Philippe. 1995. *In Search of Respect: Selling Crack in El Barrio*. Cambridge: Cambridge University Press.

Burbank, Victoria Katherine. 1994. *Fighting Women: Anger and Aggression in Aboriginal Australia*. Berkeley: University of California Press.

Chagnon, Napoleon A. 1983. *Yanomamî: The Fierce People*, 3rd ed. New York: Holt, Rinehart and Winston.

Church, Kathryn. 1995. *Forbidden Narratives: Critical Autobiography as Social Science*. Luxembourg: Gordon and Breach.

Collier, Jane, and Sylvia Yanagisako. 1989. "Theory in Anthropology since Feminist Practice," *Critique of Anthropology* 9: 27-37.

Counts, Dorothy Ayers, Judith K. Brown, and Jacquelyn C. Campbell, eds. 1992. *Sanctions and Sanctuary: Cultural Perspectives on the Beating of Wives*. Boulder, Colo.: Westview Press.

de Certeau, Michel. 1984. *The Practice of Everyday Life*, Steven Rendall, trans. Berkeley: University of California Press.

Ginsburg, Faye, and Anna Lowenhaupt Tsing, eds. 1990. *Uncertain Terms: Negotiating Gender in American Culture*. Boston: Beacon Press.

Gutmann, Matthew C. 1996. *The Meanings of Macho: Being a Man in Mexico City*. Berkeley: University of California Press.

Kelley, Heidi. 1991. "Unwed Mothers and Household Reputation in a Spanish Galician Community," *American Ethnologist* 18: 147-62.

—. 1994. "The Myth of Matriarchy: Symbols of Womanhood in Galician Regional Identity," *Anthropological Quarterly* 67, 2: 71-80.

Khare, R. S. 1996. "A Paradoxical Gift of Memory: The Pain, Pride, and History of an Untouchable 'Kitchen Poetess'," *Anthropology and Humanism* 21, 1: 19-30.

Marcus, Julie. 1992. "Racism, Terror and the Production of Australian Auto-biographies," in Judith Okely and Helen Callaway, eds., *Anthropology and Autobiography*. New York: Routledge.

Moreno, Eva. 1995. "Rape in the field: Reflections from a survivor," in Don Kulick and Margaret Willson, eds., *Taboo: Sex, Identity and Erotic Subjectivity in Anthropological Fieldwork*. New York: Routledge, 219-50.

Ong, Aihwa. 1987. *Spirits of Resistance and Capitalist Discipline: Factory Women in Malaysia*. Albany: University of New York Press.

—. 1995. "Women Out of China: Traveling Tales and Traveling Theories in Postcolonial Feminism," in Ruth Behar and Deborah A. Gordon, eds., *Women Writing Culture*. Berkeley: University of California Press, 350-72.

Ortner, Sherry. 1984. "Theory in Anthropology Since the Sixties," *Comparative Studies in Society and History* 26: 126-66.

Reed-Danahay, Deborah. 1993. "Talking about Resistance: Ethnography and Theory in Rural France," *Anthropological Quarterly* 66, 4: 221-29.

Roseman, Sharon R. 1996. "'How We Built the Road': The Politics of Memory in Rural Galicia," *American Ethnologist* 23, 4: 1-25.

Scheper-Hughes, Nancy. 1992. *Death Without Weeping: The Violence of Everyday Life in Brazil*. Berkeley: University of California Press.

Scott, James C. 1985. *Weapons of the Weak: Everyday Forms of Peasant Resistance*. New Haven: Yale University Press.

Strathern, Marilyn. 1987. "An Awkward Relationship: The Case of Feminism and Anthropology," *Signs* 12, 2: 276-92.

Tsing, Anna Lowenhaupt. 1993. *In the Realm of the Diamond Queen: Marginality in an Out-of-the-way Place*. Princeton, N.J.: Princeton University Press.

Wolf, Diane L. 1996. "Situating Feminist Dilemmas in Fieldwork," in Diane L. Wolf, ed., *Feminist Dilemmas in Fieldwork*. Boulder, Colo.: Westview Press, 1-55.

Wolf, Margery. 1972. *Women and the Family in Rural Taiwan*. Stanford, Calif.: Stanford University Press.

SHARON R. ROSEMAN

FOURTEEN

"TO RECLAIM YORUBA TRADITION IS TO RECLAIM OUR QUEENS OF MOTHER AFRICA:" RECASTING GENDER THROUGH MEDIATED PRACTICES OF THE EVERYDAY

Kamari Maxine Clarke

Margaret Mead's statement, that if a fish were an anthropologist the last thing it would discover would be water, rings in my head as I debate the relevance of "insider anthropology" to my research in Oyotunji African Village, South Carolina. Oyotunji, a village of some fifty residents, is situated approximately sixty-five miles southwest of Charleston, near Beausfort, a city with a population of nearly 90,000. Oyotunji is an intentional community of converts to Yoruba religious and cultural practices. Since its formation in 1970, residents have strengthened their ties with Nigerian Yoruba traditionalists. Artists and carpenters in the village designed a community that emulates West African rural village life. Although I am not concerned with the centrality of race as a signifier of fundamental commonalities with my African-American interlocutors in Oyotunji, I ponder the social history which often locates me as "Black" Canadian, in Toronto, "African American" in Berkeley, California, and *oyinbo* (a Yoruba word for White man or outsider) in Yorubaland, Nigeria. Yet according to Paul Gilroy (1993), still connected to a Black-Atlantic memory of transatlantic slavery. On one hand, I share the central criterion for group belonging – that of "transatlantic blackness;" on the other hand, as a non-Yoruba practitioner and an academic who claims other identities, such as "Canadianness," routed through the Caribbean, my connections to African history, via the American South, are variously located.

The relevance of which entities are seen by individuals as insiders is indeed constitutive of the forces of history by which cultural commonalities are forged. Then, Mead's fish-anthropologists, who she suggests might overlook the water variable in their life, might also render insignificant, if at all relevant, the forces of history and power in which, according to Western taxonomy, we locate them as fish in the first place. Whether the encoding of "blackness" as "former enslaved African" is used by a range of Black people as a contemporary signifier of shared ancestry raises important questions about the basis for group unity and the forces of history and social regulation that play a role in legitimizing group belonging.

When asked by a colleague about differences between the Yoruba in Oyotunji Village, South Carolina, and the Yoruba in Nigeria, I responded, "these Yoruba are Black Americans," as I pointed to the soil in front of me. When pushed further to explain how I can take seriously African Americans claiming descent from kings and queens they didn't even know, I argued that we all have interesting criteria for legitimizing ancestry and that what is interesting to me is not so much the actual identity claimed, but the forces of power that allow us to claim it as "normal."

Similarly questionable signs of normative thinking were articulated months later when I was asked by one of my relatives, as she pointed to the enlarged photo that hung in my living room displaying four masquerading figures elaborately dressed in colourful skirts and masks, "Are those African people? ... But are they even women?"

"Yes, they're African, but men dressed up as women," I responded quickly as I regretted not finding the language to explain how, during such rituals, gender differentiation is often rendered secondary to the politics of ceremonial transcendence. Yet, regardless of whether or not the signs of "Africanness" in an otherwise "black" body had been transgressed, the national origin and biological gender of the masquerades were flagged as odd.

These examples highlight the relationship between social categories and their accompanying categoric distinctions. Among anthropologists, the study of relationships between Africans on the continent and those throughout the diaspora has moved from concerns with the origins of the "primitive," to the survivals of African culture in the Americas, to the ongoing investigation into the processes through which African and African-American cultural practices are played out. Implicit in the notion of gender and culture is a presumption of particular characteristics being bounded to given territories (Grosz-Ngate, 1997: 3) and bodies. In different dimensions of studying culture, a heightened awareness of the interconnectedness of identity and the social processes through which individuals actively negotiate meaning in relation to space and time has continued to develop among scholars (Gupta and Ferguson, 1993). Constructions of diasporas as transnational multidirectional flows of people and resources have particular significance in studies that highlight how that individuals reshape the present through new interpretations of the past.

KAMARI MAXINE CLARKE

An example of transnational processes in which individuals reshape contemporary experiences by invoking the past was evident at the commencement of my second visit to Oyotunji Village and one year of fieldwork. On the first day I wore a bright yellow patterned blouse made out of a cotton fabric from Senegal with a pair of casual white cotton pants. I was greeted by the head of the women's society, a female chief,[1] who remembered me from my visit the previous summer. She took me aside and told me that she remembered that I wore such nice clothes the last time that I visited and that if I planned to live with them this year I would have to abide by the rules and wear a *lapa*, since Oyotunji was a "traditional" African village where women did not wear pants but traditional women's wraps around the bottom half of their bodies. She graciously offered to sell me some clothes from her market stall. I resisted by thanking her and explaining how comfortable I felt when I wore what I was accustomed to. To convince me to look at the clothes in her market stall, she reiterated that my dress was not "traditional" and that I should never return with "those men's clothes."

In an attempt to allude to my purpose for being there she showed me a book by Samuel Johnson, *The History of the Yorùbás* (1921), and told me I should study it if I really wanted to understand Yoruba traditions and the place of women in those traditions. Having read Johnson's work, I could not plead ignorance and told her that I simply did not bring any formal outfits with *lapas* with me. To that she responded that I was "in the right place" and, pointing to the clothes in her stall, she stated, "Forget those American clothes, show your true traditional identity, buy African clothes."

We both laughed, but for different reasons. I laughed because of the irony of my attempt to research Yoruba traditions while testing her on something as fundamental as women's traditional clothing, a signifier of not only gender but necessarily gendered traditions. Later that day, upon reflecting on the interaction, she explained that her laughter was in part to relieve the tension between us because she couldn't believe that I would stand there so blatantly wearing the "wrong clothes" and arguing about something that was so "obviously wrong."

The basis upon which the chief finally legitimized the idea of traditional Yoruba normality was through the use of sociological scholarship on Yoruba history. Samuel Johnson, a Yoruba missionary trained by British colonialists, wrote *The History of the Yorùbás* with the intention of detailing the evolution of Yoruba practices to show the influences and role that Christianity played in shaping Yoruba progress. Oyotunji practitioners refer to this text as the authorial documentation of Yoruba history, serving as a comprehensive guide for traditional Yoruba practices. Their narrativization of African traditionalism as a form of political redemption, based on the early documentation of Yoruba cultural practices, raises questions about what aspects of a given traditional practice are to be emphasized in the process of reconstructing the Yoruba past.

There remain three particularities in how the Yoruba traditional past was invoked by the chief who chastised me upon my return to Oyotunji Village. First, traditionalism was used to establish an ancestral connection with West Africa; second, it was used to highlight tropes of the female Yoruba woman as the centrepiece of the model Yoruba lifestyle; and third, its applicability for New World practitioners required a system of proof or rhetorical structure through which references to an anterior period could be established. Contemporary African-American women who are members of the growing movement of Yoruba revivalism in the United States are continually engaged in the active process of reclaiming African-based identities of which they can be proud. Ultimately this narrativization of Yoruba traditionalism as gendered and as a form of political redemption raises questions about what aspects of a given traditional practice are to be emphasized in the process of reconstructing the Yoruba past and under what conditions trust aspects are enforced and why.

The constituting features of Yoruba traditionalism are marked by a contested terrain of meaning production. While they grapple with the problem of affirming Yoruba traditionalism in their lives, they struggle with the ambiguities concerning what constitutes "traditional" womanhood in the first place and who has the right to determine its boundaries. The engendering of the African past both allows for the reproduction of patriarchy in revivalist movements and leads to the production of women's agency, in which women reshape and control the regulating and disciplining mechanisms.

One of the most important issues in the anthropology of Africa is the "invention of Africa." V.Y. Mudimbe (1988) demonstrated that colonial constructions of history and identity have informed discourses concerning how Africans understand each other and themselves. This "invention" has also been taken up by African Americans reclaiming African-based cultural practices as their own. One such location is Oyotunji African Village. For many of its residents, as well as the thousands of affiliate members dispersed throughout North America, Oyotunji Village represents a symbolic connection with the ancient Yorubaland Oyo Empire, a region seen as the symbolic ancestral home for millions of Africans exported to the New World during the transatlantic slave trade. Just as particular notions of Africa as home are driven by representations of blackness and the memory of transatlantic slavery (Gilroy, 1993), "African womanhood," as constituted within Oyotunji Village as pure, mutually constructs images of Yoruba men as noble patriarchs committed to the redemption of African-American families.

How patriarchy is reproduced in these movements raises questions about the forces of power that normalize gender relations. Here, I am exploring the constant reformulations of Yoruba tradition and the particularities of Yoruba repatriation by examining the ways that gender is necessarily central to the reformulation of the Yoruba family and consequently the diasporic nation. As such, history and the active regulation of signs of Yoruba traditions both play an important role in shaping dominant narratives of Yoruba-American womanhood and provide a framework through which women in Oyotunji Village contest the nature and relevance of Yoruba traditionalism in their lives.

Processes of constructing Yoruba traditionalism in transatlantic relations can be read through a series of instances in which particular forms of Yoruba traditions are legitimized by the disciplining mechanism of appropriate female behaviour. Through my experiences of women's rebuke, I came to understand that women's reformulations of Yoruba identity in the United States meant incorporating the gendered signs of traditionalism – clothing, social behaviour, and, more prominently, discourses of purity and polygynous marriage. Ultimately, Oyotunji women's reformulation of themselves as Yoruba was based on a range of diverse reconceptualizations of the African family through which particular constructions of Yoruba gender were played out.

The relationship between female traditionalism as a signifier and Yoruba traditions are inextricably linked to the ways that Africanness is gendered in particular ways. The power relations that surround the U.S. Yoruba signs of traditionalism and the ability of Oyotunji women to enforce their interpretations of traditional appropriate behaviour depend on the relevant social and individual forces that allow for the appearance of traditional normativity. In the process of African-American reclamation of African cultural traditions particular diasporic tropes are played out. Oyotunji women's conceptions of themselves tend to be as much about the systematic process of updating patriarchal narratives of African women as mothers and keepers of the tradition as about the implosion of gender inequalities.

In exploring theories of cultural processes, whether in revivalist communities or in communities with long histories of identity formation to a particular place, it is not just that men and women, as distinctly gendered, experience African repatriation in particular ways; it is that in the process of constructing traditionalist norms there are particular ways in which local

The Oyotunji Village Women's Society

instantiations of gender are controlled and regulated. The invention of Africa is not simply a remapping of equal social processes across national boundaries – it is an invention of the past that is gendered and regulated in particular ways.

I began this chapter with reflections on how my own experiences of Oyotunji women's discourses of traditionalism contributed to my understanding of how the canons of Yoruba history were used by women both to uphold patriarchy and to manoeuvre new meanings within it. I will now examine how, in the process of constructing the basis for contemporary cultural norms, both men and women used the Yoruba canon not only to author their practices but to construct them as legitimately gendered. In particular, through the example of a court trial held in the village, I will show how the use of traditional laws as a mediating practice provides the basis upon which larger institutional norms such as marriage and premarital sexual status can be regulated through gendered and traditional tropes.

The Ideal of the Yoruba Family: Purity, Polygyny, and Anti-Fraternization

A central value in the reclamation of Yoruba "tradition" in Oyotunji Village has been the conception of the Yoruba family through the ideal of polygynous marriage. From its founding and through to the mid-1980s, polygyny was established in Oyotunji Village to serve as the familial organization for this North American Yoruba revivalist movement. A radically different form of family was seen by the founding members as the basis for the promulgation of a Yoruba nation in North America. Enforcing interpretations of female traditionalism while maintaining the appearance of gendered distinctiveness presented challenges to standardizing notions about what constitutes the traditional Yoruba family. The existence of validating discourses for the institutionalization of traditional Yoruba marriage serves as a means of legitimacy for the way marriage is practised. To ensure that the young girls remain virgins until they marry, Oyotunji gender roles are organized and regulated by residents, especially middle-aged women, who are responsible for institutionalizing Yoruba-based traditional practices.

In an Oyotunji court trial hearing that I observed the defendant, a middle-aged female chief and mother of three, whom I refer to as Her Royal Grace (HRG) Iya Sisilum,[2] was charged for allegedly criticizing the mothering practices of the plaintiff, Iya Olayindo (also a pseudonym), thereby committing slander. Iya Olayindo, a mother of three, was popularly known by many of the town women as being unable to pay her basic living expenses and for being far too liberal (read: loose) with her daughters. Although HRG Iya Sisilum did make public allegations about Iya Olayindo and her daughter's loss of purity, she justified her actions by making intelligible particular standards of "traditional" female behaviour. In so doing, she sought to show that these allegations were justified because they were both in keeping with traditionally documented prerequisites for the Yoruba family and essential to the survival of the New World Yoruba movement.

The initial trial arguments were followed by witness testimonies and the cross-examination of the defendant by the judge. Not only did the defendant maintain that she was "not guilty," but she argued quite eloquently that as a "traditional" Yoruba woman, a mother, and village resident, she acted out of "traditionalist" obligation. HRG Iya Sisilum defended herself by appealing to values of female purity which she argued formed the basis of Yoruba "traditions" in the New World. As a rhetorical strategy, HRG Iya Sisilum repeatedly highlighted that Yoruba laws had been broken by Iya Olayindo and her girls. She argued that "Iya Olayindo ignored my advice that their behaviour was not socially acceptable among the Yorubas. These remarks were not stated to defame the family; these remarks were stated to uplift the family and to present a traditional model for Yoruba women."

HRG Iya Sisilum's reference to a traditional model of the Yoruba female behaviour during the trial was not only an effort to assert her beliefs and justify her actions, but also an effort to enforce patriarchal standards to which she believed it was the responsibility of women and girls to adhere. During an early stage of the trial she described her family's attempt to defend themselves against accusations that her young daughter was not a virgin. Knowing that there were also oppressive possibilities for the misuse of traditionalism, she argued that females had to protect themselves from unfounded accusations.

The plaintiff, Iya Olayindo, had different interpretations for appropriate enactments of traditionalism.[3] For her, "traditional" motherhood was not just based on ancient culturally specific laws but on universal notions of a mother's relationship with her daughter and the daughter's obligations to her mother. She justified this by alluding to good deeds and reciprocity in the American tradition in which she was raised. On the contrary, HRG Iya Sisilum's actions were justified by a different conceptualization of transnational traditionalism. With her invocation of "tradition" came the accompanying validation of the institution of Yoruba polygynous marriage. HRG Iya Sisilum referred to the value of policing young girls so that they could retain their bridal value by remaining virgins. Its importance? – the standard Oyotunji Village model of family emphasizes the premarital virgin. And with the rare exceptions of Oyotunji women's gender distinctions, which highlight the existence of dominant African female rulers, such as Queen Njinga and the great and powerful female deities and goddesses, Oyotunji Village narratives of "traditional" female roles focus on the centrality of female purity as "authentic" Yoruba traditionalism. With this mission, HRG Iya Sisilum tried to enforce mediating practices such as the premarital norm and polygyny in order to maintain legitimate traditions.

The irony of using traditionalism as a form of contemporary revivalism is that just as colonial constructions of "Africanness" have been selectively used to posit Africa as "primitive," so, too, notions of African "traditions" and histories are selectively gendered by the post-colonial élite in the international arena (Williams, 1991: 259). As in the selective process of using gendered signifiers of tradition to mark the past, women and men in Oyotunji Village use "tradition" to construct gendered notions of purity. The use of "tradition," seen as a product of the mutual construction between and among women and men and their notions of the past, sheds light on the complexities of interpretation through which Yoruba gender and power relations are regulated.

Audrey Wipper (1972), in her analysis of fashion and dress in relation to the selective recuperation of some African traditions in the shift to post-colonial regimes, argues that African leaders claimed superiority for their traditions over Western European "traditions" introduced during the colonial era. They publicly advocated their desires to reclaim traditional ways and openly dismissed the denigrating influences of colonialism. Yet, contradictions exist in selectively reclaiming certain aspects of traditionalism and not others. In Wipper's study, for many men who wore three-piece suits, were clean-shaven, and vied for power in the bureaucracies and parliamentary government institutions left over from the colonial era, the end to aping Western ways only meant that women were to return to the home, lower their hemlines, remove their make-up, and stop straightening their hair, wearing wigs, and using complexion lighteners (Wipper, 1972: 332-38).

Recognizing that communities and individuals are constantly engaged in negotiating and contesting meaning is critical for rethinking the complexities of African reclamation of African cultural practices. Those who produce, consume, and are marginalized by hegemonic determinants of culture on a local level are actively involved in a larger process of continual reformulation of meaning and possibilities for improvisation. These processes of reformulation, at particular times, are adequately situated as "traditional" and at other times are repudiated. HRG Iya Sisilum attempted to win the support of the jury and audience through her continual references to "traditional" codes and behaviour. Her evocative prefiguration of returning to "traditional" roots by upholding women's traditions can be seen as the enforcement of patriarchal rules previously established by the community's élite. For HRG Iya Sisilum, the different expectations of male and female behaviour were based on the fundamental teachings on the Yoruba institution of "traditional" family marriage. That is, ideas of Yoruba families are not only enforced through a state apparatus or legal institution forcing people within its jurisdiction to concede power against their conscious will; instead, they are enforced through the agents of institutions, the élite who produce cultural knowledge – in this case, priests, diviners, chiefs, authors – and because some definitions of tradition and traditional practices are already in keeping with pre-existing patriarchal alliances, they are incorporated into mediating practices and more easily defined as appropriately gendered.

The Politics of Status and Social Mobility

Even as Oyotunji imaginings of Yoruba traditionalism are imported onto new social geographies to create laws and norms – whether the goals are to reinstitute traditional practices, social hierarchy, and political power (Shaw, 1995; Ortner and Whitehead, 1978), economic inheritance, or new forms of legitimacy through the production of diasporic identity – the way the past is incorporated to contest and shape social norms is the key to understanding how gender is inextricably linked to what it means to be "traditional."

Mediating practices, such as the production of particular forms of marriage and notions of premarital purity, provide the mechanism by which social norms are played out.

The notion of purity as a mediating practice is a gendered topic with implications for social status and political hierarchies. The Yoruba female realm is itself a social construction particular to sociopolitical hierarchies and processes. Contextualizing purity through virginity and as a mode of social mobility in colonial and pre-colonial Africa is hardly new to anthropology. In *Colonial Inscriptions: Race, Sex and Class in Kenya*, Carolyn Martin Shaw argues that marriage is shaped by larger issues of inequality in which young females are used by members of their family as a form of political mobility. She argues that virginity is an indexical sign indicating a woman's physically inviolate or intact state, and on the sociocultural level virginity is an iconic sign referring to the inviolability and intactness of the group the virgin represents. Virginity is about heterosexual intercourse, or rather the absence of heterosexual intercourse. Female virginity signifies intactness, the credibility of a woman's assertion of wholeness, the lack of penetration by the other. At another level, the virginity of daughters and sisters represents in many societies the integrity of the family group or the group concerned with female fertility (Shaw, 1995: 83).

Shaw discusses the rules of sexual codes in colonial Kenya by examining how the representation of Kikuyu sexual morality had a profound effect on the ways that female sexuality was imagined. In her review of the Kikuyu literature, including the work of anthropologist Jomo Kenyatta and British colonial and anthropological writings, she argues that in particular African societies women collaborate in the control of their sexuality for themselves and the social mobility of their family. Likewise, in the Oyotunji Village, social mobility is possible through sexual purity – virgins are more likely to gain upward mobility through engaging in a Yoruba traditional marriage. Women co-operate and enforce laws and family institutions for many of the same reasons that men enforce those norms – to gain control of the political and social resources through which status and power can be achieved. Therefore, in order for traditionalism to be indexed as authentic, sexual purity as a mediating practice is inextricably linked to the categoric distinctions between Oyotunji men and women, girl and boys.

In *The King's Two Bodies: A Study in Medieval Political Theology*, E.H. Kantorowicz discusses the process of legitimizing social hierarchies by examining the idea of the transmission of a "royal race." He examines how specific forms of science invoke notions of pure bloodlines, authenticating the electoral succession of a king. This treatment of royal birth, as constituted through "blood," reiterates that notions of royalty and procreation are intricately linked to social status and the ability to become royal through kinship.

Although Kantorowitz does not explore the implications for constructions of gender, the same framework is useful in demonstrating how transmission of power is also regulated through particular practices that constitute what is seen by the majority as "proper" premarital practice. Anti-fraternization laws and royalty-commoner distinctions are instituted by Oyotunji Village elders and élite as a way both to enforce the ideal of premarital virginity for girls and to control the function of arranged marriage in maintaining class distinctions. If the relations of power through which older women institute and enforce these laws are also connected to class distinctions and mobility, then young girls function as agents through which individual and family social status is negotiated. And by maintaining the distinction between genders in which the role of Yoruba-American boys and men is not dependent on maintaining sexual purity, the mythic Yoruba female image can be constructed as legitimately "African." Therefore, just as HRG Iya Sisilum was in a position to enforce patriarchal laws at the discomfort of Iya Olayindo, so, too, was she attempting to pursue possibilities for social mobility.

The power differentials involved in creating and sustaining these family institutions raise questions about the totality and fixity of governance and power insofar as mobility and contestations to traditions are concerned. Through the type of questioning pursued by the judge, the court clearly recognized the defendant's attempt to maintain traditional gender laws, but called into question the appropriateness of her disciplinary approach. Despite her attempt to assert and justify her actions according to particular dominant "traditional" practices, the complexities of power between the judge, the defendant, and the plaintiff existed alongside patriarchal practices. As such, the trial in question was not simply about an embattled situation between two women vying for the power; it was also about the complexities of HRG Iya Sisilum's status seen in relation to the judge/king's disapproval with the way she attempted to enforce the traditional practices.

The conclusion of the trial, at 2:05 a.m. after approximately six and a half hours of deliberations in which a 4-3 vote found in favour of HRG Iya Sisilum, was marked by the judge's final reprimand of the defendant, in which he also warned the community as he counted the votes and announced the verdict, "Her Grace is then dismissed from these charges." He continued, "All members of Oyotunji are of course to be very, very careful of what you say, where you say it and of course how you say it because you do not have unlimited licence to go about making statements which you cannot substantiate or which you cannot in any way make complete sense of. This court then finds Her Grace not guilty and stands in adjournment."

HRG Iya Sisilum's insistence on enforcing "tradition" regardless of social context was not acceptable to the judge. Not only did he attempt to discipline her publicly, but he barraged her for usurping his power and making claims that she could not substantiate. Nevertheless, HRG Iya Sisilum argued her actions in enforcing traditionalism justified her means. For her, the social norms that she protected were necessarily in keeping with traditional laws.

The uses of traditionalism as a manipulable form of cultural reclamation in Oyotunji Village are bound to produce differing opinions and assertions. Differential relations of power exist where some women are able to articulate and enforce particular notions of traditionalism in public and legal spaces because they abide by dominant "traditional" interpretations; other women are not as successful in influencing the meanings and signifiers of "tradition." HRG Iya Sisilum claimed that her interpretation of "traditional" gender codes was based on the "good of tradition," therefore, the good of the community. However, for Iya Olayindo, HRG Iya Sisilum's parameters of "tradition" were ineffective and contradictory. Although the positions of the two women were neither fixed nor mutually exclusive, the position occupied by one woman attempting to enforce traditional codes is not always sustainable as dominant.

The findings indicate that more is known about gender relations in Oyotunji Village when we study the discursive articulation of how women incorporate the historical basis for gender distinctions into their own lives. The duality of authority and repudiation is central to the problem of agency and hegemony in the enforcement of traditionalism. For even though HRG Iya Sisilum was declared "not guilty" by the courts and appeared to have had the support of various women in the Oyotunji women's society, she still endured social rebuke long after the trial ended. Many residents and non-residents with whom I spoke felt the trial was based on personal vendettas and the manipulation and abuse of "truth." Some, especially the women who attended the trial, saw themselves aligned with the defendant and instead argued that the plaintiff, Iya Olayindo, was guilty and should have herself been tried for the abuse of "traditional" laws. For others, their perception of the abuse of traditions by the defendant led them to declare that Iya Sisilum should have been under scrutiny instead.

The foregoing analysis allows for a perspective on gender, culture, and power and for a rethinking of the theoretical problem of the ways that regulatory practices transmit gendered distinctions in the African diaspora. In general terms, those who claim African ancestry but do not have direct familial ties actively engage in practices that allow for a rearticulation of historical traditions. The vast majority of women in Oyotunji Village identify pre-colonial West African identity as their own through the active reproduction of "things Yoruba." And although the concluding determinations are never based on a homogeneous agreement of what constitutes Yoruba traditionalism in the Americas, the complexities of redefining local meanings in the context of globally shaped norms are precisely what makes connections between gender and power significant to the contestation of Yoruba revivalism outside of Yorubaland.

Notes

The data presented here emerged from research funded by the Social Science Research Foundation of Canada and from follow up work supported by the Wenner-Gren Foundation for Anthropological Research. Special thanks is due to the President's Office at the University of California, Berkeley, where I spent two years working on the manuscript from which this chapter emerged. I am also indebted to my reviewers, both known and unknown, and especially the intellectual insights provided by Carolyn Martin Shaw, Steve Small, Julia Sudbury, Galen Joseph, Angela Davis, Cori Hayden, and Heather Howard-Bobiwash. This chapter was presented for feedback at a range of institutions, and to those who offered suggestions I am also grateful. I thank the supportive intellectual communities at the University of Texas-Austin, the University of Toronto Ontario Institute for Studies in Education, the Congress of Black Women-Toronto Chapter, and the Canadian Sociology and Anthropology Association.

1 During the summer of 1995, there were a total of seven chiefs in the Oyotunji community. There is one ruling king, the Oba, who refers to his governmental system as a democratic dictatorship.
2 The acronym HRG, meaning Her Royal Grace (wife of the king), signifies royalty.
3 A few days after the trial, it became public knowledge that Iya Olayindo had been strongly encouraged and pressured by the king and other chiefs not only to file a letter of grievance against HRG Iya Sisilum but to enter into a formal hearing with her.

References

Gilroy, Paul. 1993. *The Black Atlantic: Modernity and Double Consciousness.* Cambridge, Mass.: Harvard University Press.

Grosz-Ngate, Maria, and Omari H. Kokole, eds. 1997. *Gendered Encounters: Challenging Cultural Boundaries and Social Hierarchies in Africa.* New York: Routledge.

Gupta, Akhil, and James Ferguson. 1992. "Beyond 'Culture': Space, Identity, and the Politics of Difference," *Cultural Anthropology* 7, 1: 6-23.

Johnson, Samuel. 1921. *The History of the Yorùbás: From the Earliest Times to the Beginning of the British Protectorate.* London: Routledge & Kegan Paul.

Kantorowicz, E.H. 1957. *The King's Two Bodies: A Study in Medieval Political Theology.* Princeton, N.J.: Princeton University Press.

Mudimbe, V.Y. 1988. *The Invention of Africa: Gnosis, Philosophy, and the Order of Knowledge.* Bloomington: Indiana University Press.

Ortner, Sherry B., and Harriet Whitehead. 1978. *Sexual Meanings: The Cultural Construction of Gender and Sexuality.* New York: Cambridge University Press.

Shaw, Carolyn Martin. 1995. *Colonial Inscriptions: Race, Sex and Class in Kenya.* Minneapolis: University of Minnesota Press.

Williams, Brackette. 1991. "Nationalism, Traditionalism, and the Problem of Cultural Inauthenticity," in Richard G. Fox, ed., *Nationalist Ideologies and the Production of National Cultures.* Washington: American Anthropological Association, 112-29.

Wipper, Audrey. 1972. "African Women, Fashion, and Scapegoating," *Canadian Journal of African Studies* 6, 2:3 29-49.

FIFTEEN

GENDER AND IDENTITY FORMATION
IN POST-SOCIALIST UKRAINE:
THE CASE OF WOMEN IN THE SHUTTLE BUSINESS

Tatiana Zhurzhenko

THE rapid growth of employment in the informal sector and the emergence of marginal forms of economic activity comprise a marked trend of the economy in transition in Ukraine in the last decade. There are women who have carried the main load of the social costs of market reforms and who have had to elaborate alternative economic strategies proceeding from their limited possibilities. Indeed, some marginal forms of economic activity may be accurately called "female," as they represent "female niches" that have spontaneously emerged in the transition economy. The hypothesis set forth on the basis of the research presented in this essay is that risk, instability, invisibility, and lack of recognition in modern Ukrainian society are inherent in such marginal types of business and specifically impact on the formation of the gender identity of women involved in this sphere of activity.

The transition from socialism to the market-oriented economy is accompanied by a revision of gender roles and by the emergence of new models of behaviour. This has resulted in radical changes in the economic strategies and lifestyles of Ukrainian women. In the present situation, where the political and economic structure of society and the cultural environment are undergoing radical transformation, the emergence of new identities for Ukrainian women reflects the instability and contradictions of society in transition.

The literature on new gender identities in the countries of former Eastern Europe (Funk and Mueller, 1993; Moghadam, 1993; Einhorn, 1993) has focused on ethnic (nationalism) and political (independent women's movement) contexts. Rarely, has the formation of new identities been examined in connection with women's new economic roles or new models of economic behaviour. An example of such an approach is the work by Marina Malysheva (1995: 22-26), which focuses on the changes in the economic strategies and self-identities of women in post-World War II and post-Communist Russia. The few works devoted to women's new models of economic behaviour, speak only about their participation in legal business. Woman's marginal economic activities have been largely ignored and have received little attention from Ukrainian sociologists and anthropologists, despite the fact that informal and marginal economic practices are undoubtedly the more common experiences for women.

In this paper I explore and document ethnographically the emergence of new gender identities among women engaged in the shuttle business – a new and increasingly common form of economic activity among Ukrainian women. What makes women take up such informal and risky work? What changes does the work bring about in their lives? What new identities do women develop through this work? How comfortable are they in their new social and economic roles?

Women in the Shuttle Business:
The Reality of the Market Economy in Ukraine

One of the marginal, shadow forms of entrepreneurship that has grown in Ukraine since the end of the 1980s has been the shuttle business. It is a specific kind of wholesale commercial business involving the delivery of foreign consumer goods to the Ukrainian market in small lots by one or a few people called *chelnoks*. In the shuttle business, profit is received as a result of the difference between prices for the goods in the country in which they were produced and prices in the local market. It is a new form of activity that emerged in the late 1980s and became possible with the opening of national boundaries, the liberalization of the economy, and the allowance of free private trading.

The Russian word *chelnok* (shuttle) refers to the part of a tool that makes rapid, regularly repeated motions to and fro. In recent years, the term *chelnok* has been given to those people who make regularly repeated trade trips to other countries, especially Turkey and China, to buy and then sell goods. The shuttle business, unlike smuggling, is a semi-legal activity. It is not prohibited by law, but Ukrainian legislation is contradictory and ambiguous concerning it. The production cycle is as follows: having accumulated necessary circulating capital a *chelnok* obtains a tourist voucher in one of the tour companies specializing in the organization of shopping tours. This voucher allows the *chelnok* to cross international borders and provides transportation and hotel accommodation. Any additional expenses are covered by the *chelnok*. The tour company forms a group of about fifteen to twenty people who go to a country such as Turkey or China to buy goods for a period of between three to seven days. In some cases (usually in the countries of the former U.S.S.R.) the trips are individually organized without the help of tour companies. Purchased at wholesale markets or directly at the factories or warehouses, goods are delivered to the Ukrainian market by the *chelnoks*, who pass it through the frontiers as private persons. Sometimes the goods are registered in the customs declaration forms as personal items, sometimes as a commercial lot. *Chelnoks* may pay both official taxes and bribes to the customs officers and frontier guards. Intermediate transport of the goods (from the market to the hotel and from there to the bus or ship) is done by porters, and if the *chelnok* cannot afford to pay a porter, she or he will transport the goods her/himself. The goods are sold, as a rule, at the local clothes market directly by the *chelnoks*, or if they have the necessary connections, in retail shops.

In the 1990s, the shuttle business fulfils important economic functions in Ukraine: it provides a considerable part (according to some estimates, as much as 50 per cent) of the clothing sold in the country; it also meets the needs of people who are economically marginalized and who make their profit because of the relatively low prices paid for the goods and, where possible, the evasion of customs duties and taxes. It is also a very important and sometimes the only possible source of self-employment under the present conditions of mass unemployment and represents an alternative strategy for survival and realization of entrepreneurial potential. In addition, the shuttle business is often the first step on the way to the creation of a legal small business. At the same time, the cheap goods from countries such as Turkey and China that comprise the major part of the commodity circulation of the business undercut the prices of goods produced by Ukraine's light manufacturing sector and contribute to high levels of unemployment, especially among women who dominate the labour force in this sector. Thus, the social and economic consequences of the development of the shuttle business are ultimately contradictory to Ukrainian families and the Ukrainian economy as a whole. However, under the conditions of a repressive tax policy, political instability, and the absence of legislative guarantees for private business, shuttle activity is virtually the only form of entrepreneurship accessible to people who do not have the necessary family connections. It offers one of the few possible adaptive strategies for households coping with the conditions of social and economic transformation.

Being accessible and democratic, and demanding relatively small amounts of start-up capital, this kind of business attracts women who are searching for any possibility to improve their economic conditions but who do not possess the powerful family connections or capital necessary for a legal business. According to various data, 60-70 per cent of the *chelnoks* are women. They hold an emergent intermediate position between the old and new economic systems by trying to use the advantages of market freedom while carrying the burden of the transition to the market economy. In other words, they are not afraid to change their lives completely, having chosen a new risky model of economic behaviour while having no opportunity to run their business legally.

For many reasons, opportunities for developing legal small businesses are limited for Ukrainian women. The first is the closed character of Ukrainian business, which is based largely on kin networks and on the use of former Communist Party connections. Second, the rigid hierarchical character of business relations and methods of conflict resolution, the undeveloped legislative base of entrepreneurship, and the semi-criminal character of a major part of Ukrainian business all make women-entrepreneurs highly vulnerable. A third factor is the "renaissance of patriarchy" in post-Communist society (Posadskaya, 1994) evident in the increasing emphasis on so-called traditional gender roles, and widely held assumptions in mass consciousness that business is a masculine occupation. Finally, institutional conditions do not exist to support women entrepreneurs: no practical aid from state bodies and non-governmental organizations (NGOs), no access to credit, and unfavourable tax laws and complex registration procedures for new enterprises.

The semi-legal character of the shuttle business and working conditions that can pose quite dangerous health and economic risks lead one to speak about this activity as entailing problems that are most acute for women. The main risk factors in shuttle activity are: (1) heavy physical work and strain caused by regular travel over long distances and carrying heavy loads without satisfactory conditions for rest; (2) psychological tensions and stresses caused by the dangers inherent in bringing in goods on routes that sometimes require going through "hot spots" and being subjected to the despotism of customs, militia, and frontier guards who often demand bribes and use blackmail; (3) the real threat of encounters with racketeers and criminals and of physical and sexual violence; and (4) excessive use of alcohol, often provoked not only by stresses and physical tension but also by unfavourable climate conditions, above all, winter.[1] Women and men involved in the shuttle business do not possess even a minimal level of social guarantees: they do not receive annual paid leaves or payment for temporary disability; their working day is not limited to set hours; women do not have maternity leaves or support for child care. Their lives, health, goods, and capital have no insurance and they are exposed to constant risk. Finally, due to the semi-legal status of the *chelnoks*, they are also deprived of legal protection.

Chelnoks remain in the informal sphere chiefly because of the excessively high costs connected with the legalization of businesses in the Ukraine. The total sum of taxes, bribes, payments for licences, patents, and allowances would consume 90 per cent of their profit. A *chelnok* who remains "invisible" from state officials and who channels capital into single-trade operations thus may have considerable advantages in comparison to the legal entrepreneur.

Methodology

The research reported here was conducted in 1996-97 in Kharkiv, Ukraine. Kharkiv is one of the largest cities in Ukraine and is a scientific and industrial centre. Today, the problem of women's unemployment is urgent due to the state budgetary crisis, especially in the spheres of education and health care, and as a result of the collapse of large industrial enterprises. The conditions of the shuttle business in Kharkiv are typical for Ukraine in general. In the course of the research twelve women *chelnoks* were interviewed. These women have different life experiences, length of work as *chelnoks*, ages, social origins, and marital status. The age of those interviewed ranged from twenty-four to forty-seven. Seven of the twelve women were married; nine had children (usually one, though some had two); four were single mothers. Half of the women (six) had a post-secondary level of education (one of whom had a Ph.D.); the others had attained either a secondary or specialized secondary education. The length of time employed as *chelnoks* varied from one to seven years. For one-third of the women interviewed this was their main and continuing occupation. The others turn to this activity from time to time and combine it with their main occupation. Among the women interviewed several were professionals, in fields such as teaching, economics, technology, engineering, child-care work, medicine, and university-level teaching. Job security and remuneration in these occupations have decreased in post-socialist Ukraine. Some of the women have prior experience working in the state-run trade sector. All the women interviewed are inhabitants of Kharkiv and either were born in the city or have lived there for most of their lives.

Life history interviewing in the form of directed conversation was chosen as a research method. Each of the respondents was told about the research purpose, agreed on a time for the interview, and agreed on the set question she would be asked to answer: "What is your experience in the shuttle business?" At the end of their narratives the respondents were asked additional questions to elaborate particular points. In the course of the interview and while analyzing their texts I was interested in the following subjects: the reason women took up the shuttle business; the problems they encounter; gender roles in the shuttle business; and the subjective experience of the respondents. A characteristic feature of this research was that the women's responses, at least initially, mirrored their experiences as semi-legal or illegal and unprotected workers: they were closed and suspicious of my interest as a researcher.

One must not forget that in this case, both the researcher and the subject are in a state of transition, even crisis, and a transitional identity is typical not only for women *chelnoks* but also for women in the academy. As evidenced by both my own experiences and those of my colleagues, at the present time the woman researcher's position in science is also marginal. We constantly have to make a choice between scientific independence and personal affection, between career and family, and between prestige and personal academic interests. We feel a constant tension in the context of the predominantly masculine academic discourse of scientific research and institutions. Ukrainian academia is in transition not only due to a crisis in funding but also because of the difficulties of negotiating new relations with Western scholarship and familiarizing ourselves with new approaches, concepts, and methods of research. Furthermore, our professional security as women researchers in this climate has become increasingly vulnerable.

Thus, at one level, researchers and *chelnoks* share experiences common to women as a group in Ukraine's transitional society: insecurity, vulnerability, and the need to be flexible, resourceful, and innovative. This provided a foundation for mutual understanding that facilitated informal interviewing, making it possible not only to reach a higher degree of sincerity but also to discuss questions that are not yet part of public or academic discourse (especially in Ukraine) and that therefore, "do not have a name" (Reinharz, 1992: 23).

At the same time, our different lifestyles and different models of professional and life success made mutual understanding problematic. Interviewing women *chelnoks*, who appear to have adapted to their social role, I felt that we were radically separated by different life experiences. "You can't get it, you know nothing about life"; "You haven't seen anything yet, you're too young"; "You know nothing but those books of yours" – such were the remarks of some of the women, though they expressed themselves in a somewhat well-wishing, even protective way. Nevertheless, when speaking to these *chelnoks* I did not feel as much tension as I experienced while talking to those women *chelnoks* who had a background of higher educational and social status, especially in the fields of education and science. In general, these women were in different ways trying to remove from their consciousness thoughts about their professional and life failures. These women suffer quite significantly in the interview situation in which they are not the researcher but rather the subject of the research. Even more problematic for them is the fact that they are being interviewed not as professionals but as *chelnoks*. Power and social prestige are always present in the research relationship, but in the case where a researcher and a research "subject" realize different models of life behaviour or belong to different social groups, this factor does not provoke such tension. However, when researcher and subject have similar education and social class background and similar ideas of what life success and social prestige are, there emerges a critical situation leading to a feeling of disappointment, awkwardness, envy, and shame and to an inequality that is difficult to overcome.

Woman *Chelnoks:* Entrepreneurs or Homemakers?

Participation in the shuttle business determines to varying degrees the economic behaviour, social status, hopes, and self-identity of women *chelnoks* and distinguishes them from women who are engaged in legal private business or hired labour. Being "pioneers" of new market relations, having chosen active strategies of economic behaviour, they have nonetheless found themselves in a situation of marginality and confront a set of contradictory conditions. The shuttle business sharply limits the possibilities of professional and personal growth or career development. The goal for women *chelnoks* is to widen and improve their family's standard of living. However, a desire for cultural and intellectual development, professional and career growth, or personal self-expression can hardly be satisfied in this sphere of activity. Such aspirations are either unrealized or remain located in their prior professional training or employment, which has been temporarily moved into the background. In both cases this leads to an identity crisis. It is extremely rare for women to identify themselves as *chelnoks*. Some women identify themselves through their main or former occupation (doctor, teacher), some through family roles (mother, wife, housewife), and some (the most successful *chelnoks*) through their entrepreneurship.

In Ukraine, it has traditionally been the woman's responsibility to organize household consumption. Generally, then, the main motivation for women to become involved in the shuttle business is not merely an abstract desire to "earn money," Rather, being familiar with the purpose of money, they enter the shuttle business to improve the financial situation of their families. In the shuttle business there is no distinct dividing line between market economic activity and housekeeping, since consumption within the family blends with the trading cycle. Through this social role – improving the material conditions of the everyday life of the family, protection of children, creation of a material base for home comfort – the woman *chelnok* most organically identifies herself, seeing herself not as a businesswoman or entrepreneur, but as a "home establisher" or housewife.[2]

Therefore, the dynamics of identity are connected with the consumer behaviour of women *chelnoks*. Above all, a woman *chelnok* tries to solve the problem of personal or family consumption, of providing the family with concrete goods and services. The shuttle business is business not only for the sake of money as such, but for the sake of obtaining consumable goods. As one of the *chelnoks* said: "Women succeed more in this sphere because they know pretty well what is necessary to bring home to their husbands and children. They know the needs of the family better than men do. After each trip I bring something home because the money I earn is usually invisibly dissolved."

The leading role of Ukrainian women in the family, their readiness to take upon themselves the responsibility for its physical survival, and their apparently greater ability than men to adapt to change all have historical roots. The specific model of family and marriage relationships, with a strong mother and weak father, was quite prevalent in the pre-revolutionary period. In the nineteenth century, Ukrainian society was based on subsistence agriculture, with the majority of the population living on the edge of poverty. As in many other agricultural societies, Ukrainian women had rigidly defined roles – to give birth, raise children, and be housekeepers. One of the characteristics typical for Ukraine, however, was that many male peasants worked as seasonal labourers far from home to earn money to pay their taxes. By the beginning of the twentieth century the urban proletariat consisted mostly of newly arrived agricultural workers (predominantly male). The result was that, in rural areas, households were often effectively headed by women, which is why patriarchal relationships showed themselves here in a different way in comparison to the idealized Western bourgeois family with a strong father. The centrality of women in rural households was strengthened by the economic and political emancipation of women brought about by the revolution of 1917. As a result of the wars, repressions, and other social disasters that led to a decrease in the male population, women's labour activity and growing economic independence became inevitable. As a rule, women took upon themselves the main burden of family responsibilities and functions while men possessed nominal authority in the family and functioned as family representatives to the external world. Women more often became the heads of households regardless of the presence or absence of men. At the same time, in the economy and society as a whole the status of women was marginal, as women were practically deprived access to management and decision-making roles. This is why, post-socialist market transformations, on the one hand, have pushed women out of the labour market and led to women losing their status in the social sphere and, on the other hand, have mobilized the historical potential of the traditional leadership of women in the family.

Social Status, Prestige, and Money

People involved in the shuttle business provide an example of how it is possible to have in a transitional society increasing and decreasing social mobility in one and the same social group. On the one hand, among *chelnoks*, there is a growth of incomes and an increase in the material standard of living. On the other hand, there is a lowering of social and cultural aspirations, and of professional and social status. The income level and consumption level of a majority of women *chelnoks* is high in comparison to average salaries in Ukraine. Indeed, this social group was one of the first to reach Western consumption standards. However, the prestige and social status of this kind of activity are very low – at least for women. Above all, this is related to a bias left over from the socialist system when private trade was regarded as "speculation." The dominant idea is that the shuttle business is associated with easy enrichment, needs no knowledge or education, and is an activity of a semi-legal character because incomes remain hidden from the state. Not only in Ukraine, but also in other countries, " the honest taxpayer" is an enemy of the informal sector, believing that she or he will win economically after its extirpation (Neitzert, 1993: 20-21). It should be noted, nonetheless, that when men are involved in the shuttle business, their relatives and friends tend to see their activity as a serious or "normal business." However, as a result of a woman's shuttle activity, her prestige and status become automatically lower. This is expressed by the language: the word *torgovets* (trader) sounds neutral and is rarely used, while the word *torgovka* (woman-trader) is used pejoratively.

At the same time, social transformations in Ukrainian society today produce new situations in which the notions of prestige, life success, and professional achievement lose their stability and significance. The status and prestige of a profession may be rather high in one social group and low in another and may be differently evaluated depending on the choice of criteria: profitability, intellectual and creative character, as well as the knowledge and qualifications necessary to carry out the work. Thus, in some sectors of the population, taking up a shuttle business is seen as a loss of social status and as ruining one's life prospects, whereas for others it is an acceptable survival strategy in the present transitional economic situation. For still others the shuttle business is a preferred lifestyle and a successful means for solving financial problems. Correspondingly, the dynamics of the formation of new identities for women *chelnoks* will be different under these distinct conditions.

Shuttle Business and Gender Roles

The identity of women *chelnoks*, as with other Ukrainian women, is formed to a great extent through the family and gender roles of mother, wife, and housewife. The social status of a man, as a rule, is determined by his personal life strategies, his personal and career development, and depends largely on himself. The social status of a woman is determined by various combinations of her personal life strategies and her husband's strategies, which may take different directions. The directions of these strategies may become a source of conflict within a family or may lead to shifts to a non-traditional distribution of gender roles. Thus, in the families of women *chelnoks* men often fulfil the role of "home health protector," because business may require that women not be at home.

From the point of view of the division of gender roles in the household, there are three observable patterns in the shuttle business: the family business, the single woman (mother), and the woman entrepreneur. In the family business, activity is run jointly by the wife and husband. Specific tasks may be distributed in a diversity of ways, but often the woman is the leader because of her business acumen and her responsibilities for household consumption and accounting. Power and privilege within these households are distributed depending on economic contribution, even if this contradicts a traditional division of gender roles that sees men as primary earners. Olga, age thirty, is married and has a seven-year-old son. She has a secondary school education, worked previously as a housewife, and has been employed as a *chelnok* for five years. Olga describes her partnership with her husband: "My husband and I have been getting goods for the last few years now – earlier in Poland and now in Russia. We have a patent and our constant place at the local market. We even met during one of our trips! It is much easier on the road with two people. And who could be more trustworthy than one's own husband? He knows how to deal with the wholesalers, customs officials, and tax inspectors. But when it comes to choosing the goods to buy, he asks my advice."

In the case of single mothers, these women have been forced to enter the shuttle business out of economic necessity. Many identify themselves primarily through the role of mother and through their notions of obligation to their children, understood primarily as providing them with an acceptable standard of living. In Ukrainian society older relatives (grandmothers) typically are actively involved in raising children. In the case where a woman *chelnok* is a divorced single mother, she has to shift the child care and upbringing of her children onto her relatives. These women usually work in groups formed around partnerships with one or two other women. Single mothers and single women who do not have the support of a male family member can more successfully overcome the difficulties of the *chelnok* business by uniting their efforts and resources The fact of having a faithful friend and partner is very important, since this may push a woman towards taking up the shuttle business or, lacking such support, keep her away from it. The critical identity of these women is often stipulated by double dissatisfaction with their lives: they may feel they have not succeeded in either the family or professional spheres. Marina is twenty-nine years old and a single mother with an eleven-year-old daughter. She is a school teacher with a post-secondary education and explains why she began to work as a *chelnok* two years ago: "I am a school teacher and I have a daughter who goes to school. The wages in schools are very low and not regularly paid. That is why it is necessary to turn to other ways of making ends meet. I used to sew for money but then my friends talked me into going to Turkey with them on one of their trips. Now I only work part-time in a school. But I do not want to completely leave because I do not want to lose my position."

The third household pattern is comprised of active and enterprising women who enjoy the role of breadwinner in the family and who feel comfortable with a non-traditional distribution of gender roles. Due to the success of their business endeavours they have gained a dominant economic position in the family. Having decided to choose a non-traditional and risky economic strategy, they have also created by their choice a gap between their lives and those of their husbands; a gap that becomes wider because of their life and business experience in the shuttle trade. Nevertheless, such families can be stable: a woman, being financially independent, strives to protect her marriage for the prestige and social status that are immediately lost if she divorces. She accepts the passive role of a man, who often turns out to be a good assistant in family matters and a convenient partner in family life. Natalia is forty-three, married, and has no children. She has been employed as a *chelnok* at various times during the past seven years. She has a secondary school education and has also worked as a waitress and a sales clerk in a state-run store. According to Natalia: "Not everyone's husband can make money. I never expected that I would rely on my husband to feed me. I was always able to deal with my own problems. But I became tired of being single."

Life Strategies and Identity Formation

Analysis of the interviews of women shuttles has made it possible to discern three main types of life strategies, what I call here the "professional," "hobby," and "survival" strategies.

Professional

Natalia, introduced above, is fairly typical of the professional shuttle worker, who has a notable entrepreneurial spirit.

> For seven years I have leased a part of a store where I previously worked as a shop assistant. I went to Turkey to purchase plastic tablewares for our store. There I have my own suppliers – everything is already settled. I typically brought home twenty to thirty boxes of tablewares per trip. Of course, it is physically difficult and there may be unexpected problems. The main thing is to be able to settle all the problems and develop personal contacts. One must be able to bargain since all questions may be settled by agreement. However, now I seldom go there – it's better to buy the goods to be sold in my store from those who bring in large lots.

Vita, a thirty-two-year-old married woman with a twelve-year-old son, has been employed as a *chelnok* for four years. She has a secondary school education and previously worked as a sales clerk. Here she describes some of the expertise required in her profession.

> The main thing is to take everything into account – how much to invest, and what your profit margin will be. Usually you have unforeseen costs. You must know many things and determine the quality of the goods. It's important to be oriented in the market situation and be able to foresee everything: which things will become fashionable and

which will not be bought. For example, there is no use buying warm coats in the middle of winter. The most difficult thing today is to sell one's goods – people do not get salaries. It's good when one has a "realizator" [retailer] to work with or you can make a deal in a store.

To this group belong women running a shuttle business on a "professional" level. As a rule, these are enterprising women with initiative who are willing to take risks. Many of them, even in the pre-*Perestroika* period, could find niches for the realization of these personal qualities. Without having a higher education they could successfully adapt to the new economic situation and realize their entrepreneurial abilities to a large extent. They could establish a network of business connections, study definite segments of the market, and cope with constantly changing conditions. For many of them the shuttle business is an intermediate stage that allows them to accumulate business experience and capital that ultimately can be transferred to legal and more stable kinds of businesses (such as private store ownership). Once they are in formal business, in time of need they may periodically return to the shuttle business, using their knowledge of the market and their connections. A majority of these women have successfully adapted to this activity, accepting it as "normal" business though complaining about physical difficulties, risk, and instability.

Women, belonging to this category of *chelnoks* are usually satisfied with their social status, the indicator of which for them is, above all, money. Their identity is most stable; disappointment and a lack of satisfaction touch only some sides of life or particular episodes, but not the activity itself and the chosen life strategy as such.

Hobby

Masha, a twenty-eight-year-old day-care worker with a secondary education, who is married with no children, exemplifies the spirit of the "hobbyist" *chelnok*: "I am very sociable; I like when there are a lot of people and crowds. I love bargaining, buying and selling – it's so interesting. I can spend all day long at the market and I get satisfaction from it. I can persuade anybody to buy anything." Irine, a forty-four-year-old medical doctor with a husband and two children, expresses the same excitement in the life of a *chelnok*, in which she worked for two years:

> When I started going to Turkey, there was a completely different life there. Everything could be found in the stores. In the evening you

could go and sit in a café. You could buy beautiful clothes that nobody had at home. If not for my children and household I would do it full time with pleasure. I love travelling, new impressions, new people. It's a different kind of life. Nobody controls you, you are your own master.

As a rule, these are women for whom economic motivation is not dominant; they are attracted by the lifestyle itself. Or, the economic motivation after meeting the first requirements has evolved into an interest in the process of buying and selling as such. These may be women who are already well-provided for by prosperous husbands but who are tired of the monotony of life as a housewife. They may have both education and occupation but sometimes use their leaves, vacations, or days off for the shuttle trade. They are ready to take all the burdens of the shuttle business for the sake of the pleasures that are not available to them in their everyday routine, that is, for the sake of new diversions and entertainment. Sometimes it is a chance to get away from the exclusive circle of family and household and to find new friends with whom to socialize. The economic aspect, as a rule, interests them only from the point of view of reimbursement of the costs of the trip. Their primary interest is in bringing gifts for relatives or updating their own wardrobes. A majority of these women identify themselves through family or profession and do not regard themselves as *chelnoks*.

Survival

For yet others, the shuttle business is a source of economic survival rather than a professional career or a means of excitement. Oksana is a thirty-seven-year-old lecturer in an institute who holds a Ph.D. As a single mother with two young sons, her three-year involvement in the shuttle trade has been out of necessity:

I always worked above and beyond what was required – I brought home my working drawings [to work after hours]. I am an architect. I had to feed my children. When I found myself alone with my children, it was very hard. There were times when we collected empty bottles in the streets. I was always betrayed by the state. Now in the Institute nobody receives salaries for several months. I'm not ashamed of what I have to do – let those in the government be ashamed. I am a candidate of science. I give lectures in the Institute and I also do research work. At home I take care of my retired mother and two children. Of course [the shuttle trade is] hard, but I can plan everything and manage. One thing I don't like: the people I have to communicate with are of such a low level! I will never give up my research work. Science and lecturing are my love, the market is my life. Initially my mother was against it and most of my friends did not understand me: how I could be a trader with such a high education! Now some of them ask me to take them with me, to show them how to start. At the moment, I don't see any other prospects of earning a living. As Lewis Carroll said: "In order to hold one's ground, one must constantly run forward."

These latter women are the most typical *chelnoks* and their experience reveals the social costs of the transition to a market economy. They were forced to take up this activity under the pressure of economic necessity, either because they had lost their jobs or because the conditions of their jobs (often including forced unpaid leaves and payment delays) or the salary itself did not provide them with a sufficient source of income. Economically, they are in the most unfavourable position because they began this business out of desperation and they usually do not have the required experience, skills, and habits or sufficient circulating capital. Not being specialists, they cannot always take into account economic fluctuations, and thus, from a commercial point of view, they risk more. There are many women who have shifted to the shuttle business from such professional positions as lecturers, doctors, or engineers, positions that were once prestigious. They are suffering the loss of their social and professional status as their personal drama. They would be happy to return to their occupation if they could make more money from it. By contrast, women with less education or no professional experience tend to accept the shuttle profession more easily. Nevertheless, all of them have feelings of dissatisfaction and disappointment; most do not see many future possibilities for themselves and most do not want to remain *chelnoks* forever.

It is necessary to note that in various stages of the development of the shuttle business in Ukraine a few of the life strategies written about above were more or less predominant. From this point of view it is possible to distinguish at least two stages in the development of the shuttle business. The first stage, following the liberalization of the economy and opening of the frontiers, between 1987 and 1994, mainly included women who had shown their entrepreneurial abilities and even a predisposition to engage in risky ventures and who had quickly decided to realize new possibilities. In this period, the decreasing standard of living had not yet touched the broad masses of the population and salaries were still being paid regularly. For women in the shuttle business, the main stimulus was not exclusively to earn money but rather to see "another life" and to emulate Western models of consumption that had been intensively introduced through the mass media, advertising, and cultural industries. Taking up the shuttle business was motivated by a desire to have fashionable clothes, purchase home appliances, and experience everything that Soviet family life had been lacking under the conditions of the deficit economy. Today, however, when practically any goods and services may be found on the Ukrainian market, this type of motivation has lost its relevance. For many who entered shuttling with this motivation in mind, the model of conspicuous consumption was typical. This model also shows the crisis of identification: in this case, purchasing consumer items and fashionable and prestigious goods becomes the only purpose of the activity, justifying the physical and moral costs of giving up professional and cultural ambitions.

The second stage, 1994 to present, is connected more with economic hardship. The growth of unemployment, lowering of the standard of living, and widespread salary payment delays forced women to become involved with the shuttle business in order to feed their families. Within recent years, economic conditions have changed – the consumer market has nearly been saturated, the population's average income has fallen, and to sell the goods has become more difficult. More and more often, large suppliers of wholesale lots are pushing the *chelnoks* out of business. Under these unfavourable conditions a majority of women *chelnoks* are forced to take up this activity by rigid economic necessity. Their goal is to meet their own and their families' material needs. But the model of consumption is different – we are speaking now about providing the basic essentials of life for the survival of a family.

At the same time, during this period certain kinds of black market activity became "professionalized." There arose the category of women *chelnoks* possessing the practical knowledge, attainments, and experience necessary to organize this business on a permanent basis, to plan their trade operations in advance, and to acquire sufficient income to invest in the expansion of the business or other types of activity.

Crisis of Identity and Lifestyle

The dynamics of women *chelnoks'* identities are determined by the informal, transitional character of the shuttle business and its semi-legal status in Ukrainian society. The temporary, unstable character of this kind of activity is recognized by the majority of women, for whom it is their only source of income. Most women *chelnoks* lack the possibility of creating their own private legal business, and even those who have managed to succeed do not see positive prospects for the development of legal business.

Such absence of future prospects in both personal and business endeavours creates disappointment and dissatisfaction, leads to intensification of the identity crisis, and creates a basis for various forms of often self-abusive behaviour. For example, many women *chelnoks*, especially those who do not completely identify themselves with this social role and lifestyle, spoke of frequent use of alcohol, promiscuous or casual sex, and wasteful, conspicuous consumption. This type of behaviour is a reaction against the limits to their other forms of self-realization and their lack of opportunity for personal and professional growth. Alcohol often creates a context for finding intimacy and establishing informal relations, and, in Soviet and post-Soviet mass culture, alcohol is associated with rituals of communication. It is also a means of relaxation after the peripatetic and physical labour required of shuttle activity. Wasteful, conspicuous consumption, alcohol, and casual sex appear to offer a way to prove to oneself and others that the stresses have not been in vain, but are compensated by moments of "joy" and satisfaction in life.

Do Women *Chelnoks* Have a Future?

The probable future for many women *chelnoks* may be defeat, accompanied by feelings of disappointment and failure. The shuttle business is a temporary form of economic activity that emerged while the economy was in transition. Already today a majority of *chelnoks* speak about the rapid decrease in the profitability of their businesses, related to a saturation of the consumer market, the fall of people's incomes, the toughening of customs measures, and new policies of taxation. In the future, the rapid growth of private business and the rise of the country's light manufacturing industry may completely eliminate the shuttle business. However, if the taxation pressures on private business decrease and the government succeeds in creating a favourable enterprise climate, then the capital, experience, and connections accumulated by the *chelnoks* may provide them with a basis for the development of their own legal businesses.

It is evident that the *chelnoks* as a social group belong to the most dynamic part of the population. Having obtained entrepreneurial skills and experience, these women (at least the most successful of them) are likely to show a desire to return to the old economic system. They represent the social base of market reforms and are the most consistent supporters of the liberalization of the economy, despite the fact that as women they bear the main burden of the transition period.

The shuttle business illustrates the social reality of the society in transition and provides a basis for criticizing the optimistic position regarding market reforms in Ukraine. On the one hand, these reforms have given the people economic freedom and opportunities for private initiative that were unattainable under the former system. On the other hand, the broad distribution of marginal economic activities and the desire to avoid state control show that the goals of the reform policy have not yet been achieved: the given freedom is rather "freedom from" than "freedom for." Institutional conditions of legal private business in Ukraine are still absent. The broad participation of women in marginal economic activities requires enterprise, courage, readiness to take risks and a willingness and capacity for hard physical labour, all of which are inconsistent with the post-socialist construction of the happy housewife well provided for by her husband. It shows the dissatisfaction of women with their economic status and their desire for change in gender roles and relations.

Conclusion

The formation of Ukrainian women's gender identity reflects a contradictory situation in post-socialist society. During the last few years of reform, Ukrainian women have lived through dramatic socio-economic transition. Under the Soviet economic system, the double burden of professional activity and securing family needs under the conditions of a deficit economy was compensated to a significant degree by social guarantees and benefits. The transitional market economy, which has opened possibilities for increasing the standard of living on the basis of entrepreneurial initiative, has also brought an end to guaranteed employment and state paternalism in the sphere of social policy. Under these conditions the sharp fall in the population's standard of living, as a result of the economic crisis, has placed additional burdens on women as they seek to meet the needs of their families.

Various forms of semi-legal entrepreneurialism (above all, the shuttle business) have turned out to be the most accessible sphere for realizing new economic possibilities and/or solving families' most urgent economic problems. The shuttle business, for some, has meant the formation of new models of economic behaviour, new lifestyles, and new gender identities. These processes are contradictory and ambiguous; they reflect the conflict between various value systems and the clash of professional, personal, and family priorities.

Risk, instability, the semi-legal status of the shuttle business, and the absence of future development prospects strongly impact the gender identities of women involved in this activity. Most women *chelnoks* do not identify themselves as "entrepreneurs" since their main motivation is to secure and organize their family needs. They are usually "ordinary women" forced into undertaking extraordinary efforts for the economic survival of their families. However, for many of them the acquisition of new knowledge and skills and the expansion of their level and spheres of communication have led to a reappraisal of their own capabilities. This self-reappraisal, along with changes in the gendered division of labour within the household (brought on by women's work as *chelnoks*), has created the conditions for the emergence of new gender identities. This was confirmed in all three models of family organization of the shuttle business. In the case where the shuttle business is a husband-wife partnership the woman plays an important and, generally, a strategic role. In the cases of single mothers and women entrepreneurs, the women independently conduct the business and, in fact, are primary earners in their households. By developing the historical potential of family leadership, which is characteristic for Ukrainian women, women *chelnoks* are forced out of the bounds of gender roles that are ideologically assigned in contemporary society.

Although the conditions of the *chelnok* business are common to all women who engage in this work, it influences gender formation in a variety of ways depending on their past social status, profession, length of time working, and age. Women without a post-secondary education, whose previous professional activity was tied to the auxiliary or service sectors, adapt to the *chelnok* business most successfully. Not having high expectations connected with professional skills and advancement and having work experience in related sectors of the economy (retail and service industries), these women accept their new economic roles more easily. Age is also a factor influencing identity: younger women, especially former homemakers or the unemployed, appear not to undergo internal conflict connected with a reappraisal of values and expectations, which is the experience for thirty- to forty-year-old women. And, for women who were forced temporarily or permanently to leave a profession, the turn to the shuttle business frequently becomes a personal tragedy viewed as the crumbling of their professional and life plans.

Generally, the identity formation of women *chelnoks* depends a great deal on whether the transition to the shuttle business was the result of a free choice and of wanting to try new possibilities and life chances or a forced abandonment of accustomed values and lifestyles that has been solely dictated by economic necessity. In the second case the woman undergoes negative emotions, that vary in intensity – from dissatisfaction to a feeling of life catastrophe. Subsequently, the dynamic of identity depends significantly on the level of business success. Business success, a feeling of self-confidence, and achievement of a new standard of living can, if not fully, change the self-identity of a woman to a significant degree and allow her to accept the losses of some of the benefits of her former social status and professional position. Nevertheless, even in this case, complete abandonment of one's former identity is impossible and the general instability of *chelnok* work lowers the sense of satisfaction or achievement.

Thus, two life strategies and types of identities ("professional" and "survival") are formed under the influence of several factors (professional and social status, age, length of time working, level of business success, personality), and at the same time reflect a process of differentiation in the shuttle business. The third strategy and type of identity ("hobby") can today be viewed as a transitional, interim pattern. The characteristics of its motivation (meeting people, an interest in travel, and the appeal of Western standards of consumption) can exist in the professional model as well. The ideology of Western consumerism, transmitted to Ukraine through mass culture, creates rigid gender stereotypes. Nonetheless, these imported images of the "pretty woman" and "ideal housewife" are unrecognizably transformed by the rigid realities of the shuttle business and the necessities of risk and struggle for survival. The sharpening of competition and professionalization of the shuttle business have formed a corresponding pragmatic motivation that leaves no room for hobbyist *chelnoks*.

These economic strategies and lifestyles are connected in one way or another with the emergence of new gender identities. Attempts to combine several social roles, difficulties in renouncing the old value system and choosing new economic strategies, problems of adaptation to the new economic situation – all are characteristic not only of women *chelnoks* but also to a considerable degree of the majority of Ukrainian women who are negotiating the transition to a market economy.

TATIANA ZHURZHENKO

Notes

1   The level of risk in the shuttle business is shown in available statistics of accidents: In 1992, during the Pridneprovsky military conflict, on the Rybnitza-Dubossary highway in Moldavia, there was an incident in which Kharkiv tourist-shuttles were shot and two people were killed. In 1996, in the Black Sea, a ship with Russian and Ukrainian tourist-shuttles was captured by terrorists from Chechnya. Luckily, no one was injured or killed. In November 1996 the most horrible tragedy occurred in Istanbul, where eighteen people were killed in a hotel fire. Dozens of people were injured and poisoned by carbon monoxide. Almost all of them were Ukrainian shuttles.

2   The Russian term "hoziayka" or Ukrainian "hospodynia" could be approximately translated as "housewife" or "housekeeper."

References

Einhorn, Barbara. 1993. *Cinderella Goes to Market: Citizenship, Gender and Women's Movements in East Central Europe*. London: Verso.

Funk, Nanette, and Magda Mueller, eds. 1993. *Gender Politics and Post-Communism: Reflections from Eastern Europe and the Former Soviet Union*. London: Routledge.

Malysheva, Marina. 1995. "Gender Identity in Russia: A Comparison of Post-World War II and Post-Communist Experiences," *Canadian Women Studies* 16, 1: 22-26.

Moghadam, Valentine M., ed. 1993. *Democratic Reform and the Position of Women in Transitional Economies*. Oxford: Clarendon Press.

Neitzert, Monica. 1993. "Marginal Notes: Women in Canada's Underground Economy," Economic Equality Workshop, Summary of Proceedings, Ottawa, 20-21.

Posadskaya, Anastasia, ed. 1994. *Women in Russia: New Era in Russian Feminism*. London: Verso.

Reinharz, Shulamit. 1992. *Feminist Methods in Social Research*. Oxford: Oxford University Press.

SIXTEEN

RURAL WOMEN AND ECONOMIC DEVELOPMENT IN REFORM ERA CHINA: THE STRATEGY OF THE OFFICIAL WOMEN'S MOVEMENT

Ellen R. Judd

THE economic reform that reshaped China's countryside in the 1980s gave no attention to women's particular roles or to gender relations. In this respect it is unusual compared with the previous major thresholds in the transformation of China's political economy. In each of the previous instances – from Land Reform (1946-52) through to Cultural Revolution (1965-76) – gender issues were prominent and in some instances were even critical components of the state's program for change. While this was conspicuously not the case for the economic reform, toward the end of the 1980s some women within the official Women's Federations moved towards taking their organizations into economic development work in the specific interests of women. This has been critically important because the official women's movement is virtually the only legitimate channel for organizing women in China; and since late 1989, other channels for organizing – which did flourish in the 1980s – have been prohibited unless officially linked with and supervised by a state body.[1]

The Women's Federations have not had a favourable reception in the West – they are not feminist in a Western sense, and they have problematic strategies and limited effectiveness (see Judd, 1995). Nevertheless, they are the only organizational vehicle for change in the interests of women that has a national presence in the countryside. More innovative urban-based groups or international non-governmental organizations all have to work with and through the Women's Federations to carry any strategy to women in the countryside. Consequently, the Women's Federations decisively shape what is actually implemented in rural China. Women do have some avenues beyond organized strategies – in market-oriented initiatives undertaken on an individual or household basis – but these are effective choices only for relatively advantaged women, those with exceptional skills or education or with access to significant household material and human resources. The official initiatives discussed here derive much of their significance from their potential to provide openings for less advantaged rural women, including the millions who are still living in poverty.

The question of whether and how the recently revitalized Women's Federations might be able to address the needs of rural women is at the heart of future prospects for women in post-socialist China. The Women's Federations mirror the central contradictions of the Chinese variant of post-socialism – they are embracing market mechanisms as key to women's prosperity and autonomy, but remain firmly rooted as "mass organizations" in the tradition and present of a Marxist-Leninist state structure.[2] The strategies and practices developed by the official women's movement involve central issues of the role of the state and the market in contemporary reform contexts. These affect the dynamic of power flows upward and downward within an official women's movement that is at the same time both a subordinate state structure and an organizational vehicle for women. In the strategies developed here, Chinese women are reworking core gender-and-development (GAD) concepts in an innovative way appropriate to their own state and society, located on the dynamic periphery of global capitalism.

Research in Rural China

I had first encountered the women's movement in China as a graduate student living in Beijing and Shanghai studying political culture at the end of the Cultural Revolution, from 1974 to 1977. When I returned to China in the 1980s, as rural fieldwork became possible, I had no idea that the women's movement was poised on the point of revival. It had certainly been inactive for some time. When Margery Wolf (1985) completed her landmark study of the early 1980s, it had been possible to argue that there was no women's movement in China. The revolutionary period was past and there was no indication that a new women's movement was emerging.

My rural field study began as an examination of the impact of the rural economic reform – and especially of decollectivization and the return of land to household management – on rural social organization, especially on households. I had a gender-inclusive concept of research design and made a point of working with women research assistants and women village leaders; and, of course, household structure is an intrinsically gendered issue. I also considered the history and structure of village women's movements a necessary element in reconstructing processes of change in the rural political economy. Perhaps these interests opened my research to a gender focus; they certainly brought me into contact with village women. It was not long before I had learned from them that their lives bore little relation to the classical rural studies done decades before, and that the rural economic reform was arguably changing nothing else as much as it was changing gender relations in every facet of life at the grassroots.

My research emphasis shifted to focus more specifically on the changes in gender and power relations in the emergent reform era political economy (Judd, 1994). I continued systematically to visit households and, where practical and negotiable, to live in village households. I thereby had the opportunity to talk directly (in Chinese, which I had learned as a student in Canada and China) with a diverse range of rural women. This is still not a common opportunity for foreign researchers in China, as most work in cities and with intellectuals and officials. Negotiating more open access, while still working as an officially approved researcher, is one of the obstacles of fieldwork in contemporary China, although it is now easier than described in Margery Wolf's report of her experiences in Shandong in 1980 (Wolf, 1985) or in my own earlier experiences.

A condition of research in China is acceptance of official supervision of the research process. It has not been unusual for me to conduct a household interview or key informant interview with representatives of national, provincial, county, township and village levels of government all present at the same time. Ordinarily, most of these depart early in the fieldwork process. I have commonly proceeded to do most of my fieldwork with local officials, and especially Women's Federation staff and village women's heads (largely because they are suitable chaperons). While this might seem constraining, it was also an unpredicted opportunity to learn about the rural women's movement at the grassroots.

Although nothing in the Western literature on China at that time would have predicted an active rural women's movement, I soon discovered that it did indeed exist. I found myself working with women in and connected with this movement as it revitalized itself during the late 1980s and early 1990s. Over the course of repeated visits, I was able to see the rural women's movement adjust to the reform context and devise new and practical strategies at the village level in connection with the emergence of a national program for institutionalizing these strategies within state policy. In the following pages, I will outline the strategies as I was able to see them emerging in the everyday practices of the women's movement and of individual rural women.

The material and the understandings are stitched together from a series of field trips in 1986, 1987-88, 1989, 1990, 1992 and 1995. The people, and especially the women's movement staff, with whom I worked changed continually during this period. While I have tried to listen attentively to all these voices, my understanding is inevitably partial and limited by my own position in the field (as an outsider) and by my own culture and personal values. Despite the dependence of this work on the work and generosity of the Chinese women I came to know in Shandong, I cannot accurately attribute the understanding presented here to anyone other than myself. The voice – and the effort to interpret these everyday practices for readers here – is necessarily my own, while the actual, substantive contributions are those of the local women.[3]

The "Two Studies, Two Competitions"

The key strategy of the rural women's movement eventually became formalized on a national level in early 1989 as the "two studies, two competitions activities" (*shuangxue shuangbi huodong*) (see Rai and Zhang, 1994). Because this is the cornerstone of recent and continuing efforts to organize rural women to transform their lives, I have concentrated on exploring this program during my field trips in the 1990s. In the project reported here (Judd, n.d.), I am examining the rationale behind this movement and exploring its concrete initiatives using some documentary materials, but primarily longitudinal field data located along a vertical slice of Chinese society extending from the national level through to the provincial, prefectural, county, township, and village levels. My emphasis is on an ethnographic encounter in one north China community.

The focus of the study is the activities of women at the lowest levels of the official women's movement (village women's heads, and township and county Women's Federation cadres) and women outside of the official movement who have had some individual economic success and are the object of attempts to draw them into a unified, officially sponsored economic development initiative. That is, the emphasis is on the points of contact between the official women's movement and rural women themselves. The purpose of this approach is to move from formal descriptions of policy initiatives on the part of the Women's Federations to an examination of the relation of these policies to concrete rural conditions, and then to identify the actual practical strategies being pursued by women at the grassroots. These will emerge as being more complex and practical than the formal statements of policy would initially suggest. The ultimate objective is to map the "genealogy" of subjugated knowledges and practices (see Foucault, 1980) through which rural women in China are transforming their conditions of life.

By the end of the first decade of reform, in the late 1980s, the official bodies charged with responsibility for "woman-work" (*funü gongzuo*), the Women's Federations, began to introduce initiatives designed to help rural women participate more fully in economic development and also to remake the Federations into bodies involved in the core economic activities of the reform. If one were to seek a familiar international analogy with what is being attempted, it could be in gender-and-development work, and certainly the main goal does appear to be the pursuit of prosperity (*zhifu*) through mainstream market activities. But it is best to start by looking at the specifics of the major Chinese initiative in this area, the "two studies, two competitions activities."

The complete "two studies, two competitions activities" phrase, hereafter the "two studies," is a conventional and compressed way of referring to this program, which literally consists of four elements: adult basic education (*xue wenhua*); practical technical training (*xue jishu*) intended to generate income very quickly; competition among local women in achieving economic success (*bi chengji*) and gaining recognition; and through that economic success making social contributions (*bi gongxian*), most commonly through helping poorer women and through paying taxes to the state. The program is not, however, literally composed of these elements. Its core is the effort to increase rural women's incomes through providing short-term training, and the remainder of the program, at least formally revolves around this element. Adjustments to a market context predicated on competition, in part structured through the promotion of officially selected models, is also a central and continuing part of the program. As will be indicated, the program has evolved somewhat over time, but it continues to operate within the same overall framework and under the same name.

Before proceeding to discuss this program itself, a few words are in order about what it does not do – and does not attempt to do. The program is not intended to produce structural change in gender relations in the countryside, or, in Molyneux's (1986) terms, to pursue "strategic gender interests." It makes little overt mention of gender equity or equality. Leaders in the Women's Federations do speak of the program contributing to raising women's status, through increasing women's income-generating potential and making this publicly recognized, but this is as far as they choose to go at present. The policy is silently – and perhaps intentionally – designed to be non-confrontational and non-threatening to the entrenched interests of androcentric and patriarchal structures in the countryside. This is presumably a condition for the support the Women's Federations seek from local branches of higher-level organs of the state.

A fundamental starting point of the national "two studies" strategy, as well as of other ones currently being pursued by the Women's Federations, is the proposition that women's "quality" (*suzhi*) is too low. This is a complex and uncomfortable starting point, but one that should be explored. Often it refers, as it does for the most part in relation to the "two studies," simply to women's disadvantages in education and training. Here it operates to identify deficiencies in education and training as the critical points at which intervention can be made that will help rural women escape poverty and move towards prosperity. In this it contrasts with other initiatives familiar from other developing countries, such as provision of credit, formation of women's co-operatives, or development of independent women's organizations. In the larger study of which this is part, I address the question of why those avenues have not been given priority in China, compared with the emphasis placed on training.

The formal argument that the leaders of this initiative present is that women are critical to rural economic growth, because although they were until recently secondary in agricultural labour, they now comprise 60-70 per cent of the agricultural labour force. Rural men have been moving out of agriculture, either to migrate to urban centres or to enter non-agricultural areas of the rural economy that are more remunerative. The result is that agricultural production is increasingly dependent on women. The Women's Federations and the "two studies" accept this division of labour – although they are also following women as they move into other sectors of the rural and urban economy – and at least one influential Chinese theorist (Meng Xianfan, 1993, 1995) working in the area has viewed this new division of labour as promising a sphere of economic independence for rural women. There are difficulties with this approach, especially in its not addressing women's limited access to the basic means of production, including land (Judd, 1994; Croll, 1994), and in its uncritical embrace of market forces. Whether or not this approach is a sound basis for a strategy, as of 1995 there were 210 million women in China primarily working in agriculture, and this figure in itself argues effectively for the practical importance of any initiative aimed at improving or transforming their conditions of life.

The official argument then proceeds to observe the importance of technical and commercial modernization in agriculture. Technical developments are the most promising means through which agricultural productivity in China can be increased at present, and this is a vital concern in light of the serious and continuing decline in arable land (see Smil, 1993).

Agricultural extension systems[4] are the main vehicle through which technical improvements can be propagated, but these are being reduced, and in places even eliminated, as part of China's massive governmental downsizing in the early 1990s. Rural women have reported inadequate access to agricultural extension services, both because of the lack of such services in general and because of the tendency for women to have less access than men. One study indicated that only 13.6 per cent of women surveyed had had any training through governmental or non-governmental channels, although almost all expressed a strong preference for training and 70.9 per cent said that they had lacked the opportunity (see He Yupeng, 1995: 110).

The Women's Federations cite this evidence in discourse directed upward towards more powerful branches of the state (for example, see Yang Yanyin, 1991) to argue the importance of the "two studies" strategy for reaching rural women and enabling them to contribute to national economic growth. There are two major implications of this discourse. The first is that the Women's Federations should be allowed to access state-controlled human and material resources to aid in their program for rural women's economic development. This has been one of the critical elements of the "two studies" program from its inception as a national policy announced by the national "two studies" co-ordinating group (xietiao zuzhi).

The co-ordinating group is a structure replicated at each administrative level from the national through to the county, and sometimes even to the township. It is co-chaired by the head of the Women's Federation at each level and one of the leading cadres of the Party or government committee at the same level, with ten or more state departments or institutions (such as the Agriculture Department and the China Agriculture Bank) represented through a leading cadre from each. The purpose of this structure is to allow the resource-poor Women's Federations to use the authority of the leading political figures at each level to access the resources of the core state bodies involved in rural economic development. In effect this is a systematic gender-and-development policy for mainstreaming women into the core of economic development planning and resource allocation. The strategy is one designed for specifically Chinese post-socialist conditions, in which state planning is still a major factor in economic development and state strategies for utilizing market forces provide the defining characteristics of the current political economy.

The second implication is that the Women's Federations should and can be organizationally strengthened by providing this organizational function for the state – but, more importantly, by providing access to economic opportunity for rural women. Rural women are not notably interested in

ELLEN R. JUDD

national economic growth targets, and the discourse of raising women's "quality" shows so little respect for rural women that it is rarely heard when the organizing work reaches into the villages. Instead the majority of rural women are seeking routes out of the poverty in which most still live. The "two studies," in practice is a response to these demands, and where it works it does so by providing concrete assistance. The Women's Federations aim, through this strategy, to reconcile their complex dual role of representing both state interests and women's interests.

Paradoxically, for a women's movement still structured and in significant ways adhering to the model of a Marxist-Leninist mass organization, the route the Women's Federations are choosing to meet both state and women's demands is through the use of the market. The "two studies" is explicitly intended to draw women into an increasingly market-driven economy and to prepare them to thrive in that milieu. Consequently, one of the major mechanisms used in the "two studies" is the recruitment of successful women entrepreneurs, who emerged in large numbers in the reform era of the 1980s, to serve as teachers and models within the strategy. This is also an organizationally astute move, because it renders the Women's Federations less dependent on state resources and provides many additional people to do the work of the strategy. In light of the extremely sparse staffing of the Women's Federations – a township commonly has one person working less than full time on woman-work (*funü gongzuo*) for as many as sixty villages – this is indispensable.

Local Strategies and Implementation

The basic features of the "two studies," announced nationally early in 1989, were actually present in earlier years in at least some agricultural areas where the Women's Federations were beginning to experiment with new initiatives. In my own fieldwork I found evidence of a precursor, then termed the promotion of "courtyard economy" (*tingyuan jingji*),⁵ dating from 1987 at the village level, and was told that this had begun in the Dezhou region as early as 1984. It accords with both the evidence and with familiar contemporary Chinese organizing practices that there would first be some practical experiments before launching a national initiative. I have also found, in the course of rural fieldwork with women, that – at the local level – some Women's Federation cadres are very closely attuned to the demands of local rural women. Whatever the political demands on higher levels of the leadership, which create a conflicted situation for the Chinese women's movement, the local network is a channel through which rural women's demands, at least at the level of Molyneux's practical gender interests, do effectively enter the agenda of at least this marginal branch of the state.

This can be indicated most effectively through detailed attention to processes of local implementation, although it might initially be misleading to refer to them in quite those terms. Such processes are creative ones in which much of the strategy implemented is locally formulated, although it makes use of openings provided by strategies articulated at higher levels. Here I will address the "two studies" as actually realized within one village I visited in 1988, 1989, 1990, 1992, and 1995. During this period the village of Huaili – and the township and county within which it is located – passed through several stages[6] of the "two studies" and experienced uneven levels of activity (see Judd, 1994). Huaili is located in Shandong province in northern China and has a population of just under 1,000 people. Its history is typical of the volatility of both politics and everyday life in contemporary China. It does not, of course, indicate the full range of possibilities within this overarching national strategy, but discussion of local processes adds the critical dimension of grassroots practices and strategies to what might otherwise appear to be an empty discussion of policy.

In reviewing the strategy as a whole, the appropriate starting point appeared to me to be an examination of the question of whether education or training could effectively promote women's economic success in the current rural context in China. In an earlier analysis of 1989 household data from Huaili, I found that specialized households (those that had successfully moved into non-agricultural production)[7] tended to have adult members with higher levels of education than did other households, and that the difference was more marked between women than between men (Judd, 1994: 149).

While this initially would appear to confirm the underlying proposition that raising women's educational "quality" could be the decisive point for intervention, closer analysis of the same and later data raised some questions and demonstrated that the situation is much more complex than a simple comparison of education and economic success can indicate. This analysis consisted of two elements: a simple comparison of education and training received by women and men of all post-school age generations in Huaili; and a detailed, longitudinal case study analysis of the education, training, and career trajectories of all those women and men in the sample who had received more than the standard education or training for their age and gender cohort (see Judd, 1996).

The first part of the analysis confirmed the existence of systemic differences in education and training between women and men in all age cohorts, although the differences were less sharp among the youngest cohorts. Arguments that women are disadvantaged in terms of education or training, relative to men in the same community, have a solid base in the evidence available for this village. This is not only a historical legacy affecting older women but applies to women in their forties, thirties, and even younger. Viewed solely from this perspective, adult education initiatives targeting younger married women, as in the "two studies," could be a very appropriately selected intervention.

However, the second part of the analysis, the part that traced trajectories of education, training, and career, indicated a more complex situation. The more highly trained women, and those given some opportunities to become village teachers (most commonly), medics, or women's heads, benefited from such opportunities only briefly in their natal villages and were almost never able to continue in the same capacities in the marital villages in which they would spend almost their entire adult lives.[8] If Huaili (and other villages for which I have less systematic but similar data) is any indication, China's villages are sprinkled throughout with women with relatively high education, by rural standards, and some experience, but whose potential is systemically wasted. It is not enough for women to be educated or experienced — it is also necessary that structures of opportunity exist to allow their education, training, and experience to be used.

Training patterns also raise questions. Women have noticeably less access to training for several reasons. The areas for which they are considered suitable trainees are more restricted than in the case of men; for example, both women and men might be trained as teachers or medics, but women will rarely if ever be trained as drivers or electricians. Rural women virtually never have the opportunity for training offered through military service, although this is a significant channel for training for young men. And, while young unmarried women might receive some opportunities for training in their natal villages, marriage into another village breaks any trajectory and is very rarely followed by opportunities in their marital villages, either for further training or for work that would use any earlier training.

Training is typically very closely tied to work opportunities, and to the extent that training has been provided by collectives in the past and villages in the present, it is linked with employment in the public sector of villages. There are evident patterns of nurturing through which a village can provide opportunities for some of its young men that include education, training and work, and these may be continuously provided through a period of many years. No comparable structure of opportunity has been available for women through collective/village channels. Despite national policies of equal rights for women, village communities remain firmly androcentric, with consequent marginalization of women (see Judd, 1994). To the extent that younger women are finding access to training, it is largely through the more diverse channels of the market and informal contacts – or through emergent new public structures being created through the official women's movement.

This suggests the – not surprising – conclusion that education and training are insufficient by themselves. Rather, they must be combined with a structure of opportunity that is either open to women or specifically targets women. This issue is not directly addressed in the official discourse of the "two studies," but it is evident in the grassroots strategies being developed locally, and perhaps increasingly so.

Practical work along the lines proposed in the "two studies" has had three identifiable stages in Huaili. All have been more concerned with immediate income-generating results than with improving rural women's quality (*suzhi*). I suspect that this may be widely true of such initiatives where they have effective local roots, although county-level Women's Federation staff are convinced that quality is a central problem.

The first initiative in Huaili was essentially a mobilizational effort personally led by a vice-head of the county Women's Federation, who organized women in Huaili to expand courtyard production (*tingyuan jingji*) in the mid-1980s. The effort focused on increasing the production of vegetables and of *xiangchun*, a tree whose leaves are an edible delicacy. Huaili had established expertise in both vegetable and *xiangchun* cultivation, so training was not immediately at issue, although the initiative did include some training classes in aspects of vegetable production.

Even though this stage preceded the formalized "two studies," it also made some effort to include the literacy training advocated in the early years of that national movement. This was not welcomed or notably successful. The women who might have benefited were among the poorest and most heavily burdened. They were not willing to undertake and did not have the time for the protracted study literacy would have required.

The township Women's Federation cadre (worker) and the women's committee members in the village who were expected to lead the way found it very difficult to identify areas of training that could be useful to local women. The demand was for training that could produce short-term results in generating income, but this required skills and economic expertise the official women's movement did not itself possess. The most they could do was to organize classes to spread knowledge that they could readily access – in seed selection, vegetable cultivation, or sewing – but these were all limited in their potential or were already familiar to many village women. As long as training was expected but local organizers were left to their own resources, they were limited in what they could offer to their fellow villagers.

The second stage of the initiative, as I was able to observe it in Huaili, took place early in the national "two studies" program. In the early 1990s Huaili had the advantage of an exceptionally energetic women's head who was being supported by an equally ambitious Women's Federation cadre at the township level. Together they drew up activity plans and registered local women for the various sectoral competitions (grain, livestock, and so on) within the program. Much of the actual activity that took place at this time was, again, less a matter of training than of organization. The women's head, who had already shown some commercial initiative on her own, rented some additional village land for a commercial crop (tree seedlings), in line with the policy that women's heads should lead by personal example in economic development. While this was not an immediate success, she was energetic and socially adept in working individually with village women. Occasional classes happened during her tenure in office and some village women reported attending them, but most of the additional economic knowledge acquired and transmitted during her tenure was through individual contact that she facilitated.

Her primary resource was the handful of village women who had already become successful through some particular skill acquired independent of the women's movement – noodle-making, mushroom-growing, sewing, or chicken-raising – but that could be promoted through its channels. These women had, in fact, already been identified as "models" as early as the courtyard economy stage in this village, and the use of models is a well-established technique in Chinese culture. This is encouraged systematically in the "two studies," and the women who are publicly endorsed as models through the competitions become living resources the women's movement uses to assist those who have not been able to break through to prosperity independently. Although this can and sometimes does result in formal classes – given as early as the courtyard economy stage in sewing – much of the assistance is given in a one-on-one form. Certainly, some of the advice or technical support provided by these models would have happened, in any event, through ties of kinship, neighbourliness, or the market, but where the women's movement is active it increases and accentuates such activity through encouragement and social pressure exerted on the "models."

However, the models rarely offer training as such. They more commonly serve as examples of what is possible, sources of advice, and (where applicable) sources of technical support. In one case of particular co-operation in Huaili, the village's leading seamstress did give training classes, through the Women's Federation, but the more effective route for women to acquire her skill was through the longer-term route of becoming her apprentice. One of the other early models, a woman whose husband privately took a course in commercial mushroom-raising offered some distance away, has also served as a channel through which mushroom-raising spread more widely in the village. She and her husband introduced this profitable line of production to the village and their household remains the sole source of spores. In both these cases, and in other similar ones, women with advantages or initiative lead the way and other women, including relatively poor and illiterate women, have been able to follow in the same direction, with some assistance informally or through the women's movement. Income-generation can then be achieved fairly directly and with little training, although the less skilled or knowledgeable women may realize less economic success and less autonomy, because they have limited control of the technical aspects of their work.

The local difficulties and limitations in accessing resources for training and economic development presumably explain the "two studies" effort to establish co-ordinating committees (*xietiao zuzhi*) through which the resources of local government can be accessed. I have not, however, found direct indications of this working in the case of Huaili and assume that it is an unevenly realized strategy.

In the third stage that I have been able to observe to date, Huaili has been on the edge of using a similar resource: training in women's classes specially run through the China Correspondence University of Rural Applied Technology (*nonghanda*) in association with local government development initiatives. This type of training targeted toward a mainstream development initiative is quite representative of what has been advocated for the second five-year phase (1994-98) of the "two studies." The move is away from literacy training and smaller-scale initiatives towards higher-level and more lengthy training, and towards mainstreaming women into areas that may be more technically demanding than those initially advocated, as in the courtyard economy.

In this particular case, the leadership of the township in which Huaili is located has identified large-scale chicken production as the area in which it would like to develop and has taken a series of concrete steps in this direction. In 1994-95, the township government brought in a professor from

Tianjin, together with a few of her students, to provide training locally. Subsequently, the township government negotiated a contract with a foreign company to raise chickens locally for frozen export to Southeast Asia. Chicken production is an area commonly considered suitable for women and, in any event, county policy was to draw women – the majority of the rural labour force – into each township's development priority. In this township, one consequence was that the Correspondence University classes for women became concentrated on chicken production in the villages targeted for the export project. Here Huaili found itself on the margins, as it was not one of the three targeted villages. Also, Huaili is no longer the priority for woman-work (*funü gongzuo*) that it had earlier been. But several households in the village have been able to make use of the presence of the professor and of the local development orientation to expand into egg production. And the pioneer egg producer in the village – a household including another early woman model – is venturing into the production of meat chickens, as well as providing a range of services to other producers, such as feed, marketing, and veterinary care.

It is too early to know whether Huaili can expect many spin-offs from this project, but at least two poorer households in the village are now raising hundreds of egg-laying chickens, and three households are operating two much larger enterprises. Women do play a major role in the chicken production in each case, especially in the poorer households with the smaller operations, which in each case are run by the wife while the husband does other work. The large-scale expansion of chicken production will almost certainly remain under male management. The questions still to be explored are those of whether and how it matters that women are being intentionally drawn into this project and receiving technical training to do so. And, perhaps more important, here is a case where the training is combined with a structure of opportunity that is at least partially opening to include women.

Implications

This brief introduction to some aspects of the "two studies," primarily in one village, does not do justice to a nationwide and complex initiative, but a few comments should nevertheless be ventured about why it is important.

There has recently been a widespread belief in Western feminist circles that the official Chinese women's movement is not feminist and is not serving the interests of Chinese women. Certainly, it rejects the label "feminism" (*fuquan zhuyi*) for the most part, which it understands as a specifically

Western construct, in favour of its own conception of "woman-work" (*funü gongzuo*). This paper in part indicates what some of the concrete content is of this woman-work in the post-socialist era of reform. If the goal of raising women's quality is problematic, it should still be recognized that a critical component of this goal is to place knowledge in the hands of rural women, including the most disadvantaged, who do not necessarily fare well in the market system without organized support. The most optimistic view of this initiative is that it may enable disadvantaged rural women to escape poverty and establish the economic independence that will permit a wider range of choices in their lives. This initiative might then provide the basis for the emergence of an expanded sector of women with economic resources and direct experience of effective organizing in relation to post-socialist state structures.

In assessing the effect of these policies the local and practical dimensions are particularly important. It is significant that at those levels the more problematic aspects of the discourse on quality fade somewhat. It is even more striking that local strategies focusing on education and training then also appear to address the practical problems of rural structures of opportunity and their persistently androcentric nature by developing means to train women systematically in areas where opportunities can be opened.

The use of state organs and mechanisms, such as township government and development plans, state-funded educational institutions, and the official women's movement itself, is a critical component of this strategy. Despite the turn towards the market, in China in general and specifically within its women's movement, effective use of the state remains decisive for creating opportunities for women to relieve poverty and improve their lives.

Notes

The research reported here has been generously supported by a series of grants from the Social Sciences and Humanities Research Council of Canada: Exchange Grants with the Chinese Academy of Social Science, 1986 and 1987; a General Research Grant, 1986; a Canada Research Fellowship at the University of Western Ontario, 1987-89, and at the University of Manitoba, 1989-92; and a Standard Research Grant, 1992-96. Writing was subsequently supported through a Visiting Scholar Research Grant at the Centre for Research in Women's Studies and Gender Relations, University of British Columbia, as well as through the facilities of the Centre, the Department of Anthropology and Sociology and Green College. An earlier and shorter version of this paper was presented at the annual meeting of the American Anthropological Association in 1996.

The author particularly wishes to acknowledge the generous gifts of time and understanding of the women of Huaili and of the many women's organizations in Shandong involved in this project. Responsibility for the interpretations in this article rest solely with the author.

1 During the 1980s women, especially urban women, spontaneously formed a variety of women's groups, including professional caucuses and networks, women's studies programs, theory and writing groups, and activist service groups. By the mid-1990s the groups still active included élite professional women's organizations, university women's studies programs, and activist groups operating with Women's Federation and/or international NGO support.

2 Marxist-Leninist organizational structures worldwide generally include women and a program for women's liberation as part of an encompassing socialist political program. Women can be members of the Marxist-Leninist party itself, as they are of the Chinese Communist Party, but Chinese Communist Party members represent a small portion of the total population, and a still smaller proportion of women. Larger numbers of people are reached through "mass organizations" attached to the party. These serve to mobilize particular constituencies (classically, these are women, trade unionists, and youth) for the party's program. The Women's Federations in China play precisely this role. Their primary task is to mobilize women to support party policy and actively carry it out. Since party policy includes the liberation of women, the Women's Federations also have a responsibility to work towards this goal and to serve as a channel through which women's concerns can reach the party. The Women's Federations cannot, without breaking the party discipline to which it and its leaders are bound, operate independently or in opposition to the party.

3 For related materials by Chinese activists and scholars, see the translations in Judd (1999).

4 The various government departments responsible for agricultural and related forms of production, including animal husbandry, fisheries, and forestry, provide technical extension services to the countryside. The technicians on staff offer a variety of services and individual advice, as well as some formal training. The staff of these extension systems are one of the main sources of technical training personnel the Women's Federations strive to access through the "two studies."

5 This initiative was directed towards building on women's traditional focus on work within the walled courtyards typical of Chinese rural homes (see Wolf, 1985), by using courtyard space for income-generating activities, such as intensive

vegetable cultivation (see Jacka, 1997).

6 As initially conceptualized, the "two studies" was a broadly based effort to promote literacy and simple training and to help women enter the market through home-based income-generation projects. It was then intended to last five years, 1989-94. It was later extended beyond that time and adjusted to allow for higher levels of technical training and more complex integration into local development plans. Identifiable stages in the implementation of the program over time became evident in the 1990s, and are discussed later in this paper as they unfolded in Huaili.

7 For a more extensive discussion of the category of "specialized household," including its meaning in Huaili in these years, see Judd (1994).

8 Patrilocal postmarital residence remains the norm in China's villages. What is commonly referred to as "uxorilocal marriage" was briefly promoted during the late Cultural Revolution, but this form of residence greatly restricts a woman's choice of marriage partner and her life options. It is no longer advocated as a strategy to improve the structural situation for women in rural China. There is an emergent trend towards intra-village marriage, which, while having some of the same disadvantages as uxorilocal marriage, may (if continued and if widespread) significantly alter rural social organization within a few generations. Women presently expect to marry outside their village and, where individual women have wider choices, may strive to move to a town or city. Women rarely prefer to marry within their own villages, except when they have no brothers and future care of their parents is a concern.

References

Croll, Elisabeth. 1994. *From Heaven to Earth: Images and Experiences of Development in China.* London: Routledge.

Foucault, Michel. 1980. *Power/Knowledge: Selected Interviews and Other Writings, 1972-1977,* ed. Colin Gordon, New York: Pantheon.

He Yupeng. 1995. "Nongcun zhengce; funü jinbu; jingji fazhan," in Li Qiufang et al., eds., *'95 di sici shijie funü dahui nongcun funü fazhan lunwenji.* Beijing: Zhonghua quanguo funü lianhehui chengxiang gongzuobu, 107-11.

Jacka, Tamara. 1997. *Women's Work in Rural China: Change and Continuity in an Era of Reform.* Cambridge: Cambridge University Press.

Judd, Ellen R. 1994. *Gender and Power in Rural North China.* Stanford, Calif.: Stanford University Press.

—. 1995. "Feminism from Afar *or* To China and Home Again," in S. Cole and L. Phillips, eds., *Ethnographic Feminisms: Essays in Anthropology.* Ottawa: Carleton University Press, 37-51.

—. 1996. "A Strategy for Economic Development for Rural Women in China in the 1990s," paper presented at the annual meeting of the Association for Asian Studies.

—. n.d. "Organizing for Quality: The Chinese Women's Movement Between State and Market," (work in progress).

—, ed. 1999. "Rural Women in Reform Era China," special issue of *Chinese Sociology and Anthropology* 31, 2.

Meng Xianfan. 1993. "Nongcun laodongli zhuanyi zhong de zhongguo nongcun funü," *Funü yanjiu* 5: 52-59.

—. 1995. "'Nangong nügeng' yu zhongguo nüxing de fazhan," *Funü yanjiu* 4: 48-51.

Molyneux, Maxine. 1986. "Mobilization without Emancipation? Women's Interests, State, and Revolution," in Richard R. Fagen, Carmen Diana Deere, and José Luis Coraggio, eds., *Transition and Development: Problems of Third World Socialism*. New York: Monthly Review Press, 280-302.

Rai, Shirin M. and Zhang Junzuo. 1994. "'Competing and Learning': Women and the State in Contemporary Rural Mainland China," *Issues and Studies* 30, 3: 51-66.

Shandong sheng fulian. 1989. *Yong kexue jishu wuzhuang nongcun funü zai zhenxing shandong zhong fahui shenglijun zuoyong*. Jinan: Shandong sheng fulian.

Smil, Vaclav. 1995 "Who Will Feed China?" *China Quarterly* 143: 801-13.

Yang Yanyin. 1991. "Shuangxue shuangbi qi dongyuan fazhan nongye zuo gongxian," *Funü gongzuo* 3: 6-10.

Wolf, Margery. 1985. *Revolution Postponed: Women in Contemporary China*. Stanford, Calif.: Stanford University Press.

SEVENTEEN

FEMINIST FIELDS: CONVERSATIONS TO BE CONTINUED

Heather Howard-Bobiwash, compiler

A PRIMARY goal of this volume has been to open up the spaces of feminism in anthropological texts and practice. Our efforts towards this goal have included the incorporation of works by both emerging and established scholars and an emphasis on narrative and reflexive modes of fieldwork analyses and presentation. Rather than close this volume with an authoritative conclusion, we have chosen instead to generate a dialogue that, in these last pages, constitutes only the beginning of conversations to be continued.

We initiated this conversation by asking the contributors to participate in the writing of this last chapter. By making use of the e-mail technology that had originally connected us across diverse locations, we created a "chat-list" among the contributors, to whom we posed the following question: Where do you place your work as a feminist within contemporary anthropology, and what directions do you see the relationship between anthropology and feminism taking in the future? While the question was focused narrowly on feminism and anthropology, we encouraged each contributor to respond to or challenge the question as broadly and candidly as she wished.

Contributors were also asked to read the brief article "Is Publishing Perishing?" by university press women's studies editors Joan Catapano and Marlie P. Wasserman (1998). This article reviews some current trends in women's studies publishing and highlights some key issues in relation to feminism as a social movement and feminist academic practice that we, as the editors of this volume, see as immediately relevant to this project. We were particularly interested in the suggestion that feminism "opened minds to new ideas and scholarship" and that this "heritage needs to renew itself." Catapano and Wasserman (1988: 22) point to the institutionalization of feminism as a major concern, echoed by the contributors to this volume, in that the reproduction of disciplinary boundaries, élitism, and hypertextualism have shifted our practice away from "engaged feminist discussion":

Early feminist writing sought to create a public discussion, not an academic argument .... Perhaps women's studies writing and publishing has succumbed to the inevitable. All revolutionary movements either dissipate or are institutionalized .... We cannot emphasize enough that writing for students, as well as non-academics, is a legitimate goal for feminist (and indeed all) scholars. Feminist discussion should be open and non-hierarchical. Women writers and scholars could perhaps experiment with the much-trumpeted "egalitarian" new communication technology.

We asked contributors to consider these perspectives as a framework for our "chat" as they read and responded to what other contributors wrote.

The "chat" was launched during the final stages of editing and submission of the volume to the publisher, at the end of a semester during which many of the contributors, including ourselves, were consumed with our teaching, research, and family responsibilities, and when some were unavailable because they were engaged in fieldwork. While we had hoped for a voluminous exchange, we found instead that replies trickled in sporadically and sparingly. Upon examination of the content, we surmised that the amplitude of our dialogue was limited by our gendered positions as women in academic roles and by the very carefulness with which we considered the question. The first issue is illustrated by the frustration that permeated some of the correspondence sent to nudge contributors to send their replies:

(May 26, 1998, 9:34 a.m.):

Hello all contributors,

Yes, it is I again, reminding you of our e-mail chat. Many of you requested extensions on this to get over the hump of the end-of-term marking period, and CASCA [Canadian Anthropology Society annual meetings], etc. That extension has now passed, and we (myself first) have been neglectful of this task. I urge you all to take the time in the next week to register your reply to our original question. We feel this type of exercise constitutes an important "experiment" in feminist practice in editing and writing, and we therefore need everyone to add their two cents. We are extending the discussion again then until Friday, June 5th. Please reply as soon as possible to ensure everyone gets a chance within this time frame. Thank you, Heather H-B.

(June 3, 1998, 6:11 a.m.):
Since the deadline is the day after tomorrow I don't know what I can say to encourage you to put in your couple of paragraphs. Originally, the idea was to generate a discussion in which we would all contribute at least twice, but we certainly have to abandon that idea. Believe me, I know you all have extremely good reasons for leaving this task by the way-side, but I find it also very sad that the state of our lives as women in academia is so full, stressful, and overworked that we can't take advantage of this experimental method of speaking to each other as contributors, as an interesting means by which we could close the book .... Heather H-B.

The substance of the contributions to the "chat" demonstrates the conscientiousness with which the contributors considered the potential personal and professional meanings of the question. Issues that surface from the conversation include ideas about the "placement" of feminism, about the contours of academic disciplines and of knowledge, about the creative potential of operating at the "margins," and about the social justice agendas of feminism. The boundaries that exist within and between feminisms are also put to task, as are the contradictions and confluences of feminisms with the many "other" emancipatory perspectives with which we work.

At the time of this writing, we were still short the voices of two contributors, Gönül Ertem and Tatiana Zhurzhenko, who were in Turkey and Ukraine respectively, and who did not have access to their e-mail. We have reproduced the replies with as little editorial intervention as possible. They are also presented in the chronological order they were received, with the exception of Sally Cole's contribution, which was submitted by fax due to technical problems with her e-mail. Our hope is that readers will be not only enlightened by the ideas generated by the contributors to this volume, but inspired to continue these conversations as well as to germinate new ones.

Deborah A. Gordon (April 20, 1998, 5:24 p.m.):

It's difficult for me to answer this question of placement of my work as a feminist in anthropology, as the borders between the inside and outside of anthropology seem unclear to me. I am struggling to think about what disciplines "are" today, because I don't believe they function as they did in the past. Anthropology, at least in the U.S., does seem to me to be functioning without a canon and certainly without a centre. The entire notion of a disciplinary centre and margin is the wrong language to capture fast-paced networking dynamics that I actually think define what I think of as "offworlds," worlds that actually are more prominent in scholarship than disciplines but define institutional reality in ways that obscure how intellectual production actually works at this moment. My sense of networks rather than disciplines defining academic space no doubt comes from my own background and training. I have never received a degree in a discipline but have undergraduate and graduate degrees in interdisciplinary fields.

For me, the question of feminism and anthropology is really one of interdisciplinarity and the range of possible intellectual and political "sites" in which "breakaway" fields that are increasingly normative are taking place. I think that the Internet has encouraged this activity, as the phenomenological experience of working on the Net can subvert the distinction between "activist" and "scholarly" intellectual activity. Most of the research I do now is on the West Bank and Jerusalem, and the literature of the occupation, Palestinian nationalism, feminism, etc. is very hybrid. I cannot depend solely on library materials, because the conditions I am studying are simply too unstable for that form of cultural literacy. The situation of Palestinians inside historic Palestine and outside is politically saturated. It has forced me to become a more hybrid writer and thinker, because I depend on the Internet for up-to-date news and information about the region.

To be honest, I probably wanted to write out of circumstances that demanded new kinds of narratives because of my disappointment with feminism in the U.S. and the way its more visible organizations have become mired in liberal political discourse at a moment when that very discourse has been eroded by alliances between the state and global capital. My academic location in Wichita, Kansas, has forced me to become both more conscious of a certain national ideology and focus, and more sceptical of the value and significance of certain visions of the nation that are articulated by legislators. One way that I am responding to a kind of over-preoccupation with the nation in my own academic institution is to leave its boundaries for another region. One of the most potent aspects of thinking about feminism and fieldwork is that it diversifies the way that feminists consider the relationship of activism and scholarship.

Rae Bridgman (May 20, 1998, 5:27 p.m.):

Following from Debbie Gordon's initial focus on the unstable ground of defining boundaries for feminist anthropology, anthropology in general, and more broadly for disciplines and departments, I'll say that I've been fascinated by the whole concept of protective boundaries. I wrote a "reflections on crossing disciplines" piece a couple of years ago (Anderson, 1996). While there are many who operate amidst wide-flung networks, through electronic media or otherwise (and I'll include myself among that number), it is still easy to come up against "hard" boundaries within the academy and other spheres. It is at those moments that canons (perhaps it should be cannons!) are manifest in the everyday practices of our colleagues and others we work with.

The most salient example of this "hardness" is exemplified by one of my graduate school experiences. We were discussing Sherry Ortner's (1984), at that time, "seminal" review of anthropology. The article was presented by the instructor as ground-breaking. Well into the seminar I raised my hand and asked why there seemed to be no reference to feminist theorizing in anthropology in this overview. I was puzzled, particularly as I had read one of Ortner's early pieces on the nature/culture: female/male divide (a formulation now soundly critiqued).

There was silence for a moment, and then the instructor said,
"That's interesting. Yes, you're right."
Silence a moment longer.
He then directed discussion along a completely different tact.
I felt silenced.

Here was a "hard" boundary defining issues acceptable for discussion, acceptable for publication. Since that time, despite having worked in a stronghold of feminist activism at York University, I have at various times felt positioned by others at the "margins" of critical thinking and practice not only within anthropology, but within many other sites of research and teaching. What can be construed as a negative, however, seems to have given me the
      intellectual freedom
        to slide
          slip
            hop
              fly
                beetle
              across
            through
          over
        under
      university boundaries

to seek correspondence with those working in other disciplines, other walks of life. That creative slipperiness that comes when you subsist on the so-called margins has now enabled me to cross over and take up a position in a department of urban planning within a faculty of architecture. It all depends on what is defined as the "centre." What may be "peripheral" for others can be "central" for you and those you are working with. It is this instability between centre and periphery that animates the practice of feminist anthropology for me. As our "centres" shift, depending on the sites of our research and the negotiations we must undertake within each new research context (and I am using sites in the broadest possible sense beyond the mere spatial) ...

> we are forced to rethink
> over and over again
> reasons behind the work
> we're undertaking
> how it will affect those
> we work with
> how it will help
> bring
> active
> change.

Heather Howard-Bobiwash (May 26, 1998, 9:34 a.m.):

Answering this question is far more daunting than asking it. For me, it simultaneously raises a profusion of other questions while suggesting we remain *disciplined* within the limits, or territory, of the field of anthropology. This challenge – to address the schism between a multidimensional perspective grounded in experience and in the consciousness of social action (feminism), and the continuous re-circumscription of self-preserving boundaries that conditions academic action – constantly informs "where I *place* my work." This challenge is at the root of both the flourishing engagement of feminist action in anthropological quests and the very practical yet perplexing quandaries we face now and in the future. These include our debates around the issues of community and/or individual empowerment; our dilemmas with the power and privilege of academic audience, writing, and editing; our concerns about the goals and directions of "consciousness-raising" in the communities in which we do research, and more importantly for me, within our academic communities; and, our ongoing reflections on the possibilities of achieving both the theoretical and practical goals of participatory research.

At the same time, then, I question how far away from, or how close to, the roots of our various feminisms are we? The transparent and shifting boundary between the personal and the political is paradoxically most visible and tangible for me when I think of this question. Margaret Mead, the undulations of her own feminisms notwithstanding, once wrote, "The strength of my conscience came from Grandma who meant what she said." I had the great fortune of spending the early years of my life within the context of extended family that included all my grandparents as well as many "aunties," most often close friends or relatives of my maternal grandmother. While the "mainstream feminist movement" took form during this same period, it was very far removed from the framework that shaped my understanding of such things as the power of knowledge, the experience of economic and social struggle and survival, the meaning of solidarity and co-operation, and the strength of women; these I gained "from Grandma." As an anthropologist and as a feminist, the goals of "my work," to promote anti-racist, cross-cultural understanding and a more equitable and just society – to practice what we sometimes call "dialogical," "cooperative," "integrative," "cross-disciplinary," and/or "applied" anthropology – are indeed intersected and grounded in experience. This pathway, snug, winding, and well-trodden by many grandmothers, is for me a most promising one to travel on in the direction of the future of the relationship between feminism and anthropology.

Cory Silverstein (May 29, 1998, 1:46 a.m.):

Because I am an interdisciplinary scholar living daily in multicultural contexts, it is difficult to isolate the two factors of feminism and anthropology from the many components that make up my life and work. When I was an M.A. student in an interdisciplinary program, feminist strategies for fieldwork, such as Pat Caplan's "action research" model (1988: 9), provided the specific guidelines I needed for doing ethical research in the politically charged climate of Ontario Native communities. As an ongoing participant in these communities, it was apparent to me that neither feminism nor anthropology was popular among these groups. Since Vine Deloria Jr. (1988), many Native people I know consider the damage done by anthropologists to be worse than that done by governments and missionaries, while they see feminism as "anti-traditional" and "White." Many of the same people, however, could easily see the value of sharing their knowledge of the power and strength of Native women in a cross-cultural forum. Ironically, although feminism provided a needed model for fieldwork, within this social context I do not place myself as a "feminist" or an "anthropologist," simply because the labels inhibit the work.

Theorizing from the grassroots up, or from the peoples studied, is another tenet of feminism that has informed my work, but it is difficult to say whether I intuited the idea from the situation and then retrospectively used feminist theory to legitimize it, or whether I got the idea from feminism in the first place. Similarly, the aspect of Anishnaabe women's concerns that my work focuses on coincides with an early project of academic feminism: the reclamation of women's history. My present research investigates the interrelations among Anishnaabek, Métis, and Euro-American women from 1800 to present through an analysis of the roles and functions of clothing in colonial relations. While this theme clearly privileges women, it also intersects with the current interest in colonialism among contemporary anthropologists. As well, my approach utilizes life histories and other forms of narrative, which is a preference that may be attributed to feminists, Native peoples and contemporary anthropologists. Thus, I see my work as integrating these various sources of inspiration. Any discomfort I feel stems from the stigmas of unequal power relations between the social categories, not from contradictions of theoretical perspectives between them.

I think we are coming into times when studies that integrate perspectives and disciplines are becoming more and more acceptable, even desirable, among mainstream scholars. Although feminism and anthropology have historically operated on the premises of different scales of hierarchy, i.e., gender versus culture, I see great potential for mutual benefit. Both streams of thought draw upon personal experience to explore a critical social issue of our times: the relationship between identity and power. It is my opinion that no single perspective on this issue is sufficient to get to the heart of the matter in the realm of either theory or practice. Some of the most insightful studies have been produced by individuals who consider themselves "feminist native anthropologists," a category that in itself challenges existing definitions of feminism and anthropology.

I think it important to continue teaching the history of feminism within anthropology, in multidisciplinary courses, and in non-academic forums. The latter is necessary to ensure the close relationship between academic and grassroots feminism, as well as to undermine popular stereotypes of feminism. I also think it dangerous, however, to allow a simplistic correlation between feminism and women to continue. The point of feminism, as I see it, is not only to consolidate women's political power, but also to analyze gender as a social category and to deconstruct it as a scale of hierarchy. One unfortunate contradiction I see in feminist anthropology is the (often hidden) assumption that, as anthropologists, we can begin to understand the cultural other, while as feminist women, we have difficulty believing that the other gender can understand us. Male anthropologists who use this reasoning as an excuse to ignore feminist work should be called into question, and institutional structures should be innovated to accommodate the inclusion of men within feminist discourse. Within anthropology, then, I think feminists should continue to focus on the production of leading-edge theory, but we should also make an effort to make feminism more accessible to both non-academics and academic men.

Ellen R. Judd (June 2, 1998, 10:18 p.m.):

I find this question very difficult, since it appears to assume that I (or we) know what is meant by the terms "anthropology" and "feminism." I see anthropology as in flux and as a discipline that ought to be intellectually and practically open. The barriers we face to opening the discipline are largely those of the nature of the academy and the marginal position so many of us occupy within it. That is, the problems are institutional ones of power structures and employment status, rather than ones that are necessarily posed by anthropology as a discipline. I rather think that within anthropology and the interdisciplinary programs in which many of us are involved, we have the intellectual – if not always the practical – space to make the discipline different.

The problem that concerns me more is not about the specifics of anthropology but about what vision of "feminism" (or women's liberation, or something else) we bring to this effort at change. Perhaps I am particularly sensitive to this because the Chinese women's movement, as well as many other women's movement activists in various parts of the world, are very critical of Western feminism. In the Chinese case, which is the one I know best, Western feminism is rejected not just as a Western cultural imposition, but as narrow and bourgeois in its predominantly liberal character. This strikes me as a quite accurate critique. Indeed, it was one often heard in the West as well in the past, when liberal versions of feminism were less hegemonic. The question for me is how – practically – to relate to this type of feminism. I wonder whether I want to consider myself a feminist any more, when it seems to have such a specifically liberal connotation.

I see a need for a more comprehensive critical vision, as characteristic of socialist feminism in previous years. Perhaps that is still the model that shapes my thinking, but I am grappling with ways of thinking of gender and political economy in an era shaped by post-socialist transitions and the global dominance of the market. This is the preoccupation of my academic work at present, but what is required is something that goes well beyond the boundaries of the academy. If we are to remake the academy, we need a more critical and inclusive vision than (liberal) feminism offers.

Sharon R. Roseman (June 3, 1998, 11:44 p.m.):

As Ellen Judd pointed out in her own words yesterday in reference to the critique of Western feminism by Chinese women's movement activists, for many women around the world, the singular labels "feminism" and "feminist" have unfortunately come to be associated with what I would describe as a limited (largely class-based and not very ethnically or politically pluralistic) group of women activists from particular states – states with governments that have worked for decades in collaboration with those who control global capital to ceaselessly insist on a world system that privileges very few and imposes increasingly precarious conditions on the rest of the earth's inhabitants.

I have described these labels as "singular" and the normally associated referents as relatively homogeneous social categories. Does it make any difference if one pluralizes the question that has been posed and asks the following? "Where do you place your work as one kind of feminist within the anthropologies of contemporary times, and what directions do you see the relationships between these anthropologies and a range of feminisms taking in the future?" As one kind of anthropologist, over the last seven years, I have been writing about how individuals in rural Galicia make a life within systems of economic and political injustice. Distrustful of welfare state promises and the wage labour market both in migrant destinations and at home, the majority of the families who have been my hosts continue to practise subsistence farming and to maintain labour exchange networks among themselves. Much of my ethnography has dealt with these activities and relationships and expressions of mistrust, particularly as articulated by women.

Another project has involved my exploration of the political struggle to situate the Galician language as a legitimized mode of communication within Spain in the post-Franco years.

"A palabra e a escrita foron desde sempre elementos de poder, úteis de marxinación." [Words and writing have always been elements of power, instruments of marginalization.]

These words were written in 1983 by the Galician feminist activist-scholar-poet-novelist-teacher, María Xosé Queizán, in reference to the internally gendered (and I have added in my work, class-based) inequality that characterized the early years of the post-Franco struggle. I quoted these same words at the beginning of an article that I published on this topic in *Feminist Studies* in 1997. I wonder now whether they are also apt in describing some feminists' arguments about having been marginalized within the anthropologies of earlier periods? Language is a double-edged tool. In North America, I have often heard feminists from the "academy" talk about the need to demarginalize the languages with which they have become comfortable and perhaps strangely complacent. The first language category about which they speak frequently is the language of feminism within universities; the goal here is to dismantle the barrier between "feminists" and "non-feminists" that is perceived (as Cory Silverstein mentioned) to be so impenetrable by some colleagues and students .... The second language is the academic language which can lead grassroots activists to justifiably decry the centring of some kinds of feminism in intellectual puzzles rather than in struggles for daily sustenance, physical safety, and political change.

In her concluding piece, Heather Howard-Bobiwash mentions that she views her own work as an anthropologist and a feminist to be in part about the promotion of "anti-racist, cross-cultural understanding." This description aptly echoes my own concern with my work as a university teacher. I have learned to play explicitly with my languages in the quest to engage my students in discussions that will not simply lead to an "appreciation of differences" but rather to a visceral understanding of how the powerful have consistently exploited differences. And students of anthropology do almost always willingly engage in the study of the histories of class and gender inequality, racism, colonialism, and imperialism. They — like grassroots activists at home and abroad — are interested in the connections between material conditions, social injustice, and yes, language. I am convinced that the emergence in the future of anthropological feminisms that may reverberate more convincingly with these activists, students, colleagues, family members, neighbours, and politicians will only come about if we are not afraid to unfold the corners of the blankets that sometimes keep our favourite words and identities cocooned and to demystify the way in which we go about doing our work.

HEATHER HOWARD-BOBWASH, COMPILER

Kamari Clarke (June 6, 1998, 5:30 p.m.):

Like Ellen Judd, I am concerned with the vision of "feminism" that we bring to the social and intellectual project. Although I do not accept that in reality the category of "Western feminism" exists in the West as monolithic, I would like to insist that as feminists we explore both the larger institutions that represent it as monolithic and the local interventions into the meanings and textures of feminism in people's lives. That said, I do not necessarily place my work within the borders of "feminist anthropology" as such. In fact, my conception of the borders of feminist anthropology is that it is integral to many components of social analysis, but if it exists alone it does so complexly and with many other entities. As a Black Canadian anthropologist living in the United States, gender oppression and various other forms of marginalization conflate theoretically with other tools of analysis – just as race, colour, gender, nationality, and class marginalization are inextricably linked in daily life.

One of the most substantial influences that "feminist anthropology" has had on anthropology as a discipline has been not only in making central the role of gender in shaping power dynamics, access to information, and the politics of representation and interpretation, but in interrogating research processes and epistemology. The late twentieth-century contestations to objectivity and anthropology as a science have not only challenged the tenets of feminist reflexivity but have also called into question the feminist approach to narrative as a process construction, as a blend between fiction and ethnography. My reflections on the future direction of the relationship between anthropology and feminism are not based on my prediction, but my hope that feminists will take seriously the connections between gender and the many other variables that shape oppression and marginalization – political economy, racism, physical ability, phenotype, poverty, criminalization etc. Perhaps the consequence will be the insistent exploration of social inequities from many dimensions.

Celia Rothenberg (June 16, 1998, 10:31 a.m.):

I have been intrigued – and somewhat tongue-tied! – by the responses contributed thus far to Heather's initial questions for concluding our collection. Indeed, I have been left with a rather sinking feeling that, considering the cross-disciplinary focus of the responses, I have little to contribute. Perhaps this feeling is due primarily to the fact that I just finished and defended my dissertation, a study firmly located in the midst of feminist anthropology.

While my dissertation has been described as "doing" many things – drawing together disparate areas of scholarship on Palestinians in the West Bank and contributing to this body of literature in specific – being interdisciplinary *per se* is not one of its tasks. There are places where my work moves towards interdisciplinary objectives (indeed, perhaps that is where it is most interesting). Yet I have the sneaking suspicion that had I approached it as an interdisciplinary task I would still be working on it! My work to date has been inspired, informed, and shaped by feminist anthropologists and anthropologists who may not call themselves feminists. Hilma Granqvist, for example, writing long before the advent of feminist anthropology, was undoubtedly both a feminist – as she worked with an eye to understanding gender relations – and an anthropologist – who utilized participant-observation and cultural explanations. It is to her and other thinkers, authors, and theorists who are committed to the goals of anthropology and feminist anthropology that I owe my inspiration. Thus, I place my work firmly within feminist anthropology, recognizing that the borders of this area of inquiry are fuzzy and shifting but its core firmly rooted in a historical trajectory of which I am now a part.

Because I am part and parcel, then, of feminist anthropology in particular and anthropology in general I see the relationship between the two as being potentially fruitful in the years to come. While well aware of the "awkward relationship" between feminism and anthropology, I believe such discomfort is best used as a source of prodding for future insight. Such are my thoughts on the subject, brief and, admittedly, distracted by a summer filled with "life" events that are providing a much needed break from my work!

Karen Su (June 18, 1998, 10:57 a.m.):

Participating in this anthology, I've bumped into some disciplinary trappings that highlighted just how much of a literature person I am – something like documentation format, for instance, required concerted effort on my part. The conscientiousness with which I had to undertake the proper formatting did spur many musings on how it reflected different emphases within literary and social science fields. Also, the Canadian context has kept highlighting for me how U.S.-based my perspectives are. Many in this concluding e-mail chat have been referring to the ways they are slipping in and out of disciplinary boundaries, so I'll start there as well.

Like Celia Rothenberg, I didn't feel very equipped to address cross-disciplinary work. And I keep wondering how my work will actually fit into this anthropology anthology – it's been a learning experience so far. I feel "out" of my literary element. I found the initial question that was posed difficult to answer because while anthropology and feminism do inform my work in Asian-American literature, I am not an anthropologist by any means nor have I ever thought of myself in very coherent terms as a feminist/women's studies person. However, I do think that the fluidity of interdisciplinary exchange has made possible the ways that I have been able to engage with anthropological and feminist work, especially since Asian-American studies itself is an interdisciplinary endeavour. I found that Sharon Roseman's rephrasing of the question – "Where do you place your work as one kind of feminist within the anthropologies of contemporary times, and what directions do you see the relationships between these anthropologies and a range of feminisms taking in the future?" – very helpful in that it allowed me to pinpoint the cross-hatchings of literary studies, feminist/women's studies, anthropology, and Asian-American/ ethnic studies that configure a position that resembles what "I do" academically. The contemporary contexts she stresses highlighted the ways in which I found recent developments within anthropology and feminism to be spaces in which I entered with more at stake than just furthering the necessitated critiques of traditional anthropology and mainstream feminism that working in Asian-American studies would require.

I hope that the work I'm doing on translation engages the interrelationships among contemporary feminist ethnography, women of colour feminism, and Asian-American women writers in ways that further push for critical and productive exchanges. If I look at how my research might be linked to my institutional positioning, I would say that the push for these new exchanges isn't so easy when working from within an institutional position that's marked as interdisciplinary. Having taught in both ethnic studies and Asian-American studies, I have found the challenges of developing curriculum and research agendas that are interdisciplinary exciting, and yet the greatest of these challenges is to negotiate the severe limitations our programs face when routinely denied the institutional operating autonomy that traditional departments are accorded.

Comparing these struggles to the ones I faced while teaching within an English department, it's becoming clear to me that it was easier to push for incremental changes while working within a well-defined and supported institutional setting such as an English department. Even though it involved struggling for legitimation and support within an alienating department and campus, because the disciplinary, departmental, and campus conventions were so clearly entrenched, I knew what I was struggling against and could rely on conventional practices within the institution to wend my way through. I also expected to make less headway overall. When teaching within ethnic studies and Asian-American studies, however, we have a "go" technically from the institution to carry out a mandate to be an interdisciplinary program on campus. This can be hugely exciting. Towards this end, for instance, within the Asian/Pacific/American studies program at NYU, we are figuring out how each of us from different disciplinary backgrounds contributes integrally to the program .... How do we form an interdisciplinary discipline? Is that what we are doing? How do I fit in as a literature person?

If I were to remain in an interdisciplinary program like Asian-American studies, perhaps in the long run, I will not be strictly a literature person. But I have found that so far we have taught and conducted research from traditional disciplines while being housed within the A/P/A program. That is, I teach the literature classes within the program, others the history, the urban planning, etc. What cross-disciplinary exchanges that we have been able to begin fostering within the program, though, and that provocatively untether me from conventional literary inquiry, are always policed by the traditional departmental units given power within the university system.

The institutional organization of NYU and most other universities keeps us strictly tied to disciplines even while within A/P/A studies, since we must be legitimated by the traditional departments on most campuses. At this point, the reality seems to be that although enough change has been brought about in that interdisciplinary programs have been started, the external structures within which they must struggle to establish themselves must be revamped as well, but it's happening very slowly. I think the alliances that seem to form between faculty who are in interdisciplinary programs and those who are pushing for change from within traditional departments may present a powerful force within universities.

Like Heather Howard-Bobiwash and Sharon Roseman and others who have discussed their goals as university teachers, my goals centre on promoting anti-racist analyses and cross-cultural negotiations of difference that are linked to practices of social change. It's fascinating to see the range of ways in which students are transformed by new programs or encouraged by traditional departments to retain old assumptions and how these jostle together in students' academic experiences. Teaching variously within new programs and traditional departments has made my experience with students constantly fresh and continually renews my commitment to implementing new pedagogies that work with new fields of inquiry.

Milagros Ortiz Barillas (June 19, 1998, 12:17 p.m.):

As a human being, a mother, and an anthropologist, what is important to me about feminist anthropology is that we are not indifferent to human suffering. Our own feelings and contradictions are taken into account as an essential part of our work. There are times, however, when I feel we have not taken risks far enough, and the perspectives of feminist anthropology are drowned within the structures of power and knowledge. My wish for the future of feminist anthropology is that we continue to remain conscious of the power of words, but not to the extent that we replace action with words. I wish for an anthropology with memory, one that does not forget centuries of history of inequality. Past and present injustices are intertwined, and it is important to me that feminist anthropology does not become blind to this. I do not forget the Aboriginal worlds I come from even if I some-times wish I could escape the pain and guilt that are part of this memory.

On some of the darker days within the context of war, when I have felt hope is very scarce, I have secretly longed to have amnesia or some form of dementia to escape the responsibilities I have chosen in my life, which are inextricably braided with my choices as an anthropologist. As Mercedes Sosa sings, I only ask:

> "que el dolor no me sea indiferente, que la reseca muerte no me encuentre vacía y sola sin haber hecho lo suficiente ... " [that I never become indifferent to suffering; that I do not shrivel and die empty and alone without having done enough ...]

I wish for all of us courage and support to continue without giving up, even if we feel silenced or that the tide in the publishing world is not favourable. As long as there are people who keep trying and learning from the many different views and perspectives we make available, the questioning heritage of feminism will renew itself in anthropology, and it is from this heritage that I see my own work being enriched in the future.

Parin A. Dossa (June 22, 1998, 11:44 a.m.):

This is a brief note to let you know that I did not participate in the e-mail chat for the simple reason that I am thinking through a vision of fieldwork and writing. It is too early for me to articulate my stance – it is not feminist (I did not get hired at one university because I could not say that my work was purely grounded in feminist thought, although I draw a lot of inspiration from its scholarship). I have found that if I adopt a feminist-informed framework of research, it distances me from women who are closely linked to families and communities, as is the case with Muslim women. I have also been struggling with the problematic of introducing the essence of sacredness into my work as many immigrant communities take this to be a vital source for reconstruction of meaning and identity in their new homeland in Canada. This aspect, together with ritual, is marginalized in social science literature. In short, I need time to work through these complex issues before I can engage in a dialogue with feminist thought. I thought I should explain this to you. For me it was not a problem of time; it is a more profound issue of reflexivity. [When asked if she would contribute this reply to the publication, Parin Dossa replied]: Yes, that is fine – I am happy that I found the space to say what I feel rather than how I think. This is one of the strengths of feminism – it is a nurturing and rejuvenating source.

Susan Frohlick (June 22, 1998, 1:37 p.m.):

As others have already noted with regards to themselves, this question about where I place my work as a feminist within contemporary anthropology is, indeed, a daunting one. It is daunting for me especially given that, while I draw more heavily from feminist scholarly work than probably any other, and while I would certainly locate my work within the disciplinary boundaries of feminist anthropology (as well as feminist geography and other critical feminist studies), I hesitate to identify myself as "a feminist." This hesitancy may have been spurred by the "kind" advice given to me as a new graduate student by a senior male faculty member not to align or identify myself too closely with "feminism" lest I find myself pigeon-holed and thus, I gathered, my professional opportunities constrained. But it also has to do with the way in which feminism, like any other "ism," is always in part a strategy and pragmatic tool as well as an epistemology, and is thus useful in some situations and not others. My general concern is about the kinds of questions it may stop us from asking.

The kinds of questions I was interested in while undertaking my Master's research on single mothers' narratives of home and loss were motivated not only by an academic interest in "identity" and "social space" but by the desire, as an emerging scholar, to locate myself directly (albeit cautiously, given the oppositional advice I had received) within feminist anthropological works such as those of Lila Abu-Lughod, Kamala Visweswaren, Sally Cole and Lynn Phillips, Ruth Behar, among others, who were writing really interesting "feminist" ethnographies in the early 1990s. Crucially, this desire had much to do, then, with my own "discovery" of a kind of anthropology (which, notably, had been sorely absent in all of my undergraduate courses) that resonated for me at that particular time in my life and enabled me to envision a "place" for me in anthropology. Therefore it was a specific genre of early 1990s, largely post-structuralist, experimental, critical feminist anthropology that provided me with a way in ... a way in to contemporary anthropology, a way in to graduate school, and a way to begin to articulate questions that were relevant to the issues facing myself and other women in my life at that time. My point here is that the strategies and politics of contributing to and maintaining disciplinary boundaries around feminist anthropology should not be undervalued, yet at the same time they require constant tracking.

The plot thickens and my own narrative becomes murkier the more I delve into my current graduate work in anthropology. While it was extremely important for me to "do" feminist ethnography for my Master's thesis, as it might be for someone else to "do" historical anthropology or medical anthropology, for example, that kind of "pedantic identification" (my term) is no longer so crucial to me in my doctoral work on the politics of space and "risk" in mountaineering. But even as I write this I hesitate to make this claim, for what I think I am doing now is hopefully a kind of more critical, less dogmatic, but nevertheless ultimately feminist work. This involves leaving aside a narrowly focused analysis of "women" to ask questions about the "other" side of gender which has largely been ignored in feminist anthropology (and for that matter, from contemporary anthropology more generally) – manhood and masculinities. I have to say that, more than anything else, being the mother of a young son has made me aware of some of the significant limitations of feminist work as well as post-structuralist work as I now grapple with the tensions between feminism and – "humanism," sort of a dirty word these days. While feminism since the late 1980s has been about examining multiple axes of difference, it strikes me that the realms of discourses and "experiences" obscured and denied by too myopic a (feminist) lens have also obstructed a more critical anthropology. For me the challenge now is to use the theoretical tools from feminist work to extend rather than impede our analytical and political visions.

Sally Cole (faxed, June 18, 1998, 2:41 p.m.):

I would divide the question into two parts to reply. Regarding my work "as a feminist within anthropology," I would have to say it is very much determined by the conditions under which I work at the present time. In the future, I plan a return to my original research interests on women and development issues. I will endeavour to design and implement that research in collaboration with women's grassroots organizations and in the context of local feminisms, aware as I am that what we call "feminist anthropology" emerged in a Western (and as Ellen Judd says, bourgeois) context. For the present, however, my identity as a feminist anthropologist is rooted in the relations of my everyday life: (1) as a teacher in a non-élite, undergraduate teaching institution where a majority of students are the children of first-generation immigrants, often the first in their families to pursue post-secondary education, and whose primary concerns are to "get a job" and who have very little interest in "feminist anthropology" as it is presently available to them; and (2) as a researcher who is engaged in historiographic research on women's writing in Americanist anthropology, in part because archival research is more compatible than fieldwork is with my other present identity: a parent with two school-age children and a non-anthropologist co-parent.

In the eight years that I have been teaching I have noticed a decline in student interest in feminist scholarship. I teach a senior undergraduate field research course where I supervise students in designing and conducting a small field research project in Montreal over the course of the academic year. Until recently, a majority of the students have chosen and designed their projects from a "feminist" perspective (locally defined). Topics included: single mothers, Latin American immigrant women, Filipina domestic workers, the South Asian women's community centre, the Iranian Women's Association of Montreal, etc. This past winter, not one student was interested in women's, gender, or feminist issues or theoretical frameworks. Topics included hip hop, the culture of skateboarding, animal rights activists, environmental activists, and martial arts clubs .... I also teach a course entitled "Gender in a Cross-Cultural Perspective," which over the past five years has become increasingly a "service course," that is, a course taken as an elective by students majoring in any discipline, with decreasing numbers of anthropology students enrolling in the course. Anthropology majors prefer, it seems, the courses "Youth Culture," "Postmodernist Anthropology," "Health, Illness, and Healing," and "Symbolic Anthropology."

I attribute decreasing interest by students and colleagues in feminist scholarship to two reasons. (1) The 1980s critique (variously called "postmodernist," "reflexive," etc.) of anthropology had, by the mid-1990s, successfully derailed the feminist project that had been building up momentum and a body of scholarship since the early 1970s, so that fewer students see feminist scholarship as providing future direction for the discipline. Further, historical research documents that feminist scholarship is intimately related to the vitality of women's movements in the wider society and to the possibilities women have "to share the stories of their lives and their hopes and their unacceptable fantasies," as Carolyn Heilbrun (1988) has written. During the 1990s, these possibilities for women were increasingly undermined both in North American society and in the academy. The fact that increasing numbers of women are obtaining faculty appointments has less to do with "equal employment" programs in universities than it has to do with the low salaries, heavy workloads and increasing emphasis on teaching over research and, hence, the low status of the work.

(2) A second reason for the relative invisibility and low level of interest in feminist scholarship in anthropology at the end of the 1990s has to do with that scholarship itself. In the February 1998 issue of the *Women's Review of Books* Joan Catapano and Marlie P. Wasserman, two feminist editors for U.S. academic presses, note the decreasing number of feminist manuscripts they see that they want to publish. While acknowledging that "it was feminists who opened minds and the canon to new ideas and scholarship," they say that feminist scholarship itself is in need of "renewal." "We see little in the way of exciting new interpretations, and ... call for more imaginative and daring forays." They find that much feminist scholarship is written in a "hyperacademic style" and that "these [feminist] scholars form an elite group, which goes against the grain of their professed inclusive philosophy." Finally, they charge that where feminist scholarship in the 1970s and 1980s sought "to create a public discussion and not an academic debate," it has today lost its ties to real people and real issues. It has become institutionalized and in doing so has lost its creative impulse, its relevance to the public world, and, ultimately, even its interest to academic publishers.

My participation in this volume was one attempt to address some of the concerns that I have about the current state of feminist scholarship. A goal of the volume was to report on research by scholars who identify themselves as feminist ethnographers, who are engaged in the everyday lives of women, who write in ways that are accessible to a wide range of readers, and who are working to keep open the intellectual and social spaces within which women can continue to "tell their stories."

References

Anderson, Rae. 1996. "Reflections on Crossing Disciplines," in Ann B. (Rusty) Shteir, ed., *Graduate Women's Studies: Visions and Realities*. Toronto: Ianna Publications and Education Inc., 70-77.

Caplan, Pat. 1988. "Engendering Knowledge: The Politics of Ethnography," *Anthropology Today* 4, 5-6: 8-17.

Catapano, Joan, and Marlie P. Wasserman. 1998. "Is Publishing Perishing?" *Women's Review of Books* 15, 5 (February): 22.

Deloria, Vine Jr. 1988 [1969]. *Custer Died For Your Sins: An Indian Manifesto*. New York: Macmillan.

Heilbrun, Carolyn. 1988. *Writing a Woman's Life*. New York: Norton.

Ortner, Sherry B. 1984. "Theory in Anthropology Since the Sixties," *Comparative Studies in Society and History* 26, 1: 126-66.

Quelzán, Maria Xosé. 1983. *Festa da Palabra Silenciada* No. 1.

Roseman, Sharon. 1997. "Celebrating Silenced Words: The 'Reimagining' of a Feminist Nation in Late-Twentieth-Century Galicia," *Feminist Studies* 23, 1 (Spring): 43-71.

CONTRIBUTORS

Rae Bridgman is an urban anthropologist (Ph.D. York University 1993) and the co-ordinator of the Women's Network/Réseau des femmes of the Canadian Anthropology Society/Société canadienne d'anthropologie (cascawn-rf@yorku.ca). She is Assistant Professor in the Department of City Planning, Faculty of Architecture, and Adjunct Professor in the Department of Anthropology at the University of Manitoba. She is co-author (with Irene Glasser) of *Braving the Street: The Anthropology of Homelessness* (1999).

Kamari Maxine Clarke, currently completing a President's Post-doctoral Fellowship at the University of California, Berkeley, is an Assistant Professor of Anthropology at Yale University. She completed her first degree at Concordia University in Montreal and received her M.A. from the New School for Social Research and her Ph.D. in anthropology from the University of California, Santa Cruz. Her past research focused on the socio-religious, legal, and linguistic/performative processes of reinventing and historicizing Yoruba traditions in Nigeria and among Black American Yoruba revivalists in the African diaspora.

Sally Cole is Associate Professor in the Department of Sociology and Anthropology at Concordia University. She is the author of *Women of the Praia: Work and Lives in a Portuguese Coastal Community* (1991) and co-editor (with Lynne Phillips) of *Ethnographic Feminisms: Essays in Anthropology* (1995). Her research interests are in gender, households, and development in Portugal and Brazil, the history of anthropology, and life-writing and ethnography. She is currently completing a book on the life and work of Ruth Landes.

Parin A. Dossa, Associate Professor of Anthropology at Simon Fraser University, received her Master's degree from Edinburgh University and her Ph.D. from the University of British Columbia. Her teaching and research interests include the anthropology of diaspora and migration with a focus on gender, aging, mental health, and disability among Muslim minorities in Canada. Her exploratory research project on the impact of development on Muslim women on the coast of Kenya has focused on the life narrative approach.

Gönül Ertem is an instructor at Kennesaw State University in Georgia. She is interested in configurations of ethnicism, nationalism, and gender in post Cold War politics of identity constitution. Her dissertation, completed at the University of Texas at Austin, is entitled "Dancing to Modernity: Cultural Politics of Cherkess Nationhood in the Heartland of Turkey."

Susan Frohlick is a doctoral candidate in social/cultural anthropology at York University. Her doctoral research focuses on the spatial politics of gender, danger, and risk in high altitude mountaineering. She is currently working on a co-edited volume of anthropological papers addressing the broad themes of women, bodies, and space.

Deborah A. Gordon is Associate Professor in the Center for Women's Studies at Wichita State University. She is the co-editor (with Ruth Behar) of *Women Writing Culture* (1995) and the author of the forthcoming volume, *A Troubled Border: Feminism and the 'Literary' Turn in Anthropology*. Her present research concerns Palestinian feminism in the occupied territories of the West Bank.

Heather Howard-Bobiwash is a doctoral candidate in social/cultural anthropology and a teaching assistant with the Women's/Gender Studies Program at the University of Toronto. She is the co-editor of the Native Canadian Centre of Toronto's monthly newsletter and is the co-ordinator of the Toronto Native Community History Project's Resource Centre. She is co-editor (with Frances Sanderson) of *The Meeting Place: Aboriginal Life in Toronto* (1997). Her doctoral research examines women's history in the development of the social service infrastructure of the contemporary Native community in Toronto, as well as concepts of community, gender, class, and identity politics.

Ellen R. Judd is Professor of Anthropology at the University of Manitoba. She first went to China as a student from 1974 to 1977, and has been doing research related to China since that time. Since 1986 much of her research, including her book, *Gender and Power in Rural North China* (1994), has focused on the reconfiguration of gender in the countryside of China during the reform era. Her current work based on field research in rural Shandong, examines women's local organizing initiatives.

Milagros Ortiz Barillas received a Master's degree in anthropology from the Université de Montréal (1992). Her thesis focused on the ethnohistory of the Miskitos in her native Nicaragua. She is currently a Ph.D. candidate at Simon Fraser University. Her research focuses on the schooling system in northern British Columbia and the experiences of Aboriginal youth.

Celia Rothenberg is a Rockefeller Fellow (1998-99) in the Department of Religion at the University of Toronto. She is currently pursuing a research project in the Palestinian community of Toronto focused on how Islamic practices and beliefs are maintained, negotiated, and created. This work builds on and lends a comparative perspective to her previous research examining village women's ideas about gender, morality, and family. This research was carried out in the Palestinian West Bank.

Sharon R. Roseman (Ph.D., McMaster University, 1993) is Assistant Professor of Anthropology at Memorial University of Newfoundland. Her past field research in Spain has dealt with such topics as how rural Galicians have responded to their marginalization within Western European industrial capitalism, the unregulated labour of Galician seamstresses and dressmakers, and language and feminist politics within the context of the Galician nationalist movement.

Cory Silverstein received her M.A. in interdisciplinary studies from York University. Her thesis, "Gifts of Nokomis: Spiritual Power in the Arts of Ojibwa and Cree Women," drew on fieldwork among urban Anishnaabe beadworkers and traders in the Ontario pow-wow circuit. She is currently a doctoral student in anthropology at McMaster University. Her interests span women's arts ("crafts"), clothing, narratives, and spirituality, as well as issues of social justice in power relations of gender, ethnicity, class, and age.

Karen Su is currently a visiting faculty fellow in the Asian/Pacific/American Studies program at New York University. Her research and teaching interests focus on Asian-American literature, U.S. writers of colour, and feminist/anti-racist pedagogy. She has also taught at Mills College and the University of California, Berkeley.

Tatiana Zhurzhenko is Associate Professor of Philosophy at Kharkiv State University and vice-president of the Kharkiv Center for Gender Studies. She graduated from Kharkiv State University, Department of Economics and earned her Ph.D. in philosophy in 1993. Her interests lie primarily in the fields of business ethics, gender theory, and feminist economics and sociology. She is the author of *Businessman: A Money-Grabber, Gambler or Creator? The Formation of Entrepreneurial Ethos* (1993) and is currently a participant in the first

Ukrainian collective research project on gender issues, "Ukrainian Women in the Transition Period: From Social Movement to Politics" (funded through the J. and K. MacArthur Foundation).

INDEX

Asian-American writing; Ethnographic Authority; Narratives; Identity; and Representation

Chinese language, 33, *See also* Mother tongues

Chodorow, Nancy, 49 n.3

Class: 16, 29, 47, 55, 60, 63-64, 64-66, 67, 71, 75, 82, 86, 94, 98, 158, 160, 161, 163, 166, 168, 179, 197, 199, 201-202, 205, 239, 247, 264-265, 275, 291; and feminist anthropology, 4, 29, 90, 197; 'performative,' 4, 55; and small village life, 9-10, 212, 218, 272-275; and women's work, 7, 9, 10-11, 91-92, 199

Clifford, James, 42, 62, 66-67, 75-76, 78, 81

Cole, Sally, 42, 298

Collier, Jane, 62-63

Colonialism (and colonization), 38, 43, 66, 71, 74, 75, 77, 81, 121, 129, 133, 158, 160, 170, 196-201, 202, 205, 209, 232, 236-38, 241, 289, 292; anti-colonialism, 64; colonized peoples, 38, 77, 89, 129, 197-198; decolonization, 66

Columbia University, 3, 13, 17, 18, 22-23

Committee on International Exchange of Persons, 27

Compartmentalization, 15

Consciousness, 21, 28, 118-119, 120, 161, 183, 224, 287; Historical 4, 8; Cultural 7, 8, 134; Oppositional, 47, 61, (revolutionary) 203

Corporatization, 55, 59

Cultural continuity, 117, 118, 120, 123, 130, 133

Cultural Studies, 38

Cultural traveller, 206

Dance, 187, 190

De Aguerri, Josefa Toledo, 201-202

De Alva, Klor, 205

Deconstruction, 64, (indigenous), 212, 213, *See also* Anthropology and the native perspective; and Disruptions (social)

Deloria, Ella Cara, 14, 37

Deloria, Vine Jr., 288

Dialogue, 59, 63, 76, 98, 282, 288

Diaspora, (Cherkess) 182, (Ismaili) 160, (Palestinian) 150, (African), 28, 230, 233, 237, 240, *See also* Identity

Difference, 24, 38, 41, 44, 47, 48, 70, 82, 83, 90, 160, 180, 292; gender and education, 272-273; within feminism, 29, 49 n.2, 173-193, 184, 277-278; political, 71, 79, 264, *See also* Politics

Differential knowledge, 37, 44, (positions) 47, 48, 49 n.3, 82, 171, 200, 223, 284, 295, *See also* Difference with feminism, and Knowledge

Discourse, 15, 21, 63, 89-90, 150, 154, 158, 170-171, 175, 179, 191, 196-210, 233, 235, 248, 270, 271, 285; anthropological, 104; ethnographic, 40; of home, 86; and marginalization, 89; social, 71

Displacement, 75, 81, 82, 127, (dislocations) 87, 89, 91, *See also* Identity and location, Narratives and location; disembodiment, 170

Disruption (social), 212, 213-214, 221, 222, 224-225, 226 n. 4; tactics, 218

Dittmar, Helga, 109

Divorce, 17, 40-41, 89, 163, 164, 177, 226 n. 5, 253

Economic development, 158, 159, 161-162, 168, 259, 261, 264, 267, 270, 275, *See also* Gender-and-development (GAD)

Economic reform, 245, 264

Écriture feminine, 49 n.3

Eickelman, Dale, 141

Embodiment, 71, 74, 82, 157, 158, 160, 162, 164-165, 169, 171

Employment, in anthropology, 18, 19-25; informal sector, 243, 245, 249, *See also* Women and work

Empowerment, 103, 104, 105-107, 223; defined, 106-107, 115 n. 1; feminist theory of, 107, 222, 287

Enriques, Magda, 203

Environment, 71-72, 75, 80, 82, 95, 97

Equality, 58; egalitarian, 24

Eskişehir (Turkey), 174

Essentialism, 41, 45-47, 70

Ethnicity, 15, 29, 174, 183, 191-192, 243, 291; and literature, 34; pride, 40, 184

Ethnic Studies, 62

Ethnographic authority: 33-34, 38, 38-39, 49 n.1, 63, 66; and Asian-American, 4, 33-52, 35, 40; and critical revisioning of, 43;

and textual representation, 5, 33, 35-36, ('writing culture'), 44; and translation practices, 43, *See also* Feminist ethnography

Ethnographic imperative, 33

Ethnography, rejection of, 33-36; 'of reading,' 118-119, See Reading, and Feminist ethnography

European Enlightenment, 38

Evans-Pritchard, E.E., 140

Experience, 14, 21, 24, 86, 87, 97, 133, 151, 157, 158, 169, 174, 199, 202-204, 208, 222-223, 248, 286-289; Chinese-American 34; in Nicarguan politics, 196-197, 199, 202-204

Experimental writing, 11, 34, 38, 39, 59, 72, 119, 123, 282-301, housing project, 105, *See also* Fiction

Family, 17-18, 29, 63, 88, 92, 94, 95, 97-98, 99, 108, 123, 125, 126, 127, 130, 133, 148-150, 155, 164, 183, 190, 199, 200, 204, 220, 233-237, 239, 245, 248, 250, 251, 253, 260, 288

Feminism, and anthropology, 2-3, 28-30, 55, 61, 62, 64, 137, 139, 142, 157, 213, 221-225, 282, 285, 287, 288-290, 293-294, 296, 298, 300-301; and class, 4-5; and cultural translation, 4, 293; and ethnography, 4, 34, 37, 55, 149, 213; and historical perspective, 3-4; and knowledge, 40; and post-modern perspective, 5; socialist, 291; and solidarity, 41, 48, 127, 179, 208, 288; and the state 8, 67, 264-280, 285, 173-193; and struggle, 41, 264, 266, *See also* Difference and feminism, Women's movements

Feminist ethnography, 4, 34, 37, 38, 44, 45, 47, 54, 61, 63, 64, 66, 67, 89, 106, 140, 213, 221-225, 291, 293, 295, 298, 301

Feminist epistemology, 44, 47, 48, 58, 87, 118-119, 123, 132-134, 139, 183, 265, 293, 298

Feminist paralysis, 213, 221, 222, 224

Feminist practice, 14, 48, 171; approach, 6-7, 9, 212, 213-214, 221-225, 286, ('grounded theory') 117, 213; and shelters, 109

Feminist scholarship, 1, 14, 15, 55, 58, 62, 170, 213, 282-284, 298, 300-301; and democratization, 2; and literary criti-cism, 34, 296-297; and U.S. influences, 4, 54, 284-285, 294; and personal narratives, 117-118, 120, 299

Feminist Studies, 38, 49 n.1, 295, 298, *See also* Women's Studies

Feminist theory, 29, 38, 55, 62, 63, 65, 71, 79, 104, 180-181, 213, 286, 289

Fiction, 33, 35, 36, 37, 40-42, 43, 72, 293, *See also* Experimental writing

Fieldwork, 17, 22, 23, 24, 54, 60, 64, 76, 88-90, 98, 103-104, 137, 138, 141, 146, 148, 152, 153-154, 159-160, 161, 173, 174, 185, 213, 214, 222-225, 247-249, 265-267, 285, 289, 297, 300; and trust, 112-113, 222, 231, 291

Fletcher, Alice, 14

Food preparation, 123-126

Four Directions, 78, 79, 82, 84 n.3

Fox, Mary, 118, 122, 125-126, 127-128

Galicia (Spain), 9, 212-226, 291

Gender, 15, 49 n.3, 71, 75, 82, 89, 100, 170, 173, 174, 175, 182-183, 184-187, 189, 190-191, 222, 224, 231-236, 238-240, 243, 244, 248, 261-262, 265-266, 268, 289-290, 291, 293, 299; and-Development (GAD), 161, 265, 268, 270, 300; and division of labour, 166-169, 261, 268-269, 277, 283, 291, *See also* Women and work; and national identity 8-9, 173-193, 197, 203, 264, 268-269, 270; and power 9, 61, 106, 177, 182, 191, 203, 233, 240, 272, (differentials) 47, 197-198, 199, 226 n. 1, 230; roles 7, 13, 16, 29, 120, 125, 129, 149, 164, 229, 231, 235, 237, 239, 240, 250-253, 260, 264; and seg-regation, 158, 159, 165, 167, 168, 175, 176, *See also* Seclusion; sex/gender system, 62, *See also* Male, manhood and masculini-ties

Genealogies, 146-147, 149, 150, 154

Geography, 99; of the body, 73; biography, 75; social, 150-151

Gilbert, Kate, 60

Gilroy, Paul, 229

Global capitalism, 265, 291

Globalization, 60, 81

Gordon, Deborah, 34

Granqvist, Hilma, 7, 137, 138-142, 143-144, 146-148, 150-154, 294

Group interviewing, 119, 134 n. 2

Guerrero, Marie Anna Jaimes, 133
Handler, Richard, 28
Harding, Sandra, 142
Harrington, Mona, 14
Harraway, Donna, 47
Heilbrun, Carloyn, 301
Herrera, Rafaela, 201, 202
Hierarchy, 28, 29, 70, 160, 175, 177, 246; spatial 73, 78, 289-290
History, as authority, 42, 79, 118, 132, 151, 229-233, 250; reclaiming women's, 142, 289
Home, and meaning of, 5-6, 54, 62, 86-100, 87, 90-91, 93, 94, 95, 99, 100, 103, 104, 108; and feminist practice, 6; homemakers, 249; and nostalgia, 94-95, 99
Homelessness, 6, 103, 104, 112, 123; chronic, 105-106; history of in Toronto, 107-108; and women, 108-110
Homes First Society, 104, 105
Homogenization, 42, 58, 81, 131, 154, 160, 163, 196, 198, 205, 241, 291
Homophobia, 91
Hostels, history of, 109
Hosting behaviour, 217-218, *See also* Female visiting
Housing, 6, 93, 96, 104, 107, 109, 112; Native, 122
Household, 92, 93, 95, 249, 251, 253, 261, 265, 272, 280 n. 7
Housework, 91, 168, *See also* Women and work
Huaili (China), 272-277
Hurston, Zora Neale, 14, 37
Identity, 45, 55, 62, 70, 71, 82, 91, 112, 119, 121-122, 128-129, 133, 149, 152, 174-175, 184, 196-197, 200, 205, 208, 243, 249, 252, 253, 254, 258-262, 289, 292, 298, 300; African/Black, 21, 230, 232, 233, 237, 241; Asian-American, 33, 34; Chinese 41, 45-46; disabled, 94, 95, 97; fragmentation, 71, 82, 160; Jewish, 16, 17, 21, 23, 26, 30 n. 1, 153-154; and location, 5, 81-82, 87, 152-153, 160, 161; and marginalization, 89, 243-263; Mestiza, 8, 196-210; and motherhood, 87-88, 92, 95, 97, 98, 200; multiple 70-71; Muslim, 157, 160, 161, 162-163, 170, 174, 175, 177, 182, *See also* Gender

and segregation, Seclusion, Veiling; and nationhood, 8, 9-10, 174-193, 196-198, 243; narratives of, 86, 119-121, 160-161; and neo-colonialism and neo-patriarchal relations, 5, 175, 197, 198-201, 205; and performance, 9-10; and post-socialism, 10, 181, 248; and reading, 6-7; and socialism, 23, 252, 174; Turkish, 174-193; and Western culture, 5, 75, 77, 175, 199, 201; and women's economic roles, 243-244, *See also* Self
Immigrant community, 43, 298
Imperialism, 55
Individualism, 21
Informants, 59, 64, 139-140, 142, 148, 152; and anonymity, 113; native, 35, 37, 40, 42, 289, *See also* Anthropology and the native perspective
Insider/Outsider debate, 4, 6-7, 8, 71, 158, 160-161, 267, 284
Interdisciplinarity, 57, 59, 70, 285, 286, 288-289, 294-296
Internet, 11, 285
Intervention/non-intervention, 105, 110, 159, 284; in fieldwork, 6, 9, 213, 222, 225, 293
John, Mary, 54-55
Johnson, Samuel, 231
Johnston, Verna Patronella, 118, 119-120, 121, 127, 129, 130
Kantorowicz, E.H., 238-239
Kehoe, Alice, 131
Kemal, Mustafa (Kemalist), 176, 178, 179-180, 181, 184, 190, 191
Kenya, (Lamu) 7, 157-171, (Mombasa) 158, 160, 162, 164, 167; 238
Kim, Elaine, 35
Kingston, Maxine Hong, 4, 33, 34, 35-36, 37, 38, 39, 43-48, 49 n.1
Kinship relations, 178, 183, *See also* Genealogies and kinship studies, 62-63
Knowledge, 22, 131, 139, 140, 159-162, 165, 166, 169, 170, 208, 237, 251-252, 255, 261, 267, 274, 275, 278, 284, 288, 297; 'Situated', 47, 64
Kondo, Dorinne, 99
Kroeber, Theodora and Alfred, 66
Laframboise, Teresa, 133

Landes, Ruth, 3, 13-30
Landscape, 71, 73, 78, 93, 96
Language, 43, 291-292
Lee, Virginia, 35
Life stories, 86, 247, *See also* Narratives
Life strategies, 254-258, 262
Linton, Ralph, 18
Lionnet, Francoise, 196, 199
Literacy, 274, 276; cultural, 285
Literary criticism, 4, 6-7, 65, 123-124, 295-296; and feminist critique, 34
Long, Elizabeth, 118-119, 133
Lorde, Audre, 47
Male, alcoholism, 215-218, 219-221, 222-223, 226 n. 2 and n. 3; behaviour, 9; manhood and masculinities 299; 'missing,' 90, 94, 95, 96, 97; space, 166, 168, 170; power, 177, 181; patron, See Patronage
Malinche, 200, 209, 210 n. 3
Malysheva, Marina, 243-244
Map, 75-76, 79, 83
Maracle, Lee, 129
Marginality (marginalization), 21, 58, 79, 82, 86, 89, 90, 93, 106, 142, 170, 179, 213, 225, 237, 243-245, 248, 249, 260, 274, 284, 286-287, 290, 292, 293, 298, *See also* Identity and
Marriage, 16, 17, 20, 24, 28, 95, 119, 140, 149, 163, 183, 188, 190-191, 214-217, 237-238, 239, 250, 280 n. 8; joking courtship, 184-187; marriageability, 9, 212, 222; and polygyny, 233-236; polygamy, 177
McMaster University, 28
Mead, Margaret, 3, 5, 14, 18, 25-28, 29, 72-74, 80, 81, 84 n. 2, 141, 229, 288
Mediated practices, 229, 237, 238
Mentoring, 3, 14, 15, 22, 23, 25, 26, 29
Mestiza, 8, 196-210
Mimetic verisimilitude, 36
Miscegenation, 199
Misogynism, 200
Modernism (modernity, modernisation), 13, 21, 28, 29, 174, 179, 181, 183, 191
Molyneux, Maxine, 197, 268, 272
Monture-Angus, Patricia, 133
Moraga, Cherríe, 47, 65-66, 199
Morrison, Toni, 30 n. 2
Motherhood, 63, Chinese, 33, 41-42; and

daughters, 33, 40, 42; and Nicaraguan identity, 200, 204; single, 5-6, 86-100, 86, 87, 89, 92, 94, 95, 97, 107, 226 n. 5, 247, 253, 254, 256, 298; Turkish, 179; in Ukraine, 253; Yoruba, 233, 235-236, *See also* Narratives of
Mother tongues, 33, 40
Narayan, Kirin, 161
Narratives, 24, 40, 56, 74, 88-89, 96, 120, 121, 123, 130-131, 134 n. 1, 149, 157, 158, 164, 165, 169, 222, 247-248, 289, 293; critical, 212, 214, 222, *See also* Disruptions; of displacement, 81-82, 96; emotional quality of, 119, 123-129; of home, 5, 90-98; and homelessness, 108, 111-112; of identity (Asian American) 4, (Native Canadian) 6-7, 117-134, (Yoruba) 233, 236; of location, 5, 70, 75, 160-161, (North American) 74-82; master, 42; (Mestiza) 8; meta-, 70, (ruling) 56; of motherhood, 41-42, 43, 86, 98; Muslim, 162-171, 175, 177; personal, 72, 87-88, 117, 118-123, 131, 206-209, 299; and social disruption, 9; and work 8, 166-169
Nation, 60, 71, 197, 203, 264, 268-269, 270
Nationalism, 8, 174, 201, 285
National Women's Studies Association, 62
Native Canadian Centre of Toronto, 118, 122
Native Canadians, 6-7, (Native Americans) 66, 117-134, 288-289
Native perspective, See Anthropology, and
Neo-colonialism, 75, 197-201, 205, *See also* Identity and
Networks, 56, 162, 165, 167, 246, 255, 285, 286, 291
Nicaragua, 8-9, 196-210
Nicarao, 200, 207
Niranjana, Tejaswini, 38
Nishnawbe Homes, 122, 128
Okely, Judith, 71
Ong, Aihwa, 59-60, 224
Oppression, 88, 149, 170, 171, 197, 199, 202, 205, 293
Orientation, 71-72, 79; egalitarian, 78; and landscape 73-74, 76, 82
Ortega, Daniel, 202
Ortner, Sherry, 286

Other, the, concept of, 15, 42, 70, 87, 299
Ottoman Empire, 176
Oyotunji African Village (South Carolina, U.S.), 9, 229-241
Palestinians, See West Bank
Palma, Milagros, 200, 204
Parezo, Nancy, 14, 15
Parsons, Elsie Clews, 14, 15
Participatory research, 288
Partido de la izquierola erótica (PIE), 204, 205
Patriarchy, 70, 71, 79, 133, 149, 160, 170, 175, 177, 178, 179, 232-235, 237, 239, 250; Chinese, 40, 268; post-Communist, 245
Patronage, 3, 14, 15, 25
Personal/political, 288, See also Public/private
Phillips, Lynn, 298
Photographic realism, 74
Place, sense of, 55, 81-82, 93
Politics, 18, 28, 71, 78, 81, 82, 92, 152, 157, 243, 299; of home, 91, See also Power
Political economy, 264, 265-266, 270, 278, 291, 293
Polygyny, 10; polygamy, 177
Post-civil society, 57
Post-colonial, studies, 38; discourse, 196-201, 201, 205; theory, 38, 210 n. 1
Post-modernism, 74, 83, 300-301; and theory, 72, 75; and writing, 37
Post-socialism, 10-11, 243-262, 265, 270, 278, 291
Post-structuralism, 67
Poverty, 23, 24, 91, 92, 127, 159, 161, 170, 250, 265, 275, 278, 293
Power: 33, 43, 65, 76, 86, 93, 96, 178, 203, 214, 230, 236-241, 249, 287-288, 289, 293, 297; 'negative' 106; relations, 47, 48, 121, 131, 197, 199, 233, 239, 266, 290, See also Knowledge and
Pratt, Minnie Bruce, 78-79
Public education, 56
Public/private, 8, 24, 59, 60, 118, 158, 159, 170-171, 173-174, 176-178, 180-182, 184-187, 188-190, 191, 212, 215-217, 220, 235, 236, 240, 248, 274
Pun, 39
Queizán, María Xosé, 292
Quintales, Mirtha, 63-64

Race, 15, 23, 29, 49 n.3, 62, 64, 71, 82, 86, 89, 115 n. 2, 197, 229, 238, 293
Racism, 61, 63, 64, 70, 110, 112, 127-128, 129, 199, 202, 293; (anti-racism) 61, 63, 64, 288, 292, 296
Radcliffe-Brown, A. R., 18
Reading, 117, 118-119, 121, 123, 127, 128-129, 130, 133
Reciprocity, 169
Reflexivity, 6, 7, 9, 29, 54, 64, 87-88, 98-99, 103-104, 112, 133-134, 137, 142, 152, 199, 206-209, 213, 221-225, 249, 293, 298, 300-301
Reichard, Gladys, 14
Representation, 33, 58, 71, 76, 79, 83, 104, 117, 157, 293; and cultural (African) 232, (Asian –American), 4, 34, (Anishnaabe) 77, 118; of women in anthropology, 1, 3, 13-30, 138-142
Resistance, 95, 103, 104, 105-106, 127-128, 168, 198; strategies of, 38, 133
Revolution, China, 265; Nicaragua, 196, 197-198, 203, 205-206; Turkey, 179-180; Ukraine, 250
Rich, Adrienne, 70, 75, 82
Roosens, Eugene, 207-208
Rosaldo, Renato, 207, 208, 209
Rossiter, Margaret, 15
Rubin, Gayle, 62
Rural women, (China) 265-280
Safety, 109, 110, 112, 292
Sanad, Musa, 143-144, 151
Sanderson, Frances, 118, 122, 125-126, 127-128
Sandinista Front, (Sandinistas) 196, 205
Sandoval, Chela, 47, 61-62, 66
Sands, Kathleen, 123-124, 127, 133
Sapir, Edward, 18
Savard's, 104, 105, 107, 110-112, 114
Scott, Joan, 157
Seclusion, 163-164
Self, 15, 28, 55, 157, 187; and identity formation, 5, 8, 17, 71, 76, 83, 87, 93, 95, 96, 97, 98, 169, 249; multiple selfhood, 70, 76, 88, 94; personhood, 183, 188, 259, 261-262
Semerkho, 184-187, 190
Sexism, 15, 91
Sexuality, 24, 27, 45, 90, 92, 96, 134 n. 3, 163-

164, 179, 181, 188, 190, 203, 204; Kikuyu sexual morality (Kenya), 238; and purity, 233-236, 238; sexual tension, 178, 183

Sexual orientation, 71, 75, 82, 87, 96

Shaw, Carolyn Martin, 238

Shostak, Marjorie, 63, 64

Shuttle business, 10, 243-262

Sisterhood, 48, 62, 174, *See also* Feminism and solidarity

Slavery (transatlantic), 25, 229, 232, 233

Social action, 71

Social conditions, 56

Social control, 214, 223, 230, (social order) 191

Social facts, 140

Social justice, 284

Social mobility, 58, 237-239, 251

Social relations, 15, 24, 60, 63, 71, 75, 82, 175, 212, 250, 259

Social status, 94, 97, 212-213, 238, 239, 249, 251-252, 257, 261-262; and Muslim women, 161, 170, 175

Social structure, 72, 73, 74, 75

Social welfare, 56

Somoza, (dictatorship) 196; Anastasio Somoza Garcia, 197; Somoza Debayle, 201

Sosa, Mercedes, 297

Space, hierarchy, 73; and home, 86, 93, 94, 95, 99; and identity, 158, 164-165, 230; female, 13, 15, 169, 170-171, 191; male 166, 168, 170-171, 177; ; (spatial) orientation, 73, 87

Stacey, Judith, 48, 62

Stone, Merlin, 61

Strathern, Marilyn, 9, 213

Strobel, Margaret, 159

Struggle, feminist, 41; for home, 88, 91; identity 70, 89; and resistance, 106, 205

Subjectivity, 45, 59, 63, 66, 80, 86, 88, 92, 94, 95, 99, 118, 120, 191, 196, 223, 248

Sugimoto, Etsu, 35

Surveillance, 106

Swahili, 158-159

Tan, Amy, 4, 33, 34, 37, 38, 39, 40-42, 48

Taussig, Michael, 54

Tekeli, Şirin, 178

Textiles, 72

Textualization, 42, 119

Theriault, Madeline Katt, 118, 120-121, 124, 129, 130

Third World Feminism, 47, 64, 174, 196

This Bridge Called My Back, 61-62

Tomas, Annabel, 109

Tong, Benjamin, 35, 36

Toronto (Canada), 5, 76, 98, 104, 119, 121, 122, 123, 126

Tourism, 159, 162, 167, 168, 244-245

Tradition, conceptualization of, 6, 9-10, 15, 125, 127, 149, 160, 174, 175, 183; oral, 119, 123, 129-132, 231-236, 239-241, 296, ("anti-traditional") 288, (non-traditional) 253

Training, 163, 247, 249, 255, 285, (and economic development, China), 268-277, *See also* Literacy

Translation: 44, 45, 47, 48, 121, 149, 295; Cultural, 4, 33, 34, 35-38, 40, 41, 43; Critique of, 38; mis-, 39; Practices, 43; Studies, 38

Trinh Minh-ha, 42-43, 156-157

Turkey, 8, 173-193, 244, 245, 253, 254, 255

Turner, Pat, 118, 121-122, 125-126, 127-128

Two Studies, Two Competitions (China), 267-277, 280 n. 6

Ukraine, 10, 243

Unemployment, 220, 223, 243, 245, 247, 258

United States, 3-5, 9

Universals, 42, 48, 174, 236, *See also* Homogenization

Vancouver (Canada), 5, 87, 99

Vanderburgh, Rosamond, 118, 120, 127, 128, 131

Veiling, 158, 164, 166, 168, 171

Vincent, Joan, 160

Visiting, 166, 168, 184, See Zexes

Visweswaran, Kamala, 37, 38, 44, 45, 47, 64-65, 88, 89, 98, 207, 298

Voice, 104, 120

Walker, Alice, 47

Wasserman, Marlie, 2, 282-283, 301

Watkins, Evan, 55-56, 57

Watson, Sophie, 108

West Bank (Palestine and Palestinians), 11, 137-155, 285, 294

Western consumption standards, 251-252, 258